THE ELITE
AGAINST ALL ODDS

THE NAVAL UNITS

Other National Historical Society Publications:

THE IMAGE OF WAR: 1861-1865

TOUCHED BY FIRE: A PHOTOGRAPHIC PORTRAIT OF THE CIVIL WAR

WAR OF THE REBELLION: OFFICIAL RECORDS
OF THE UNION AND CONFEDERATE ARMIES

OFFICIAL RECORDS OF THE UNION AND CONFEDERATE NAVIES
IN THE WAR OF THE REBELLION

HISTORICAL TIMES ILLUSTRATED ENCYCLOPEDIA OF THE CIVIL WAR

CONFEDERATE VETERAN

THE WEST POINT MILITARY HISTORY SERIES

IMPACT: THE ARMY AIR FORCES' CONFIDENTIAL HISTORY
OF WORLD WAR II

HISTORY OF UNITED STATES NAVAL OPERATIONS IN WORLD WAR II
by Samuel Eliot Morison

HISTORY OF THE ARMED FORCES IN WORLD WAR II
by Janusz Piekalkiewicz

A TRAVELLER'S GUIDE TO GREAT BRITAIN SERIES

MAKING OF BRITAIN SERIES

THE ARCHITECTURAL TREASURES OF EARLY AMERICA

For information about National Historical Society Publications, write:
The National Historical Society, 2245 Kohn Road, Box 8200,
Harrisburg, Pa 17105

THE ELITE
The World's Crack Fighting Men

THE NAVAL UNITS

Ashley Brown, Editor
Jonathan Reed, Editor

Lisa Mullins, Managing Editor, NHS edition

A Publication of
THE NATIONAL HISTORICAL SOCIETY

Published in Great Britain in 1986 by Orbis Publishing

Library of Congress Cataloging-in-Publication Data
The Naval units / Ashley Brown, editor, Jonathan Reed, editor.—NHS ed.
p. cm.—(The Elite)
ISBN 0-918678-52-8
1. Navies. 2. Submarine warfare—History. 3. Naval history.
Modern—20th century. I. Brown, Ashley. II. Reed, Jonathan.
III. Series: Elite (Harrisburg, Pa.)
VA10.N363 1990
359.3'1—dc20 89-13864
CIP

CONTENTS

INTRODUCTION

Around the world the single word "Dive!" conjurs exactly the same mental images . . . brave submariners taking their ship down to the chilly bottom to carry out some of warfare's most dangerous and dashing missions. In a ship barely more than 200 feet long and twenty feet wide, forty or more brave men ran silent and deep to take sudden terror and destruction to their foes. Surviving terrible depth charge attacks when submerged, and bombing and strafing attacks from the air when on the surface, these dauntless men blazed their own special chapter in the annals of the ELITE.

Few exploits could compare with the daring of the British submarine E11 when she ventured alone into Constantinople's harbor in 1915 to attack the enemy's shipping. One war later, the most daring of the German U-Boat commanders, Kapitanleutnant Otto Kretschmer and his U-99 sank more than 350,000 tons of British shipping, becoming thereby the greatest U-boat ace of the war. Equally as daring were the British sailors who piloted the X-Craft, midget submarines that attacked the German battleship *Tirpitz.* And few exploits could surpass Gunther Prien and his U-47's attack on the British navy at Scapa Flow, where he sank the *Royal Oak.*

Not all of the Naval Units were submariners. The coastwatchers who served as the eyes of the U.S. and British Navy in the Pacific braved incredible hazards. Special Boat Squadron (SBS) units of the Royal Navy did hazardous duty in the Falklands War of 1982 just as they had forty years before in the Mediterranean. In Vietnam, the "Brown Water Navy" of the United States carried on the first serious river war efforts since the Civil War.

Whether using submarines or helicopters, as divers or special naval "infantry," the men of the world's Naval Units have taken that extra step, dived that extra foot, and endured the extra risk that separates them from the majority. On land, sea, and air, they have earned the right to stand among the ELITE.

In May 1915 the British submarine *E11* ran the gauntlet of the Dardanelles and mounted a daring raid in Constantinople harbour

IN THE EARLY hours of 19 May 1915, the British submarine *E11* slipped out of harbour at Kefalo Burun to begin its hazardous mission: to sail up the narrow, mine-strewn channel of the Dardanelles into the Sea of Marmara, where it would intercept the Turkish forces' shipping supplies to the Gallipoli Peninsula. Standing on the conning tower, Lieutenant-Commander Martin Nasmith peered through the darkness as *E11* entered the Dardanelles, which separated the Gallipoli Peninsula off his port bow from the mass of Asiatic Turkey to starboard. While night artillery duels lit up the sky over Cape Helles, Turkish searchlights swept the narrow channel at regular intervals: it was time to dive.

Nasmith gave the 'Diving Stations' order and below him the crew scurried into activity: hatches and ventilators were closed, air circulating fans turned on and the two diesel-engine clutches opened, disconnecting them from the propeller shaft. While Nasmith looked around him one last time, the diesels were shut down and the underwater electric motors made ready. Leaving the conning tower, Nasmith clamped the hatch tight and climbed down into the operations room where he was met by his two fellow officers, Lieutenant D'Oyly Hughes (*E11's* First Lieutenant) and Lieutenant Brown, responsible for general navigation. The vents to the main ballast tanks were opened, and, as the water rushed in, *E11's* bow dipped downwards and the boat steadily submerged, levelling out at a periscope depth of 30ft.

Once submerged, *E11* began the process of negotiating the deadly obstacle course of Turkish mines, anti-submarine nets, patrol boats and destroyers. The submarine also faced the natural dangers of swirling cross-currents, which constantly threatened to knock the boat out of trim, and a multitude of poorly-charted shoals and underwater banks. In addition, if the submarine were located the Turks could call upon massed batteries of guns of all calibres, using carefully sited searchlights for illumination.

Despite these hazards, the submerged *E11* nosed up the Dardanelles at a steady pace of around three knots – moving slowly to conserve the electric motors' batteries – and rounded Nagara Point at 0530 hours. Dawn had broken, and, as the light improved, Turkish observers spotted the tell-tale wake of *E11's* periscope and shells began to fall near the submarine, forcing Nasmith to dive to a safe level of around 70ft below the surface. A further periscope observation was made and Nasmith kept *E11* well below sea level for the long, but relatively safe, haul from the end of the Narrows to the town of Gallipoli, where the Dardanelles began to open up into the Sea of Marmara. At 0930 Nasmith came up to periscope depth and found himself alongside Gallipoli; he rapidly dived again to pass below the minefield by the town.

After more than eight hours submerged the batteries were running low, and conditions for the men were progressively worsening as the air deterio-

Top left: The officers and crew of *E11*, photographed at their base at Kefalo Burun in the Aegean Sea. During the course of the Allied campaign on the Gallipoli Peninsula, *E11* and her sister E-class submarines sought every opportunity to destroy Turkish vessels bringing reinforcements and supplies to the Turkish defensive line on the peninsula. Despite their efforts, however, the Turks successfully contained the British invasion force on the peninsula's steep coastal fringe (above). Above right: The fortifications and heavy guns of Seddulbahir at the entrance of the Dardanelles were installed by the Turks to prevent enemy naval incursions into the Sea of Marmara. Below: A British E-class submarine in search of Turkish merchantmen.

rated. In order to conserve the air, those men not on duty either slept or rested; condensation increased rapidly, dripping down the steel-sided hull and soaking the men, who were already drenched in sweat. As the morning wore on, a grey mist began to rise up from the bilges, creating a miniature fog throughout the vessel. Although the Turks had spotted *E11* in the Narrows, Nasmith was determined that they should get into the Sea of Marmara unobserved, and he pressed on submerged until 1130 when a periscope observation revealed that they were well into the sea. Any movement would give their position away, however, and with failing batteries *E11* limped to shallow water to rest on the bottom at a depth of 80ft until nightfall.

The main hatch cover was eased and with an ear-splitting whistle the air rushed into E11

As the light faded, Nasmith made preparations for surfacing. The ashen-faced crew were now having trouble breathing, the air so foul that even a match would not ignite. At 2100 the order was given to blow the tanks and regain positive buoyancy. The submarine rose slowly to allow just the conning tower to be above the surface. The main hatch cover was eased and with an ear-splitting whistle the air rushed into *E11*, to the relief of the suffering crew. Once on the conning-tower bridge, the boat's officers checked their positions according to the low-lying hills surrounding the inland sea, which were visible by the moonlight. As the men recovered, the batteries were recharged and a wireless signal sent towards the destroyer HMS *Jed*, positioned in the Gulf of Xeros on the other side of the Gallipoli Peninsula, to inform Nasmith's superiors of *E11's* safe arrival. A failure in the set prevented contact, however – a fault that was not to be rectified for several days.

At 0400 hours on 20 May the batteries were at full charge and *E11* set off eastwards into the Sea of Marmara to carry out Nasmith's orders. The Turkish forces on the Gallipoli Peninsula relied mainly on maritime supply, the road and rail links being inadequate. By cutting off the sea route it was hoped that the Turks would experience a significant problem in keeping their forces up to strength. The Sea of Marmara is roughly lozenge-shaped, stretching 110 miles in length by just under 50 miles in breadth, a large enough area for a submarine to roam at large.

Aware that a submarine had probably penetrated the Dardanelles barrier, the Turkish authorities limited maritime traffic while gunboats and destroyers were sent out to try and track it down. Thus, merely by its presence, *E11* was having a disruptive effect on the flow of supplies to Gallipoli. That was not

DARDANELLES PATROL

THE DARDANELLES CAMPAIGN

Turkey's decision to join the Central Powers (Germany and Austria-Hungary) in October 1914 was of immediate concern to the British, as the strategically vital Suez Canal now lay under direct threat from Turkish forces in Palestine. Rather than just defend the canal, it was decided to take the war to the Turks through a direct attack towards Constantinople itself. In January 1915 a British plan was put forward to mount a naval operation to force the Dardanelles and capture the Gallipoli Peninsula prior to an attack on the Turkish capital. The plan was followed through in a highly desultory manner, however, and a series of long-range bombardments only alerted the Turks to the danger of an imminent Allied attack. Consequently, the Turks strengthened their defences, and when Allied landings were made on 25 April 1915 the men were held on the beaches. Both sides reinforced their troops on the peninsula but the only result was rising casualties and trench stalemate. Submarine activity, by the Allies in the Sea of Marmara and the Germans off the Dardanelles, restricted conventional naval operations, imposing renewed hardships on the ground forces. By November 1915 the Allied commanders were beginning to realise that the plan could never succeed and a break-out from the Gallipoli beach-heads was an impossibility. The disastrous campaign came to end during December and January when all the remaining troops were evacuated.

ADMIRAL SIR MARTIN NASMITH

Born in 1883, Nasmith entered the Royal Navy aged only 13 and, following promotion to lieutenant, volunteered for duty in the new submarine branch. In the years leading up to the outbreak of war in 1914 Nasmith established himself as an expert in the field of submarine warfare, becoming chief instructor in underwater tactics, and once war was declared he was appointed commander of the submarine *E11*. After a number of minor setbacks during 1914 (including the failure in October to negotiate the Kattegat and sail into the Baltic) Nasmith was despatched to the Mediterranean to operate in support of the Gallipoli landings. On his first patrol he successfully breached the Dardanelles and spent over two weeks in the sea of Marmara harrying and destroying Turkish shipping. The success of this patrol was followed by others, during which *E11* sunk a large number of Turkish vessels, including the battleship *Heireddin Barbarossa.* After the last patrol Nasmith was awarded the Victoria Cross for the courage and initiative he had displayed as commander of *E11* while operating in conditions of great difficulty and danger. Promotion to captain followed, and after the war Nasmith held a variety of appointments, reaching the rank of admiral and becoming Second Sea Lord. During World War II Nasmith was Commander-in-Chief of the Western Approaches and Flag Officer in Charge, London. Nasmith was highly respected throughout the Royal Navy as an officer of great integrity, who combined courage and modesty in equal measure.

Below: Crewmen experiment with the gun that has been installed on the deck of their submarine. When the E-class boats arrived from Britain they had no deck armament and this was soon found to be a severe limitation on the destructive potential of operations in the Sea of Marmara. Many of the Turkish cargo vessels were too small to merit one of the submarines' limited complement of 10 torpedoes, and they escaped unscathed until the 12-pounders were introduced. Right: After careering around in Constantinople harbour, the first of *E11's* torpedoes finally crashed into the waterfront and shattered a dock. But it was *E11's* sinking of a large merchantman moored in the heart of the Turkish capital that gave Britain its much-needed propaganda victory. Far right, above: Petty officers enjoy a meal in the cramped eating quarters of an E-class submarine, while (below) torpedoes gleam in the fore torpedo tubes.

enough for a commander like Nasmith, however, and the hunt for suitable vessels was on. The *E11's* torpedoes were too valuable to be wasted on small sailing vessels and so these were stopped by the submarine after surfacing, their cargoes inspected for contraband, and the torpedoes saved for warships or larger merchantmen.

While a sailing vessel was being searched on 23 May, one of *E11's* lookouts spotted a torpedo gunboat some miles distant. Quickly disengaging, the submarine dived to periscope depth and advanced towards the gunboat, its bow tubes flooded and the torpedoes made ready. The gunboat was unaware of the submarine's presence and presented *E11* with a perfect target. Looking through the periscope, Nasmith crept to within 600yds of the Turkish vessel before the order was given to fire the starboard bow tube. While Nasmith had the luxury of watching the torpedo race towards the gunboat, the crew waited patiently until, after 30 seconds, they heard a dull explosion. A wild cheer went up throughout *E11* in celebration of the hit. The torpedo had struck the vessel squarely amid-ships and it listed to starboard before slowly sinking. The *E11* had been bloodied in battle after nine months of war and the morale of the crew soared correspondingly. When Nasmith came into the wardroom he was presented with a bottle of beer and a cigar by Brown and D'Oyly Hughes; after a second's surprise he remembered the vow he had made while on a frustrating North Sea patrol the previous year – never to drink or smoke until he sank an enemy warship.

More successes followed this first action. The cargo vessel *Nagara* was intercepted carrying artillery ammunition and then sent to the bottom after her

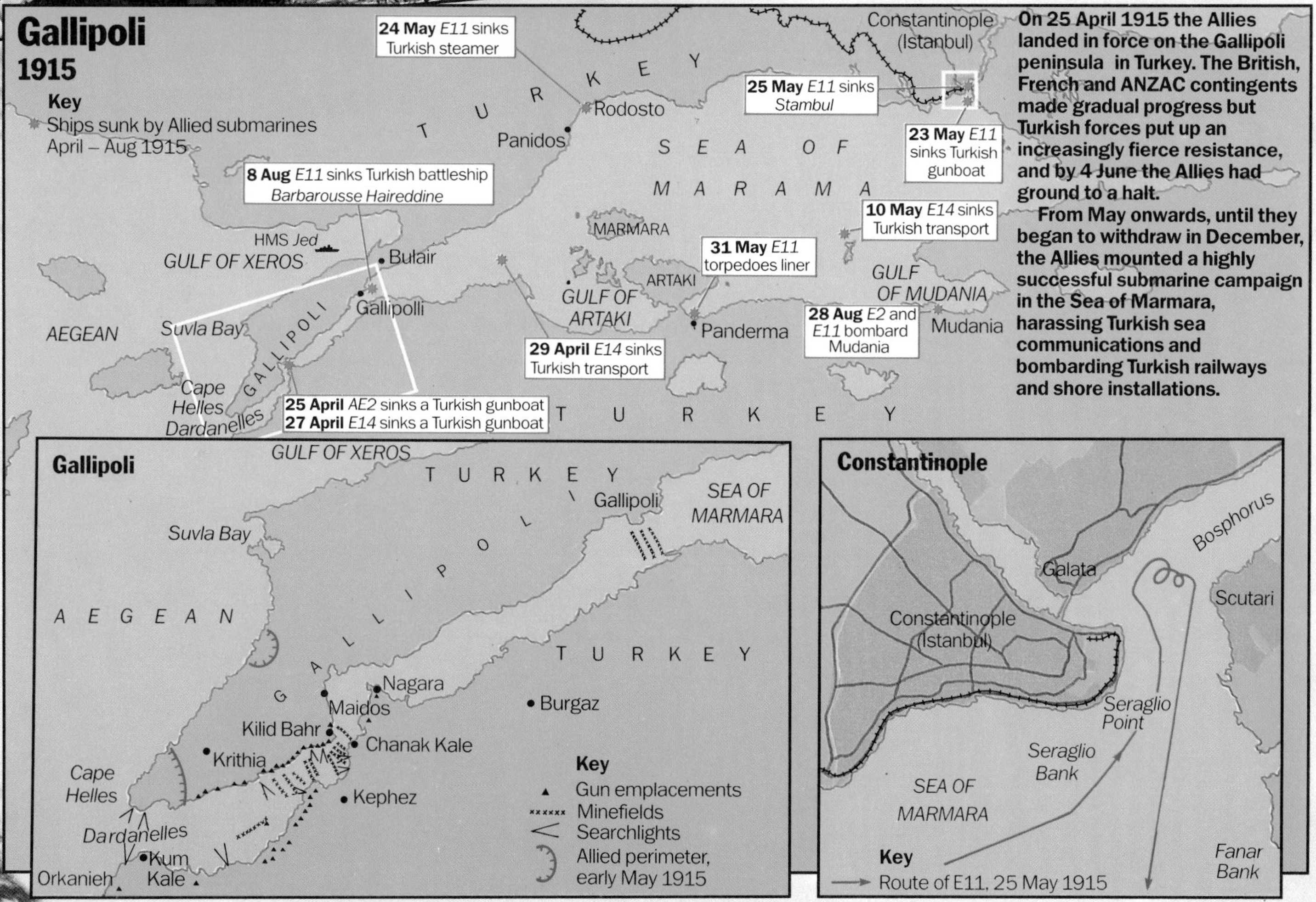
Gallipoli 1915
Key
Ships sunk by Allied submarines April – Aug 1915
24 May E11 sinks Turkish steamer
25 May E11 sinks Stambul
23 May E11 sinks Turkish gunboat
8 Aug E11 sinks Turkish battleship Barbarousse Haireddine
10 May E14 sinks Turkish transport
31 May E11 torpedoes liner
28 Aug E2 and E11 bombard Mudania
29 April E14 sinks Turkish transport
25 April AE2 sinks a Turkish gunboat
27 April E14 sinks a Turkish gunboat
Constantinople (Istanbul)
TURKEY
Rodosto
Panidos
SEA OF MARAMA
MARMARA
HMS Jed
GULF OF XEROS
Bulair
Gallipoli
GULF OF ARTAKI
ARTAKI
GULF OF MUDANIA
Mudania
Panderma
AEGEAN
Suvla Bay
GALLIPOLI
Cape Helles
Dardanelles
Gallipoli
GULF OF XEROS
TURKEY
SEA OF MARMARA
Suvla Bay
AEGEAN
GALLIPOLI
Nagara
Maidos
Kilid Bahr
Chanak Kale
Krithia
Burgaz
Kephez
Cape Helles
Dardanelles
Kum Kale
Orkanieh
Key
Gun emplacements
Minefields
Searchlights
Allied perimeter, early May 1915
Constantinople
Bosphorus
Galata
Scutari
Constantinople (Istanbul)
Seraglio Point
Seraglio Bank
SEA OF MARMARA
Fanar Bank
Key
Route of E11, 25 May 1915

On 25 April 1915 the Allies landed in force on the Gallipoli peninsula in Turkey. The British, French and ANZAC contingents made gradual progress but Turkish forces put up an increasingly fierce resistance, and by 4 June the Allies had ground to a halt.

From May onwards, until they began to withdraw in December, the Allies mounted a highly successful submarine campaign in the Sea of Marmara, harassing Turkish sea communications and bombarding Turkish railways and shore installations.

crew had been ordered into lifeboats. A second deeply-laden ship was chased into Rodosto harbour and torpedoed at the quayside from a range of 1000yds; the enormous explosion which followed the torpedo strike indicated that she too was carrying ammunition. A further ship was forced to beach to avoid being sunk. Nasmith now began to look eastward towards the then Turkish capital of Constantinople (Istanbul). If *E11* could sneak into the harbour there and sink a vessel of reasonable size, the propaganda victory gained would be enormous. It would be a vivid demonstration to Turkey (and the world) that even her capital city was not safe from attack.

Early in the morning of 25 May, *E11* edged into the harbour at Constantinople, the great walled city visible through the morning mist on their port bow. Taking every care not to be discovered, Nasmith gently probed further northward into the Bosphorus, the channel which connects the Black Sea to the Sea of Marmara. The *E11's* entrance was not without incident, however, as Nasmith recorded:

> 'Our manoeuvring was rather difficult because of the cross-tides, the mud, and the current, but most particularly on account of a damn fool of a fisherman who kept trying to grab the top of my periscope every time I raised it to take an observation. I don't think he had any idea what it was, but to get rid of him I gave him a chance to get a good hold on it. Then I ordered "Down periscope quickly" and almost succeeded in capsizing his boat. When I looked at him a minute later he wore the most amazed and bewildered expression I ever hope to see.'

A target was eventually located, a large transport vessel which lay alongside the Topkhara Arsenal. A torpedo was fired but a defect in the gyro caused it to leap out of the water and race madly off course. A second torpedo was prepared and loosed off and as Nasmith watched the weapon's track heading straight towards the transport, to his sudden and complete astonishment he saw the first torpedo swing round back towards *E11*. The submarine crash-dived, just in time to allow the wildcat torpedo to carry on at 47 knots along its eccentric course. The harbour was in uproar: the second torpedo hit home and the transport began to settle in the water while the harbour craft tried desperately to avoid being hit by the first torpedo which eventually struck home, exploding by the Galata Bridge.

Turkish guns opened up in all directions, splinters hitting *E11's* hull as she dived down to get out of the harbour at as deep a level as possible. Disaster almost struck when she bounced around on the bottom off Leander Point, grounding on a loose sand shoal, only to be caught in a cross-current which sent the submarine spinning round on her axis. Eventually the helmsman restored the boat's trim and at a depth of 85ft she headed seaward.

After resting the crew and carrying out running repairs to the submarine, Nasmith set out to find new targets. On 28 May a convoy was spotted crossing the sea, amongst which was a large steamer, duly selected as first victim. Edging carefully under the destroyer escort, Nasmith let loose a torpedo at a close range, sending the merchantman to the bottom within a minute of the torpedo hitting the ship's hull.

Supplies were now running low, and with only one torpedo left *E11* looked carefully for one last target. Nasmith hoped to catch the battleship *Barbarossa* which was thought to be in position in the Dardanelles. On the night of 3 June, *E11* developed a major fault in the transmission and turned for home, intending to loose her last torpedo against *Barbarossa* if she could be found. The *Barbarossa* remained hidden, but the last torpedo successfuly sank a transport vessel at the entrance to the Dardanelles.

The return trip began without trouble, *E11* rounding Nagara Point before proceeding to dive down below the minefields strung across the Narrows. Alongside Kilid Bahr the helmsmen began to have problems holding the boat's trim. Coming up to periscope depth to determine the source of the

Below right: The sortie into the Sea of Marmara of May 1915 was not the last episode in the illustrious career of submarine *E11* (shown below). She is seen here being applauded by the crew of HMS *Grampus* while returning from sinking the Turkish battleship *Barbarossa* on 8 August 1915. Below left: *E11's* periscope after the raid in Constantinople harbour; it sustained a strike by a 6-pounder shell from a Turkish patrol boat.

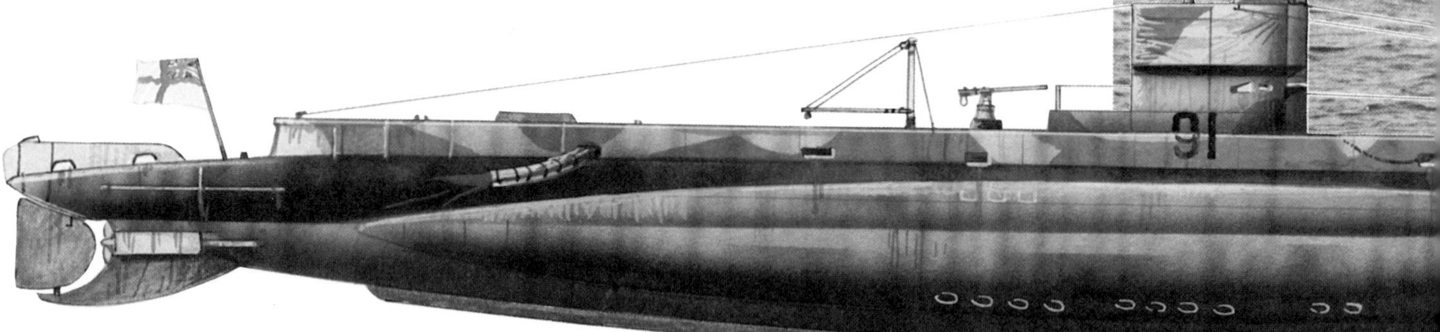
91

problem – probably a piece of wreckage fouling one of the hydroplanes – Nasmith was horrified to see that *E11* was trailing behind her a six-horned mine that had attached itself to the port hydrophone by a trailing wire. If one of the horns knocked against the vessel, a glass tube inside would break and release acid. This would complete the circuit required to detonate the 80lb of high explosive inside the mine. With the mine dragging behind her, *E11* slowly made her way under the remainder of the minefields until at last they were past Cape Helles and out of the Dardanelles. Now clear of the Turkish defences, Nasmith was able to free the mine and, hoisting the white ensign, he surfaced to the cheers of the British escort vessels awaiting *E11's* arrival.

The patrol of *E11* was a triumph for the Royal Navy's submariners, and it was welcomed by the troops on the ground as one of the few operations that had gone the Allies' way during the otherwise disastrous Dardanelles campaign. First Sea Lord Winston Churchill paid full compliment to *E11* when he wrote of the Submarine Branch's contribution during the campaign: 'The naval history of Britain contains no page more wonderful than that which records the prowess of her submarines at the Dardanelles.'

THE AUTHOR Adrian Gilbert has edited and contributed to a number of military and naval publications. His book *World War I in Photographs*, which is soon to be published; covers all aspects of the Great War.

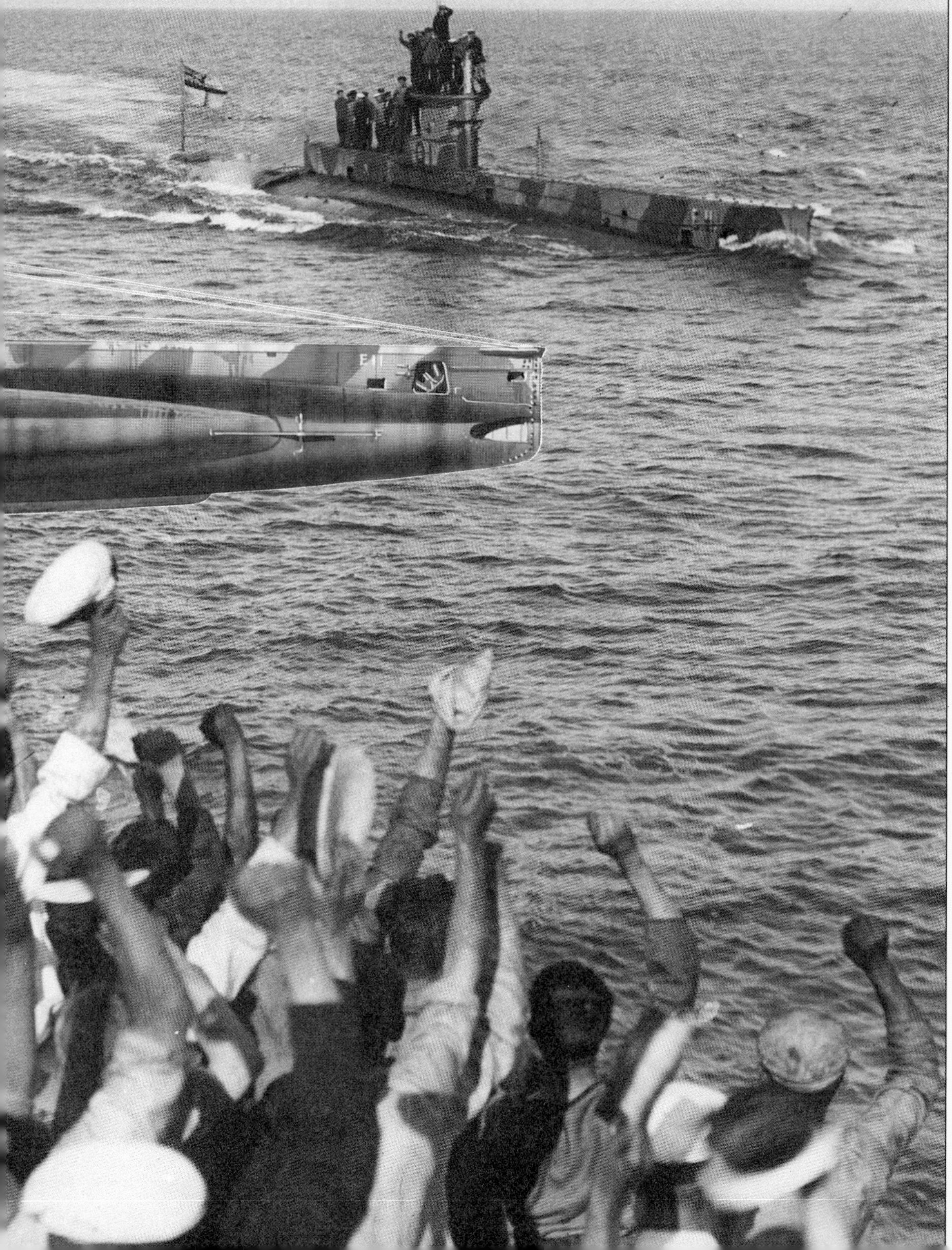

E-CLASS SUBMARINES

The first E-class ocean-going submarine was completed in 1913, and over the following three years some 55 boats were commissioned. A generally successful design, the 'E' saw service in most of the World War I theatres of submarine warfare, including the North Sea, Baltic and Mediterranean. While moving on the surface, the submarine was powered by twin diesel engines (of eight cylinders each), while two electric motors enabled the craft to travel underwater for up to 75 miles. The submarine had five torpedo tubes and could carry 10 torpedoes, a total which was found inadequate for long-range patrols. A more serious restriction, however, was the lack of deck armament, for a gun was by far the most economical and effective means of dealing with unarmed merchant vessels, the main victims of submarine warfare. Several attempts were made to rectify this shortcoming: 2-pounder, and later 12-pounder, guns were adapted for submarine use, and one E-class boat was even fitted with a 6in howitzer, a useful weapon for shore bombardment. Following the capture of a German minelaying submarine in 1915, six British E-class boats were converted as minelayers. Equipped with three torpedo tubes and 16 vertical mine tubes, they carried a total of 32 mines.

UPHOLDER

CUTTING THE LIFELINE

LIEUTENANT-COMMANDER MALCOLM DAVID WANKLYN

Malcolm David Wanklyn was born in London on 28 June 1911. He joined the Royal Naval College in Dartmouth as a cadet at the age of 13 and a half, and subsequently gained the maximum number of five first-class certificates in his lieutenant's examinations. 'Five ones' did not always signify the best kind of officer, but Wanklyn had a strong, resourceful personality to go with his brains. He was practical as well as intelligent: courageous determination was his finest characteristic and he was to demonstrate an uncanny flair for being in the right place at the right time.

Volunteering for submarines in 1933, he was just 29 years old when, after briefly commanding the elderly *H-31* on war patrols in the Channel and the North Sea, he commissioned HMS *Upholder* in August 1940 at Barrow.

Wanklyn had a keen, studious face with an untidy beard which gave him a rather Old Testament appearance. When going to sea he wore a thoroughly disreputable uniform, the trousers shiny with age and the two and a half gold stripes on his monkey jacket tattered and torn: but that in no way deprived him of authority.

Many admiring words were spoken of Wanklyn. Special operations Corporal 'Dicky' Bird said, 'he was respected as a skipper second to none by everybody that knew him', and when *Upholder* failed to return from her last patrol Captain Simpson wrote to the Admiralty, 'it seems that Wanklyn was a man whom the nation can ill afford to lose'.

Below left: With his submarine HMS *Upholder* in the background, Lieutenant-Commander Malcolm David Wanklyn stands with his officers on the Lazaretto quayside. Below far left: Wanklyn points from the conning-tower. Below: Two U-class boats of the 10th Submarine Flotilla await operations in Valletta's Quarantine Harbour. Bottom: *Upholder's* sister ship HMS *Unrivalled* sails into Valletta flying the Jolly Roger after a successful raid.

SIMONDS
ALES & STOUT

HMS *Upholder* achieved more than any other British submarine in the campaign to strangle the supply line to Rommel's Afrika Korps

THE SMALL SUBMARINE HMS *Upholder* arrived at Malta on 14 January 1941. With the least possible number of telegraph orders her captain, Lieutenant-Commander Malcolm David Wanklyn, manoeuvred the craft alongside her berth in Lazaretto Creek, where a new submarine base had been established within the ancient Lazaretto itself. This last was a massive stone building which had been used for quarantine purposes in the days of the bubonic plague. Facing south on to the deep harbour, it was bordered to the north by a sheer rock face that offered a degree of protection from the island's constant air raids. The Lazaretto periodically took a battering but, somehow or other, the base always managed to keep functioning under its dynamic leader, Captain 'Shrimp' Simpson, and his engineer officer, Commander Sam MacGregor.

Captain Simpson was commander of the British 10th Submarine Flotilla, established in Malta to strike out and sever the vital Axis supply line from Italy to North Africa. As the land battles of the Desert War surged back and forth along the North African coast, both sides were desperate for reinforcements and supplies. While the Allied armies, based in Egypt, had to be supplied by ships steaming 12,000 miles around the Cape, Rommel's forces in Libya were receiving material from across the short sea route to Italy. Simpson knew that if supplies to Rommel were allowed to flood in unchecked, the Germans would win control of North Africa: it was as simple as that.

She carried a full load of eight torpedoes, four of them ready in the tubes

As Lieutenant-Commander Wanklyn briskly climbed down from his submarine, it was 'Shrimp' Simpson who greeted him at the gangway. *Upholder* was the first boat to join the newly established flotilla, and more were on their way. Everything was in short supply on the beleaguered island, including torpedoes. 'Shrimp' made the point to Wanklyn that the 'fish' had to be conserved very carefully. In the light of what followed, perhaps he emphasised the need too strongly.

Upholder sailed on 24 January for her first patrol, heading for an area west of Tripoli. She carried a full load of eight torpedoes, four of them ready in the tubes. Soon after midnight on 26 January, while the submarine's batteries were recharging on the surface, the officer of the watch sighted the vague shapes of a supply ship guarded by a single destroyer. Wanklyn commenced a surface attack: at 0130 he fired two torpedoes at the merchant vessel, but they missed. Evading the escort, he saw a second supply ship coming up astern, but two more fish aimed at this vessel also missed their mark.

At this point it might be as well to recall the fire-control problem that faced submarine captains in World War II. Wartime torpedoes were straight-running at 45 knots and they had no homing devices. They were fired in 'hosepipe' salvoes, one following another along the same path, and the submarine itself had to be pointed at the future position of the oncoming enemy. The firing interval between each fish was such that, in effect, the target's own movement created the spread. Nowadays, torpedoes are discharged on divergent courses like a slightly opened fan.

Two torpedoes alone were seldom sufficient to allow for the margin of error in the captain's calculations which was bound to occur. Fire-control calculations were entirely dependent, when dived, on the captain's own observations through the slender attack periscope which could only be raised, cautiously, for a few seconds at a time. During those brief glimpses, preceded by an 'all round look' for escorts, the captain had to take an accurate relative bearing (which was converted to true bearing by referring to the gyrocompass). He would judge the inclination by angle-on-the-bow (which, combined with true bearing, gave the target course), and then measure the range on a part of the target of which the height was known – the funnel or masthead as a rule – by means of a miniature range-finder incorporated in the periscope.

When the captain's observations were plotted, a fairly reliable estimate of enemy speed could be obtained; but a propeller revolution count by the Asdic operator was also useful, and so was intelligence about the enemy's capabilities. Sometimes it helped to gauge the distance of the second bow wave from the bow (when visible) because that, too, gave an all-important indication of speed. The results gained by these procedures were fed into an elementary calculator called the ISWAS or, as the war progressed, into a slightly more advanced torpedo director known as the Fruit Machine. Either way, the calculator produced a DA (Director Angle) – that is to say, the lead angle which the submarine would have to steer for the torpedoes to intercept the target.

A good captain could usually produce a target solution correct to within a couple of knots for speed and 10 or 20 degrees for course. He then endeavoured to fire so that the torpedoes ran at more or less right angles to the enemy's course from an ideal range of about 1000yds. At that range, the fish took only 40 seconds to cross the enemy's track or, hopefully, impact on the target: this gave little opportunity for the ship under attack to take evasive action if the torpedo wakes were sighted, while the chances of him altering course in the normal way, on a standard zig-zag pattern, were minimised. But, of course, there were escorts to be evaded on the way in, and the approach was by no means easy.

Paradoxically, although submerged attacks presented plenty of problems, nocturnal attacks on the surface were, in some ways, more complex still. The captain on the bridge, divorced from his periscope, had no range-finder, and it was exceedingly difficult to estimate a darkened ship's inclination. It was thus often impossible to develop a meaningful plot down below. The resultant DA was therefore usually no better than a good guess – although some old hands said it was always 10 degrees whatever, and more often than not they were right! Attacking was both a science and an art. Hitting depended very largely on the captain's personal skill, judgement and courage. Some captains had a natural 'periscope eye' or acquired it in time: others never did get the hang of the game. Wanklyn was certainly not one of the latter, but his early attacks were almost all failures.

On his first Mediterranean patrol he did succeed in hitting the German transport *Duisberg* but 'Shrimp', necessarily a miser, did not reckon that a fair return for a total of eight valuable torpedoes.

U-CLASS SUBMARINES

The British U-class submarines were originally intended to be training boats, but it was quickly realised that they had great operational potential . Only 191ft long, with a draught of 14ft 5in and displacing 720 tons submerged, they were agile and relatively difficult to detect either on the surface or dived. Moreover, they were economical in manpower: the normal wartime crew consisted of four officers and 27 ratings. Unfortunately, they had disadvantages as well. Their top speed on the surface was 12 knots: time and again lack of speed robbed the Malta-based submarines of the 10th Flotilla of opportunities to attack. Their range, 3800 miles, was short, but that was unimportant in the Mediterranean theatre. Underwater, the U-class could make eight knots, though only for the limited period of about one hour. At two and a half knots (the normal patrol speed) endurance was an adequate 60 hours.

Another principal restriction of the design was its nominal maximum diving depth of 200ft – although HMS *Ultimatum*, late in the war, went to 400ft without collapsing.

Eight torpedoes were carried for the four bow tubes, and at close range the 12-pounder gun gave effective fire. Habitability was poor, but patrols seldom lasted longer than a week or two. The junior ratings lived with the torpedoes in the stowage compartment, while the officers, petty officers and engine room artificers had tiny messes of their own. HMS *Upholder*, ninth in a line of more than 50, was launched on 8 July 1940. She sailed for work-up in September of that year before leaving for the Mediterranean in December.

After the last – and abortive – attack of this initial patrol *Upholder* also had her baptism of fire. The escorting destroyers saw the torpedo tracks and pounced. The depth-charges sounded like gigantic hammer blows on the hull, reminding the crew all too forcibly that they were locked inescapably in a fragile steel tube separated from the crushing sea by a mere half-inch thickness of metal. But, listening intently at 150ft to the Asdic operator's reports – 'bearing drawing slowly right... getting fainter' – Wanklyn was able to steal quietly away. Retrospectively, though, *Upholder's* 'hammering' had a beneficial effect: it reassured the crew that their captain could get them out of trouble.

Upholder had to go deep in a hurry while a 'wanderer' circled, clattering noisily, overhead

Morale was high when *Upholder* sailed on the next three successive patrols, but success continued to elude Wanklyn. By the middle of April, 30 torpedoes had been fired with only one certain hit – and even then the *Duisberg* had not sunk. Simpson was forced to ask himself whether he could afford to keep such a poor shot in the flotilla. Wanklyn's leadership, mathematical ability and meticulous accuracy were obvious to all. Why, then, were his initial patrols so unproductive?

Firstly, he heeded the order to conserve torpedoes too literally, for his salvoes should have been larger and spread wider. Secondly, some of the fish were elderly and unreliable: on one occasion *Upholder* had to go deep in a hurry while a 'wanderer' circled, clattering noisily, overhead. Furthermore, the touchy weapons seemed to resent being fired on the surface in anything but a flat calm sea, and a fair number probably careered off course after being discharged. However, Wanklyn's keen analysis of his situation gradually led him to realise the causes of his early failures. When *Upholder* set out on her fifth patrol he coolly resolved to put matters right, even if that meant disobeying his directives concerning economical use of torpedoes.

To make sure of hitting the next target, the 5500-ton *Antonietta Laura*, he decided to use all four of his bow tubes from the very close range of 700yds. The first fish of the salvo hit amidships – which suggests, incidentally, that the target's speed was underestimated, because the torpedo from No. 1 tube would have been deliberately aimed to pass ahead on the calculated DA with a spread for errors. Despite the natural upsurge of relief and excitement at that moment, Wanklyn had the presence of mind to stop the automatic firing of the third and fourth torpedoes (number two was already on its way), thereby reserving them for the next opportunity.

Opportunities for *Upholder* now at last started to come, and steadily the submarine went into the kill. The symbols on her Jolly Roger pirate's flag, traditionally flown by submarines on return from sea to signify their successes, clearly showed how the enemy tonnage sunk was totting up.

Upholder's luck had changed through the dogged determination of her captain; but St Ambrose, the patron saint of submariners, was off watch for a while in May. The Asdic set – the captain's only means of knowing what was happening 'up top' when deep – became defective when the submarine was patrolling off Sicily in the Straits of Messina. A lesser man would have turned back to base, which was only a day or so distant, but not Wanklyn when an important convoy was expected.

On 20 May an attempt was made on two tankers at the extreme range of well over two miles, but without results. However, when a third tanker appeared nearer the submarine three days later it took a torpedo in the stern. Stealing away from the ensuing mêlée, Wanklyn found himself, quite by chance, right in the path of a much bigger target. It turned out to be the liner-troopship *Conte Rosso*.

The last pair of torpedoes would have to be fired at virtually point-blank range

It was impossible to count the number of escorts surrounding this very important ship and Wanklyn did not try to do so. Just two torpedoes remained and there was to be no help from the silent Asdic set. He calculated that his quarry was making 20 knots, which allowed him scant time to generate a fire-control solution. But that was the kind of mathematical problem at which Wanklyn excelled.

If the last pair of torpedoes were to find their mark they would have to be fired at virtually point-blank range. There was no time to waste: Wanklyn could not afford to wriggle and deviate from the optimum closing course in order to avoid escorts. The only thing to do was to ignore them and disregard the very real danger of being rammed on the run in. Wanklyn calmly accepted the risk, refused to be distracted and focussed his whole attention on the target. Following a tense period when his submarine was forced deep by a charging destroyer, he found his moment. The loss of life from the *Conte Rosso* when *Upholder's* weapons hit was heavy: out of 3000 Italian soldiers on board only 1432 were saved.

Now came the inevitable counter-attack. Over the next half-hour the depth-charges plunged down, some of them exploding very close indeed, but not quite within the lethal 30ft of *Upholder's* hull. Inside

Left: Resplendent in their Mediterranean blue livery, *Upholder* and her small sister submarines were ideal craft for operations in clear, shallow waters. Above left: The cramped engine room of a U-class submarine, with (inset top) a commander using the search periscope in the control room and (inset bottom) hydroplane operators with an Asdic operator in the background.

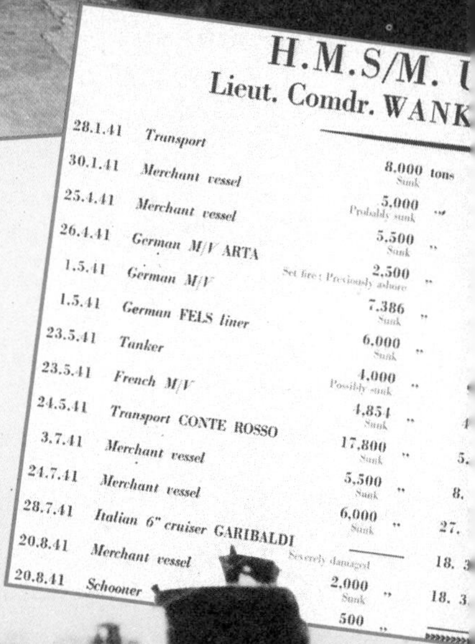

H.M.S/M. U
Lieut. Comdr. WANK

28.1.41	*Transport*	8,000 tons Sunk		
30.1.41	*Merchant vessel*	5,000 Probably sunk	"	
25.4.41	*Merchant vessel*	5,500 Sunk	"	
26.4.41	*German M/V* ARTA	2,500 Set fire: Previously ashore	"	
1.5.41	*German M/V*	7,386 Sunk	"	
1.5.41	*German* FELS *liner*	6,000 Sunk	"	
23.5.41	*Tanker*	4,000 Possibly sunk	"	
23.5.41	*French M/V*	4,854 Sunk	"	4
24.5.41	*Transport* CONTE ROSSO	17,800 Sunk	"	5.
3.7.41	*Merchant vessel*	5,500 Sunk	"	8.
24.7.41	*Merchant vessel*	6,000 Sunk	"	27.
28.7.41	*Italian 6" cruiser* GARIBALDI	Severely damaged		18. 3
20.8.41	*Merchant vessel*	2,000 Sunk	"	18. 3
20.8.41	*Schooner*	500	"	

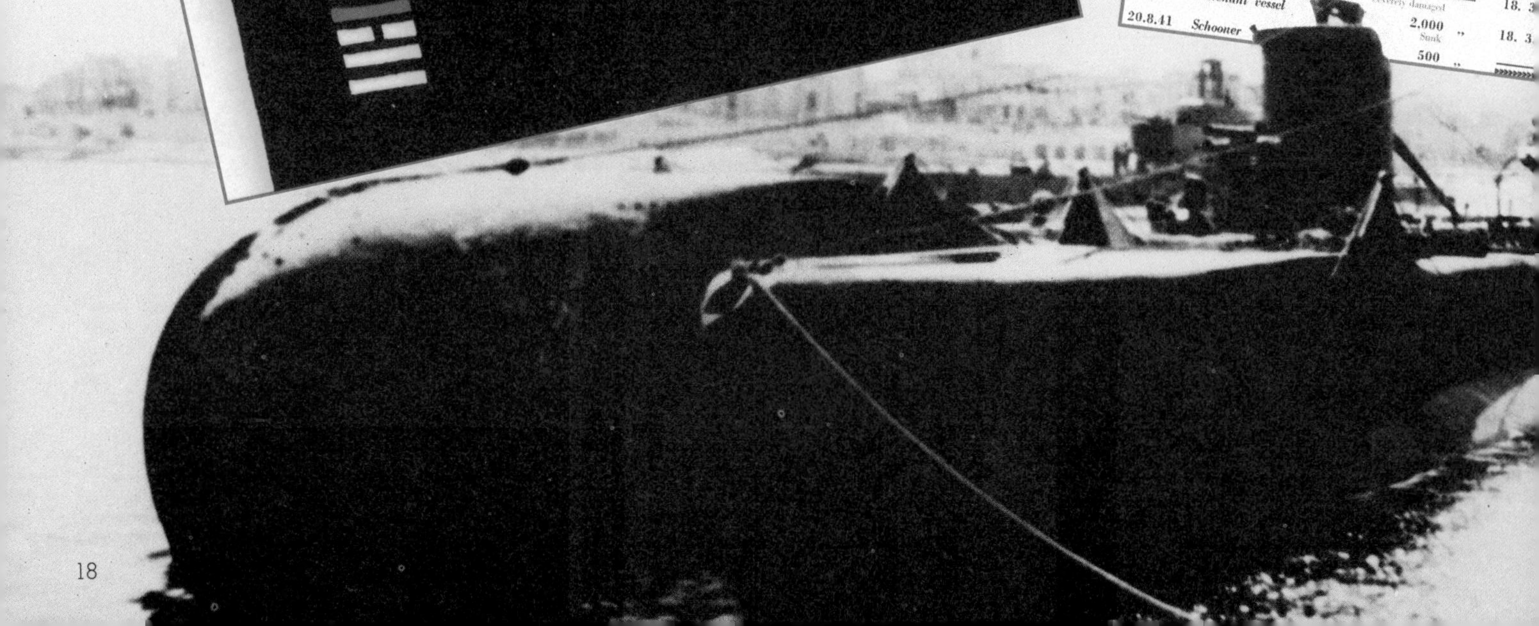

eft: Lieutenant-Commander lalcolm David Wanklyn is hotographed with some of pholder's officers and crew llowing his award of the VC. elow left: *Upholder's* ombat record and (below far eft) the submarine's Jolly oger. The bars on the left of ie flag stand for ships sunk split bar indicates a ship hit ut not sunk, while red enotes a warship and white a ipply ship). On the right of ie flag, the star above rossed guns indicates a iccessful gun action, the agger marks a special peration, and the three red mbols denote three U-boats ink. It was later discovered iat one of the U-boats icceeded in escaping *pholder's* torpedoes. ottom: *Upholder* lies ongside her sister ship HMS *rge*. Although both belong the 1939 Programme of U-ass submarines, there is a arked difference in their onstruction. *Upholder* (left) as a raised, rounded bow nd is armed with a 12-ounder gun. *Urge* has a flush ow and carries a 0.3in gun.

the boat there was complete silence, save for a few quiet helm orders from the captain in the control room where, apparently unconcerned, he stroked his beard thoughtfully from time to time as he listened to the express-train noise of destroyers racing overhead. All too audible, even without artificial Asdic 'ears', the screws indicated that the next shattering and potentially fatal pattern of explosions would arrive in an exact number of seconds. Time after time, the submariners ticked off the seconds on their fingers before the next wave of explosions flung their craft aside.

One man's nerve broke. The signalman suddenly dashed at the lower conning-tower lid and started to ease back the clips – a futile gesture because, even if he had been allowed to climb the tower, the external pressure on the upper hatch was more than 20 tons. He was reverted to general service – the worst, in fact the only, punishment on board *Upholder* – but back at Malta Simpson understandingly assured him that there was nothing to be ashamed of.

For this attack on one of Rommel's troopships, under the most testing and dangerous circumstances imaginable, Malcolm David Wanklyn was awarded the Victoria Cross. His fellow submariners, the most critical judges anywhere, applauded.

Throughout the rest of 1941, *Upholder's* assaults on the enemy continued unabated. Meanwhile, losses at sea amongst other boats of the 10th Flotilla were growing. The submarines were also attacked in harbour when the Luftwaffe stepped up their bombing raids shortly before Christmas and, with showers of bombs plastering the anchorages, the boats were forced to lie on the bottom by day in the hope of escaping damage.

In September, with *Upholder* still miraculously unscathed, Wanklyn conducted what was arguably the most skilful attack ever made by a submarine commanding officer. Three large troopships, escorted by four or more destroyers, were the targets. But then *Upholder's* gyro-compass failed, causing the boat to lurch and swing wildly at speed on the surface in the long swell, while the coxswain struggled vainly to maintain a steady firing course by the erratic magnetic compass. In spite of this serious handicap and the very long range of about 5000yds, two of the massive liners – the *Neptunia* (19,330 tons) and the *Oceania* (19,405 tons) – were sunk by *Upholder's* torpedoes before the crucial convoy reached Tripoli. It was an irremediable loss for Rommel: in the space of five hours, Wanklyn had accounted for as many enemy men as the total number of Allied submariners employed in the long Mediterranean war.

Wanklyn did not trouble, in his patrol report, to underline the fact that the attack was uniquely tricky with the boat yawing several degrees either side of the true course. He simply remarked that he had been forced to spread his torpedoes over the full length of *both* overlapping targets, with the first fish aimed, as normal, at the leading target's bow. Then a violent yaw to starboard obliged him to fire his second where normally the fourth would have been aimed; and Nos. 3 and 4 tubes were fired to fill the gap on the swing back to port. The modest account did not deceive Captain Simpson, who now fully appreciated his finest commanding officer's exceptional skill and bravery.

The story of *Upholder* finishes in sadly low key. Having despatched still more supply ships in January and March 1942, she sailed for her 25th patrol in April. On her return, Wanklyn was to take her home

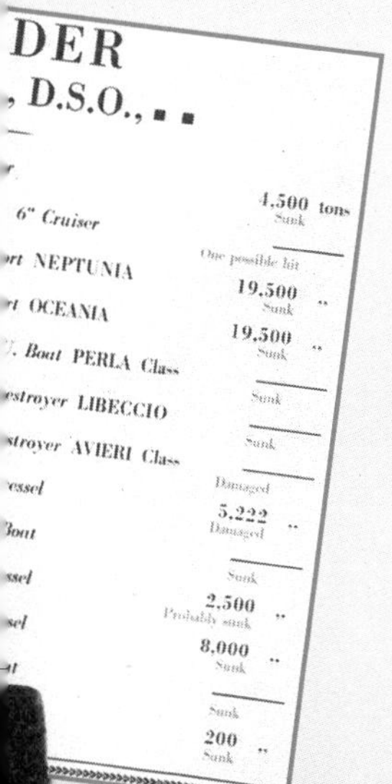
DER
, D.S.O., ■ ■

6" Cruiser	4,500 tons Sunk
rt NEPTUNIA	One possible hit
t OCEANIA	19,500 " Sunk
. Boat PERLA Class	19,500 " Sunk
estroyer LIBECCIO	Sunk
stroyer AVIERI Class	Sunk
essel	Damaged
Boat	5,222 " Damaged
ssel	Sunk
sel	2,500 " Probably sunk
t	8,000 " Sunk
	Sunk
	200 " Sunk

Below: A German transport ship in dazzle camouflage unloads supplies in North Africa. Such vessels were prime targets for Malta-based submarines aiming to sever Rommel's link with Axis resources in Italy.

to England for a refit and a much-needed rest for himself and the crew.

But *Upholder* never came back. While making a submerged approach on a convoy off Tripoli on 14 April 1942, she was seen from the air in clear, calm water. The seaplane marked the spot with a smoke float and the small Italian torpedo boat *Pegaso* sped to the location, dropping a random pattern of depth-charges without ever gaining firm contact. At least one charge must have struck home.

Ironically, the captain of the seemingly unimportant little vessel – much less formidable than the foes that *Upholder* had previously enountered – did not know what he had done and made no claim; but in fact *Pegaso* had put an end to the short but glorious life of the Royal Navy's most hard-hitting submarine, together with her gallant crew and captain. None of them was saved.

Upholder was a tiny submarine by the standards of today: a modern nuclear attack boat is seven times the size. But being small had been a positive advantage in the confined waters of the central Mediterranean. In less than 16 months, from January 1941 to April 1942, *Upholder's* torpedoes had sent two Italian U-boats and a destroyer to the bottom, damaged one cruiser and one destroyer, and had either sunk or damaged 19 Axis transport and supply vessels. The total bag amounted to 133,940 tons, including a luckless trawler that fell victim to the 12-pounder gun. During her brief wartime career, she had destroyed or disabled a greater tonnage than any other British boat, and had topped the achievements of the most successful American submarine by one third. Even compared with the best of the German U-boats, which were preying on much easier targets in the broad Atlantic, *Upholder* ranks as one of the most destructive submarines in World War II.

THE AUTHOR Commander Richard Compton-Hall, MBE, RN, (ret'd) is director of the Submarine Museum at HMS *Dolphin*, the Royal Navy's submarine base at Gosport. During his naval service he commanded three submarines, including an X-Craft.

Left: *Upholder's* sister ship HMS *Utmost* lies alongside the Lazaretto submarine base. The tall radio mast (used to transmit reports of sightings of the enemy) and the attack periscope are raised, and a Lewis gun has been mounted on the starboard side of the bridge. Bottom: The crew of *Upholder* line up to cheer their captain as he is piped aboard following the award of the Victoria Cross. As a tribute to the gallant men of the small submarine, the first of Britain's new class of Type 2400 diesel-electric submarines will be named *Upholder* when she is launched at the end of 1986.

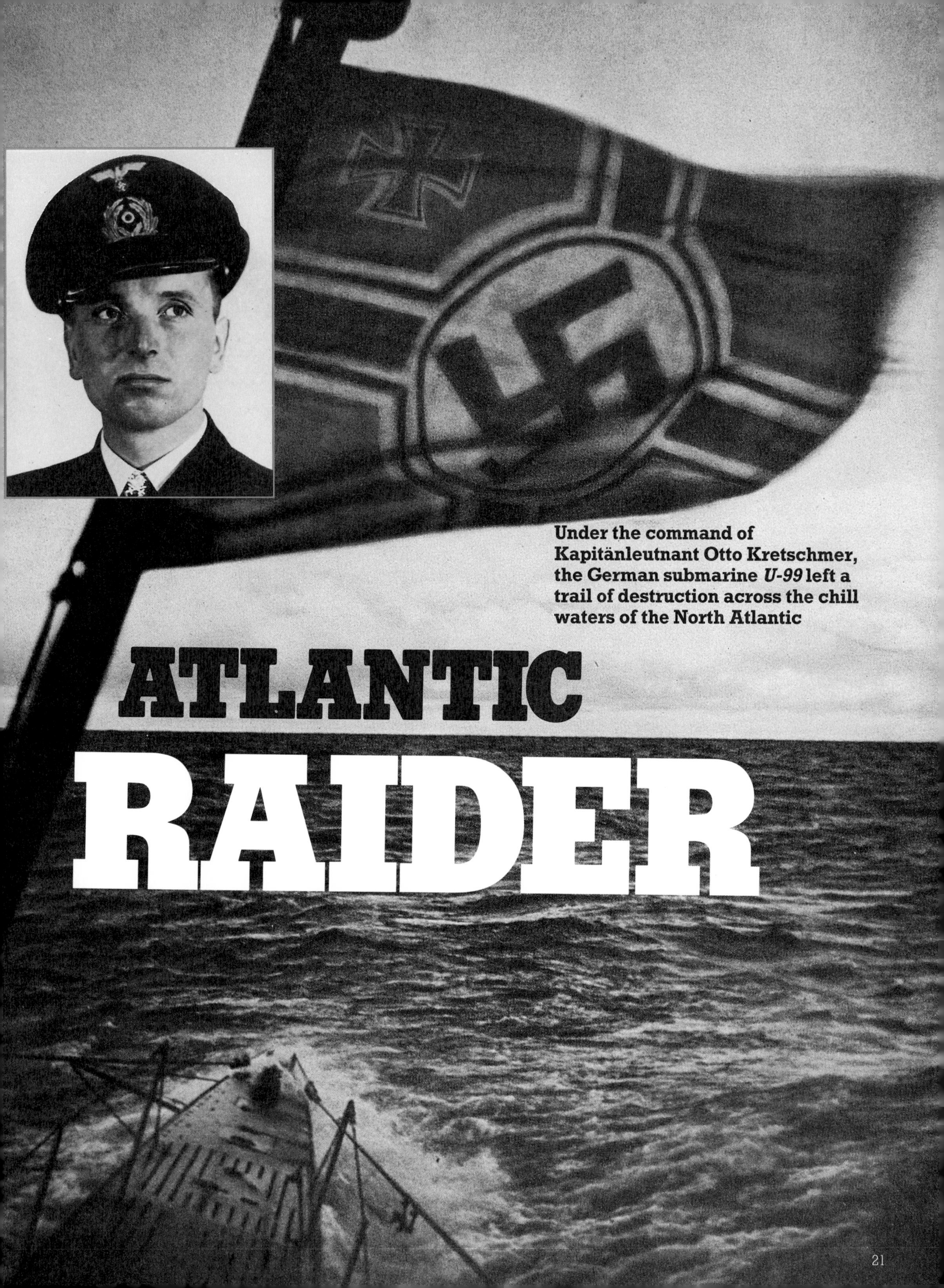

Under the command of Kapitänleutnant Otto Kretschmer, the German submarine *U-99* left a trail of destruction across the chill waters of the North Atlantic

ATLANTIC RAIDER

OTTO KRETSCHMER

In 1936, at the age of 24, Otto Kretschmer, shown above with Hitler, volunteered for training in Germany's new expanding U-boat force. Cool, confident and dedicated to his chosen career, Kretschmer rose rapidly to the command of his own boat, the *U-23*, a 250-ton coastal attack craft. From the start of World War II, he was involved in operations in the North Sea and around the Orkneys and Shetlands, scoring some notable successes, particularly the sinking in February 1940 of the British destroyer *Daring.* On 30 April 1940 he assumed command of the newly commissioned ocean-going submarine *U-99*. His exploits in the Atlantic over the following year made him famous. Kretschmer did not affect the relaxed, somewhat indisciplined style adopted by some U-boat commanders, always maintaining his crew in strict military dress and behaviour whenever possible.

His only self-indulgence was a taste for cigars – he chain-smoked on the conning-tower throughout the course of surface operations. By the time his career was brought to an end by his capture in March 1941, he is reckoned to have sunk over 350,000 tons of British shipping, making him probably the greatest U-boat ace of the war.

As a prisoner of war, Kretschmer was promoted to full captain while in the camp and was finally released in 1947.

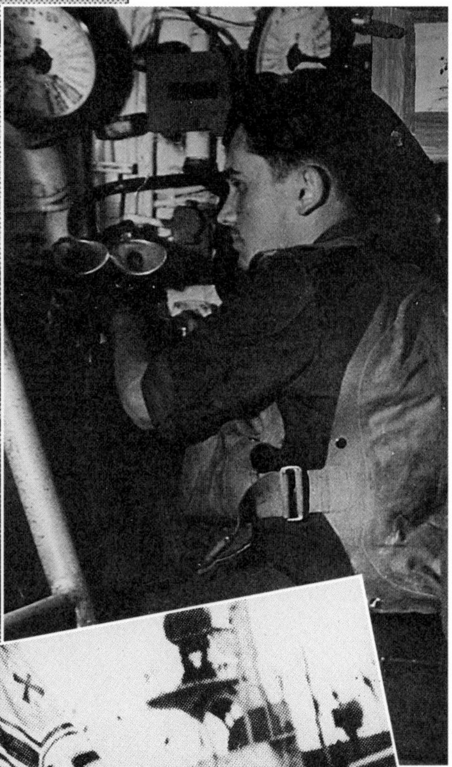

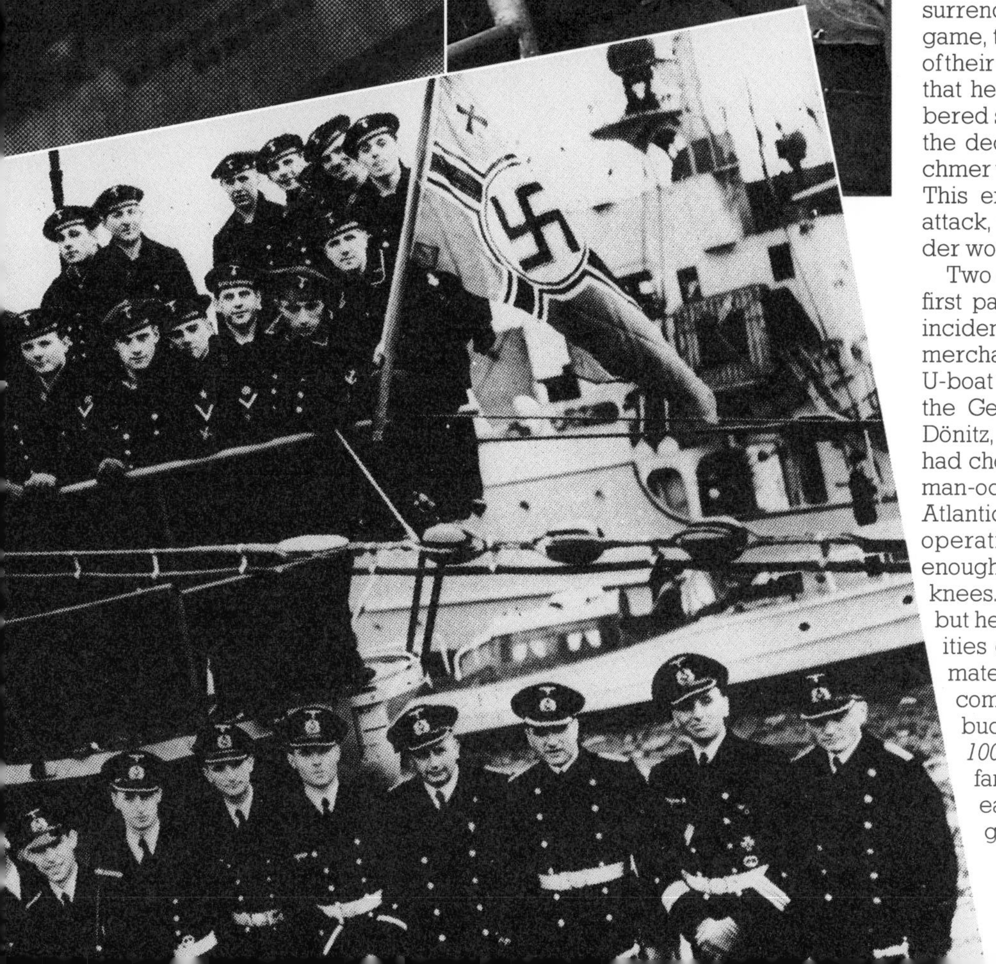

Page 21 : Its flag billowing in the wind, a Kriegsmarine raider heads for the atlantic in search of a convoy, and (inset) Otto Kretschmer, one of Germany's top U-boat aces. Left: Kretschmer's *U-99* returns to base on 10 November 1940 after a successful patrol. The flags commemorate a seven-hour tussle with two British escorts. Bottom: Officers and crew of *U-99* pose for the camera in Kiel during May 1940. Below: Life on a U-boat was cramped and uncomfortable.

AT 0806 HOURS on 8 July 1940, Kapitänleutnant Otto Kretschmer, commander of the German submarine *U-99*, then on its first marauding patrol in the North Atlantic, recorded in his war diary:

> 'Propeller noises heard approaching to starboard. I order depth to be trimmed at 100ft. I believe my crew are going to get their baptism of depth-charging this time. Escort approaching fast as though to attack.'

Minutes later, the U-boat shook violently as the first depth-charges exploded. It was the start of an ordeal that would last almost 20 hours. Completely at the mercy of their attackers, Kretschmer and his crew, their unshaven faces pale and drawn in the dim electric light, could only sit and sweat it out, cramped inside their narrow vessel. Chief Radio Operator Jupp Kassel, at the U-boat's hydrophone set, listened intently to the churning screws of the vessels above. Each time his cry of 'Attackers above, sir' rang out, the men braced themselves for the worst. Each time, the charges fell wide of their mark.

After two hours of depth-charging, the U-boat's oxygen supply failed. The crew donned their rubber oxygen masks – attached to air purifiers – and lay on their bunks to conserve what air remained. Gradually, the U-boat's electric batteries, which could only be recharged on the surface, were running down. As the U-boat lost power, it sank deeper, unable to maintain sufficient forward momentum to hold level. If the vessel sank below a critical depth, the weight of the ocean would split its hull plates, consigning the crew to certain death.

Kapitänleutnant Otto Kretschmer was the most gifted and innovative submariner of them all

Knowing that if he surfaced within sight of the British escort vessels, he would have no choice but to surrender, Kretschmer played a desperate waiting game, taking both his boat and the crew to the limits of their endurance. It was not until 0330 hours on 9 July that he finally felt safe to surface. The crew clambered stiffly out of the stinking interior of *U-99* on to the deck, gasping lungfuls of fresh sea air. Kretschmer wrote, 'We all felt like children at Christmas.' This experience of being the passive object of attack, the hunter hunted, was not one the commander would quickly forget.

Two days later, *U-99* was ordered to terminate its first patrol which, apart from the depth-charging incident, had been a great success: a total of seven merchant vessels had been sunk in a week. The U-boat was not to return to its original base at Kiel on the German Baltic coast, however. Admiral Karl Dönitz, mastermind of Germany's underwater war, had chosen a new headquarters, at Lorient in German-occupied France, from which to attack the Atlantic convoys. Dönitz was convinced that by operating from Lorient his U-boats could sink enough merchant shipping to bring Britain to its knees. As yet, his fleet was still short of submarines, but he depended on the outstanding fighting qualities of his officers and men to make up for any material deficiency. Foremost among his U-boat commanders were the three 'aces', the swashbuckling Joachim Schepke, commander of *U-100*, Günter Prien, a dedicated Nazi already famous for sinking the *Royal Oak* in Scapa Flow early in the war, and Kretschmer, the most gifted and innovative submariner of them all.

On 24 July, *U-99* slipped out of Lorient on its

ATLANTIC HUNTERS

In an attempt to inflict even more crippling losses on the Allied merchantmen sailing the convoy routes of the North Atlantic, Admiral Karl Dönitz, Hitler's submarine chief, developed the concept of the 'wolf pack': the use of several U-boats to launch co-ordinated attacks on the convoys.

For the first few months of the war, the German Navy had too few submarines to make the technique worthwhile and the invasion of Norway in April 1940, precluded the use of wolf packs until the latter quarter of the year.

The fall of France gave Dönitz the opportunity to put his theory into practice. With the capture of France's Atlantic ports, his U-boats, previously based in the Baltic, would be able to reach the key convoy routes more readily and could remain on station for a much greater period.

By mid-September, the presence of the wolf packs was being felt by the British merchantmen. On the night of 21 September U-boats attacked a convoy, consigning 12 of its 41 ships to a watery grave. Losses mounted steadily: in two separate attacks on 18 and 19 October, two wolf packs stalked convoys *SC7* and *HX79*, sinking 32 out of 84 vessels.

During the following winter, atrocious weather reduced the impact of Dönitz's wolf packs, but in 1941, the U-boats returned to the fray.

second Atlantic voyage. Bizarrely, the crew were kitted out in British uniforms, captured during the German invasion of France in 1940. No suitable German uniforms had been available to replace their outfits that were hopelessly soiled on the first patrol.

At 1100 hours on 31 July, Kassel detected the sound of a convoy's propellers on his hydrophones. A deadly game of hide-and-seek began between the lone hunter and the pack of merchant vessels with its watchful escort. At 1400 hours *U-99* found itself right in the path of the convoy and was forced to submerge to about 300ft as the merchantmen passed overhead. When Kretschmer brought the boat back up to periscope depth, he could not resist picking off a slow-moving freighter, the *Jersey City*, which he found in his sights, and in return *U-99* was subjected to an hour-and-a-half's depth-charge attack by a destroyer. Having survived this onslaught, *U-99* then surfaced to put on speed and catch up with its quarry, only to be immediately forced to crash-dive as a Sunderland flying-boat swooped down on a bombing run. By 2100 hours, when Kretschmer could at last surface, all contact with the convoy had been lost.

But the crew of *U-99* had a masterly flair for tracking merchantmen in the wastes of the Atlantic. All night, Kretschmer made full speed on the surface in the convoy's estimated direction. Just at daybreak, he submerged momentarily to allow Kassel to take a hydrophone bearing on the enemy and then, back on the surface, set off once more in pursuit. Soon his look-outs, reputedly the best in the U-boat force, sighted smoke.

It took all of the remaining daylight hours for *U-99* to manoeuvre ahead of the convoy. When night fell, the boat was in perfect attacking position, but still Kretschmer held off. Then, at midnight, the escort vessels slipped away to protect another, supposedly more vulnerable, convoy. For Kretschmer, the ideal chance to experiment with new tactics had come. To the astonishment of his experienced crew, he ordered them to sail directly into the convoy on the surface. With the U-boat cutting across the bows of 20

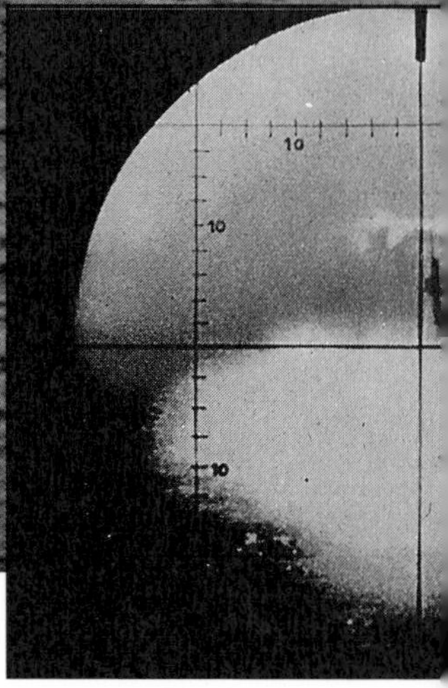
10
10
10

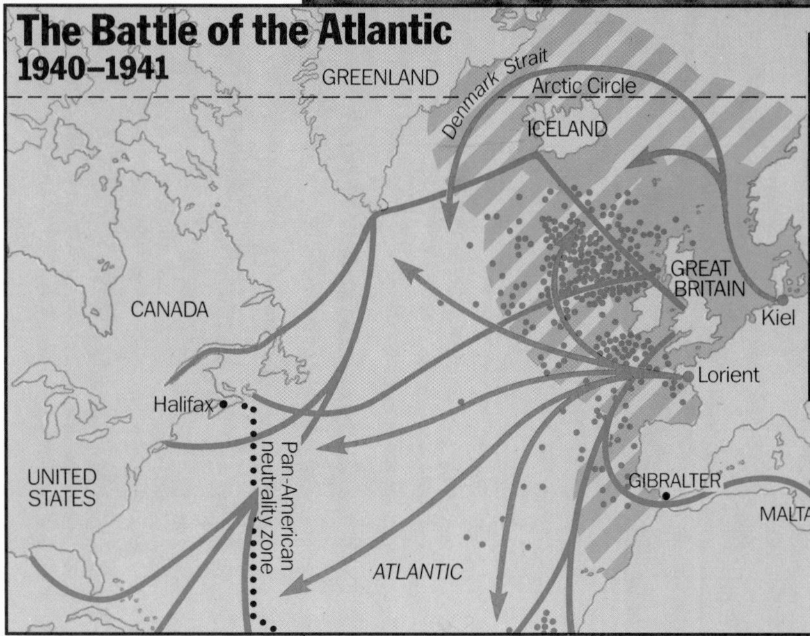
The Battle of the Atlantic
1940–1941
GREENLAND
Denmark Strait
Arctic Circle
ICELAND
GREAT BRITAIN
Kiel
CANADA
Lorient
Halifax
Pan-American neutrality zone
UNITED STATES
GIBRALTER
MALTA
ATLANTIC

Unlike any other World War II battle, the Battle of the Atlantic lasted from the beginning of the war to the end. But it was during 1940 and 1941, when the United States was still neutral, air cover was limited, and many merchant ships had to cross the mid-Atlantic without even the benefit of surface escorts, that the German U-boat offensive came closest to defeating Britain.

Key
- U-boats
- Allied convoy routes
- Allied ships sunk, June 1940–March 1941
- Allied air cover up to March 1940
- Allied air cover after March 1940

Right: The calm before the storm: an engineer checks over machinery in a U-boat's diesel room. Above: Unaware of its impending fate, a heavily laden British freighter is framed by a submarine's periscope. Top: Great plumes of spray and acrid smoke signal the end of another merchantman. Despite their escorts, the ships remained vulnerable to torpedo attacks.

Above: The Submariner's War Badge was adopted in January 1918 and re-introduced in 1939 for U-boat crews who had either carried out two operational sorties or one particularly successful mission.

merchant vessels as they plunged forwards through the darkness, the chances of a collision seemed high. However, Kretschmer was determined to go in close to chosen targets and maximise the number of hits. As his first torpedo struck the stern of an oil tanker, the other ships began manoeuvring furiously to avoid attack. It was in vain. Within 30 minutes, two other tankers were sinking in flames, and another two ships had collided heavily in the general confusion. The approach of a British destroyer at high speed forced *U-99* to withdraw, but Kretschmer considered his experiment a success.

When *U-99* returned to Lorient on 8 August, each man received a hero's welcome. They had sunk a greater tonnage of shipping than any other U-boat had previously achieved in a single mission. Still wearing their British uniforms, they were inspected by the German Naval Commander-in-Chief, Admiral Raeder, who congratulated the men and decorated Kretschmer with the Knight's Cross.

U-99's record of success continued through September, and the crew were full of confidence when they set out for their fourth patrol on 14 October. By the 18th, nine U-boats were stealthily tracking convoy *SC7*, exchanging signals, keeping in close contact, occasionally losing touch with their prey only quickly to pin it down once more. Among the other U-boats was *U-100* with Schepke in command. The convoy was well defended, with substantial destroyer escort, so the wolf pack took its time. Finally, at dusk on 19 October, the onslaught began. It was to be Kretschmer's classic night surface raid.

While the other U-boats launched their torpedoes from outside the convoy, *U-99* slid towards the British escort screen. Two British destroyers were clearly silhouetted against the moonlight, one at the head of the convoy and the other on its starboard beam. Kretschmer headed straight for the gap between them, praying that no sharp-eyed lookout would spot his boat's low profile. Within a matter of minutes *U-99* was through and into the thick of the convoy. Kretschmer directed operations from the conning tower as merchant ships loomed out of the darkness all around him. First, Lieutenant Bargsten entered details of targets on the automatic aiming device. Then, as *U-99* went into the attack, at full speed, merchant ships began to go under. The freighter *Sedgepool*, hit by a torpedo in the bows, dived straight down into the sea like a giant whale. Another ship, broken in two, sank almost immediately. A third vessel exploded spectacularly in a huge ball of smoke and flame. On several occasions, Bargsten's aiming mechanism apparently misfunctioned and targets were missed at close range. When Kretschmer chose to order a snap shot to be fired by guesswork, however, the success rate was virtually 100 per cent. At one point, Kretschmer shouted instructions to the helmsman for a sharp turn and, almost simultaneously, ordered the firing of one of the stern torpedoes. Some 300yds behind the U-boat, a freighter was hit amidships and began to sink.

Officers and look-outs had to be chained to the boat or risk being swept away by waves

The British escort vessels concentrated their attention on the other U-boats attacking from outside the convoy. The crew of *U-99* could see the illuminating flares and hear the depth-charges exploding as the destroyers moved outwards to defend the convoy. Nothing had taught the Royal Navy to expect a raider within its protective screen. Kretschmer knew the enemy would eventually realise what was happening, however, and at around 0130 hours on 20 October he reduced speed, allowing the convoy to pull past him and disappear ahead – an elegant and simple means of disengaging from action. A small freighter which had dropped behind the convoy fell victim to *U-99's* last torpedo before the submarine set course back to port. Of 17 British vessels sunk that night *U-99* had accounted for no less than nine.

By now, Kretschmer was famous. In November, after one more patrol in which *U-99* sank two armed merchant cruisers, he was flown to Berlin to be decorated by Hitler himself. Back in Lorient, Prien, Schepke and Kretschmer celebrated their success in a restaurant, frivolously placing bets as to which would be first to sink 250,000 tons of shipping.

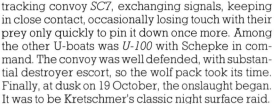

But as winter closed in over the North Atlantic, the mood darkened. On patrol once more from 27 November, *U-99* struggled against awesome weather conditions. For days on end, officers and look-outs in the conning tower had to be chained to the boat or risk being swept away as waves broke over the deck. Surviving against the ocean almost took precedence over the search for the enemy. However, despite the conditions, *U-99* still managed to sink almost 35,000 tons of shipping on this patrol, but not without coming close to disaster. On 8 December, the U-boat was surprised by British escort vessels and forced to crash-dive. The bad weather had put Kretschmer's main periscope out of action, so once underwater he was effectively blind. Hearing nothing on the hydrophones, after a short time he took the risk of surfacing again, only to find two of the British vessels waiting for him, less than a mile off with engines stopped. *U-99* dived again, but it had been spotted and was subjected to a depth-charge attack that it was extremely fortunate to survive.

Kretschmer picked out a tanker at the rear of the convoy and broke it in two with a hit amidships

Dönitz was well aware of the incredible strain imposed on U-boat crews and their commanders by constant patrolling in the Atlantic. When *U-99* arrived back in Lorient, the admiral tried to persuade Kretschmer to accept a shore posting. Kretschmer refused, but agreed that he and his men should take a spell of leave to shake off their war-weariness. It was a welcome break from combat, and when the crew reassembled at Lorient in late January 1941, they were visibly refreshed. Schepke and Prien were there to welcome Kretschmer back and to pay up – for Kretschmer had won the race to reach 250,000 tons sunk. Supplies of brandy and cigars were plentiful, and by the time they returned to action, *U-99*'s commander and crew were in high spirits. On 22 February the U-boat slid out of Lorient serenaded by a military band playing the specially composed *Kretschmer March*.

It was to be their last voyage. From the outset, periods of fog and heavy seas made the submariners' lives difficult. Also, the British anti-submarine forces were ever increasing in strength and vigilance. On 7 March *U-99* once more narrowly survived a depth-charge attack; Prien's *U-47* had no such luck, being sunk by the escorts of the same convoy. As days went by without Prien making radio contact, Kretschmer became inescapably aware of his fellow ace's fate.

By 15 March, *U-99* was drawing towards the end of a relatively fruitless patrol when it received a message that a convoy had been sighted south of Iceland. By the following morning, Kretschmer and Schepke were both with the pack of U-boats moving around the convoy, harassed by Sunderlands and the destroyer escorts. Because of uncharacteristically careless work by a look-out, *U-99* lost contact with the convoy in the afternoon, but shortly after dark the boat caught up with its quarry once more, and immediately attacked. Forging through a gap in the escort screen, Kretschmer torpedoed a tanker which exploded in a sheet of flame. Afraid he might have been spotted in the glare of the burning vessel, Kretschmer momentarily dropped back into the darkness behind the convoy, but then he began a devastating run forwards through the formation, leaving another two tankers and two freighters sunk or sinking. *U-99* now had one torpedo left. Kretschmer picked out a tanker at the rear of the convoy and broke it in two with a hit amidships. There was nothing left for *U-99* to do but turn away from the wrecked and burning ships and head for Lorient.

Unknowingly, however, as Kretschmer moved away from the convoy, he drew close to the position of Schepke's *U-100* which was in difficulties. Schepke had surfaced to inspect the damage after being depth-charged by the destroyer HMS *Walker*. Despite its being a moonlit night, he had not expected to be spotted. But, for once, the British escorts' primitive radar equipment, normally useless for locating a U-boat, picked up a target. Guided by its radar operator, the destroyer HMS *Vanoc* bore down on *U-100* at full speed. The U-boat had no time to take evasive action and was struck by the destroyer's bows directly alongside the conning tower. The impact crushed Schepke behind his periscope and tore his legs from his body. *U-100* quickly sank, as *Walker* steamed up to join *Vanoc* on the scene.

At this point, unaware of the drama being enacted, Second Lieutenant Petersen, in the conning tower of *U-99*, sighted the two destroyers a mere half-a-mile away and immediately ordered a crash-dive. Instantly *Walker's* Asdic revealed the

Kretschmer's remarkable career was cut short by HMS *Walker* (bottom left), a destroyer commanded by Captain D. MacIntyre (below left). Brought to the surface by depth-charges (below), *U-99* was then blasted at close range and Kretschmer ordered his crew to surrender. Below right and far right: Kretschmer and his crew dock at Liverpool to a less than friendly reception. However, after the war old animosities were forgotten. Right: MacIntyre (right) returns Kretschmer's binoculars at a reunion in London in 1955.

U-boat's presence, and the destroyer raced in to depth-charge. The first pattern of explosions threw *U-99* about wildly. The second attack was still more accurate. Water and oil poured into the U-boat as tanks and pipes split. The shuddering blast-waves shattered gauges and instruments, and the engineer reported that the propellers had stopped. Without power, Kretschmer faced a stark choice: either to fill the ballast tanks with air and rise to the surface, or to sink inexorably to the bottom of the ocean. He chose the surface and inevitable surrender.

Fortunately for the crew, when *U-99* bobbed to the surface it was listing heavily away from the *Walker,* giving the men shelter from the destroyer's machine-gun and tracer fire during the time it took to signal their surrender. Kretschmer would not allow *U-99* to fall into British hands, however. As *Walker* drew near, he scuttled the U-boat; the surge of water as the vessel sank swept him clear of the conning tower. He was hauled up on to the destroyer, along with all but three of the crew.

Three days later, *Walker* docked in Liverpool. *U-99*'s crew were forced to march through the streets of the city, reviled by an angry crowd who regarded them as murderers. Kretschmer was driven off separately for interrogation. None of them would play any further part in the war. However, Kretschmer and the crew of *U-99* had, by their dedication to duty and combat skills, wrought havoc on the convoys plying between America and Britain.

THE AUTHOR R.G. Grant graduated in Modern History from Trinity College, Oxford. He has written extensively on military campaigns.

In September 1943 a small force of midget submarines launched Operation Source – a daring attack on the battleship *Tirpitz*

HMS *TRUCULENT*, a Royal Navy submarine, cut through the North Sea at a steady 10 knots, on course for Altenfjord on the northern tip of Norway. It was 14 September 1943: a clear, fine day with the sea sparkling under the autumn sun. The submarine's commanding officer, Lieutenant Robert Alexander, DSO, stared aft at the taut 2in-thick nylon hawser that carried a telephone cable to a four-man midget submarine, *X-6*, trailing 200yds behind and 40ft beneath the surface. The officer standing next to Alexander, Lieutenant Donald Cameron, RNR, studied the towing rope with even keener interest. He was to take charge of *X-6* once they had reached their destination. Cameron had insisted on using one of the only two nylon ropes available as he was wary of using hemp lines, believing that they were more likely to part under any strain.

To the port and starboard of *Truculent*, running on parallel courses about 20 miles apart, were four other submarines: *Syrtis*, *Thrasher*, *Seanymph* and *Stubborn*. These were towing four of the *X-6's* sister craft, *X-9*, *X-5*, *X-8* and *X-7*, to a pre-arranged rendezvous, 75 miles east of the Shetlands. The armada had left Loch Cairnbawn, a naval base on the northwest coast of Scotland, at two-hour intervals during the late afternoon of the 11th. A sixth pair, HMS *Sceptre* and *X-10*, had sailed 24 hours later, having a shorter route to the meeting point.

The X-craft were on their way to carry out Operation Source, a daring attack on three German capital ships, the *Tirpitz*, *Scharnhorst* and *Lützow*, as they lay at anchor in Norwegian waters. The driving force behind the raid was the British prime minister, Winston Churchill. He had first proposed the idea of attacking the *Tirpitz* in 1942, but the X-craft were not ready for delivery until January 1943.

Lieutenant Cameron, the first man to be accepted for X-craft duty, and a number of fellow officers and ERAs began training in earnest on *X-3* and *X-4*; first at Loch Striven, then at Loch Cairnbawn, where the 12th Submarine Flotilla was formed around the depot ship HMS *Bonaventure*. Loch Cairnbawn, remote from prying eyes, was ideal for simulating the conditions likely to be encountered in the small fjords leading off Altenfjord, where the German battleships lay. The Admiralty, 'progged' on by Churchill, was already drawing up plans for an attack on the *Tirpitz*. Net-cutting was practised day after day and, in mock attacks against the capital ships of the Home Fleet, the craft had to negotiate anti-submarine nets and avoid the look-outs, keeping a careful eye out for underwater attack.

By the time the six X-craft were delivered in January 1943, the naval planners had finalised the details of Operation Source. It was hoped to send the midget submarines against the *Tirpitz* before 9

Below: An X-craft ploughs through the sea during trials for Operation Source, the attack on the *Tirpitz* in September 1943. Below left: Lieutenant Donald Cameron, RNR, commanded *X-6*, one of the two craft to lay charges near the target, and won a well-deserved VC for his part in the raid. After becoming a submariner in August 1940, he served with HMS *Sturgeon* before volunteering for service in midget submarines.

X-CRAFT

March as, after that date, the daylight hours at the 70 degree parallel would be too lengthy for any chance of success. However, it soon became obvious that the crews of the X-craft could not be worked-up in time, and that the operation would have to be postponed until early September, when the northern nights would again be sufficiently long to hinder detection. This last-minute setback was a blessing in disguise as it not only gave the crews more time to get accustomed to their often temperamental craft, but also allowed them to improve their teamwork.

The delay also gave the authorities more time to arrange aerial reconnaissance sorties and collate the information radioed to London by the Norwegian resistance. In fact, it was not until the beginning of September, just eight days before the X-craft were scheduled to leave Loch Cairnbawn, that three Spitfire PR VII high-altitude reconnaissance aircraft began to fly twice-daily sorties from the Russian airbase at Vaenga. The Russians had finally, with the greatest reluctance, given permission for these sorties, but had delayed the photographers' visas. To the horror of the pilots and the consternation of the Admiralty, the first reconnaisssance flight on 6 September revealed that the German fleet had disappeared – the ships had sailed to bombard Spitzbergen. When, however, on 9 September the battleships were photographed lying in their berths, the mission was given the go-ahead and the attack force sailed from Loch Cairnbawn two days later.

The midget submarines X-5, X-6 and X-7, towed by *Thrasher*, *Truculent* and *Stubborn*, were to attack the *Tirpitz* in Kaafjord. *Syrtis* and *Sceptre*, with *X-9* and *X-10* in tow, had the *Scharnhorst* as their target; *X-8*, towed by *Seanymph*, was to attack *Lützow*. Both the *Scharnhorst* and *Lützow* were berthed in Langefjord. The X-craft were to be slipped at Söröy Island on D-day 20 September, and hide on the bottom during the daylight hours of the 21st. They were to enter their respective fjords for the attack at dawn on the following day.

The passage to the targets was to be in three stages. During the first part of the journey, the towing submarines would make good time by

The men who attacked the *Tirpitz* got a clutch of medals for their bravery. Right: Sub-Lieutenant Aitken of *X-7* won the DSO for his part in the operation. The crew of this craft laid two charges under the ship, and then escaped detection until forced to clear the anti-submarine nets on the surface. Hit by gunfire, *X-7* sank; Aitken escaped three hours later. Below: Lieutenant Godfrey Place, DSC, the CO of *X-7*, earned a VC for his inspired leadership. Below right: Sub-Lieutenant Richard Kendall, the diver and cook of *X-6*, gained a DSC. Bottom: Engine Room Artificer Edmund Goddard, one of *X-6's* crew, was awarded the Conspicuous Gallantry Medal.

MIDGET RAIDERS

The craft used against the *Tirpitz* were developed from a prototype, known as *X-3*, built by Commander Cromwell Varley, a former member of the Royal Navy who had set up a marine engineering business near Southampton. After her launch in 1942, the *X-3* underwent a series of successful trials, and Vickers Armstrong Ltd was contracted to supply six production models by early 1943.

In many respects the X-craft (shown below) were scaled-down versions of conventional submarines, but with two important differences. First, they were constructed with a watertight space, the 'wet and dry'. Situated between the forward compartment and the control room, the wet and dry allowed each crew's diver to make underwater sorties against obstacles. The second difference lay in armament. Unlike larger submarines the X-craft did not carry torpedoes, but were fitted with two detachable charges on either side of the hull. Each charge was filled with two tons of high explosive and could be detached from inside the craft. A timing device allowed the crew up to 36 hours leeway before detonation.

The X-craft were not designed for comfort or speed. With a length of 51ft, they were extremely cramped and the crews had to work in a pressure hull that was a mere five-and-a-half feet high. The midget submarines displaced 27 tons on the surface and had a diving depth of 300ft. Speed on the surface was some six knots; underwater, this was reduced to two knots. Propulsion was provided by a Gardner diesel engine. With full fuel tanks and charged batteries, the operational range was some 1500 miles, but on-board conditions meant that no crew could work efficiently for any great length of time.

travelling on the surface, while the X-craft remained submerged at 40 to 50ft. Two days before sighting the Norwegian coast, the mother submarines and their X-craft would travel submerged to avoid detection by German aircraft and patrolling U-boats. (It says much for the overall security and vigilance of the British look-outs that the Germans had no inkling that Source was afoot). The final stage would come off Söröy Island, where the X-craft would slip their lines and make their way independently through the minefields into Altenfjord, under the direction of their operational crews.

All went well until the early hours of 15 September, when a heightening wind lashed the sea into a frenzy that the submariners laconically logged as a 'rough to very rough' sea. As the towing submarines rose precipitously in a following sea, the X-craft, wallowing along 200yds astern, yawled wildly from side to side in a sickening corkscrew motion: rolling, pitching and heeling to every movement of the mounting waves. The stern of a submarine, crashing into a trough, would plunge its tiny companion into a headlong dive. Retching with seasickness, the passage crews fought to control the X-craft, their clothes and hair saturated by condensation, their bodies chilled by the increasing cold as they headed further and further north.

Almost inevitably there was trouble: *X-8* broke loose from *Seanymph* which, unaware of the break, ploughed on through the heaving seas. Later, *X-8* made contact with *Stubborn* and *X-7;* this combination had also had a break in their hemp cable. *X-8* lost contact later, but was eventually picked up by a frantically searching *Seanymph*. The craft, however, was doomed. Her two explosive charges, found to be leaking, had to be jettisoned. The starboard one, exploding at 1000yds, did no damage, but the port one, detonating all of 600yds away, so badly damaged *X-8* that she had to be scuttled. It also smashed lights and gauges on the *Seanymph*. At 0120 hours on the 16th, after 'guffing through' (drawing in fresh air) and recharging her batteries, *X-9* dived, and was never seen again. Later, the hemp towline to *Syrtis* was found to have parted.

Dusk on D-day saw the remaining submarines in their respective slipping zones – operational crews had already taken over from passage crews on the evening of the 19th – and *X-5*, *X-6*, *X-7* and *X-10* began their hazardous trip through the minefields, which they cleared without incident. The air was still and clear, but bitterly cold, as they made their way on the surface towards Altenfjord by the light of an uncertain moon. However, the nine days of pitching and tossing at the end of a towline were beginning to take their toll.

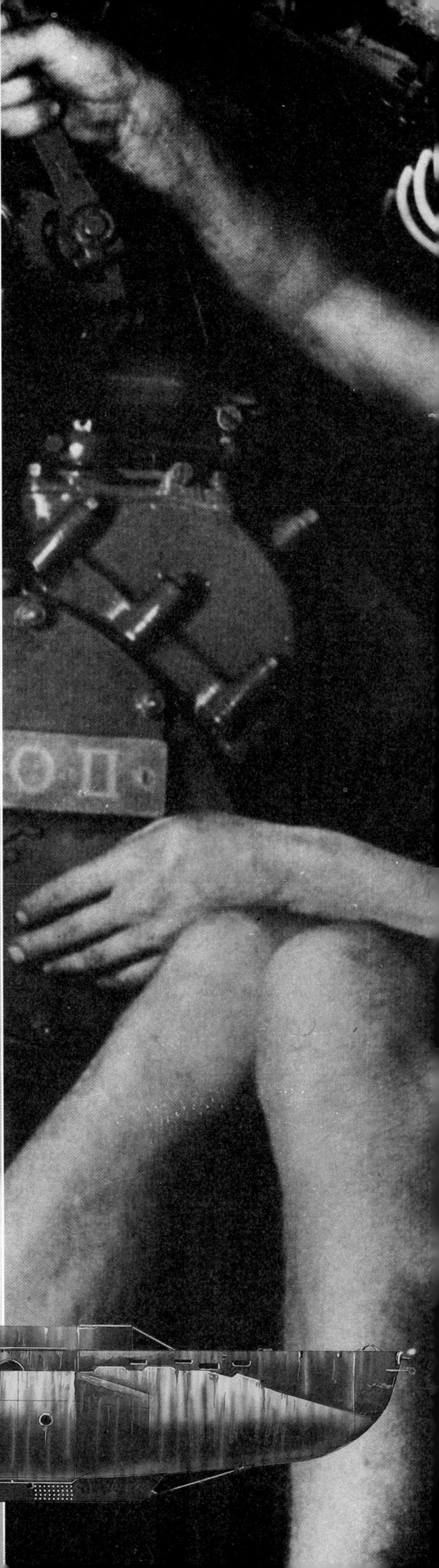

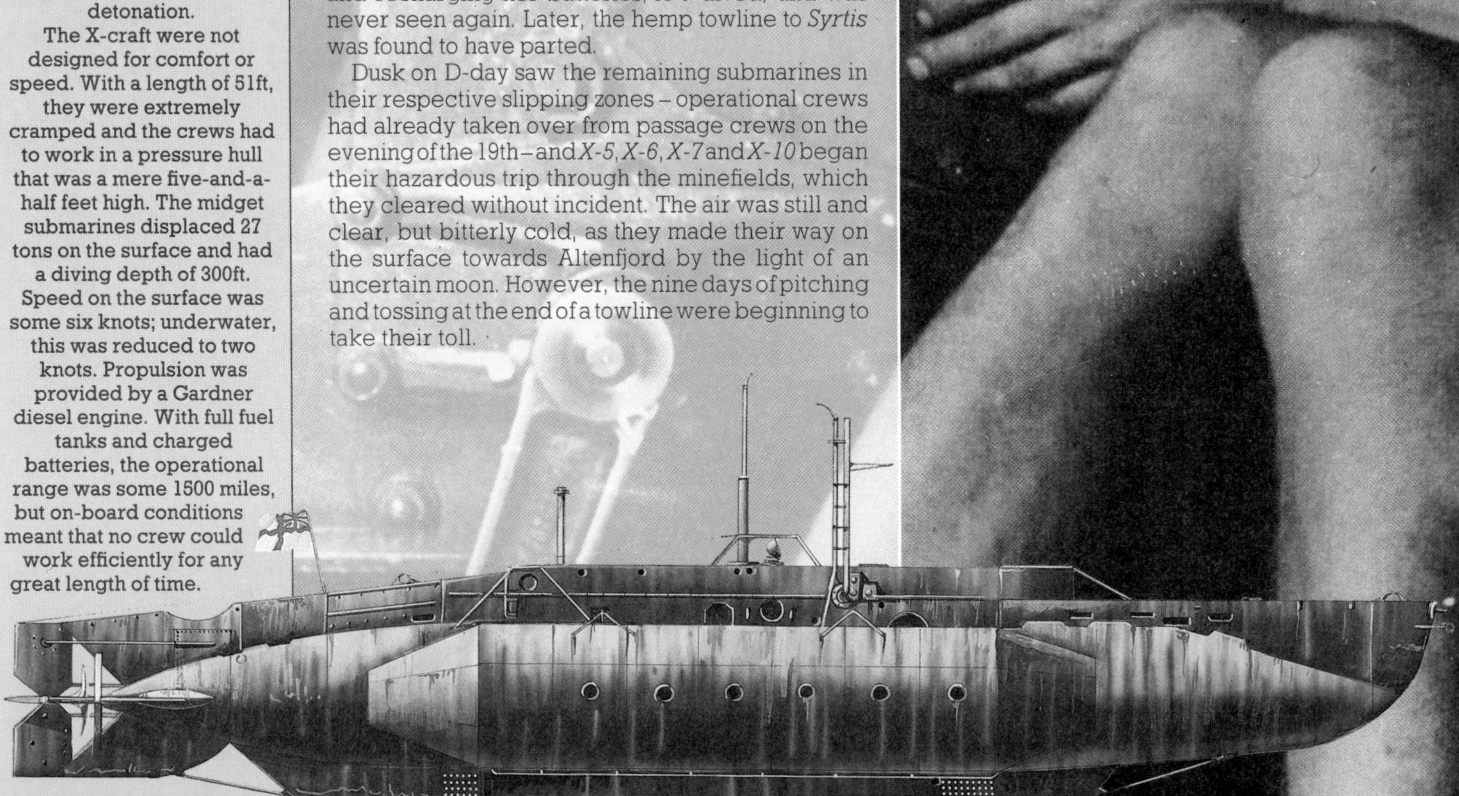

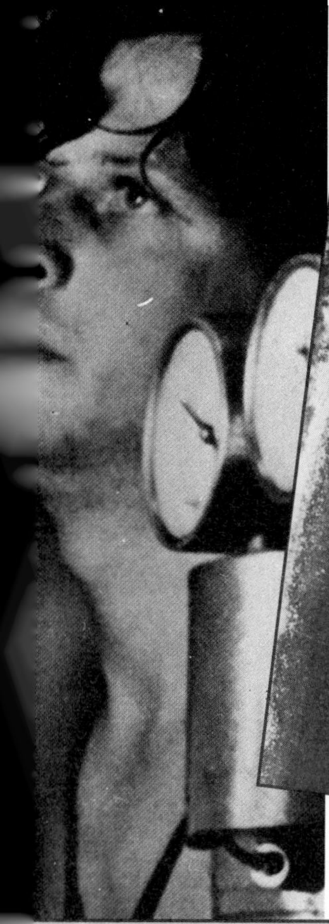

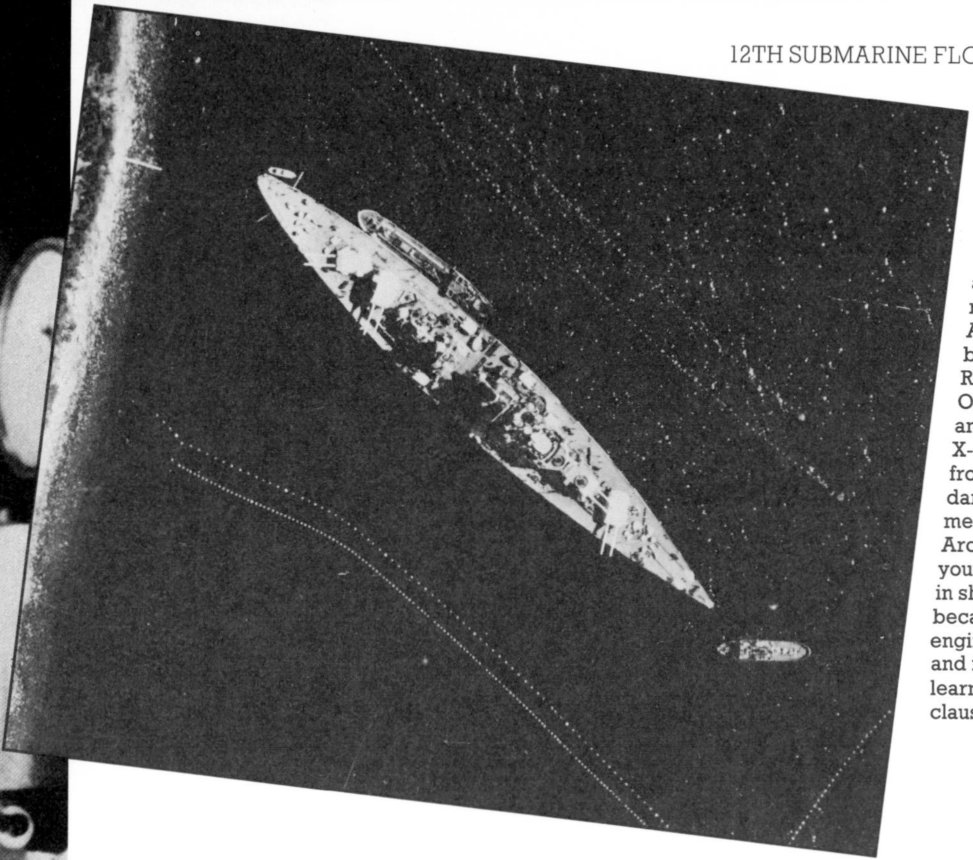

Left: Protected by massive lengths of anti-submarine netting, the mighty *Tirpitz* lies at anchor in the chill waters of a Norwegian fjord. One of the finest ships afloat, the *Tirpitz* remained a threat to the Allied convoys plying between Britain and Russia for much of the war. Only frequent air attacks and the daring raid by the X-craft prevented the ship from inflicting catastrophic damage on the merchantmen sailing the Arctic sea-lanes. Far left: A youthful stoker, dressed only in shorts and gym shoes because of the heat, tends his engine. Submariners, a tough and individualistic breed, learned to live with the claustrophobic conditions.

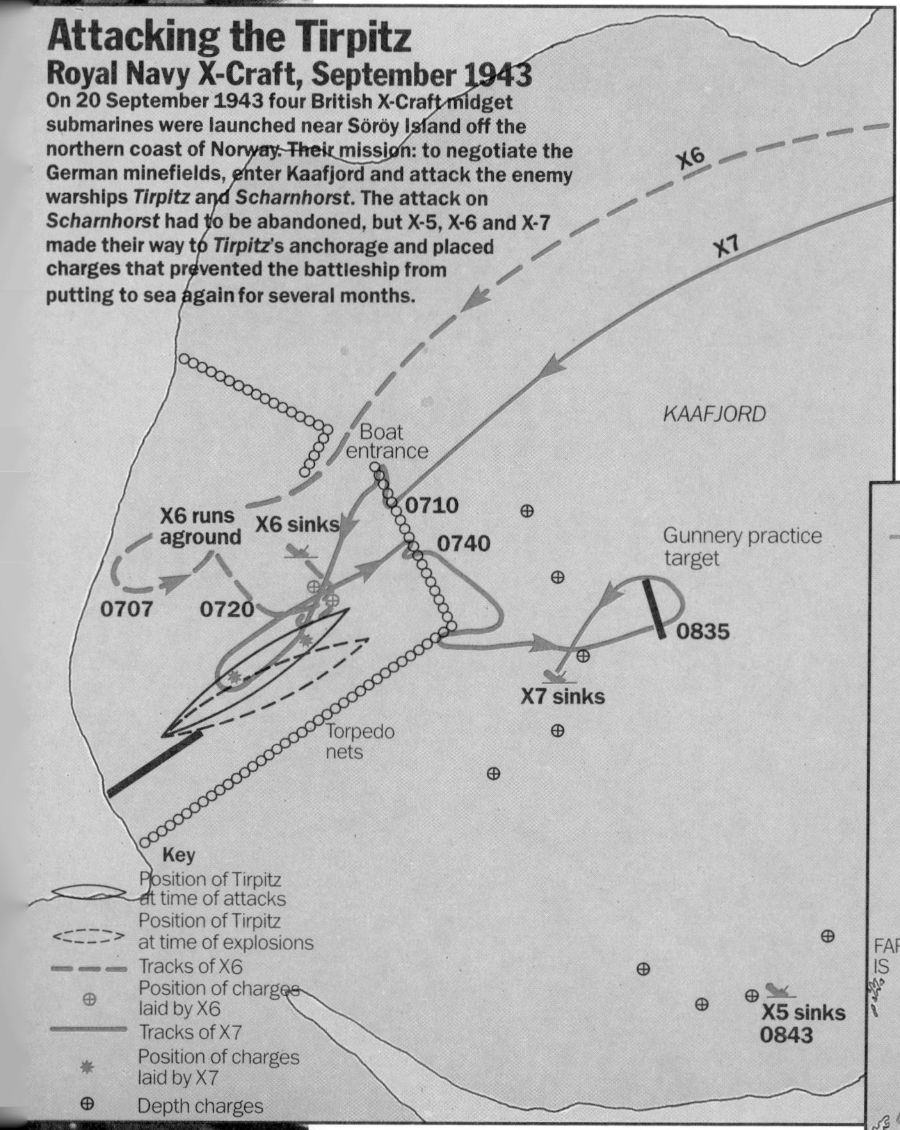
Attacking the Tirpitz
Royal Navy X-Craft, September 1943
On 20 September 1943 four British X-Craft midget submarines were launched near Söröy Island off the northern coast of Norway. Their mission: to negotiate the German minefields, enter Kaafjord and attack the enemy warships Tirpitz and Scharnhorst. The attack on Scharnhorst had to be abandoned, but X-5, X-6 and X-7 made their way to Tirpitz's anchorage and placed charges that prevented the battleship from putting to sea again for several months.
X6
X7
KAAFJORD
Boat entrance
0710
0740
X6 runs aground
X6 sinks
0707
0720
Gunnery practice target
0835
X7 sinks
Torpedo nets
X5 sinks 0843
Key
Position of Tirpitz at time of attacks
Position of Tirpitz at time of explosions
Tracks of X6
Position of charges laid by X6
Tracks of X7
Position of charges laid by X7
Depth charges

By standing on the seat of the toilet in the W & D (wet and dry – a waterproof space), with only his head above the open hatch, Lieutenant Cameron in *X-6* was able to conn the craft with some protection from the elements. Nonetheless, when he slammed the hatch shut and gave the order to dive at 0125 hours, on 21 September, he was soaked to the skin and numb with cold. Stripping off his wet clothes, he changed into long flannel underwear, dry clothing, thick wollen stockings and tennis shoes, hanging his wet gear in the engine room – the 'Chinese laundry'.

In spite of the growing problems aboard *X-6*, Cameron was confident of reaching his lying-up position off Tommelholm Island shortly before midnight, ready to attack the *Tirpitz* at first light. However, the craft was having problems: 'George', the automatic helmsman, had ceased to function, ERA

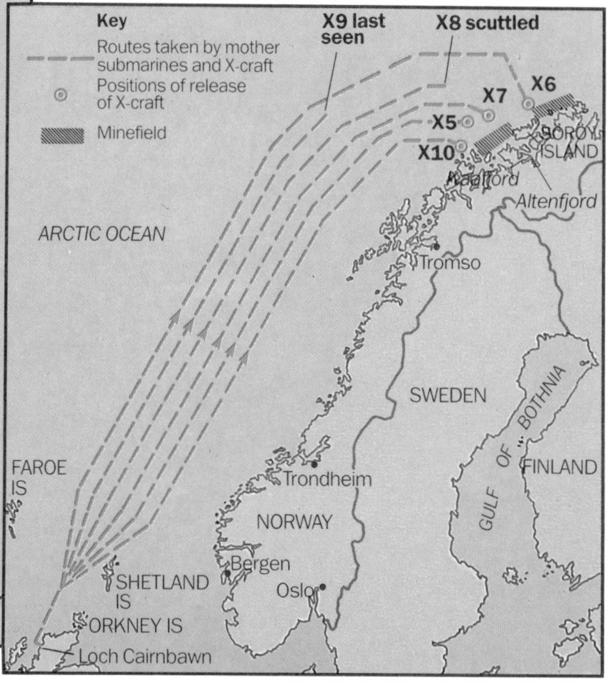
Key
Routes taken by mother submarines and X-craft
Positions of release of X-craft
Minefield
X9 last seen
X8 scuttled
X7
X6
X5
X10
SÖRÖY ISLAND
Kaafjord
Altenfjord
ARCTIC OCEAN
Tromso
SWEDEN
GULF OF BOTHNIA
FINLAND
FAROE IS
Trondheim
NORWAY
Bergen
Oslo
SHETLAND IS
ORKNEY IS
Loch Cairnbawn

Goddard was stripping down the periscope which had begun to flood, and the craft had taken on a 10-degree list to starboard due to the side-charge flooding. The crew had to throw all their unnecessary gear overboard, mainly tinned food, to achieve even this degree of stability. At 0145 hours, after a meal of hot stew and cocoa, they dived to 60ft and set course for the *Tirpitz*. Cameron hoped to attack at 0630. It had been agreed that the charges should be laid under *Tirpitz* between 0500 and 0800 on 22 September, and that no X-craft should attempt to breech the anti-torpedo net before 0100.

Kendall, clad in his rubber diving suit, squatted on the seat of the toilet. Alone in the claustrophobic W & D, cut off from his shipmates by a watertight bulkhead, he was sweating despite the cold. Kendall's job was to flood the compartment, open the hatch and cut a passage through any German nets that the sub might encounter. As *X-6* dived, the floodlit, 155ft-deep Kaafjord net and its 33ft-deep 'gate' could be clearly seen, about four miles directly ahead. The barrier stretched from shore to shore, and beyond it lay the *Tirpitz*, protected by her own double anti-submarine net. This was 50ft deep but, below this, a net of looser mesh reached down to the fjord's bed; the only way in was through a 66ft-wide gate, where the net had a maximum depth of 110ft. As chance would have it, the *Tirpitz's* ship-to-shore telephone had broken down the night before and the gate had been left open to allow a continuous flow of boat traffic. Small, fast submarine chasers patrolled the area and *Tirpitz's* commander, Captain Meyer, had ordered a continuous hydrophone watch until 0600 hours.

As Cameron approached the battleship's protective net at 0705, his periscope flooded and the hoist motor burnt out. The submarine was in a perilous state but, hearing the rhythmic thud of a ship's engines entering the net, he decided to press on. 'Surface. Full ahead on the diesel,' he ordered. With unbelievable luck, *X-6* got through unseen and then dived, only to run aground on the German ship's port beam. Again Cameron's luck held out, the look-outs aboard the *Tirpitz* took *X-6* for a porpoise. Diving, Cameron made his way blind and released his charges abreast *Tirpitz's* 'B' turret. Minutes later, the German look-outs were astonished to see a small submarine burst to the surface less than 50yds away; too close to depress the ship's guns, the crew poured a hail of smallarms fire and tossed grenades at the target. Aware that the detonation of the side-charges would blow *X-6* out of the water, Cameron had taken the craft to the surface, opened the sea-cocks and was waiting to surrender to a boat from the *Tirpitz*. It was 0722 hours.

Below: Preparing for future missions. Dressed in waterproof overalls, the captain of an X-craft relays orders to his helmsman via a speaking tube during a training run. After Operation Source, X-craft were employed in the Far East, one sinking a Japanese cruiser, the *Takao*, in the Jahore Strait and others were used for reconnaissance and navigational duties on D-day.

At that very moment *X-7*, commanded by Lieutenant Place, DSC, was laying charges: one near those of *X-6* under 'B' turret; the other between the engine room and 'C' turret. Earlier, *X-7's* crew had spent an hour extricating their boat from a net enclosure formerly occupied by the *Lützow*, and did not wriggle through the *Tirpitz's* net until 0715. Having laid his charges, Place attempted to clear the nets on the surface, but, at that distance, close-range anti-aircraft guns were brought to bear. Once again blundering into the nets, *X-7* was thrown clear of the barrier by a violent explosion at 0812. His craft badly damaged, her ballast tanks leaking, Place had no choice but to surface close to a practice target. With bullets ricocheting off the hull, Place decided to leave the craft first, waving his white sweater in surrender. He just had time to step on to the floating target, before *X-7* sank at 0835. Only Sub-Lieutenant Aitken escaped three hours later; Sub-Lieutenant Whittam and ERA Whitely died, having exhausted their oxygen supply.

To the four prisoners on *Tirpitz's* upper deck, covered by eight machine-pistols, it was a scene of chaos: alarm bells shrilled, orders were shouted only to be immediately countermanded, wires were dragged along the ship's keel, and reluctant divers prepared to go over the side. At 0812 they and the crew were flung off their feet by two immense explosions: *Tirpitz* leapt up several feet, whipping violently. The damage was severe: two of her 15in-gun turrets were immobilised and her engines were badly damaged. The ship would never be fully serviceable again, and it would take several months to bring her anywhere near full seaworthiness.

At 0843, another X-craft, surfacing 650yds from *Tirpitz's* starboard bow, was hit by heavy and light anti-aircraft fire and sank; two minutes later she was depth-charged. This craft must have been the *X-5* but little is known of its fate. Later, rumours led to the belief that she may have survived. *X-10*, plagued by incurable defects, was forced to jettison her charges, and make her way back to the open sea, where she was eventually picked up by *Stubborn*. During the passage home, she too had to be scuttled.

Although none of the X-craft returned to base, the casualties were remarkably light. For the loss of nine men killed and six captured (the POWs returned home after the war), the mighty *Tirpitz* was put out of action for six months, and the morale of her crew was irreparably undermined.

THE AUTHOR Bernard Brett left the Royal Navy at the end of World War II, and has since written several books on ships, sea power and naval warfare.

SUBMARINE KOMMANDO

Right: A Neger midget submarine is prepared for a mission. While the perspex dome provided the pilot with good visibility, it left him very vulnerable to Allied strafing attacks. Left: A beached Neger at Anzio is examined by men of the US Fifth Army. Above left: A German Biber midget submarine.

Riding into battle in midget subs, the 'K-men' of the German navy fought a desperate campaign against Allied shipping in 1944

BY THE SECOND half of July 1944, the Allied bridgehead along the Normandy coast was being rapidly expanded: the US Third Army had cleared the Cherbourg peninsula to the west, while on the other flank, the shell and bomb-blasted ruins of Caen had fallen to the British and Canadians after prolonged fighting. But Hitler, if not his generals, remained convinced that victory in the west was still within reach. By the 20th of the month, some eight panzer divisions were concentrated against the Normandy perimeter, mostly in opposition to the British forces in the east. If the flow of war materials across the Channel could be halted, then there might still be a chance of throwing the invaders back into the sea.

Only the question of how to enforce a blockade remained to be answered. The Luftwaffe lacked air

Left: Mission accomplished – Neger pilot returns to base. Below and right: The twin-torpedo configuration of the Neger. Bottom left: Admiral Helmuth Heye, commanding officer of the Kleinkampfverbände, decorates one of his courageous volunteer submariners.

superiority over the beaches and, already badly mauled, could do little more than launch small-scale hit-and-run raids. The remnants of the Kriegsmarine were ill-equipped to carry out the Führer's bidding: its surface fleet was too vulnerable to air and sea attack to be effective, and its conventional ocean-going submarines were too clumsy to negotiate the extensive Allied minefields or operate close inshore where a vast array of troop transports and supply ships were moored. The only viable option was to deploy the midget submarines of Admiral Helmuth Heye's Kleinkampfverbände (small battle units). Yet the chances of success were slim. Heye's 'K-men', all volunteers, operated primitive craft that in previous missions had exacted a heavy toll of their crews. To make matters worse, the Allies were well aware of the existence of these small battle units.

The midget submarines had first been deployed against the Allies the previous April. Elements of Flotilla No.261, a unit equipped with the cigar-shaped Neger (Negro) submersibles, had attacked shipping off Anzio on the western seaboard of Italy, south of Rome. The raid had gone wrong from the start: during the launch from the beaches of Practica di Mare, a small resort 20 miles north of the operational area, 14 Negers stuck fast in the muddy shallows with one pilot dying from asphyxiation before he could be rescued. After travelling for three hours on a southerly course parallel to the coast, guided by flak batteries firing tracer in the direction of Anzio, the remaining craft, their skippers suffering from exhaustion and carbon dioxide poisoning, altered course and headed inland. Three separate groups carried out attacks in the Bay of Nettuno and Anzio. The results were uniformly disappointing: most Negers failed to find a target and only two small patrol craft were torpedoed. Most of the Negers were scuttled to avoid discovery, their

NAVAL SPECIAL FORCES

Senior German naval officers had discussed the creation of special forces in the opening stages of World War II but it was not until early 1943, when the Kriegsmarine's surface fleet had been effectively silenced and the Allies had introduced a very successful range of anti-submarine devices, that Hitler gave the go-ahead for the raising of a number of Kleinkampfverbände (small battle units).

The man tasked with the job, Admiral Helmuth Heye, was given wide powers to requisition all that was needed to get the programme started but, unlike both the Italians and British, the Germans lacked the resources, technical experience and men needed. The Italians helped out and a captured British midget submarine provided some answers, but the equipment deployed by the small battle units was often substandard.

By the close of 1943, the first batch of volunteers, some 30 officers and men, had assembled in a compound close to the Baltic port of Heilingenhafen, and were being put through a tough training programme. Men were taught to operate small motor-boats and midget submarines, and to carry out commando-style raids.

While the men underwent training, Heye oversaw the development of their specialist craft. Given the limited resources available and believing that the Allies would quickly counter any one design, the admiral decided to produce a wide variety of attack craft. In the event many proved to be unsatisfactory and his battle units were mostly equipped with the Neger and Biber midget submarines, and the Linse explosive motor-boat.

The special forces were first used in action against the Anzio beachhead in Italy during early 1944. Moved to northern Europe in mid-1944, the small battle units opposed the Normandy landings; losses were high and Heye's men, for all their courage, were unable to save the Third Reich from defeat.

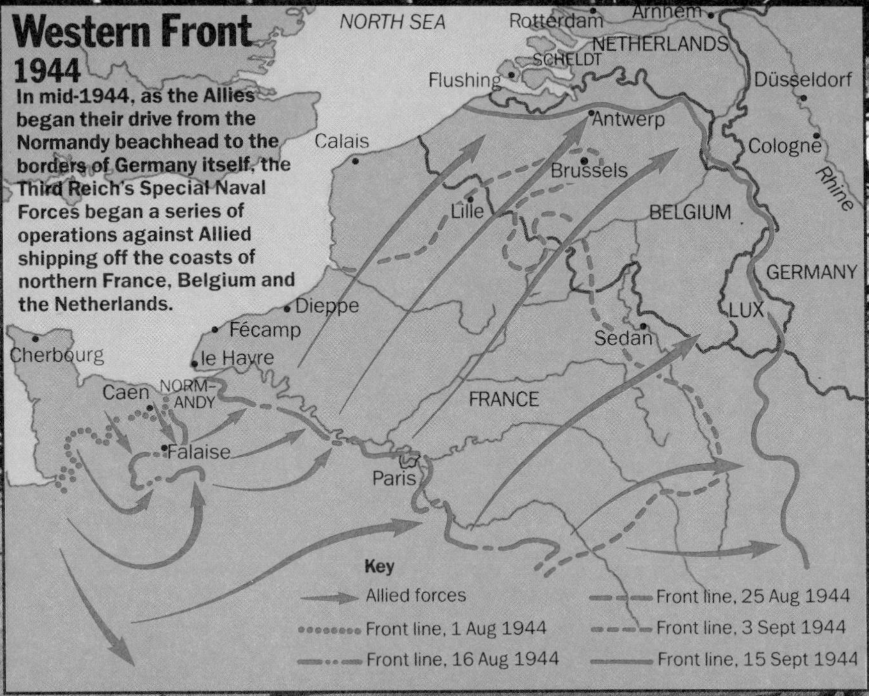
Western Front
1944
In mid-1944, as the Allies began their drive from the Normandy beachhead to the borders of Germany itself, the Third Reich's Special Naval Forces began a series of operations against Allied shipping off the coasts of northern France, Belgium and the Netherlands.
NORTH SEA
Rotterdam
Arnhem
NETHERLANDS
SCHELDT
Flushing
Düsseldorf
Antwerp
Calais
Cologne
Rhine
Brussels
Lille
BELGIUM
GERMANY
Dieppe
LUX
Fécamp
Sedan
Cherbourg
le Havre
Caen
NORMANDY
FRANCE
Falaise
Paris
Key
Allied forces
Front line, 1 Aug 1944
Front line, 16 Aug 1944
Front line, 25 Aug 1944
Front line, 3 Sept 1944
Front line, 15 Sept 1944

UNDERWATER RAIDERS

In their campaign to prevent the build-up of Allied forces in northwest Europe, Germany's naval special forces deployed a number of midget submarines to strike against ships at anchor off the Normandy coast. Rushed into full production after little evaluation, these crudely designed and rudimentary craft were often barely seaworthy and it was only through the skill and bravery of their crews that they were able to notch up any successes against enemy shipping.

The first and most widely used midget submarine was the Neger (Negro), consisting of two G7e electric torpedoes slung one beneath the other. In action, the pilot sat in a cramped compartment in the upper torpedo, sheltered from the elements by a perspex dome that could only be removed from the outside. The Neger could not submerge completely, but cruised to its target at a top speed of four knots with only the pilot's head showing above the surface. To launch an attack, the pilot first selected a target and then estimated its course, speed and distance. The craft's aiming device comprised a graduated scale etched onto the perspex dome and a spike-like foresight attached to the front of the upper torpedo. When these were in line with the target, the clamps holding the live G7e were released; once disconnected, the torpedo's engines started automatically.

The Neger was a difficult and dangerous craft to operate. It was unusable in all but the calmest seas and its lack of range (some 35 nautical miles at two-and-a-half knots) meant that its base had to be very close to the target area. Many pilots died from asphyxiation or drowning when their vessels were overwhelmed by rough seas. A later version of

the Neger, known as the Marder (Marten), could submerge.

Developed in parallel with the Neger by Leutnant Hans Bartels, the Biber (Beaver) was much more like a conventional submarine: it could submerge to a depth of 90ft and was armed with a pair of torpedoes placed on either side of the hull. Weighing six tons, the Biber was powered by either batteries or a single petrol engine and had an operational range of 90 nautical miles at a cruising speed of seven knots. Although safer to use than the Neger, the Biber suffered from several design faults, not least the cramped compartment occupied by its one-man crew. Over 300 saw service during the war; most were lost in accidents.

The other three main types of midget submarine used by the navy's small battle units were the Seehund (Seal), Molch (Salamander) and Hecht (Pike). The Seehund, like the Biber, could carry two torpedoes, but had a two-man crew. A much larger vessel (15 tons), it had a greater diving depth (150 ft), and a range of some 270 nautical miles at a top speed of five knots. The Seehund was a development of the Hecht, a much less seaworthy submarine that was used primarily as a training craft. Although the Hecht had a similar diving depth to its successor, its range was limited to 60 nautical miles and it carried a single torpedo and a mine. Because of its poor performance, the production run was ended after 50 craft had been constructed. The third craft, the Molch, saw service off the Italian coast and in the waters of the Channel. Crewed by one man, the submarine carried two torpedoes and had a diving depth of 100ft. Its radius of action, at a sedate five knots, was some 105 nautical miles. Like its contemporaries, the Molch proved difficult to operate in battle conditions.

Main picture: A flotilla of two-man Seehund midgets at the German naval facility at Kiel. Inset top: Hans Bartels, designer of the Biber. Bartels' creation (above left) weighed six tons and was only slightly larger than the torpedoes it carried, one fitted on either side of the lower hull. Above: A Molch one-man midget submarine rolls off the production line. The Molch weighed 10.5 tons and, like the Biber, was armed with two torpedoes mounted along the length of the lower hull. In keeping with many of the German midget submarines, the Molch was a dangerous and difficult craft to operate and required considerable courage on the part of the pilots.

SURFACE RAIDERS

Apart from midget submarines, Germany's naval special forces also made use of explosive motor-boats during the latter stages of World War II. The idea was nothing new, similar vessels having been used during the invasion of Russia in 1941, but when they were transferred to Admiral Heye's command in early 1944, they were found to be unsuited to ocean conditions and had to be refitted. By July these up-rated craft, given larger fuel tanks and more powerful engines, were ready for use against the Allied invasion fleet lying off the Normandy coast.

The basic operational group used in action was the three-boat Rotte consisting of two explosive-carrying Linsen and a single command craft. Because of their short range, each Rotte was usually towed to within three miles of its target. Once on station, the pilot of the command craft selected a suitable enemy ship and one of the attack craft would then move much closer to the objective. At a distance of 100yds, the Linse would accelerate to its top speed and, as it headed for the target, the craft's pilot would switch control of his Linse to the command boat via a radio-control device and then abandon his craft. When it struck home, a small explosive charge would blow off the Linse's bow, and the stern, containing the main charge, would sink beneath the target to detonate a few seconds later. By this time, the second attack Linse would already be on its way to the same target. Once the two pilots had been picked up, the command craft would head for home.

crews swimming ashore behind German lines. In the morning, however, Allied troops found one craft afloat, its crewman dead. The element of surprise, so vital to the success of future missions, had been lost.

Three months after the Anzio operation, the Negers of Kapitän zur See König's Flotilla No. 361, some 30 craft in total, launched the first attack against shipping off the coast of Normandy. The flotilla was based at the secluded port of Villers sur Mer, a few miles south of Trouville, only a short distance from the Allied beaches. With their limited range (about 35 nautical miles) and poor handling characteristics, the Negers needed to be launched as close to their targets as possible. The objective of the mission, scheduled to take place during the night of 4/5 July, was the destruction of shipping lying off Sword beach.

Villers sur Mer had been chosen as the launch site to prevent a repetition of the disastrous Anzio mission. The port facilities included two concrete ramps which, when covered with water at high tide, would make for easier launching. If the right moment was chosen, favourable tides would take the slow-moving submarines to the target. The attack began at 2300 hours on the 4th and everything went well. Guided by a friendly moon, the raiders reached Sword between 0300 and 0500 on the following morning, and several attacks were made with the Negers' torpedoes. The scale of the flotilla's success remains uncertain, but official British records indicate that a frigate and a coastal minesweeper were sunk. The commander of Kleinkampfverbände operations in France, Kapitän zur See Böhme, claimed that many more ships were destroyed, and added that seven Negers returned to their base. Many of the others were caught and strafed by Allied aircraft as they made their homeward journey to Villers sur Mer; others simply sank in rough water as they struggled to make headway against the tide.

Squadrons of fighters and ground-attack aircraft circled over the Channel like birds of prey

Although the first attack had only been a qualified success, the submariners remained optimistic. With more time to train and better craft, they might still achieve great things. However, the total failure of the next mission, on 7/8 July, cast a deep shadow over future midget-submarine operations. Initially, everything went according to plan: the 21 craft allocated to the mission were launched without difficulty and in record time – yet not one returned to base. After the first attack, the Allies had tightened up their anti-submarine procedures – measures that proved highly successful against the slow-moving and vulnerable Negers. Explosive charges lobbed into the sea would force the pilots to veer away from their intended victims, while heavy smallarms fire, directed against a Neger's perspex dome, which always poked out of the water, was often enough to kill the skipper and sink his vessel. Squadrons of fighters and ground-attack aircraft circling over the Channel like birds of prey had little difficulty in blasting the Negers out of the water. An estimated 200 midget submarines of all types, many of them Negers, fell victim to strafing attacks during the small battle units' campaign against the Normandy beachhead. With an acute shortage of both replacement craft and trained crews, Heye's flotillas could ill-afford these losses.

Some ran aground on sand-banks, where they were exposed to the full fury of the Allied defences

Following the heavy defeats of July, the Germans introduced a new, more sophisticated submarine, known as the Biber (Beaver), into service. Unlike its predecessor it could travel fully submerged – though it could only fire its torpedoes from the surface – and with two torpedoes was capable of inflicting a great deal more damage. With its greater range, the Biber could be based well away from the centre of the fighting, less vulnerable to surprise attack. Rushed into service in mid-August, the first of the new submarine flotillas established its base camp at Fécamp, a coastal town between Boulogne and Le Havre. After settling in, the first raid, consisting of 18 Bibers under the boat's designer, Leutnant Hans Bartels, was launched on the night of 28/29 August. The run-in to the target area was made difficult by a force-five gale, and all but two craft were forced to abort the mission. Two Allied transports, one a US-built Liberty ship of 8000 tons, were reported sunk. Operations from Fécamp had to be abandoned, however, as the Allies pushed out from Normandy in late August.

Over the next few months, operations by the midget submarines were limited by the speed of the Allied advance as well as the need to find new bases and train replacement personnel. In November, the Bibers of Flotilla No. 261 began to operate out of the massive concrete submarine pens of Rotterdam in Holland; their mission was to prevent the flow of supplies moving down the river Scheldt to the Bel-

Right: High and dry. A Biber lies abandoned on a beach on the North Sea coast. Clearly visible is the concave port torpedo station in the submarine's lower hull. Left: A flotilla of Linsen explosive-carrying motor boats. Once aimed at a target, the crew would open up to full throttle and bale out as the launch streaked away on a collision course.

gian port of Antwerp. At least a score of flotilla-sized sorties were launched by the small battle units during the last weeks of 1944.

The missions usually followed a set pattern. After the technical staff had given the boats a thorough check and the pilots had been briefed in full, the Bibers would be towed to a point off the island of Goeree, near the lock at Hellevoetsluis on the Maas river, to conserve fuel for the journey to the Scheldt. At the lock, the towing vessels would release their charges, which would receive a last-minute shakedown. The attack craft were at their most vulnerable at this stage, which was carried out in daylight so that the slow-moving Bibers could make use of the ebb tide during their outward journey, and if all went according to plan, use the flood tide for the return leg later in the day.

Once out into the North Sea, the attack boats turned to the southwest and headed down the Dutch coast to the West Scheldt. From there they would travel past the outlying islands of the estuary and the town of Flushing before entering the Scheldt proper to search for suitable targets among the convoys headed for Antwerp. The outward journey was rarely that easy. For all the precise calculations of the planners, many Bibers failed to reach the area of operations. Some ran aground on sand-banks, where they were exposed to the full fury of the Allied defences at low tide, while others were swept to destruction by adverse currents. Nevertheless, the arrival of a pack of midget submarines in the Scheldt often halted, at least temporarily, the flow of war materials into Antwerp and forced the Allies to divert considerable resources to the area in order to combat their activities. Although the flotilla's activities were often cut short by adverse weather conditions, the Bibers despatched an estimated 90,000 tons of shipping to the bottom between December 1944 and the following January of 1945.

But these triumphs were bought at a high price. Statistics compiled from after-mission reports indicated that up to 80 per cent of the craft taking part in any operation failed to return. With such a high rate of attrition, the small battle units could not be maintained at full battle readiness. To make matters worse, two self-inflicted wounds during the first months of 1945 virtually destroyed the flotillas operating out of Rotterdam. The first accident, in January, involved a runaway torpedo while an attack force of 30 Bibers was waiting for a favourable tide at Hellevoetsluis. During the usual pre-attack routine, a technician set off a live torpedo which exploded with devastating effect, creating a small tidal wave which swamped all but five of the 30 boats present. On 6 March 1945 a similar disaster occurred. This time, however, the pilots were on board their craft – few survived the resulting explosion.

The deployment of the inexperienced Kleinkampfverbände was a last-ditch attempt to save Germany

Within the space of two months the heart had been torn out of the most experienced small battle units, not by the Allies but through the negligence of their own men. It was a double blow that marked the end of Biber operations in Holland. Other midget submarines, such as the Seehund (Seal) and the Molch (Salamander), were used in operations off the Normandy coast and in the North Sea, but they too failed to halt the build-up of Allied forces on the continent. As the British and American forces swept eastwards, the small battle units, short of equipment due to the scarcity of raw materials and short of trained crews once the Baltic training depot had been overwhelmed by the Red Army, gradually disappeared from the Kriegsmarine's order of battle.

The deployment of the inexperienced Kleinkampfverbände against the Allied forces in northern Europe was a last-ditch attempt to save Germany from defeat. The men who joined these units knew that they stood little chance of success. Their craft were of poor quality and their training was often frighteningly brief, yet they were willing to pay the ultimate price to defend their homeland. For all their efforts, they were too few and much too late.

THE AUTHOR William Franklin is a military historian who has contributed to several specialist military magazines and publications. His interests include the history of special forces of World War II.

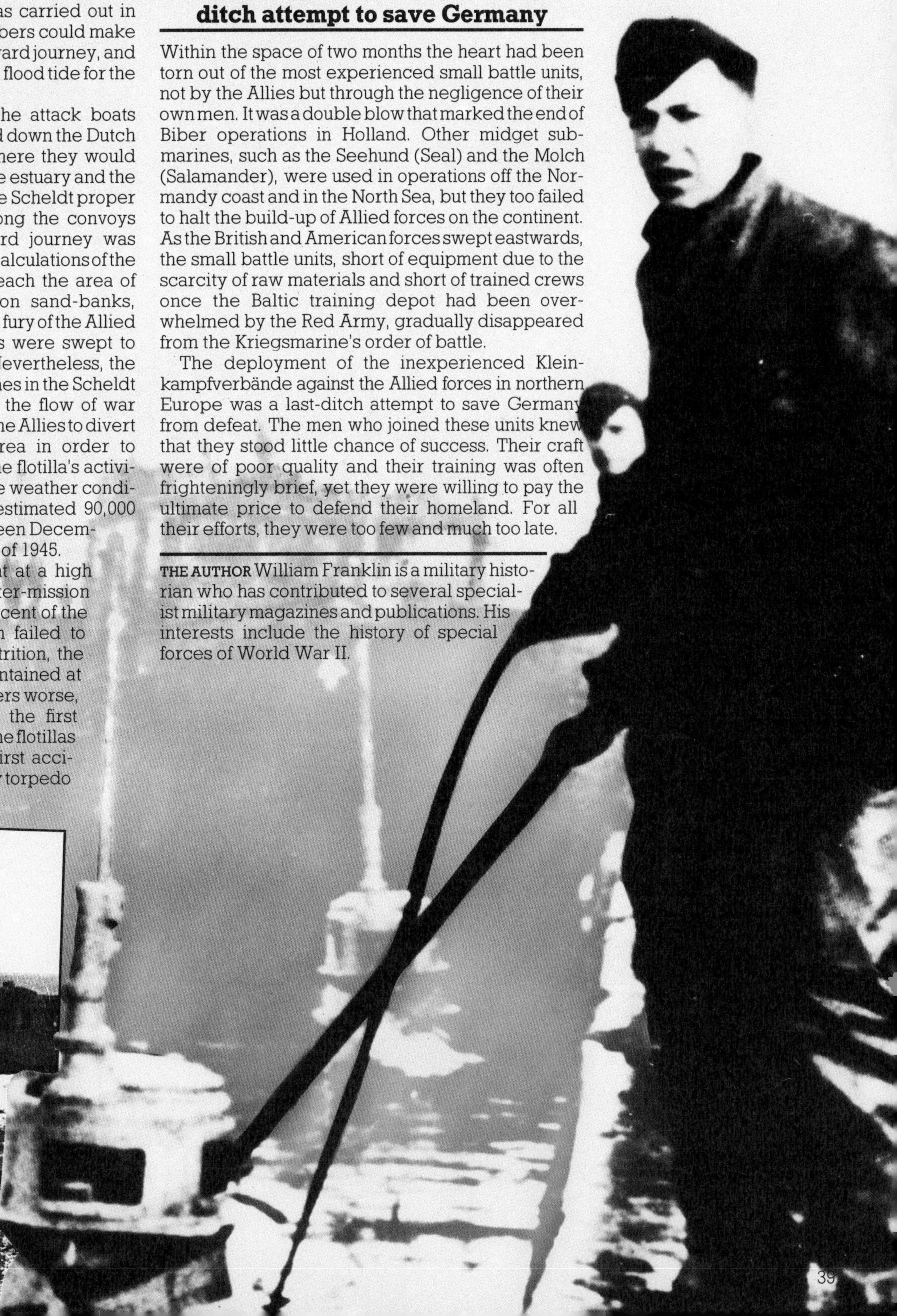

Below: German naval personnel bring forward a pair of Bibers of Flotilla No. 261 at Rotterdam submarine base.

KILLER FROM THE DEEP

Günther Prien's *U-47* made its way stealthily towards the Royal Navy's anchorage at Scapa Flow, with a daring plan to slip through the British defences

ON THE evening of 12 October 1939, barely six weeks into World War II, a German submarine, the *Unterseeboot-47*, surfaced off the Orkney Islands at the northern tip of Scotland. As the officers stood in the conning tower, observing twinkling lights on the land to their west, only the captain, Günther Prien, knew the object of their mission – so total was the secrecy surrounding the operation. Prien was aware that the moment was fast approaching when the men would have to be told. After a night of observation, *U-47* withdrew eastwards and submerged. As the submarine settled on the bottom and the motors were cut, Prien ordered the crew to assemble in the forward mess. They waited expectantly, their young faces – their average age was 20 – pale in the crude lighting. With no preamble, Prien delivered the extraordinary news: 'Tomorrow,' he said, 'we shall enter Scapa Flow.'

Scapa Flow had been the Royal Navy's major naval base since World War I. A superb natural harbour, 10km from north to south and 17km from east to west, it provided protection for the large numbers of warships that made up the British Home Fleet, and its strategic position was ideal for dealing with German forays into the North Sea and for intercepting enemy vessels attempting to escape into the Atlantic. (Until the defeat of France in 1940, the English Channel remained an impassable seaway for German ships.)

For Germany, too, Scapa Flow had a special significance, since it was there that the proud German High Seas Fleet had been ordered after the defeat of Germany in 1918. And it was there, in 15 fathoms of water, that the High Seas Fleet had been scuttled – a last defiant act to prevent German warships coming under Allied control.

At the outbreak of World War II the German Navy was the Cinderella of the German armed forces, and while the army and air force were gaining victory after victory in the war against Poland, the navy's

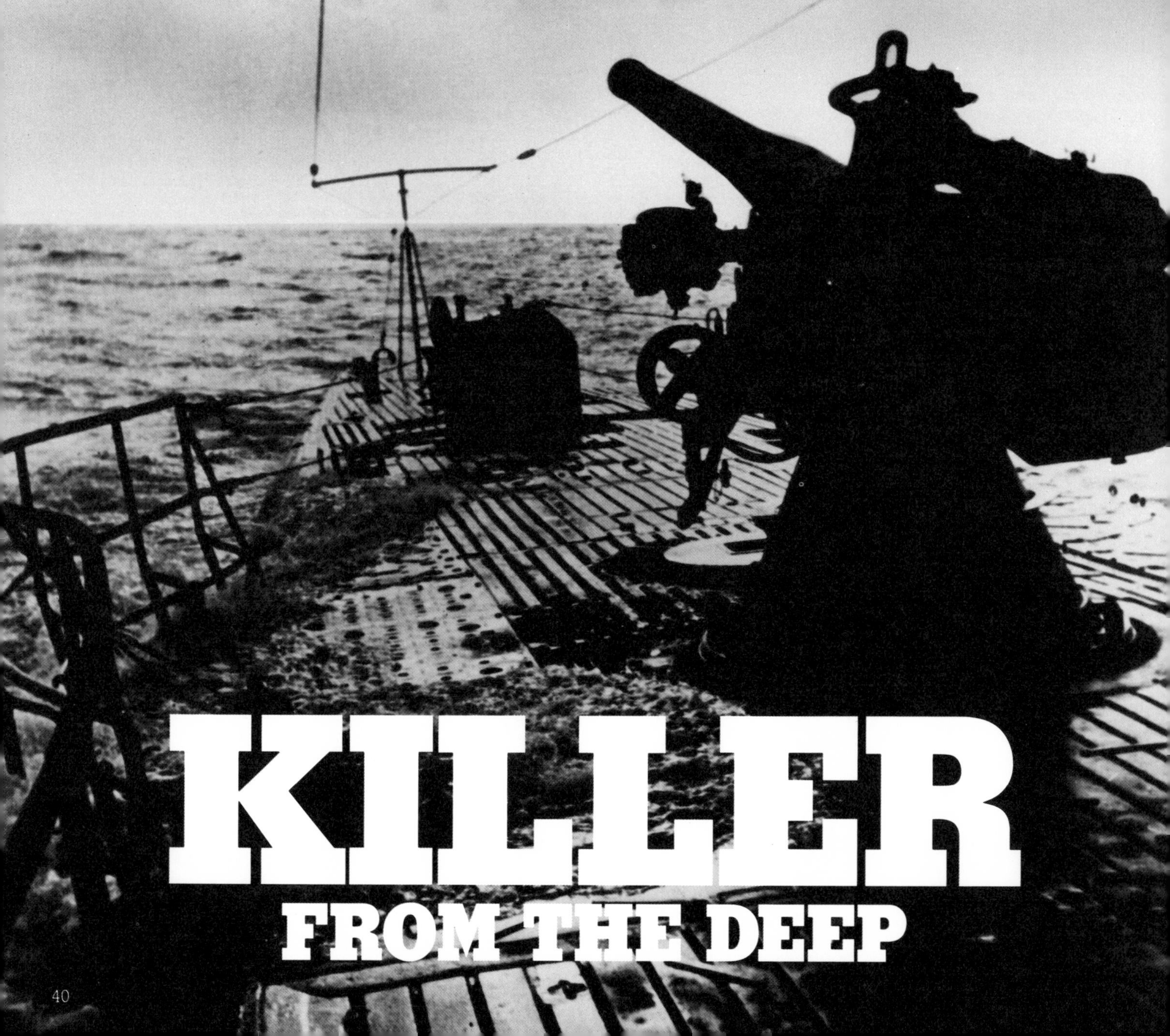

Below: The view forward from just below the conning tower of a Type VIIB U-boat – the same model as *U-47*. The 8.8cm gun was used to finish off lone merchant vessels on the surface, and was far more reliable and much less costly than the torpedoes in use during this period of the war. Although of the same calibre as the dual-purpose 8.8cm used by the Army and the Luftwaffe, the U-boat gun bore no relation to this model, and could not even accommodate the same ammunition.

Günther Prien, commanding officer of U-47

Günther Prien wears the standard German Kriegsmarine officers' navy blue service dress: peaked cap, reefer jacket, trousers and black shoes. The cap bears the badge worn by officers, warrant officers and midshipmen, consisting of eagle and cockade with embroidered gold wreath, and the peak is decorated with the gold waved rim worn by officers below the rank of Korvettenkapitän (Lieutenant-Commander). Prien's rank of Kapitänleutnant (Lieutenant I) is indicated by the gold lace rings on the cuffs of his reefer jacket. Decorations consist of the red, white and black ribbon to the Iron Cross 2nd Class, the Iron Cross 1st Class and, below that, the Submarine War Badge awarded to crews who had been engaged in at least two operational sorties or one particularly successful mission. At his throat he wears the Knight's Cross awarded to him personally by Hitler for the Scapa Flow raid.

successes were much more modest. In addition, obsessed with land warfare, Hitler had little interest in the Navy (apart from being impressed by the size of the heavy units, especially *Bismarck* and *Tirpitz*). He completely failed to appreciate the war-winning potential of the submarine.

The head of the U-boat arm Captain Karl Dönitz, needed a spectacular victory to impress upon the German Navy and Hitler the importance of developing his U-boat programme. Dönitz had been a U-boat commander himself in World War I and, posted to the Mediterranean, he had slipped his boat into a defended harbour in Sicily and got out again without being detected. Dönitz reasoned that such a feat might be possible against Scapa Flow. If a U-boat could manoeuvre past the British defences undetected, it could launch a series of attacks against the assembled ships that would be both a grievous blow to the Royal Navy and a superb advertisement for Germany's submarines.

For the plan to have any chance of success Dönitz had to instigate a major information-gathering programme. *U-16* was despatched to patrol the waters around Scapa Flow, to assess the state of water defences, currents and tides, while detailed hydrographic maps and charts were assembled alongside aerial reconnaissance photographs. By 11 September – with the information in hand – serious planning was under way. Close examination of the aerial photographs suggested to the planners that Scapa Flow was not as well defended as they had been led to believe. The series of anti-submarine booms and sunken blockships had worked during World War I (when two German submarines had been lost attempting to penetrate the anchorage), but gaps were evident to Dönitz and his men.

The man to lead such an operation would need to be an expert seaman with nerves of steel

The most favourable route lay through Holm Sound, within the eastern approach to Scapa Flow. Holm Sound was divided into smaller channels and one of these, Kirk Sound, was incompletely defended by a number of sunken blockships. For the German planning officers, two of the gaps between blockships seemed highly promising. If the timing was right, then on a dark night, at slack water, a resolute U-boat commander could guide his fully-surfaced boat between the blockships and into Scapa Flow. The plan was risky and dependent on British patrols not spotting the German submarine – but it was possible.

The man to lead such an operation would need to be an expert seaman with nerves of steel. Casting around amongst his most experienced submariners, Dönitz came up with the name of Günther Prien. The 31-year-old Prien was one of the new men of the German Navy: he had no connection with its Imperial past and was, instead, a fervent Nazi. Observed by Dönitz as a fine submariner, Prien combined his sea-faring skills with the calculating boldness and 'sixth-sense' that made a great U-boat commander. A man with the common touch, he was both respected and liked by his men. The crew under his command, like all U-boat men hand-picked volunteers, had already proven their ability to handle the intense strain of submarine warfare.

Having just returned from a successful voyage sinking Allied shipping in the Atlantic, Prien was relaxing in the mess on 1 October when he was summoned to Dönitz's office. There Dönitz revealed

GÜNTHER PRIEN

One of the most outstanding of Germany's submariners, Günther Prien was born in 1908 and spent his early years in Leipzig in conditions of considerable poverty. A childhood hero was the famous Portuguese navigator Vasco de Gama, and at the age of 16 he left home, attracted by the lure of the sea. Prien learned his seamanship the hard way, working his way up from a cabin boy on a sailing clipper to merchant captain. Thrown out of work by the Depression he was only able to get back to sea through the expansion of the Navy as Nazi Germany began its massive rearmament programme after 1933. His maritime experience ensured officer rank and after volunteering for the U-boat arm he was appointed commander of *U-47* just before the outbreak of the war in September 1939. Officially credited with the first U-boat victory of the conflict on 5 September, he achieved overnight success when he sent the *Royal Oak* to the bottom on the 14 October. Awarded the Knights Cross for this exploit Prien became a national hero, although he was soon back at sea creating havoc in the shipping lanes of the North Atlantic. A natural U-boat ace, Prien sank 28 ships totalling 160,939 tons. His luck ran out on 8 March 1941, however, when the *U-47* was sunk by the British destroyer *Wolverine*. There were no survivors. Shown above: the 'snorting bull' insignia of *U-47*. This insignia was later adopted by the 7th U-boat Flotilla, renamed as the 'bull of Scapa Flow' in honour of Prien.

Sinking the Royal Oak

U-47, Scapa Flow, October 1939

On the night of 13 October 1939, six weeks after Britain's declaration of war against Germany, Günther Prien and the crew of *U-47* penetrated the British Home Fleet's anchorage in Scapa Flow. They torpedoed the 31,250 ton battleship *Royal Oak*, which sank with over 800 of its crew still on board. *U-47* made good its escape and returned to a heroes' welcome in Germany.

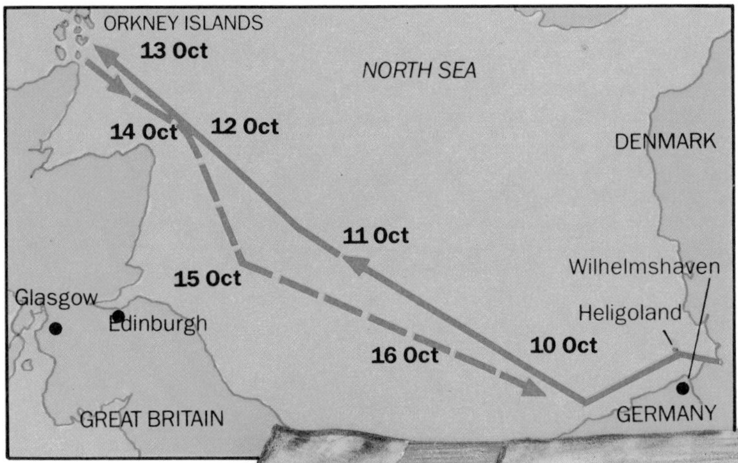
ORKNEY ISLANDS
13 Oct
NORTH SEA
14 Oct
12 Oct
DENMARK
11 Oct
15 Oct
Wilhelmshaven
Glasgow
Edinburgh
Heligoland
16 Oct
10 Oct
GREAT BRITAIN
GERMANY

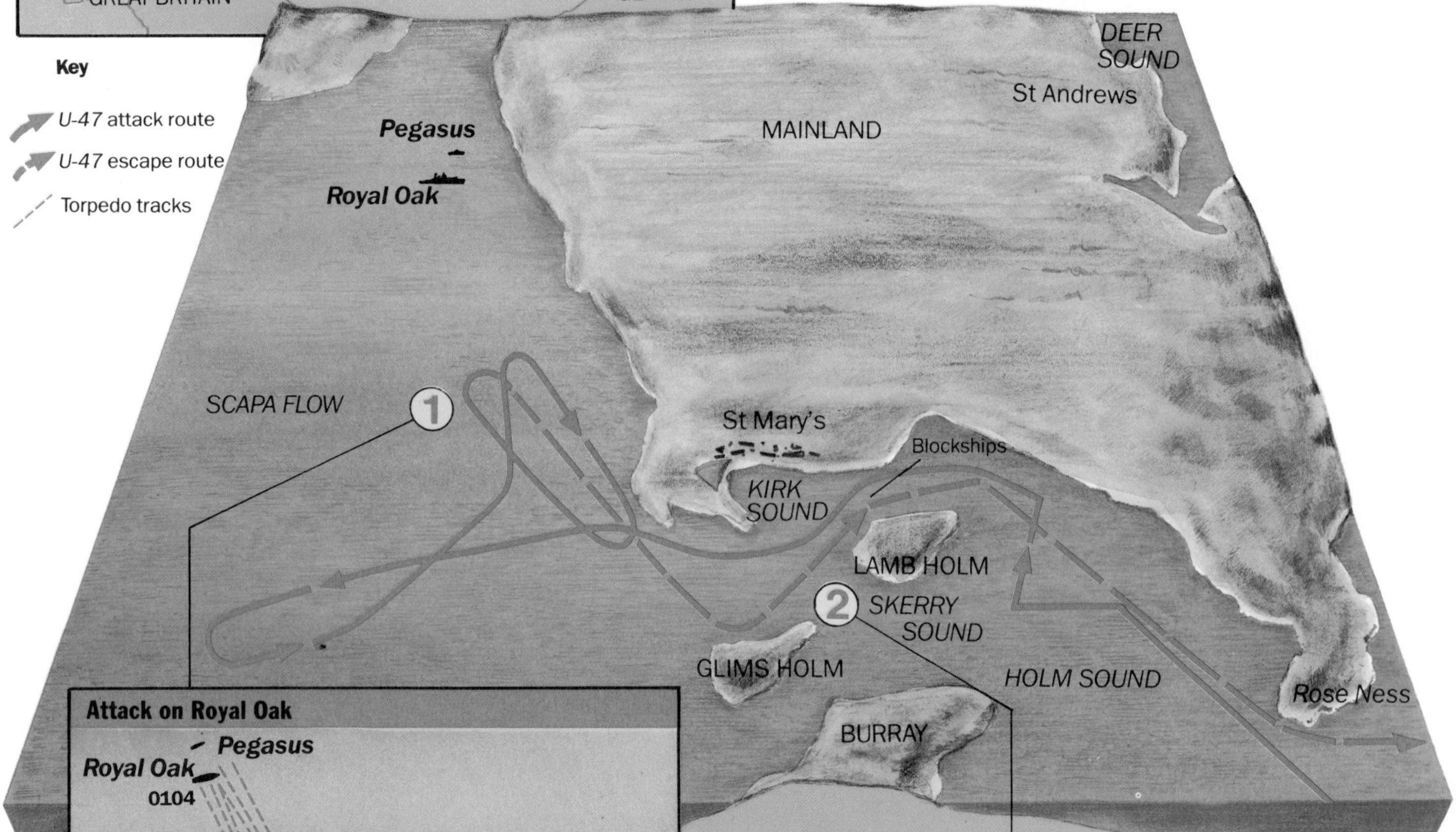
Key
U-47 attack route
U-47 escape route
Torpedo tracks
DEER SOUND
St Andrews
MAINLAND
Pegasus
Royal Oak
SCAPA FLOW
1
St Mary's
Blockships
KIRK SOUND
LAMB HOLM
2
SKERRY SOUND
GLIMS HOLM
HOLM SOUND
Rose Ness
BURRAY

Attack on Royal Oak

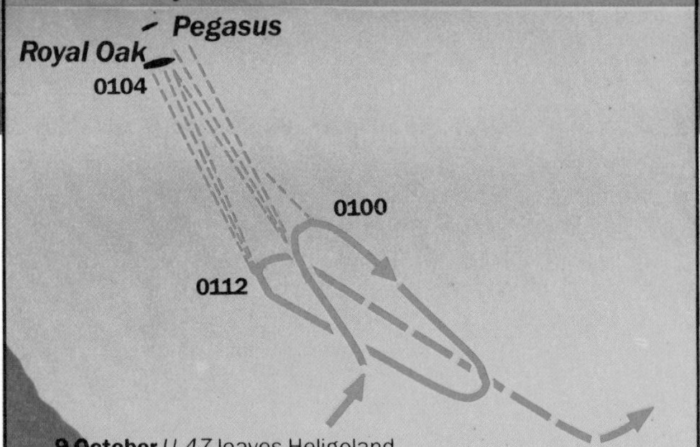
Pegasus
Royal Oak
0104
0100
0112

9 October *U-47* leaves Heligoland.
13 October 1900 *U-47* surfaces off the Orkney Islands and heads for Holm Sound.
14 October 0027 *U-47* inside Scapa Flow after negotiating Kirk Sound.
0100 Having sighted *Royal Oak* and *Pegasus*, *U-47* launches a salvo of torpedoes. She turns about and fires a torpedo from the stern tube which misses.
0104 *Royal Oak* is hit in the bows by a torpedo.
0112 *U-47* fires a second salvo. All three torpedoes hit *Royal Oak*.
0133 *Royal Oak* sinks.

The Escape

14 October 0133 As *Royal Oak* sinks, *U-47* makes off towards Kirk Sound.
0215 *U-47* passes beyond Rose Ness into the North Sea.
15 October British minesweepers are sighted. *U-47* crash-dives and escapes intact after being depth-charged.
17 October 1100 *U-47* reaches Wilhelmshaven in Germany.

the plan and asked his U-boat commander to assess its feasibility and give him his decision. After detailed examination Prien accepted the proposition.

On 8 October, Prien and the crew of *U-47* prepared to set out from the harbour at Kiel. After steering through the Kiel Canal, the submarine entered the North Sea and during the night of the 8th travelled to the offshore island of Heligoland, where the final trim trials took place. *U-47* was a Type VIIB U-boat and although it was the most advanced submarine in the German Navy it was hardly a submarine in the modern sense, in that it could only travel underwater for short distances and then at slow speed. Normally U-boats sailed on the surface and only submerged if attacked by enemy aircraft or surface vessels; and while U-boat assaults against well-guarded convoys were often carried out under water, engagements against single ships were delivered on the surface, more often than not by the single 8.8cm gun mounted on the U-boat's hull.

Explosive charges were placed around the boat in case the order was given to scuttle it

Absolute secrecy was essential, and so, to avoid being sighted by enemy or even neutral vessels and aircraft, Prien submerged *U-47* during the day and resurfaced when it was night, to travel on the surface only during the hours of darkness. For the 44-man crew of *U-47* night and day were reversed as they slept during the day and awoke for breakfast in the evening. All the crew – mechanics, electricians, cooks, wireless operators, torpedoers, stokers – were used to the unnatural routine and claustrophobic conditions.

During the nights of the 10th and 11th, *U-47* sailed across the shallow waters of the North Sea without incident. The sighting of the Orkneys on the evening of the 12th marked the end of their journey. After Prien had told the crew of their destination, he dismissed them to their bunks, although few could sleep in the knowledge that in a few hours' time *U-47* would attempt to breach the defences of Scapa Flow.

In his autobiography, Prien relates how he carried out his final preparations: 'Once more I went through the boat and gave my instructions. During the whole of the action no-one was to smoke and, even more important, no-one was to speak unnecessarily. Everyone inspected his life jacket. I cast a last glance at the escape hatch; the navigator fixed his chart.' The torpedoes were armed and prepared for firing, while explosive charges were distributed around the boat in case the order was given to scuttle it to avoid capture.

At 1900 hours the electric motors were started up and *U-47* rose slowly to the surface. Once above sea level, the main diesels were gunned into life. Clad in oilskins, Prien emerged onto the bridge of the conning tower with his bo'sun and two watch officers to check that all was clear. To their surprise the night was not very dark; the northern lights cast a glow across Scapa Flow and its approaches, enough to make the U-boat considerably more visible than expected. Prien thought of postponing the operation

Above: The crew of *U-47* in relaxed mood as they set out for the Atlantic. Moving on the surface, and only submerging to avoid Allied aircraft, Type VIIB U-boats were capable of a maximum speed of just over 17 knots. Below: HMS *Royal Oak*. The eight 15in and 12 6in guns of this ageing battleship proved no defence against the stealthy German raider that attacked her in Scapa Flow.

SUBMARINE WARFARE

Karl Dönitz, a former U-boat commander of World War I, was given command of the new submarine fleet of Nazi Germany in September 1935. Although there had been clandestine work on submarines since the Nazi takeover in 1933 (under the cover of an anti-submarine warfare school), the signing of the Anglo-German Naval Treaty of June 1935 gave the Kriegsmarine the formal permission it wanted to build more of the 'wolves of the sea' that had proved so frightening and dangerous during World War I. Drawing on his experience, Dönitz, a clear-thinking and ambitious commander, believed that Britain would not be defeated by the isolated successes of a few powerful submarines, but by the gradual attrition exerted by a large submarine fleet, acting in flotillas – the famous 'Wolf Packs'.

Dönitz wanted submarines that would be able to sweep an area of sea, and then concentrate for a co-ordinated night attack when a convoy was sighted. They would attack on the surface (at night, a U-boat's profile was practically invisible) and then break off the engagement during the day. They would need a high surface speed to keep ahead of the convoy (convoys generally travelled at about seven knots) to move in for the kill the following night. Underwater manoeuvres would be undertaken only to avoid enemy escort vessels or aircraft.

Type VII boats suited this requirement perfectly. They were fast (*U-47* had a surface speed of 17 knots) and easy to produce in quantity (over 600 had been put into production by the end of the war).

***U-47* was a Type VIIB, displacing 750 tons on the surface and crewed by 44 men. Armed with 15 torpedoes – four bow firing tubes and one in the stern – the *U-47* also had one 8.8cm deck gun and a 2cm anti-aircraft gun. It was 218ft long and had a beam of 20ft 3in.**

to the following night, but the morale of his men was high and setting back the attack would only dampen spirits. He decided to press on. Off Rose Ness a merchant ship was spotted, forcing *U-47* to crash dive and stay submerged for 30 minutes. Then, at 2331 hours, the submarine resurfaced and entered Holm Sound.

As the boat neared the coast, the orange and blue rays of the northern lights shot upwards in the sky and the dark silhouettes of the low hills around Scapa Flow could be easily discerned. Twice, the submarine skirted disaster. First, mis-sighting of a blockship by Prien nearly had *U-47* sailing towards the impassable Skerny Sound, but the navigator spotted the error in time and, with the course corrected, the submarine slipped into Kirk Sound. Then, *U-47* grated noisily across the cable of one of the blockships, and was momentarily forced aground. Reacting quickly, Prien ordered the opening of the air-pressure valves and the flooded diving-tanks blown. *U-47* trembled in the water and shook free. They were in Scapa Flow.

Edging past the village of St Mary's, the German submarine was suddenly caught in the headlights of a car on the mainland. Staring in horror at the shore the small group on the conning tower feared the worst, but to their relieved amazement no alarm was raised and the boat sailed on unnoticed. Prien now began to look for his prizes, but as *U-47* advanced into Scapa Flow, his anxiety began to grow, for nowhere could he see the mass of battleships, cruisers and destroyers of the British Home Fleet.

While German aerial reconnaissance had observed several large warships at anchor during the previous week, these had steamed out towards the North Sea just after *U-47* had left harbour, in response to a German naval sortie. Instead of returning to Scapa Flow, the main body had anchored at Loch Ewe. Only the ageing *Royal Oak* had returned to Scapa, unable to keep up with the other ships in the force-nine gales which they had encountered. The *Royal Oak* had been commissioned in 1916 as one of the Royal Sovereign-class battleships and by 1939 she was strictly a 'second-line' battleship, even though her eight 15in guns and displacement of 31,250 tons made her an impressive sight.

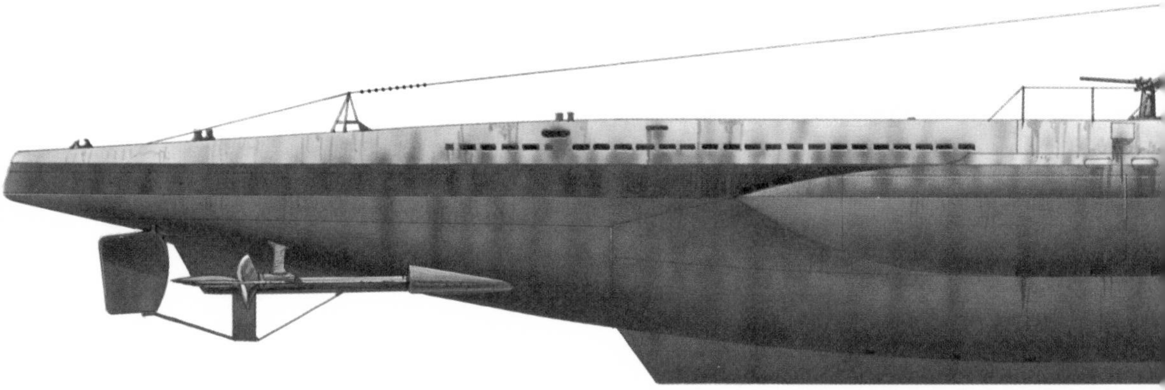

Below: The Torpedo Mate on a Type VII withdraws one of his 'eels' for maintenance. One of the five tubes would normally be worked on each day, to make sure that the torpedoes were always ready.

Bottom centre: A crewman hangs on grimly in heavy seas. The U-boats had to operate under the most difficult weather conditions, and, in addition, the crew had to exist for long periods in cramped and uncomfortable living quarters.

The *U-47* had entered Scapa shortly after midnight, travelled over three nautical miles westwards and seen nothing. Not daring to travel further westwards for fear of being spotted by British patrol boats in Hoxa Sound, Prien ordered *U-47* into an 180-degree about-turn and then, against a rising tide of desperation from his crew, turned to port and began to advance northwards. Just before 0100 hours the Germans' luck changed, for directly ahead the shadowy bulk of a battleship began to emerge. As *U-47* moved in, the battleship was correctly identified as a Royal Sovereign-class vessel. Behind it Prien claimed he saw a further warship, the battlecruiser *Repulse*, but in this he was mistaken: the second ship was only the 6900-ton seaplane tender *Pegasus*.

The torpedoes were loaded into the tubes and on Prien's order a salvo of three was fired, two at the *Royal Oak*, the third at *'Repulse'*. The range was long (about 3000m) – and the men of *U-47* waited anxiously as the electrically-powered weapons sped towards their targets. A full three-and-a-half minutes later, at 0104, one hit the bows of the *Royal Oak*. Although the explosion was felt throughout the battleship, it caused surprisingly little consternation; many on board thought it must have been a small-scale explosion in the oxygen and paint store. No one was expecting an enemy attack by submarine.

The explosion had been spotted from the *U-47* but the *Royal Oak* remained uncannily quiet. In fact, Prien thought he had struck the *'Repulse'*, the distance being too great to correctly identify the hit. Fearing detection, *U-47* turned about to reload its forward torpedo tubes, while loosing off a further torpedo from the stern tube this went wide.

Torpedoes loaded, *U-47* again turned into the attack. About 12 minutes after the first strike the submarine fired a second salvo of three torpedoes. The first hit the starboard side of the *Royal Oak* under the 'B' gun turret, sending up a large column of spray. Seconds later the other two torpedoes smashed into the hull of the battleship. The *Royal Oak* lifted then settled, and began to list to starboard.

Aboard the battleship, there was chaos. All power had been lost and the broadcast system destroyed. Below decks the crew staggered blindly in the dark,

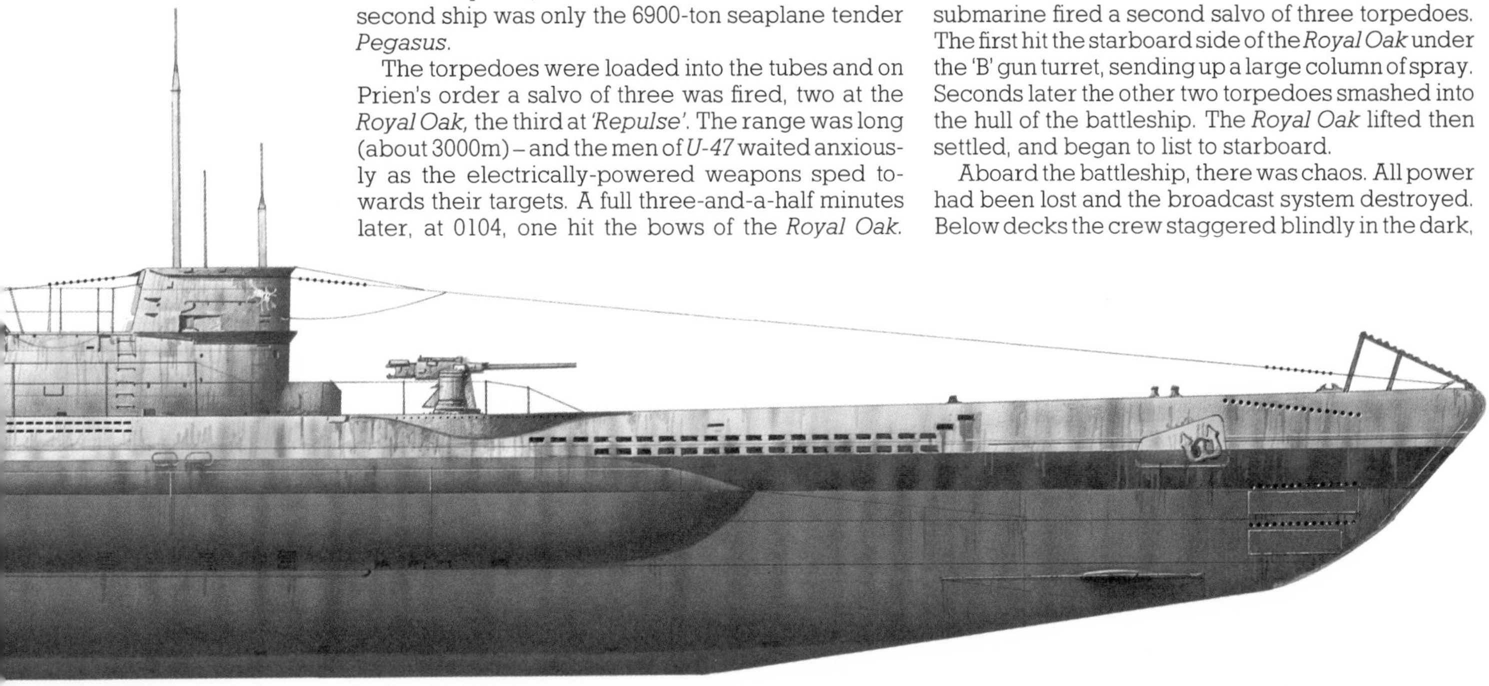

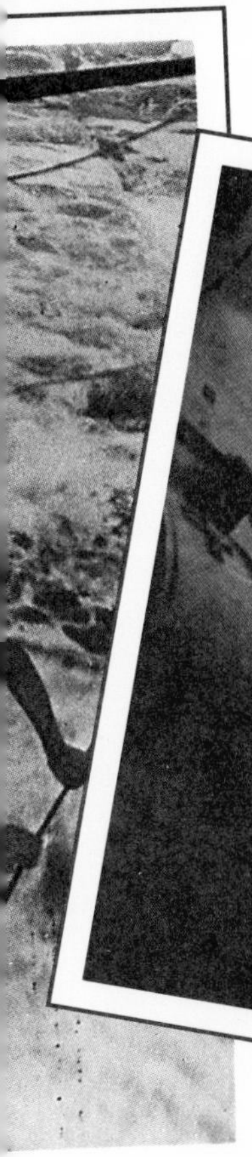

Below: Preparing to use the electric motors underwater while tracking an Allied merchant vessel in the Atlantic.

many trapped by the fires raging throughout the ship and others by the power-operated hatches now jammed shut. The *Royal Oak*'s starboard list grew more severe and about ten minutes after the second set of explosions the ship turned turtle, going under completely at 0133. Out of the 1200-strong crew, 833 men went to their deaths.

As the *Royal Oak* was going down, *U-47* turned to make its escape. The current was running against it as it clawed its way back into Kirk Sound. Deciding against the northern channel through which he had entered Scapa Flow, Prien chose the deeper, though tighter, southern channel. Negotiating the twisting channel with great skill, the *U-47*'s helmsman took his boat past the blockship and out into Holm Sound. By 0215 hours *U-47* was beyond Rose Ness Point and heading into the North Sea. A crate of beer was produced and the crew celebrated their audacious victory – the sinking of a 31,000-ton battleship in the Royal Navy's major home anchorage by a 750-ton submarine.

U-47 set course for home and, after surviving a depth-charge attack by minesweepers on the 15th, sailed into port at Wilhelmshaven at 1100 hours on the 17th. The German authorities had quickly picked up the sinking of the *Royal Oak* so that when *U-47* docked the crew received a hero's welcome. *Grossadmiral* Raeder and

Left: Karl Dönitz, architect of Germany's U-boat arm, inspects the crew of *U-47* on their return. Below left: Some of the officers of *U-47* during the same inspection. Bottom: Günther Prien, in white cap, with his crew after the triumphant reception at Wilhelmshaven. Nazi propaganda made great play of the sinking of the *Royal Oak* and Prien was awarded the Knight's Cross. In Britain, there was suspicion that the German vessel had been guided into Scapa Flow by traitors, and stories that the car headlights that had so frightened the German submariners had been a secret signal, circulated freely. Only after the war did it become clear that aerial reconnaissance and not treason had been the Germans' main intelligence source.

Dönitz were there at the quayside to award the entire crew the Iron Cross 2nd Class, while their leader, Günther Prien, was to receive the Knight's Cross from the Führer himself.

The sinking of the *Royal Oak* by the *U-47* provided Dönitz with his proof that the submarine was a potent war-winning force, and that the expansion of the U-boat arm was an urgent priority. Fortunately for the Allies, the U-boat-building programme was never quite sufficient to cover U-boat losses, and in the end the submarine menace was defeated.

Prien was destined to have little time to savour his triumph. He continued to command *U-47*, leading it for a further 18 months in a successful career attacking Allied merchant shipping, but on 8 March 1941 the Royal Navy was avenged. The destroyer HMS *Wolverine,* escorting Atlantic convoy OB 293, sank the submarine with depth-charges after a lengthy pursuit. *U-47* went down with all hands, eight of them, including Prien, members of the Scapa Flow crew.

In all, only 15 of the 44 submariners involved in the sinking of *Royal Oak* were to survive the war – a typical example of the dreadful losses eventually suffered by the U-boats as the tide of conflict turned against them. Ironically, the youngest member of the crew, torpedo mechanic Herbert Herrmann, later became a naturalised British subject, living with his Scottish wife in Dumfriesshire.

THE AUTHOR Adrian Gilbert has edited and contributed to a number of military and naval publications and is a co-author of *Vietnam: The History and the Tactics.*

SEA WOLF

Operating in the Mediterranean during World War I, the German U-boat *U-35* sank 535,900 tons of shipping, making it the most successful submarine of all time

WHEN WAR WAS DECLARED in August 1914, the young German naval officer Lothar von Arnauld de la Perière found himself constrained to a desk job on the staff of Admiral von Pohl. Desperate for action, he applied for a command in the naval Zeppelin branch, but on being refused he turned his attention to the other end of the spectrum and requested a transfer to the submarine branch. A torpedo expert, von Arnauld's wish was granted and in the autumn of 1915 he was given command of *U-35*. A Mediterranean-based submarine, *U-35* had previously been commanded by Kapitänleutnant Kophamel, but his promotion to commander of the new naval base at Pola, on the Adriatic coast of Austria-Hungary, left a vacancy which von Arnauld was now appointed to fill. While *U-35* returned to its forward base – the Adriatic port of Cattaro – von Arnauld travelled down to assume his new command.

Below left: The crack German submarine *U-35* claimed 224 ships sunk during her career in World War I, a total far in excess of the 52 ships sunk by *U-48*, the top-scoring German U-boat of World War II. Below right: The crew of *U-35* contained some of the best submariners in the Mediterranean. Behind the deck gun is their commander, Lothar von Arnauld, the coveted Pour le Mérite at his neck.

The startling success of the submarine as a strategic weapon had surprised both Germany and the Allies, and in 1915 Germany increased the size of her submarine branch as rapidly as the supply of vessels would allow. Almost simultaneously, the Mediterranean assumed a new importance as a theatre of war: first, it was a major supply route for the Allies and, second, the Dardanelles campaign had brought Turkey into the war – Germany felt that it must provide support for its far-distant ally. Consequently, *U-35* set out from Germany on 4 August 1915 along with the *U-34*, to be followed shortly by *U-33, U-39* and *U-38*. The five 'Thirties' were amongst the German Navy's best submarines, led by daring commanders, with top-notch crews. The Allies, by contrast, were poorly prepared for the arrival of these sea wolves, and suffered heavily as a result. The Austrians allowed the German Navy the use of the base at Cattaro and, operating from its southerly

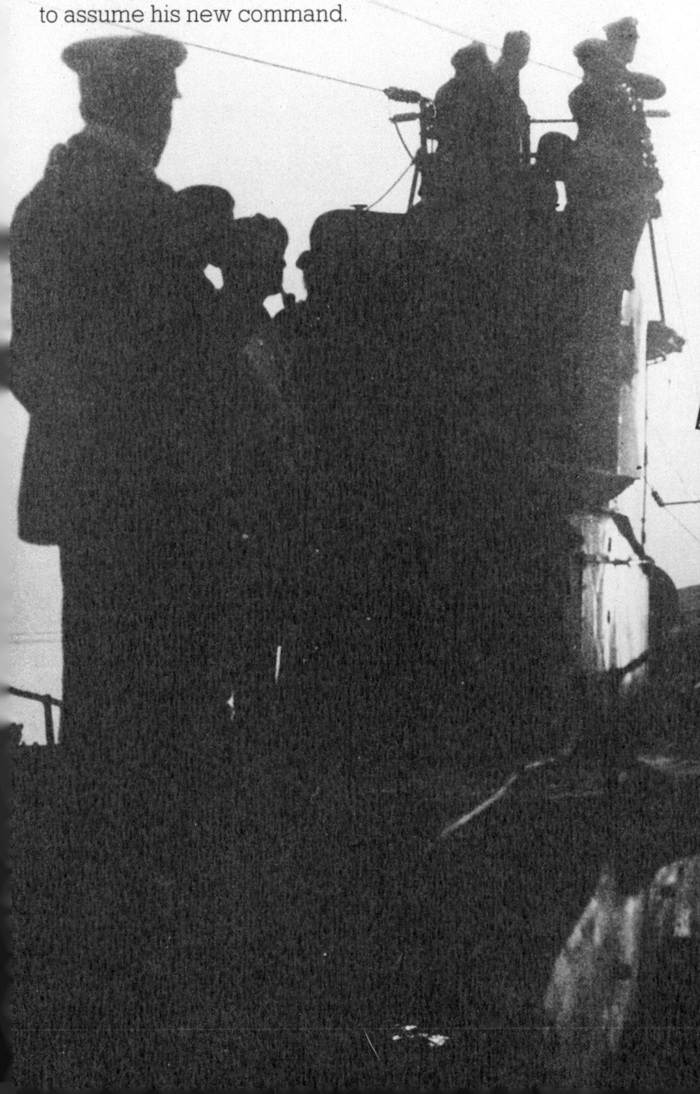

U-35

The *U-35* was one of a batch of 11 U-boats (numbered *U-31* to *U-41* inclusive) ordered by the German Navy in June 1912 and completed between October 1914 and February 1915. The first German U-boat, *U-1*, had been constructed in 1906, and experience with *U-1* and subsequent models had caused several improvements to be introduced. The calibre of the torpedoes had been increased from 450mm to 500mm, and the early 8.8cm deck guns had been uprated to 10.5cm pieces. Conditions were still cramped however, with 35 ratings and four officers crammed into a boat displacing 870 tons submerged, and 212ft in length.

It was imperative to the German Navy that her submarines could operate far into the North Sea. The twin diesel engines of *U-35* were designed to give full ocean-going capability, and their range of 4440 miles at eight knots allowed the U-boat to make the voyage from her home port in the North Sea to the forward base of Cattaro in the Adriatic. With a full operational complement of only six 500mm torpedoes, *U-35* had limited capability for submerged anti-shipping warfare. However, the submarine carried 900 rounds for the 10.5cm deck gun, and these were quite adequate for *U-35's* unarmed merchant targets. *U-35* spent her wartime career in the Mediterranean, and after being interned in Barcelona in November 1918 she was handed over to the British. She was just one of the 105 U-boats surrendered to Britain after the war which were either broken up for scrap or used for target practice.

Below: Various German submarine types are made ready in Cattaro for operations. Left: Torpedoes are hoisted aboard *U-35*, while (below left) spent 10.5cm deck-gun cartridges are unloaded on the return to port. Below right: Crewmen of *U-35* and a UB-class submarine watch an approaching aircraft, while (bottom) German submariners are photographed ashore on a Spanish quayside.

position on the Adriatic, the U-boats were easily capable of slipping through the feeble Allied barrage at Otranto and penetrating into the heart of the Mediterranean.

U-35's first patrol was undertaken in the eastern Mediterranean. Partnered by *U-34*, it began to attack the Allied shipping lanes around Crete, sinking five vessels that included an Indian Army troopship. Kapitänleutnant Kophamel was a fine submariner (achieving Germany's sixth highest score), and after the success of this first cruise he set off alone into the northern Aegean, where he correctly assumed there would be rich pickings from the supply of troops and stores that were being ferried to the Allied base at Salonika. In addition to the primary objective of sinking Allied shipping, Kophamel and *U-35* also engaged in cloak and dagger operations by shipping over German and Turkish officers, along with supplies of munitions, to Bardia on the Libyan coast. The Turks were providing aid to disaffected Senussi tribesmen against their Italian colonisers in this region, spreading alarm among the British authorities in neighbouring Egypt.

By the time Kophamel received his promotion, *U-35* had sunk an impressive 49,000 tons of shipping, its complement of four officers and 35 men now fully experienced in the techniques of underwater warfare. The crew quickly accepted their new comman-

The War in the Mediterranean
1914–1918
BAY OF BISCAY
FRANCE
AUSTRIA-HUNGARY
Genoa
Marseille
BLACK SEA
ADRIATIC SEA
ITALY
Cattaro
SPAIN
Naples
TURKEY
Otranto
Cartagena
GIBRALTAR
Athens
MALTA
CRETE
MEDITERRANEAN
Key
U-boat routes into Mediterranean
Allied merchant shipping routes
Areas of heavy Allied losses
Bardia
Alexandria
Port Said
LIBYA
EGYPT

Far left, above: Trapped by *U-35*, an Allied merchantman awaits the gunshots that will send it to the bottom, while officers on the submarine's bridge scan the horizon for signs of Allied warships. Far left, below: One of Germany's small Type UB submarines moors alongside *U-35* during a mission in the Mediterranean. Some of these small coastal submarines were transported in sections by railway from Germany to such ports as Pola, and then assembled for immediate action in the Adriatic. The incongruous figure pacing the deck of *U-35* in British Army uniform is Captain Wilson, King's Messenger, who was captured earlier in the mission. Top, left and right: Victims of *U-35*: one British steamer is holed by surface gunfire, while another slides out of sight. Von Arnauld was a humane commander, however, and allowed merchant crews to escape before despatching their ships. Above right: Crew members in two lifeboats are interrogated by the officers of *U-35* after a sinking.

der, and during the winter of 1915-16 von Arnauld supervised *U-35* as she underwent a refit. Submarines had originally been envisaged as vessels whose prime function was to attack surface warships, with the torpedo considered as the main armament and the deck gun added as an afterthought. By 1915, however, the U-boat was proving its effectiveness as a weapon of economic warfare; while the opportunities to destroy warships arose relatively infrequently, the vast merchant fleets that sailed the major waterways were easy to locate and sink. Merchant ships were generally too small to merit an expensive torpedo (in the Mediterranean a typical merchant ship was a sailing vessel of under 2000 tons), but they could be readily despatched by a few accurate shots from a 10.5cm or 15cm deck gun. Von Arnauld was quick to grasp the importance of this, and placed great emphasis on gunnery, bringing with him a top gunner from the Fleet. Indeed, he often returned from an operation with torpedoes on board, so that, for example, on his most successful patrol he used only four of 10 torpedoes but completely exhausted his 900 rounds of 10.5cm ammunition. In addition to his tactical prowess, von Arnauld was a humane commander, preferring to give the defenceless merchant ships a warning of their impending fate, so that before his prey was sunk its crew could lower the lifeboats.

Von Arnauld led *U-35* out on his first patrol on 20 February 1916, and, taking his lead from Kophamel, sailed eastward to operate between Malta and Crete. On 26 February *U-35* chalked up her first kill, with von Arnauld torpedoing a French troopship with 1800 men aboard, over half of whom drowned. Three days later the young commander launched an attack on a British 'submarine-chaser' called the *Primula*. The action that followed was fraught with danger, as von Arnauld later recounted:

'The toughest nut to crack was the *Primula*, and I shall never cease admiring her skipper. She was a small craft, scarcely worth a torpedo, but the situation was such that if we did not get her, she might possibly get us. The first torpedo hit her in the bow and her foremast went clattering down. We gaped with wide eyes at what the boat proceeded to do. Her engines reversed and she started back at full speed, coming at us and trying to ram us with her stern. The *Primula* steamed backwards with such speed that it kept the pressure of water from her shattered forepart, else she would have sunk at once, and at the same time we had to step lively or she would have crashed into us.

'I loosed another torpedo. The *Primula*, still with reverse speed, swung around so as to avoid the missile. The torpedo missed, and the damaged boat continued trying to ram us. Another torpedo; it missed. That sort of thing could not go on forever. The fourth torpedo hit, and to my immense relief the *Primula* sank, at last.'

A second patrol in the eastern Mediterranean was undertaken in March and April but proved disappointing, the only sinking of note being that of the 13,400 ton *Minneapolis*. After a refit at Cattaro, the *U-35* sailed on a third patrol, this time towards the western Mediterranean – where her luck changed dramatically. During a two-week operation, beginning on 10 June, *U-35* sank 40 enemy vessels, totalling 57,000 tons – an amazing feat even in the crowded waters between France, Italy and North Africa. Von Arnauld even found time to break off from commerce raiding to enter the Spanish port of Cartagena and deliver a personal message from the Kaiser to the King of Spain. Since the Allies controlled the surface waters, U-boats could be highly effective as a special delivery service, capable of taking messages or selected individuals into and out of Germany.

Incredibly, the next patrol yielded an even higher figure: over a period of 25 days some 54 assorted merchant vessels, amounting to 90,000 tons, were despatched to the bottom. The high point of the patrol was 14 August when *U-35* sunk 11 Italian coastal vessels in quick succession, although von Arnauld only just managed to escape being intercepted by a flotilla of French anti-submarine ships.

On 15 August the *U-35* almost fell prey to the Italian decoy ship *Citta di Sassari*, but managed to dive to safety in time

As a result of the high losses inflicted upon Allied shipping, various methods were adopted to counter the U-boat threat. One of the most dangerous of these to *U-35* was the introduction of decoy ships (called Q-ships by the British): 'merchant' vessels were fitted out with a number of powerful but concealed guns, the intention being to lure the unsuspecting submarine to short range. At the appropriate moment, the decoy ship's guns would be revealed and the submarine blasted out of the water before the commander had a chance to submerge. On 15 August the *U-35* almost fell prey to the Italian decoy ship *Citta di Sassari*, but managed to dive to safety in time when the Italian captain made the common error of opening fire at too great a distance. Although it took great nerve, the key to success in this form of warfare was to wait until the U-boat was virtually alongside the decoy ship before opening fire.

By now the leading scorer in terms of tonnage sunk, success followed success for von Arnauld, the unprotected merchantmen falling to him like flies. His next patrol, conducted during the autumn of 1916, yielded 22 ships with a gross displacement of 70,000 tons. The Kaiser's propaganda machine made good use of Germany's new hero of the deep, and, following the award of the Pour le Mérite, von Arnauld was rapidly becoming a household name.

At the close of 1916, *U-35* was withdrawn to Cattaro for a major refit: engines were overhauled and faulty or broken equipment was replaced. As a result, when the new 'hunting season' got underway *U-35* was ready for action. By early 1917, the enormous and ever increasing shipping losses being inflicted upon the Allies belatedly forced them to adopt the convoy system, the only really effective counter to the U-boats. However, while the gradual introduction of convoys in the Mediterranean during 1917 made things more difficult for von Arnauld, he still managed to amass very high scores. A five-week patrol, beginning in April 1917, eventually led to the sinking of 20 vessels of 65,000 tons displacement.

The two officers of the watch suddenly saw, to their horror, the distinctive mast of a periscope looking straight at them

The shortage of victims in the Mediterranean forced von Arnauld to take *U-35* past the Straits of Gibraltar and adopt a station on the western approaches to the Straits, a decision that was vindicated in the destruction of 17 ships in less than two weeks. On this patrol, *U-35* had a 'cinematograph' cameraman assigned to it, who, despite suffering from acute sea sickness, managed to film the submarine in action – including the sinking of the British merchantman *Parkgate*. The finished film was despatched to Germany where it was shown to the Kaiser, and to frontline troops in cinemas along the Western Front, much to the chagrin of the master of the *Parkgate*, who was depicted as being under the influence of alcohol upon his capture by von Arnauld. During the two-week patrol a total of five British captains found themselves imprisoned together, von Arnauld's policy being to take only the captains of destroyed enemy ships prisoner. In contrast to a number of other U-boat commanders, von Arnauld was scrupulous in his observance of military and naval conventions at sea, and even though he inflicted massive losses upon the British, his opponents always held him in the highest regard. Thus, in one instance, von Arnauld was sent a letter of appreciation from the master of the *Patagonier*, thanking him and the crew of *U-35* for his treatment during 23 days aboard the submarine.

U-35's next patrol was another triumph for von Arnauld, again operating to the west of Gibraltar and sinking 11 ships of around 31,000 tons off the coasts of Spain and Morocco. A subsequent patrol nearly ended in disaster for the German submariners, however, when *U-35* narrowly escaped being sunk by a British submarine in an extraordinary episode that confirmed the *U-35*'s reputation as a 'lucky' boat.

When *U-35* came into home waters at the end of a long patrol, the two officers of the watch suddenly saw, to their horror, the distinctive mast of a periscope looking straight at them. Almost immediately there appeared a streak on the water – a torpedo was racing directly towards them. Petrified, the two officers knew that there was no time to take evasive action and braced themselves for certain destruction. But to their complete amazement, the torpedo leaped out of the water only 10yds from the U-boat. The British torpedo had been set for a shallow run to

ensure a hit against the U-boat's own shallow draught, but the operator had over-set the torpedo, causing it to become temporarily airborne. The torpedo described a graceful arc through the air before landing with a crash on the U-boat's foredeck, its detonating nose just missing the deck gun, before bouncing harmlessly into the water. The loud bang of the torpedo on the *U-35*'s deck alerted the whole crew, and with an instinctive shout of 'Helm hard aport!' von Arnauld guided his submarine out of danger, with further torpedoes racing alongside them, albeit harmlessly.

That patrol was to be one of von Arnauld's last as commander of *U-35*. Early in 1918 he was recalled to Germany to take command of *U-139*, one of a new class of giant cruiser-submarines designed to operate for long periods in the Atlantic against American shipping. Von Arnauld had one notable engagement against a convoy west of Spain, where he sank a number of vessels despite being heavily depth-charged by the convoy's numerous escorts. *U-139* returned to Kiel on 14 October 1918, only to find the High Seas Fleet disintegrating into outright mutiny, a dismal end to von Arnauld's distinguished war career.

U-35 remained in the Mediterranean throughout 1918, continuing to operate against Allied shipping. During the autumn of 1918 it became increasingly clear to the German Navy in the Mediterranean that Austria-Hungary was finished, and during October plans were made to withdraw the remaining U-boats to Germany. Although the majority of U-boats slipped through the Straits of Gibraltar, the commander of *U-35* decided upon internment rather than eventual surrender, and sailed *U-35* into Barcelona habour shortly before the Armistice on 11 November 1918. The most successful submarine of all time, *U-35* sank 224 ships totalling 535,900 tons, the vast majority gained under the command of Kapitänleutnant von Arnauld de la Perière, in his turn, one of the most successful submarine aces of all time.

THE AUTHOR Adrian Gilbert has edited and contributed to a number of military and naval publications. His book *World War I in Photographs*, which is to be published this year, covers all aspects of The Great War.

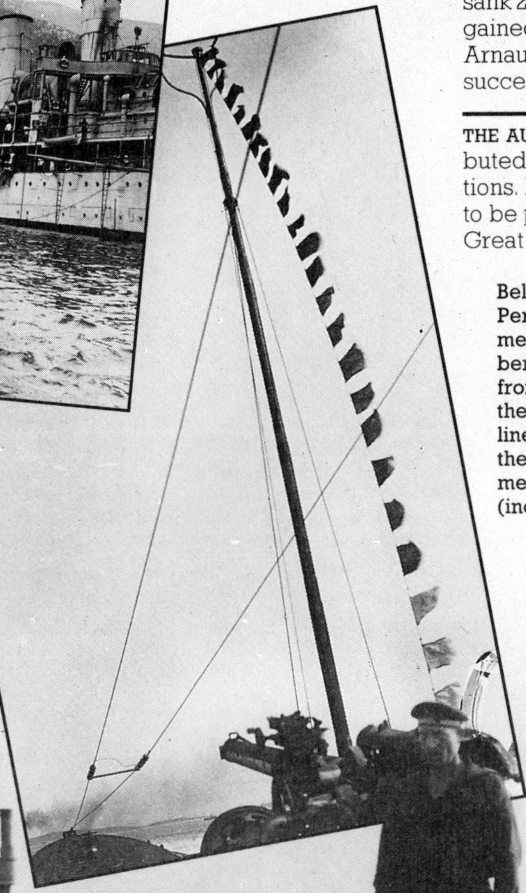

Below: Kapitänleutnant Lothar von Arnauld de la Perière stands near an aft hatch of *U-35*. Top left: The men of von Arnauld's submarine salute a vessel berthed in the Adriatic port of Cattaro as they return from a successful patrol in April 1917. Seen beyond the 10.5cm gun (left), a telescopic mast supports a line of pennants, each one marking a vessel sunk on the cruise. The submarine's 'bag' is typically high – 21 merchant steamships sunk, plus three sailing vessels (indicated by white pennants).

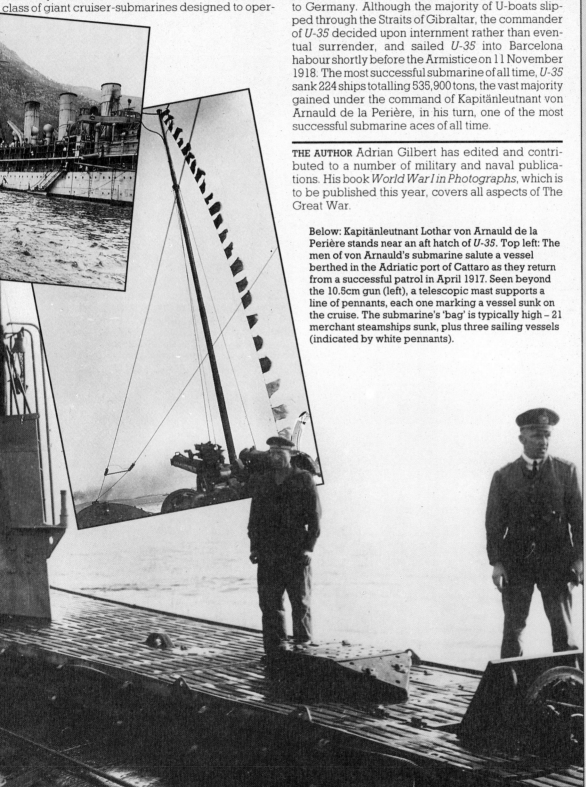

LOTHAR VON ARNAULD DE LA PERIÈRE

Born in 1886, Lothar von Arnauld de la Perière came from a famous Prussian family with a long tradition of military service. The French surname came from his great-grandfather who, entering the service of Frederick the Great in 1757, had risen to the rank of lieutenant-general and won the coveted Pour le Mérite.

The young Lothar was enrolled as a cadet at the naval school at Wahlstadt at the age of 10, spending seven years there before joining the navy proper in 1903. After gaining general experience of naval command, von Arnauld specialised as a torpedo officer and spent two years on SMS *Emden*, the German cruiser which was to gain a formidable reputation as a commerce raider during World War I.

When war broke out in 1914, von Arnauld was serving on the staff of Admiral von Pohl. Craving active service, he attempted to gain command of one of the navy's new Zeppelins, and when this failed he applied for U-boat service. His pleas were answered at the end of 1915 when he was given command of *U-35*.

During the next two years he amassed the greatest score of ships sunk by any submarine commander, before going on to command *U-139* in the closing stages of the war.

Following World War I, the Treaty of Versailles banned the German Navy from operating submarines, and so von Arnauld was given a variety of surface commands, including a naval brigade in Straslund and Stettin. He became navigation officer on the battleship SMS *Elsass*, before being appointed to the naval staff at Wilhelmshaven. In 1931 Germany reintroduced submarines into her navy and von Arnauld joined the new command as an instructor, training the young officers who were to become the U-boat aces of the next world war.

SUB KILLER

HMS *Starling*, proved a ruthless foe of the German U-boat 'wolf packs' during the Battle of the Atlantic

AFTER 10 DAYS without sighting a target, Kapitänleutnant (Lieutenant) Hartwig Looks, commander of the Type VIIC U-boat *U-264*, was undoubtedly relieved when he made contact with an Allied convoy on the night of 18/19 February 1944. His U-boat was equipped with the new schnorkel air mast, enabling him to recharge her batteries without coming to the surface, and U-boat Command was expecting a major success in the Battle of the Atlantic, now entering its fifth grim year.

If Looks had any hope of scoring an easy success against the slow ships of the convoy, it vanished when a destroyer of the close escort broke from the screen at high speed, forcing him down with patterns of depth-charges. For two hours *U-264* was forced to

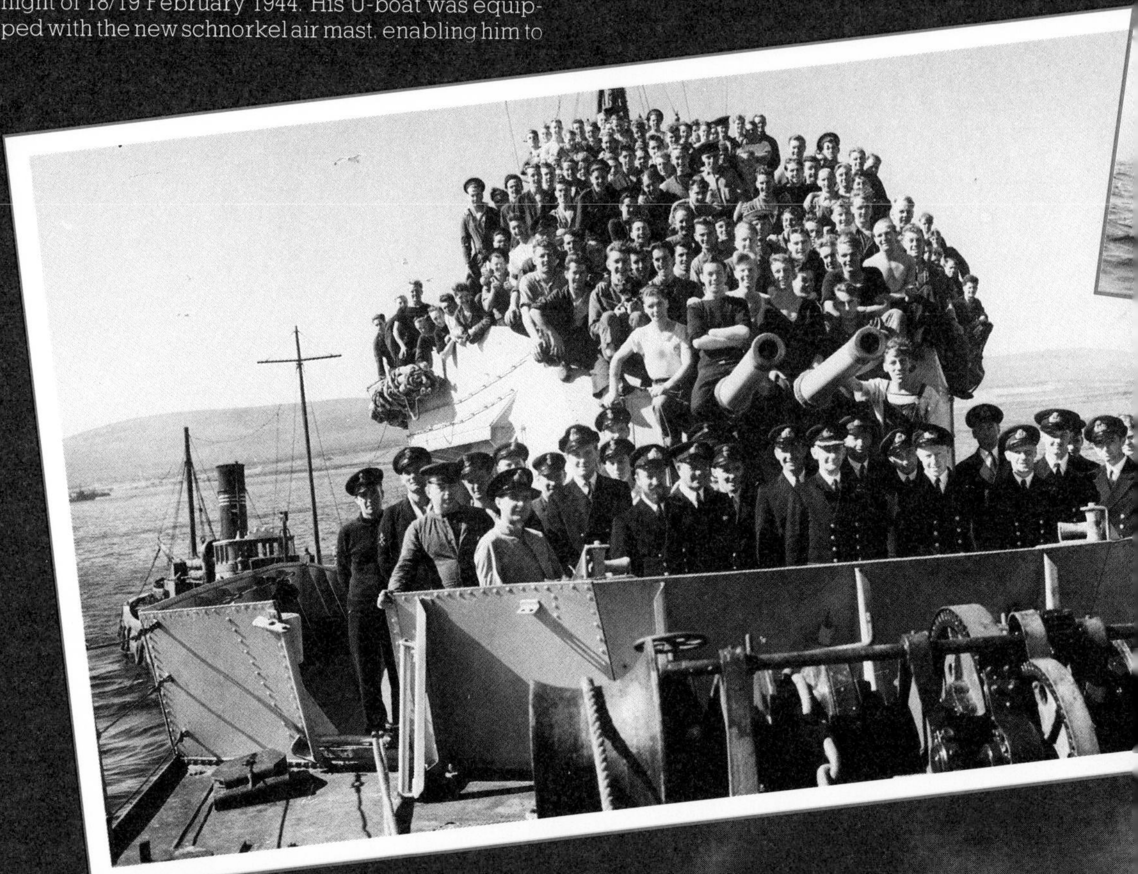

BREAKING THE STRANGLEHOLD

By the end of 1942, Germany's U-boats had sunk a staggering total of 3862 merchant vessels for a loss of only 152 submarines. Beginning the war with 46 operational U-boats, Admiral Dönitz had expanded the force to over 600 submarines, and the entry of the US into the war had produced a rich harvest of unescorted supply ships. However, the period known to U-boat crews as the 'happy time' was drawing to an end, for the Allies were now able to greatly increase their anti-submarine activity.

In 1943, Dönitz's 'wolf-pack' attacks in the Atlantic, in which around 20 U-boats on the surface would converge on a convoy at night, were being made increasingly difficult by a number of factors. American aircraft and escort vessels, equipped with radar and other target-seeking equipment, were being deployed in intensive patrols over the U-boat hunting grounds, forcing the submarine flotillas underwater where their speed and operational flexibility were much reduced. Also, coded German intelligence reports were being intercepted, allowing convoys to make early alterations in their routes to avoid U-boat concentrations. Finally, the Atlantic Convoy Treaty of March 1943 brought together all the Allied anti-submarine commands in a determined bid to drive the U-boats from the Atlantic. The death knell for Dönitz's Atlantic operations was sounded by the formation of hunter/killer support groups

creep along at slow speed, with her crew tensely listening for the rumble of explosions and the metallic 'pinging' of the destroyer's Asdic. But *U-264* was lucky and the destroyer eventually gave up the hunt, allowing her victim to move clear of the danger.

Following standard 'wolf pack' tactics, Looks made his way to the rear of the convoy, hoping to remain astern during the daylight hours; he would then report any alterations in course so that other U-boats could reinforce him before he went in again the following night. But morning brought no respite; instead of merchant ships the look-outs saw the distant silhouettes of a Royal Navy support group closing at high speed. Despite poor Asdic conditions and a high wind, the sloops of the support group harried the U-boat mercilessly for hours, keeping *U-264* at maximum depth, her light-bulbs broken by continuous explosions, engines shaken loose from their mountings and one propeller shaft jammed. By 1600 hours the hunters were certain of victory, but it still took an hour before Looks decided to blow tanks and come to the surface.

The U-boat surfaced about a mile from the warships, which immediately closed in for the kill with guns blazing. Looks and his men abandoned ship after setting scuttling charges, and he and his six officers, nine petty officers and 35 ratings were rescued. Only then did they learn that they had fallen victim to the most successful U-boat hunter of World War II, Captain Frederick Walker RN, leading the 2nd Support Group in the sloop *Starling*. Since leaving Liverpool on 29 January, Walker's Group, comprising *Starling* and her sisters *Wild Goose*, *Kite*, *Wren*, *Woodpecker* and *Magpie*, had sunk six U-boats in the most successful anti-submarine operation of the Atlantic battle. By V-E day in May 1945, *Starling* would be credited with sinking 16 U-boats, and Walker's personal score included another nine submarines sunk by ships under his command.

Starling started life as Job No. 11701 in the Fairfield

Far left: The exultant crew of *Starling* after a cruise which claimed three U-boats. Top: The sloop *Starling* at anchor. Above and left: Captain F.J. Walker watches *Woodpecker* as she closes for the kill. Centre left: The lives of Allied convoy crews depended on the constant vigilance of their escorts and support groups.

ANTI-SUBMARINE TACTICS

Of all the men involved in the development of British anti-submarine warfare in World War II, none made a greater contribution than Captain Frederick Walker. Not only was he Britain's top-scoring U-boat hunter, he also formulated highly successful tactics which were passed on to all the Royal Navy's escort commanders.

By the end of 1942, U-boat commanders had learnt to exploit the deficiency of Asdic at close range and make their escape under cover of the explosions of inaccurate depth-charges. Walker evolved the 'plaster attack', in which one slow-moving ship operating Asdic carried out a normal attack while two others positioned themselves, with their Asdics turned off, 150ft out on either beam. All three then released a wide pattern of charges that caught the U-boat unawares. When Asdic conditions were poor and a deep U-boat seemed likely to escape contact, Walker adopted a technique called the 'creeping attack'. One ship maintained a 1000yd gap with the target, without attempting to close in: at the same time it directed another escort along the submarine's bearing until it was sailing just ahead. The leading ship's commander would then drop 26 charges in pairs at nine-second intervals. The U-boat, aware only of the distant Asdic 'ping' of its tracker astern, would steer straight into a descending carpet of high-explosive. If the submarine was following an evasive zigzag course, Walker would detail three ships, guided from astern, to lay a 'creeping barrage'.

shipyard at Clydeside. She was a 'sloop' or general-purpose escort vessel of the Black Swan class, ordered with 10 sisters under the 1940 Supplementary War Programme. These tough little ships had been developed before the war and their design showed remarkable foresight: there was heavy anti-aircraft armament in the shape of three twin 4in guns and a multiple 'pom-pom', a heavy outfit of depth-charges and an Asdic underwater sensor. If they had a fault it was that they were too good – they were too complex for mass production and simpler types of frigates had to be designed to make up numbers.

When Walker joined his new command early in March 1943 she was still fitting out, but such was the pressure of wartime urgency that she was formally commissioned on 21 March and accepted on 1 April. After an intense 'work-up' in the Western Isles she headed for Liverpool, where she became part of Western Approaches Command.

The Battle of the Atlantic had reached its crisis point in March, but with escort vessels now pouring out from shipyards on both sides of the Atlantic it was possible for the Royal Navy to form five support groups. Their purpose (similar to the American 'hunter-killer' groups) was to cruise independently of the convoys, ready to go to their rescue when called upon, but otherwise free to pursue U-boats on the way to their hunting-grounds. Another advantage of the support groups was their freedom to persist in lengthy attacks on U-boats; convoy escorts were frequently forced to abandon promising contacts in order to rejoin their convoy's screen.

For Walker it became a personal fight, using all his remarkable intuition to co-ordinate the weapons and sensors in his ship

With Walker and *Starling* as their leader, the sloops *Cygnet, Woodpecker, Wren, Wild Goose* and *Kite* sailed from Londonderry on 28 April 1943. After only two days they received a call for help from a convoy bound for Britain from Canada, but there were teething troubles with the new ships and hurriedly trained men, and the first cruise yielded no results. Not until their second cruise did Walker's training methods begin to show results. On 1 June, a clear and sunny day, a U-boat was detected by high-frequency direction-finding equipment (H-F/D-F or 'Huff-Duff').

Within seconds Walker was issuing orders, getting the group into line abreast along the bearing of the U-boat, increasing to full speed. As half-dressed seamen ran to 'action stations' the six ships came to life, and with at least 15 miles to cover there was time to get the ships fully ready. For Walker it became a personal fight, using all his remarkable intuition to co-ordinate the weapons and sensors in his ship. When he learned that his Asdic operator had a contact at about two miles' range, he ordered the *Cygnet, Woodpecker* and *Wren* to maintain a patrol at two miles' distance, and *Wild Goose* and *Kite* to stay in support while he attacked first.

Aboard *Starling's* bridge the 'pinging' of the Asdic could be heard clearly, the shortening interval between the transmitted signal and the sharper-toned echo indicating that the ship was closing rapidly with her adversary. When the two signals were almost merging the order came, 'Stand by depth-charges', followed a second later by 'Fire'. A pattern of 10 depth-charges was dropped, using both stern racks and the four throwers on the quarterdeck. After a seemingly endless interval, the sea suddenly erupted as the 10 charges detonated at pre-selected depths around the estimated position of the U-boat. But as the cascades of water and spray subsided there was no tell-tale sign of a hit.

Walker's quarry was *U-202*, whose captain had taken her down to 500ft, and then up to 400ft to confuse the hunters. Walker had ordered a barrage attack, code-named Operation Plaster, which subjected *U-202* and her crew to a total of 76 depth-charges in three minutes, but Kapitänleutnant Poser was a wily opponent. He took his boat down to 820ft, 100ft more than her official safety limit. At that depth the current pattern of British depth-charge would not function, as a maximum diving depth of about 700ft had been assumed.

All day the hunt went on, with the escorts unable to reach *U-202* and the U-boat unable to escape her tormentors. Walker tried dummy attacks to trick

Below: For the dedicated U-boat hunter, a momentary lapse of concentration could mean the escape of his quarry. Here Captain Walker has resorted to a sandwich on the bridge rather than leave his compass. Below right: The deafening blast of depth-charges came as a welcome relief after the strain of a hunt.

Submarine killers

On 29 January 1944, HMS Starling and four other Royal Navy sloops of Captain Walker's 2nd Support Group put to sea to begin a tour of convoy escort duty in the Atlantic off the coast of Ireland. The group patrolled the Western Approaches for nearly a month, and by the time the tour was over the ships under Walker's command had sunk six German U-boats.

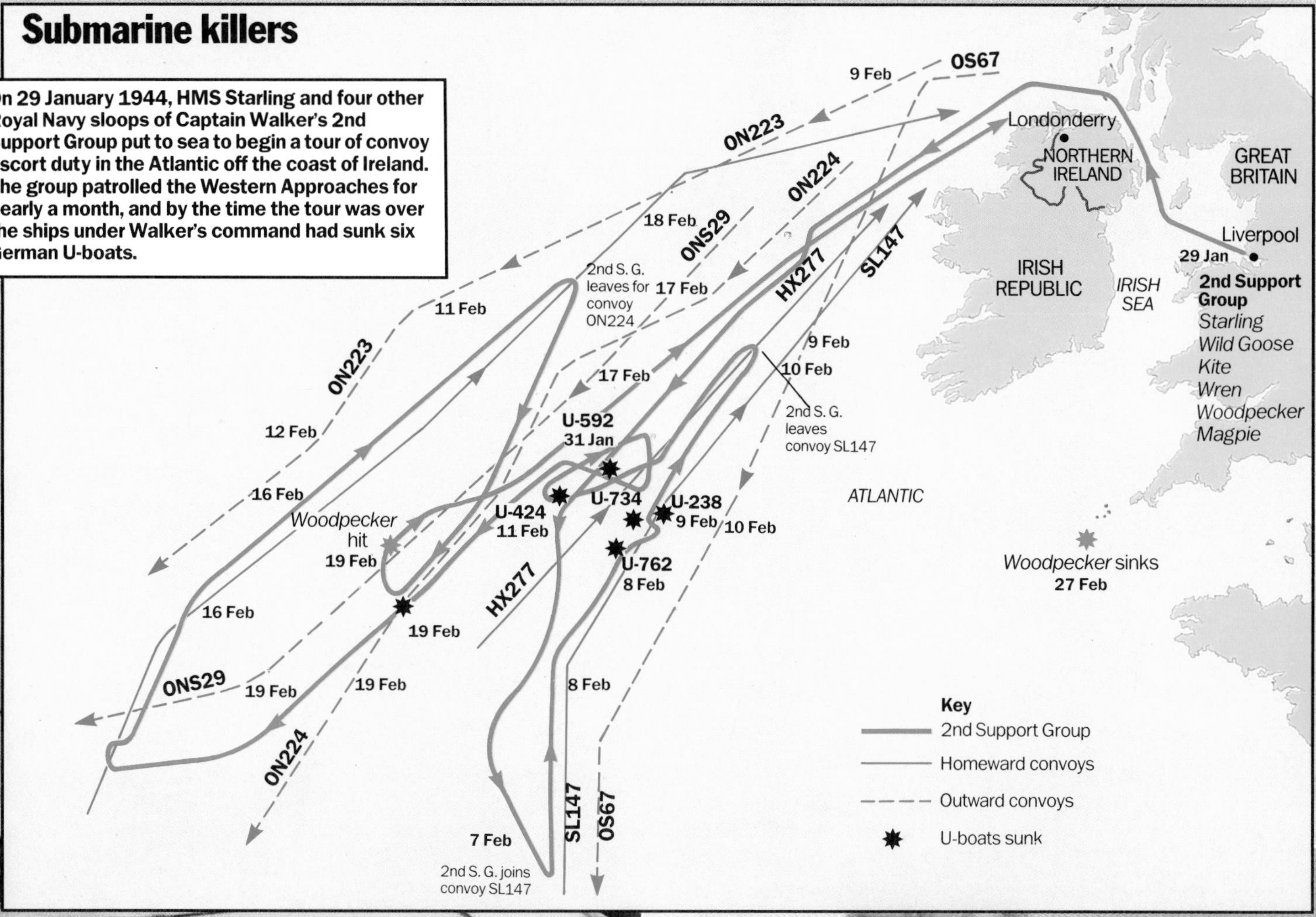
OS67
9 Feb
ON223
Londonderry
NORTHERN IRELAND
GREAT BRITAIN
ON224
18 Feb
ONS29
SL147
HX277
Liverpool
29 Jan
IRISH REPUBLIC
IRISH SEA
2nd Support Group
Starling
Wild Goose
Kite
Wren
Woodpecker
Magpie
2nd S. G. leaves for convoy ON224
17 Feb
11 Feb
9 Feb
10 Feb
17 Feb
2nd S. G. leaves convoy SL147
ON223
12 Feb
U-592
31 Jan
16 Feb
U-424
11 Feb
U-734
U-238
9 Feb
10 Feb
ATLANTIC
Woodpecker hit
19 Feb
U-762
8 Feb
Woodpecker sinks
27 Feb
16 Feb
19 Feb
ONS29
19 Feb
19 Feb
8 Feb
ON224
7 Feb
2nd S. G. joins convoy SL147
SL147
OS67
Key
2nd Support Group
Homeward convoys
Outward convoys
U-boats sunk

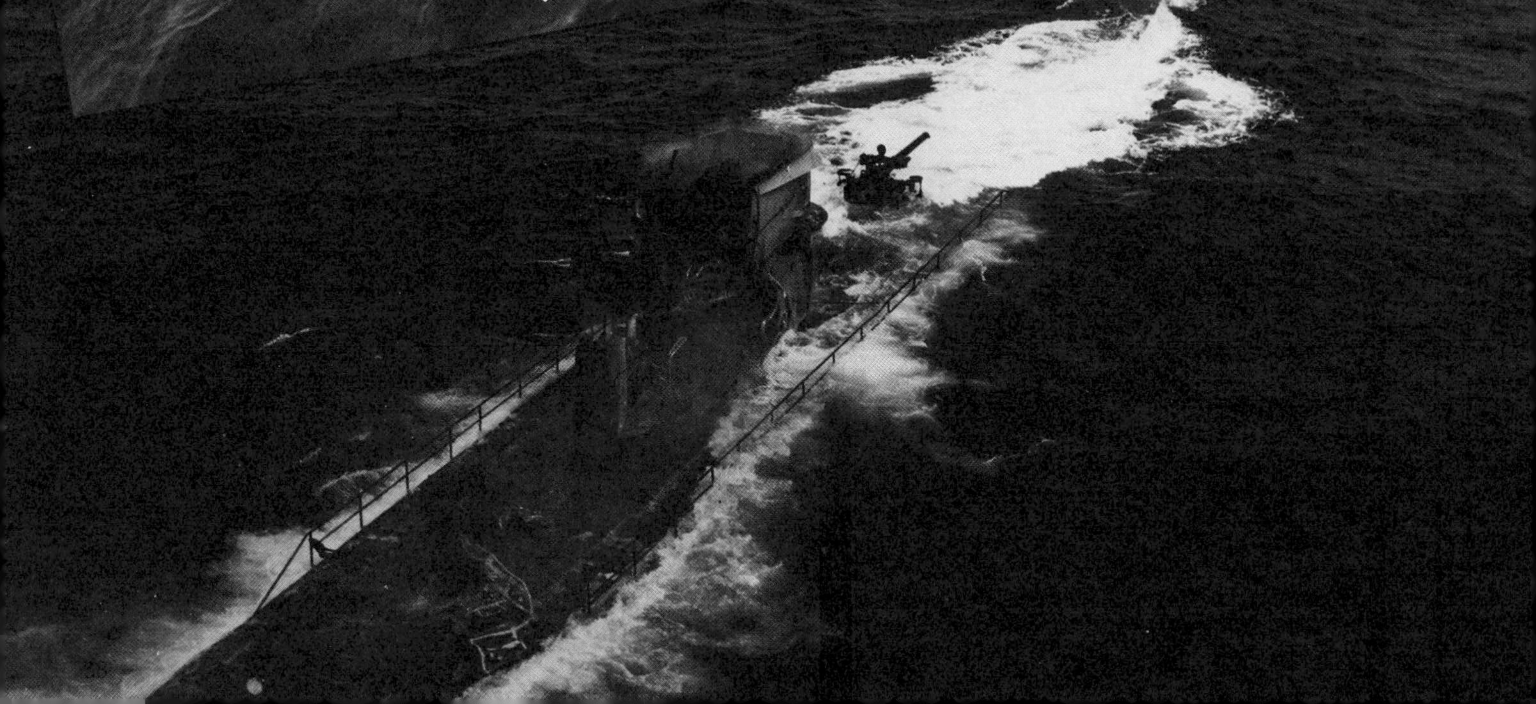

Left: Crewmen reload a Thorneycroft Mk II depth-charge thrower. When this early type was fired, the gases of a 2lb cartridge expanded to force both the depth-charge and its carrier out of the launcher. In the later Thorneycroft Mk IV the carrier became an integral part of the thrower. Below left: Two lucky survivors from a U-boat sunk by the 2nd Support Group await rescue in the chill Atlantic. Bottom: One that did not get away. A U-boat, its conning-tower shattered, flounders helplessly on the surface after a successful anti-submarine operation.

Poser into starting his motors, and Poser launched decoys – bubble targets which created false echoes. Such was Walker's instinct for anti-submarine work that he predicted that *U-202* would run out of air at midnight, and at two minutes past midnight she blew tanks, surfaced and tried to make her escape. It was hopeless, with six well-armed sloops waiting, and by 0030 hours the dazed survivors were being picked up while their shattered U-boat sank. It was to be the only 'kill' of the cruise but it was a heartening sign of things to come.

On 17 June *Starling* led her group to sea again, bound for the Bay of Biscay, where a major air and sea offensive against the U-boats was in full swing. On the morning of 24 June the Asdic operator reported an echo about 1000yds ahead, and Walker ordered an immediate attack with depth-charges. Much to his surprise, as the noise and blast of the last depth-charge died away, the U-boat appeared astern, trying to make her escape on the surface. Walker ordered the rest of the group to cease firing, and ordered *Starling* to ram.

The 1400-ton sloop struck the U-boat abreast of the conning-tower, rolling her over, and to make her destruction certain a pattern of shallow-set depth-charges was dropped as the U-boat slid clear. There were no survivors from *U-119*, but *Starling* had paid a heavy price. Her bow was badly crushed, her Asdic dome had been scraped off and the forward magazines were flooded. In addition, during the first frantic moments of the action she had been struck on the bow by a 'friendly' 4in shell. But Walker was still full of fight, and he took over *Wild Goose* to allow *Starling* to limp back to Plymouth. As the battered little ship moved off he signalled, 'Goodbye, my gallant *Starling*. God be with you.'

Starling's departure was soon followed by another 'kill', *U-449*, and like the *U-119* she was sunk with all hands. This time Walker used his 'creeping attack', using one ship's Asdic to provide data for a slow-speed attack by other ships; it meant that the U-boat was sunk without realising that it was under attack.

Starling's repairs were finished by the beginning of August but the ensuing three months produced no more 'kills'. Admiral Dönitz had pulled his U-boats out of the battle after their severe defeat in the spring, and now they were returning with new weapons and tactics. The schnorkel air mast was intended to reduce the heavy losses from radar-equipped aircraft at night, but there was also a fearsome new weapon for use against escorts. The formidable *Zaunkönig* acoustic homing torpedo locked on to the fast-running propellers of warships, and Dönitz hoped that his U-boats would be able to sink attacking escorts. German aircraft were also beginning to use radio-controlled glider bombs against warships in the Bay of Biscay.

In order to improve its response to the changing tactics, the 2nd Support Group was sent to Tobermory for intensive training in early October, and it did not go back to sea until the 15th. This time it was to operate with one of the new small escort carriers, HMS *Tracker*, on a hunting mission in mid-Atlantic. A week later it joined another successful group, Commander Peter Gretton's B7, to provide joint support for the westbound convoy ON207. The resulting total of two carriers and 16 escorts ensured that no U-boats got near the convoy until just before midnight on 5 November, when the sloop *Kite* signalled to *Starling* that she could see a U-boat on the surface two miles ahead of her.

The attacks forced the U-boat to submerge and Walker was content to wait until dawn to enable her 'to be destroyed before breakfast', as he put it. Once more the 'creeping attack' worked with textbook simplicity, and the Asdic operators reported the grisly crunching sound of *U-226*'s hull breaking up. It remained only to retrieve some of the 'trophies' floating in the water (needed for such intelligence purposes as the confirmation of the identity of the boat) before the three sloops rejoined the others in the patrol line.

It was typical of Walker's leadership that he should invite his 'new boys', the sloops *Magpie* and *Wild Goose*, to join him in the next attack, only two hours later, when an aircraft sighted a diving U-boat 20 miles away. Guessing that the U-boat commander would move north of the convoy route, he ordered a sweep in that direction, and just after 1400 hours his judgement was vindicated by an Asdic contact from *Wild Goose*.

From the debris which came to the surface it was learned that the two ships had sunk *U-842*

As always, Walker went into the attack quickly, with a pattern of 10 depth-charges set to explode at between 150 and 300ft, but the U-boat took evasive action and escaped. He then directed *Wild Goose* in a 'creeping attack', with 26 charges set to between 500 and 700ft, but she was fractionally late in releasing them, dropping only 22 charges and incidentally putting *Starling's* gyro-compass out of alignment. Walker was seen literally stamping on his cap in fury and calling down imprecations on the head of *Wild Goose's* captain. He was in the middle of drafting an acidulated reprimand when his Asdic operator calmed him down with the good news that he could detect a hull breaking up and an underwater explosion. From the vast amount of debris which came to the surface it was learned that the two ships had sunk *U-842*.

The group was now too low on fuel to remain on patrol, and it headed for Argentia in Newfoundland. There the sloops were treated to a heroes' welcome; as *Starling* led them in, a band struck up the 2nd Support Group's signature tune 'A-hunting we will go', and an embarrassed Walker had to face scores of newspaper reporters and photographers. He and his ship had suddenly become known to the press, which was delighted to hear the group's good news after a diet of unrelieved gloom for three years. The scenes were then repeated when *Starling* and her group docked at Liverpool in time for Christmas leave.

The ship was now adopted by the town of Bootle on the outskirts of Liverpool, where the escorts of Western Approaches Command were based.

The 2nd Support Group did not put to sea again until the end of January 1944, by which time it was fully rested, repaired and re-equipped after the exhausting autumn patrol. Only two days later the ships sank their first victim, *U-592*. Then it was the turn of *U-762* on 8 February, *U-238* and *U-734* the following day, and *U-424* on 11 February. The sinking of *U-264* on 19 February, mentioned previously, brought the total to six U-boats sunk within three weeks, and *Starling* had contributed directly to four of them. It had not all been one-sided, however. Before she was sunk, *U-734* had fired two *Zaunkönig* acoustic homing torpedoes (known to the British as 'Gnats') at her tormentor, and only Walker's quick thinking saved his ship. A pattern of shallow-set

ASDIC

When German submarines began to claim shipping early in World War I, two French scientists, Chilowski and Langevin, began to enquire into ways of detecting them from surface vessels. They were joined by the British Board of Inventions and Research, and in 1917 a prototype was produced by the Anti-Submarine Detection Investigation Committee (ASDIC). All subsequent British developments from the prototype were known as Asdic until 1948, when the US Navy's term Sonar (deriving from Sound Navigation Ranging) was adopted.

The Asdic sets installed in Captain Walker's escort sloops were located in retractable pear-shaped domes situated close to the bow. Extended below the hull when in use, the dome contained a quartz oscillator; when activated by a transmitter the oscillator emitted a sound impulse, known as a 'ping', which would be returned as an echo by any solid object it encountered in the water within the Asdic's range.

The sonic echo was converted by the oscillator into an electrical pulse which could be 'read' by the Asdic operator. The interval between transmission and receiving the echo would give him the distance to the underwater object, and from the character of the echo an experienced man could estimate its size and identity. When he located a moving target, the operator could determine its speed and bearing by adjusting the angle at which the Asdic transmission left the ship. During World War II, escort vessels would set up an Asdic screen around a convoy. Each ship would direct its Asdic transmissions over a given sector, thus maximising the chance of detecting a U-boat within the device's 2500yd range.

depth-charges countermined a homing 'Gnat' and caused it to detonate prematurely, only five yards away. That night the *Woodpecker* was hit by a 'Gnat' which blew her stern off, and she subsequently foundered in heavy weather while being towed back to Liverpool.

Walker took his group to sea again at the end of February to find a U-boat which was signalling weather reports, and a month later it left for Murmansk. By the war's end *Starling* was to participate in the sinking of a further six U-boats, but only two of them were sunk under Walker's command. While on leave in Liverpool on 7 July 1944 he was taken ill, and two days later he died of a cerebral thrombosis, undoubtedly brought on by the appalling strain he had been under. He was buried at sea on 11 July, from the destroyer *Hesperus*, as his beloved *Starling* was at sea.

For *Starling* the war continued much as before. In August 1944 she joined the re-formed 2nd Escort Group, composed largely of newer frigates, and she helped to sink *U-482* in January 1945. Her hard war service left her hull and machinery worn out, and after the defeat of Germany it was decided to disarm her for subsidiary duties. With her sister *Redpole* she was converted to a navigational training ship, with deckhouses for use as classrooms. She was finally sold to be scrapped in 1965.

As a class, the Modified Black Swan must rank as one of the most successful designs of World War II. Although heavily loaded with wartime additions, their novel Denny-Brown stabilisers enabled them to function successfully in the worst North Atlantic winter seas. Even as originally designed they carried a greater proportion of armament than any other escorts, and the addition of radar from 1941 onwards did much to enhance their fighting value.

Apart from the additions of gunnery and search radar sets, the principal wartime changes to the ships were increases in depth-charge stowage and in close-range anti-aircraft guns. The depth-charge stowage went up from 40 to 110, and as an extreme measure the Bofors magazine was used to stow another 50 charges, an indication of the demands of continuous U-boat hunting.

In the years of peace the surviving ships of the Black Swan class were re-rated as frigates, and many saw service overseas. In 1949 *Amethyst* made her dash down the Yangtze River after being held captive by the Communist Chinese for three months, and during the Suez operations *Crane* drove off an attack by Israeli aircraft in the Red Sea. Three were transferred to Germany in the mid-1950s but these, together with two built for India during the war, have all been scrapped. The sole survivor of the class is the Egyptian *Tariq*, formerly the *Malek Farouk* and before that *Whimbrel*, which was transferred to Egypt in 1949. An attempt to preserve the *Starling* as a museum ship in the late 1960s failed due to lack of funds. It was hoped to moor her at Bootle as a floating memorial to the Battle of the Atlantic, but sadly the British public seemed to have forgotten the unique part which she played in the Allied victory.

THE AUTHOR Anthony Preston is naval editor of the military magazine *Defence* and author of numerous publications including *Battleships, Aircraft Carriers* and *Submarines.*

Below: *Magpie*, one of the six sloops of Captain Walker's 2nd Support Group, sails proudly into Liverpool. When the group returned from Newfoundland in late 1943, the nation turned out in force to give the ships a rapturous welcome, and they were greeted by the First Lord of the Admiralty, A.V. Alexander. During four long years the U-boats had been taking a deadly toll of the slow-moving Allied merchantmen, and at last Britain had unleashed a devastating weapon of retribution.

The USS *Barb* was the scourge of Japanese sea lanes, and sank a record amount of enemy shipping during the war in the Pacific

UP PERISCOPE!

USS BARB

The USS *Barb* was the ninth unit of the Gato class, the US Navy's standard submarine at the start of World War II.

Laid down at Groton, Connecticut, in June 1941, the boat was launched in April 1942 and commissioned only two months later.

Gato-class submarines had a displacement of 1525 tons and a maximum speed of 20 knots. With a crew of 80, each boat carried 10 21in torpedo tubes, one 5in and one 40mm gun.

After commissioning, the *Barb* completed her sea trials at the New London base in September 1942. A few weeks later she, and five other boats, were formed into Submarine Squadron 50 to take part in the invasion of North Africa. In the summer of 1943, after a spell in European waters, the *Barb* was sent to the Pacific theatre.

Sailing from bases at Pearl Harbor, Guam and Midway until the end of the war, the *Barb* mounted a series of very successful patrols against Japanese surface ships operating in the western Pacific. By August 1945, the *Barb* had sent 90,000 tons of enemy shipping to the bottom of the ocean.

The boat was briefly decommissioned in early 1946 but resumed service as a training submarine in 1951. In December 1954 the *Barb* was transferred to the Italian Navy under the Mutual Aid Program. As the *Enrico Tazzoli*, she served without incident until 1972, when she was finally decommissioned and scrapped in 1973.

Shown above is the US Navy Submarine Combat Insignia, awarded to officers and men who completed one or more missions in which their vessel sank at least one enemy ship, or completed an equally important combat mission.

BARB

IN EARLY 1944, two years after the catastrophic attack on Pearl Harbor, US armed forces were driving into the very heart of the Japanese empire in the Pacific. At sea, mighty amphibious assault groups were 'island-hopping' to victory and battlewagons were reducing the enemy's defences to ruins. In the air, fighters and bombers flying from carriers were inflicting their own special brand of defeat on the Imperial Japanese Navy.

The war in the Pacific, however, had another dimension: the silent warfare carried out by the US submarine fleet. Alone or in wolf-packs, these shadowy raiders roamed at will, stalking enemy merchantmen and warships plying between far-flung Japanese outposts. One submarine in particular, the USS *Barb*, was to gain a fearsome, almost unequalled reputation as a hunter. Commanded by Lieutenant-Commander Eugene B. Fluckey, whose nickname was to change from 'Gene' to 'Lucky' as the boat notched up more 'kills', the *Barb* was to become one of the top-scoring submarines in World War II.

Previous page above: With flags flying, the USS *Barb* glides smoothly down the slipway on 2 April 1942 at the outset of a remarkably successful career during which she despatched over 90,000 tons of Japanese shipping to the bottom. Previous page below: The final moments of a Japanese cargo ship. Above: The *Barb's* crew proudly display their battle flag in 1944. The flag claims the demise of two warships, 13 merchantmen and one German ship. Below: The USS *Barb*, scourge of the Pacific.

Commander Eugene B. Fluckey, Captain USS *Barb*, 28 April 1944 – 17 August 1945

Commander Fluckey wears US Navy light khaki summer uniform, officers' summer working cap and black leather shoes. The silver leaf on the shirt collar denotes the rank of Commander, and above the left breast-pocket is the submarine officers' metal insignia.

One of the *Barb's* most successful patrols began on 21 May 1944. After slipping its moorings at the naval base on Midway, the boat headed for the Kurile Islands in the North Pacific in search of prey.

Ten days after sailing a lookout made the first sighting, a large tanker in the Sea of Okhotsk, but she was identified as being Russian. Later that day another ship was sighted but, as the submarine moved to an attacking position, she was spotted by enemy aircraft and Fluckey had to take the boat down to avoid bombs and depth-charges. Instead of breaking off the attack, however, he came back to periscope depth and fired a salvo of three 'fish' which hit the target. The *Barb's* stricken victim was the 1053-ton *Koto Maru*.

The *Koto Maru* had scarcely disappeared when the smoke of another ship was sighted, and Fluckey brought the boat to the surface in the hope that he could catch and sink it. Ignoring machine-gun fire he drew within torpedo-range and then submerged to fire another lethal salvo of three torpedoes. The second victim was the cargo liner *Madras Maru* (3802 tons).

After an unsuccessful attack on 2 June, the *Barb* suffered a severe counter-attack with gunfire and depth-charges, for her target turned out to be a naval escort, but she escaped damage and headed for the icy waters around the northern Kurile Islands. Here, amid ice floes up to 60ft high, and with visibility reduced by thick haze and fog, Fluckey managed to penetrate the anchorage at Sakayohama but found it empty of shipping. On 11 June, he chased two trawlers through the ice floes and sank them with gunfire. Immediately afterwards, two plumes of smoke were sighted on the horizon and Fluckey went in pursuit.

After a four-hour chase, the targets were close enough to be identified as two merchant ships. Fluckey fired the usual triple shot at the leading ship. One torpedo hit in the stern, bringing her to a stop, but the *Barb* then turned to port to fire three torpedoes at the second ship, and hit her abaft the funnel and at the stern. This was the 3823-ton *Totem Maru*. Fluckey was still determined to sink the first ship and, using his stern tubes, he fired two more torpedoes. One hit set off a huge explosion, destroying the 1161-ton *Chihaya Maru*.

Two days later, with only two stern torpedoes left, the *Barb* was able to sink the 5633-ton cargo liner *Takashima Maru*. The *Barb* then returned to Midway on 5 July, having sunk seven enemy ships in just over six weeks.

In spite of these successes, when Fluckey took the *Barb* to sea on her next patrol she was part of a new group trying out new tactics. Known as Task Group 17.6, it was a three-boat version of the German U-boat 'wolf-pack', under the command of Captain 'Ed' Swineburne. Inevitably, the crews of the *Barb*, *Tunny* and *Queenfish* came to describe themselves as 'Ed's Eradicators', and the *Barb* and *Queenfish* became known as the 'Boob' and 'Queerfish'.

As the boat dived, the Japanese warship roared overhead, missing the submarine by only a few feet

The three submarines left Pearl Harbor for Midway on 4 August, and left the island on 10 August after a day spent refuelling. They were bound for the Luzon Straits, an area already known as the 'Convoy College', in scouting formation, 20 miles apart. The *Barb* passed through the Straits on 23 August and headed for the Manila-Hong Kong shipping route, where the 'Eradicators' were to join 'Ben's Busters' and 'Donk's Devils', two other wolf-packs, in an attack on a convoy of eight Japanese ships.

With more submarines than targets, positioning was important. Fluckey had manoeuvred the boat to a position ahead of the port and centre columns of the convoy when his sonar operator reported torpedoes approaching on a constant bearing. Realising that they must be 'fish' fired by one of the other boats, Fluckey ordered 'down periscope' to avoid the torpedoes, and, miraculously, they passed overhead without detonating.

Alerted to the attack, the convoy made a sharp turn to the east, but this took the ships into the *Barb's* line of fire and presented Gene Fluckey with a submariner's dream shot – overlapping targets. The first 'fish' of his three-torpedo spread hit a tanker and the other two hit a cargo ship. Fluckey did not rest on his laurels, and spent the next five hours stalking the surviving ships. To his chagrin, as soon as he worked

TORPEDOES

During the early stages of the war in the Pacific, the efforts of the US Navy's submarines to sink enemy shipping were blighted by faulty and unreliable torpedoes. When fired, many ran 10ft below the depth for which they were set and passed under a target without exploding. In addition, magnetic detonators malfunctioned and torpedoes often failed to run on the correct course.

Part of the reason for this poor showing was that peacetime exercises were carried out with dummy warheads, fitted to torpedoes adjusted to pass under a ship. Although these measures were unimportant in tests of propulsion and directional equipment, they were a weakness in evaluating the destructive power of a torpedo.

US torpedoes were fitted with two types of detonator: impact and magnetic. The former was activated as the torpedo struck a target, the latter by alterations in the earth's magnetic field produced by a ship's hull. Both systems were unreliable and prone to failure.

By a process of trial and error, these weaknesses were gradually ironed out, but it was not until the introduction of the electric torpedo in the final stages of the war that US submarines were finally armed with a fully effective weapon.

The new torpedo's entry into service was delayed, however, because of doubts about its low speed of 28 knots which compared unfavourably with the 40 knots of the older types. This shortcoming was offset by the introduction of a fire-direction computer and the fact that the new torpedo, unlike its predecessors, did not leave a tell-tale wake to identify its path.

into a firing position, a seabird landed on the periscope and draped its tail feathers over the aperture. The order to 'down scope' forced the bird to fly away, but 'up scope' merely attracted the bird back to its perch. After several failed attempts to drive the bird off, the solution was found: the search periscope was raised, offering the bird a perch, and this left the attack periscope unmolested for the rest of the attack. After such vicissitudes, the attack on the 5633-ton *Okuni Maru* was successful, and the *Barb* escaped a depth-charging by the escorts.

On 15 September 'Ben's Busters' discovered to their dismay that they had sunk two troop ships loaded with British and Australian prisoners and, in response to orders from Commander Submarines Pacific (COMSUBPAC), the *Barb* and *Queenfish* headed for the area to pick up survivors. While rushing to the rescue, the two boats ran into a convoy. As the *Queenfish* attacked submerged, the *Barb* went in on the surface under the cover of darkness, using radar to track the convoy.

As he manoeuvred to get an 'overlap' shot, Fluckey identified two top-priority targets, a tanker and a small aircraft carrier. Even so 'Lucky' Fluckey had to earn his nickname; as he moved in for the kill a lookout sighted an enemy Chidori-class escort bearing down at top speed, less than a 1000 yards away. Fluckey kept his head, and gave the order to fire all six bow tubes before 'pulling the plug'. As the boat dived, the Japanese warship roared overhead. missing the submarine by only a few feet. An interval followed while the torpedoes ran towards their targets and then there were two explosions, followed by three more and the unmistakable sounds of a large ship breaking up. The first torpedoes had sunk the 11,177-ton tanker *Azusa Maru* and the second, the 20,000-ton escort carrier *Unyo*.

Late next afternoon, lookouts reported several small liferafts, and these turned out to be the hapless prisoners the *Barb* had been sent to find. The 14 survivors were in dreadful condition, having suffered five days of exposure on top of the ill-treatment they had received during three years of captivity. After the *Queenfish* picked up another eight survivors, the two boats headed for Majuro Atoll at top speed.

In one month, the three new wolf-packs had sunk 150,000 tons of Japanese shipping as well as a

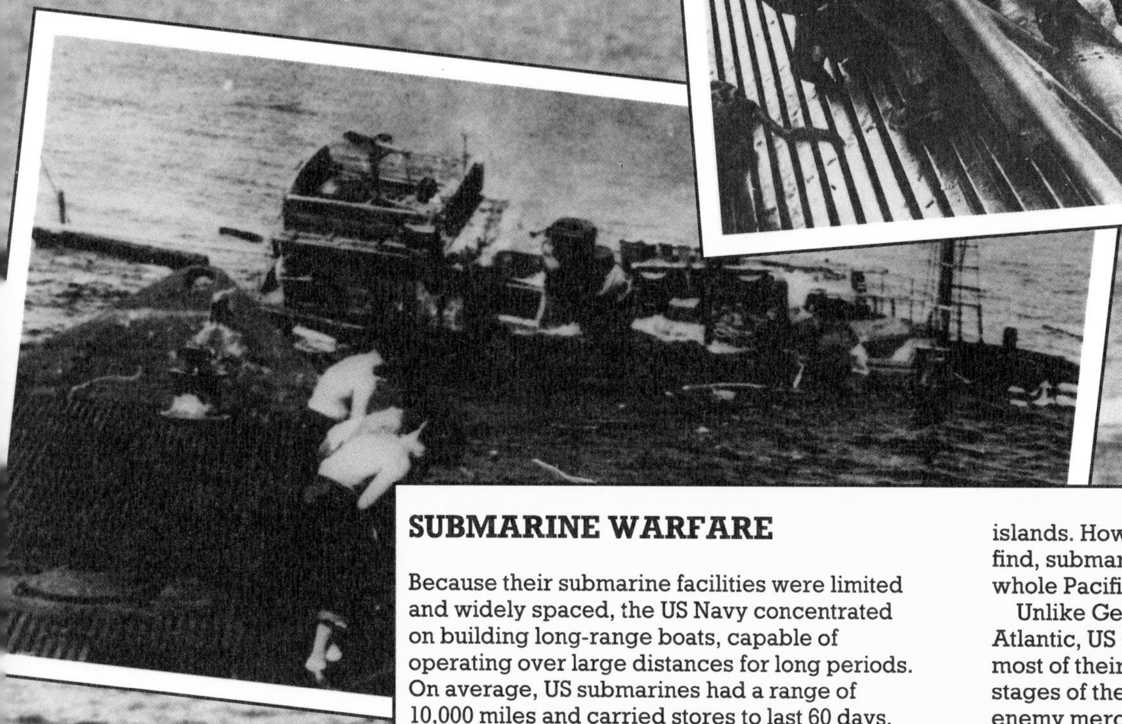

SUBMARINE WARFARE

Because their submarine facilities were limited and widely spaced, the US Navy concentrated on building long-range boats, capable of operating over large distances for long periods. On average, US submarines had a range of 10,000 miles and carried stores to last 60 days.

The submarines' operational area was primarily the Pacific where they were employed offensively to sever Japanese supply lines and sink merchant ships.

Initially, patrols were confined to the area around the Philippines, the waters east of Japan and the straits separating the enemy's home islands. However, as targets became harder to find, submarines began to operate across the whole Pacific, including the China Sea.

Unlike German U-boats operating in the Atlantic, US submarines were able to carry out most of their attacks on the surface in the early stages of the naval campaign. Until March 1942, enemy merchantmen sailed independently, without the protection of warships. In the following July the Japanese made their first attempts to operate a convoy system, but it was not until November 1943 that they organised a regular service protected by purpose-built anti-submarine escorts. To counter these measures, the US Navy formed wolf-packs of up to five

Far left below: Taking a leaf from the German text book, US submarines took to patrolling in 'wolf-packs'. Here a unit of a wolf-pack pulls alongside a stricken Japanese merchantman to pick up survivors. Left: Rescue mission. Exhausted Allied POWs are hauled aboard the *Barb* following the unfortunate sinking by 'Ben's Busters', of two Japanese troop ships loaded with British and Australian prisoners. Below: Dark and menacing, the bow of the USS *Barb* breaks surface during a patrol in the Pacific.

number of warships. In his report. Gene Fluckey did nothing to minimise the risks that the *Barb* and the other boats had run. His boat had suffered five bombings, 141 depth-charges and gunfire, to say nothing of torpedoes from the *Redfish* and *Sealion*.

Still supported by a submarine tender at Majuro Atoll, the *Barb* left on her tenth war patrol at the end of October 1944. She was now part of a new wolf-pack known as 'Laughlin's Loopers', in company with her old pack-mate *Queenfish* and the *Picuda*, nick-named 'Peculiar'. On 10 November she hit the 10,438-ton armed merchant cruiser *Gokuku Maru* with two torpedoes and, when the listing ship tried to beach herself, the submarine surfaced and fired her deck gun. Two further torpedoes missed, but after a third hit the luckless ship rolled over and sank.

During the night of 11/12 November, while on 'lifeguard' duty to rescue aircrews shot down during attacks on Japan, the *Barb* discovered a convoy of 11 ships, escorted by four destroyers. Four torpedoes were fired at two targets in the first attack, but heavy seas caused the torpedoes to run erratically and no hits were recorded. A second attack, two-and-a-half hours later, produced another 'overlap', but this time Fluckey's torpedoes sank the large merchantmen *Gyokuyo Maru* and *Maruo Maru*.

On her next patrol, the *Barb* sailed from Guam reached the southern part of the East China Sea and, while patrolling at the northern end of the Formosa Strait at mid-day on 8 January 1945, she made contact with a southbound convoy. After a gruelling five hours of stalking, she was finally able to fire a full salvo of six torpedoes at two targets. Four hits were noticed, but the third caused an explosion big enough to rock the submarine bodily. In Fluckey's own words, it was a 'stupendous earth-shaking eruption. A high vacuum resulted in the boat. Personnel in the control room said they felt as if they were sucked up the hatch.' He himself felt the air being wrenched from his lungs but somehow managed to give the order, 'All ahead flank' (full speed). The target looked more like a phosphorus bomb than a ship – splinters and debris splashed into the water as the explosion lit up the night sky. The victim was the *Shinyo Maru*, apparently loaded with ammunition.

As the Japanese were now suffering heavy losses to the radar-equipped US submarines, they were running coastal convoys close inshore during the day and holing up in shallow anchorages during the night, trusting to the shallow depth of water to keep the big US submarines out. Early on the morning of 23 January, *Barb* succeeded in entering Namkwan Harbour and found an estimated 30 ships at their moorings. She fired her four remaining bow torpedoes and the four stern torpedoes into the anchorage, and eight explosions were heard. Unfortunately, the Japanese kept no records of the results, and the only officially-identified victim was the 5244-ton freighter *Taiku Maru*. It was after this raid, however, that Lieutenant-Commander Fluckey received the Congressional Medal of Honor and the entire crew of the *Barb* received the Presidential Unit Citation.

By now the hard-worked boat was in need of an overhaul and, after her return to Midway on 10 February, she was sent home to Mare Island Navy Yard for overhaul. When the *Barb* emerged, she had been fitted with 5in rocket launchers on deck to supplement her 4in deck gun. In May 1945 she headed back to the western Pacific.

By the time the *Barb* started her last war patrol on 8 June, Japanese shipping had all but disappeared. Mines laid by aircraft and submarines had virtually sealed the main harbours, and the losses of tankers meant that there was little fuel available for the enemy's warships. The noose was tightening, and *Barb's* patrol area was in the Japanese home islands, north of Hokkaido and east of Sakhalin (Karafuto). She sank two small craft with gunfire on 21 June, and that evening moved into position three miles off the small port of Shari on the north coast of Hokkaido and fired a dozen 5in rockets into the town, the first use of such weapons by an American submarine.

After sinking a small ship and carrying out two more bombardments, the *Barb* sank the 2820-ton cargo ship *Sapporo Maru* on 5 July, followed by two more small craft. On 18 July she sank an 800-ton escort, the *Kaibokan No.112*. Despite these successes, Fluckey seemed destined to lose his bet that he would sink 15 ships on the patrol. A trawler hit by gunfire on 26 July obstinately refused to sink, and, when she was discovered still afloat, the *Barb* fired away all her ammunition to no avail. To sink her and win his bet from the First Lieutenant, Fluckey rang down for five knots' speed and gently rammed the burned-out hulk to send it to the bottom.

It was the last hostile act of the war for Fluckey and his men, and *Barb* returned to Midway on 2 August. She had sunk over 90,000 tons of Japanese shipping, one of the highest scores of any US submarine.

THE AUTHOR Anthony Preston is naval editor of Jane's Defence Weekly and author of numerous publications including *Battleships, Aircraft Carriers* and *Submarines*.

boats to stalk the enemy's merchantmen. Technical superiority, particularly in the field of radar, ensured that US submarines always had an invaluable edge in any encounter.

The scale of the losses inflicted on the Japanese was enormous. Apart from sinking over 200 warships, US submarines accounted for 1079 merchant vessels of over 500 tons, virtually annihilating the enemy's supply fleet. Their underwater offensive, mainly directed against oil tankers, ruined the Japanese war effort and had a decisive impact on the outcome of the war in the Pacific. Remarkably the cost to the Americans was light; only 45 submarines were destroyed by the Japanese.

VOYAGE OF THE CONQUEROR

Beneath the icy waters of the South Atlantic, the hunter-killer submarine HMS *Conqueror* stalked her prey before unleashing a devastating attack

CONQUEROR

SILENT CONQUEROR

HMS *Conqueror* was laid down in 1967 and was commissioned four years later as one of the C-type (Churchill) follow-ons to the Valiant-class, the first all-British-built nuclear-powered submarines. The length of the submarine is 285ft, its beam is 33ft 2in and it has a draught of 27ft. When submerged, *Conqueror* has a displacement of 4900 tons. The crew comprises 103 men and, although conditions are cramped, they are much improved since the days of World War II.

A small nuclear reactor is housed amidships, and the heat generated by the reactor is converted into steam which drives a turbine, coupled to the main shaft (through a reduction gearbox). The 15,000 horsepower that is generated turns a single propeller. The submarine is capable of a maximum submerged speed of 28 knots but on the surface, this is reduced to between 15 and 20 knots depending on sea conditions.

***Conqueror* is armed with both short-range Mark 8 torpedoes and long-range Tigerfish torpedoes which are wire-guided and allow the submarine commander to guide the weapon to a chosen target, at ranges of up to 20 miles, before the torpedo's own active homing head takes over. Some doubt has been cast on the reliability of the Tigerfish and this may have been a subsidiary reason for the decision to use the Mark 8 to sink the *Belgrano* . The third weapon system carried by *Conqueror* is the Harpoon anti-ship missile which can be fired while the submarine is submerged.**

The maximum range of Harpoon is around 60 miles and it is armed with a 500lb warhead.

ON THE EVENING of 30 April 1982 the sonar operators on board the nuclear-powered hunter-killer submarine HMS *Conqueror* made long-range contact with a group of ships some 50 miles from the Isla de los Estados, off the Argentinian mainland. *Conqueror's* captain, Commander Christopher Wreford-Brown, instructed the submarine to close on the contact. On the morning of 1 May *Conqueror* came up to periscope depth to find its quarry of three Argentinian warships, the two destroyers *Hipolito Bouchard* and *Piedra Buena* and the cruiser *General Belgrano*, undergoing a replenishment at sea from an oil tanker. The sea was calm and, with excellent visibility, the submarine was able to observe their movements at a distance of 4000 yards. Wreford-Brown reported their presence back to Fleet Headquarters in Britain via satellite and, as the Argentinian vessels were outside the Total Exclusion Zone, settled down to trail them patiently from a discreet distance of 10,000yds and await further orders.

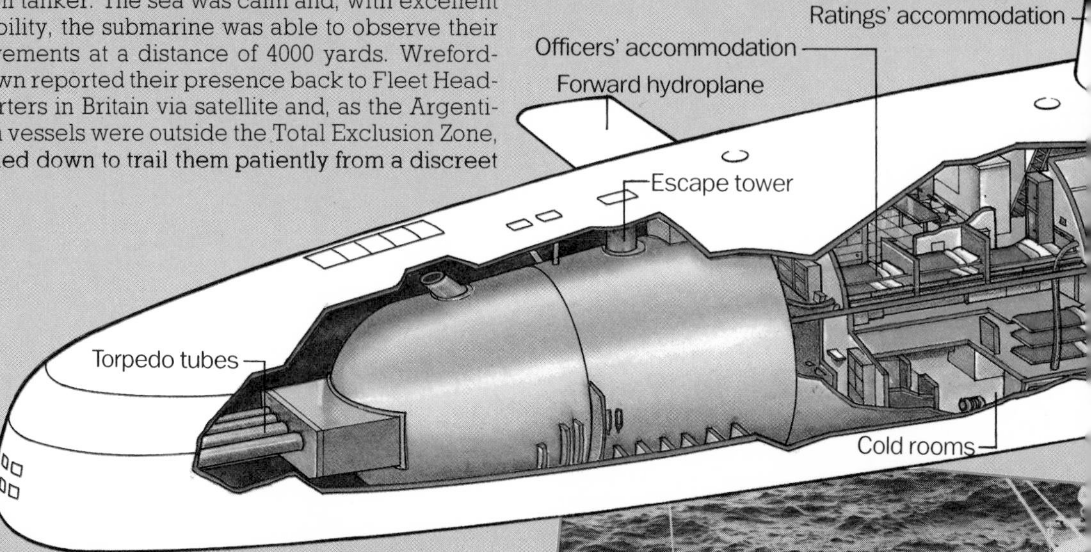
Ratings' accommodation
Officers' accommodation
Forward hydroplane
Escape tower
Torpedo tubes
Cold rooms

The Royal Navy regarded the *Belgrano* and her two escorts as a potentially grave threat to the Task Force, now positioned just to the northeast of the Falkland Islands. Requests were made to eliminate the *Belgrano* group, but in view of the complex political situation at that time – with peace negotiations still in progress – any decision to attack had to be referred to a higher authority. Chief of the Defence Staff, Admiral Sir Terence Lewin, arrived at Chequers to discuss the situation with the Prime Minister and found that she too favoured direct action. At 1400 hours local time on 2 May, Wreford-Brown received the order to proceed with offensive operations and, having decided upon the cruiser, began his attack sequence. The signal from London was a death sentence for the unsuspecting *Belgrano*.

The British reaction to the Argentinian invasion of the Falklands on the night of 1/2 April had been remarkably swift. On the day following the capture of Port Stanley HMS *Conqueror* lay at her base at Faslane in Gare Loch, on the west coast of Scotland, taking on stores in preparation for a voyage to the South Atlantic. Also on board were 14 men of the Special Boat Service (SBS), included amongst the submarine's company for covert amphibious operations. On the evening of 4 April the submarine sailed out of the Gare Loch and submerged, setting out on her long journey to the South Atlantic. Capable of a 24-hour-a-day speed of over 25 knots, the *Conqueror* made a rapid passage down the length of the Atlantic. Sailing mainly at depths of around 400 feet, the submarine would only come up to periscope depth at intervals of 30 hours.

On 10 April *Conqueror* received orders to proceed to South Georgia. From this point on, preparations for the forthcoming conflict were stepped up: the SBS studied the landing drills to be implemented on South Georgia, while the submarine's workshop improvised a gun mounting, should she be attacked on the surface while acting in an amphibious role. On 19 April the *Conqueror* arrived off South Georgia and put her SBS patrol ashore on a reconnaissance mission, before pulling back from the island and commencing her main anti-shipping task around the approaches to South Georgia.

The next few days were spent in routine patrols up to 100 miles north of South Georgia: no enemy vessels

Page 67 : Exploiting their three-dimensional environment, the Royal Navy's SSNs performed an invaluable role during the South Atlantic conflict. Capable of remaining submerged for up to 112 days, the presence of the hunter-killer submarines confined the Argentinian Fleet to port after the sinking of *General Belgrano.*

Conqueror

Type C-type modified Valiant Class hunter-killer submarine
Length 285ft
Displacement 4900 tons
Propulsion 15000shp nuclear-powered steam turbine
Maximum speed (submerged) 28 knots
Maximum speed (surface) 20 knots
Complement 103
Armament Six 21in torpedo tubes capable of firing Mark 8 or Tigerfish torpedoes; Harpoon anti-ship missiles

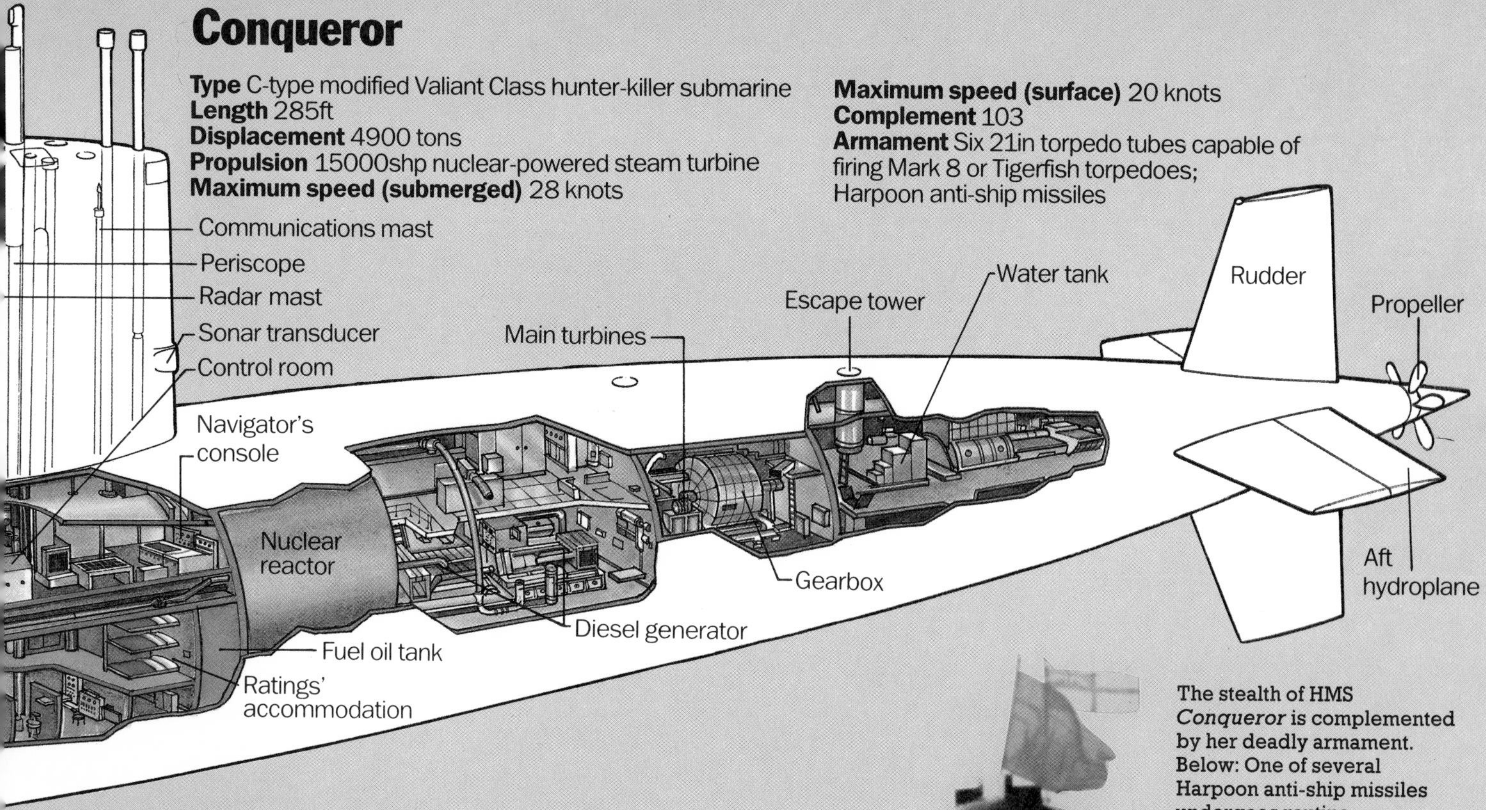
Communications mast
Periscope
Radar mast
Sonar transducer
Control room
Navigator's console
Nuclear reactor
Fuel oil tank
Ratings' accommodation
Main turbines
Diesel generator
Gearbox
Escape tower
Water tank
Rudder
Propeller
Aft hydroplane

The stealth of HMS *Conqueror* is complemented by her deadly armament. Below: One of several Harpoon anti-ship missiles undergoes routine maintenance. Although not used in the South Atlantic, this weapon provides submarine commanders with the option of a long-range attack should the threat of surface vessels prevent him from closing on his quarry. Far left: A vintage Mark 8 torpedo of the type used with devastating effect on *General Belgrano.*

were spotted and on 23 April *Conqueror* was ordered to join the main battle group now off the Falklands. The following day, however, those orders were rescinded and she was ordered to return to South Georgia to deal with the Argentinian submarine *Santa Fé*. *Conqueror* was unable to make contact with the enemy submarine, but the threat was averted when, on 25 April, the *Santa Fé* was crippled on the surface by attack helicopters from the British surface ships. On the same day a British landing on South Georgia brought about an Argentinian surrender of the island. There was now no need for the SBS men to remain on *Conqueror* as she would return to straightforward anti-shipping work, and on 27 April a helicopter lifted them off and flew them back to HMS *Antrim*. This left *Conqueror* free to sail for the Falklands and take up a position southwest of the islands.

'I spent more than two hours working my way into an attack position on the port beam of the cruiser'

The *Belgrano* and her two escorts had left the port of Ushuaia on Tierra del Fuego, on 26 April and, under the command of Captain Hector Bonzo, they began to patrol the 'gap' between Tierra del Fuego and the 200-mile radius Total Exclusion Zone. Equipped with sophisticated Dutch surveillance radars, the *Belgrano*'s function was to monitor any possible threat from the south: whether an incursion by the British or even an opportunist entry into the conflict by Argentina's hostile neighbour Chile. The *Belgrano* zig-zagged across her patrol area and, lacking the latest sonar equipment, she and her escort ships were totally unaware of the presence of *Conqueror*, silently stalking them since the early hours of 1 May.

As the submarine began to close on the *Belgrano*, Commander Wreford-Brown ordered his torpedo officer, Billie Budding, to load the tubes with World War II-vintage Mark 8 torpedoes, in preference to the more advanced wire-guided Tigerfish Mark 24s, which possessed a maximum range of 20 miles. This decision was based on Wreford-Brown's confidence in *Conqueror*'s ability to get within close range of her quarry. Although the Mark 8 had a shorter range than the Tigerfish, it carried a larger warhead and, in the commander's estimation, this would be necessary in order to penetrate the *Belgrano*'s thick armour plate and anti-torpedo bulge. Looking through his attack periscope and directing operations, Wreford-Brown was very much in command. He recounts the complex business of a submarine attack:

> 'I spent more than two hours working my way into an attack position on the port beam of the cruiser. It was still daylight. The visibility was variable; it came down to 2000yds at one time. I kept coming up for a look – but when at periscope depth we were losing ground on them – and then going deep and catching up. I did this five or six times. They were not using sonar – just gently zig-zagging at about 13 knots. Twice I was in reasonable firing positions but found they had moved off a few degrees. We eventually got them – ourselves on the cruiser's port beam with the two destroyers on her starboard bow and beam.'

The atmosphere within the submarine was electric, crew members in the control room straining to hear Wreford-Brown's instructions. At 1557 the order was given to fire and three Mark 8 torpedoes were loosed. The men waited silently as the seconds ticked away and the torpedoes sped towards their target 1400yds away. After 43 seconds two hits were heard and, looking through the periscope, Wreford-Brown saw an orange fireball on the *Belgrano*, followed shortly by a second explosion. The third torpedo hit the escort vessel *Hipolito Bouchard* but failed to explode. On board the jubilant *Conqueror* a junior officer wrote in his diary:

'The control room was in uproar, 30 people shout-

FORE ENDS TEST SET

Below: The graceful profile of an SSN as it breaks surface, its nuclear-powered engines pushing the submarine effortlessly through the water. Bottom, left to right: Below the conning tower, or fin as it is known in the Royal Navy, submariners man the weapons control panel which guides Harpoon missiles and Tigerfish torpedoes to their target; at the fore-end of the SSN two members of the crew await instructions to fire; as the commander checks his position, a choice of two periscopes is available to him – the search periscope, which provides excellent vision but is highly visible from the surface, and the smaller, attack periscope which would be preferred if he considered his submarine to be in any immediate danger; a Tigerfish torpedo in the rack on board an SSN.

SUBMARINE TACTICS

The nuclear-powered hunter-killer (SSN) submarines of the Royal Navy are primarily intended to fulfil an ASW (anti-submarine warfare) role against submarines of the Soviet Navy but, in addition, they have an independent attack and reconnaissance capability to be used against surface vessels.

Designed to operate at maximum efficiency while fully submerged, the nuclear-powered submarine has an endurance limited only by stocks of food and supplies. In addition, the SSNs have impressive underwater speeds.

The key to submarine warfare is the mastery of sound: while water acts as a barrier to radio, radar, light, X-rays and infra-red, it allows an easy and very rapid transfer of sound. In water, sound travels at over four times the speed it does through air, and by using sophisticated sonar equipment, signals can be picked up over long distances. There are two kinds of sonar: passive (listening) sonar and active (transmitting) sonar. Passive sonar provides the SSN with an underwater early warning system which detects targets at long distances and, significantly, does so without giving away the submarine's position. Its limitation is its inability to provide accurate details of range and bearing. This failing can be overcome by active sonar which is used to provide a precise location of the target prior to an attack. Active sonar has one great drawback, however, in that the 'ping' of the sonar burst can be picked up by other, hostile sonar operators, thereby giving away the submarine's position.

Capable of diving to 1000ft, the SSN is able to hide behind an invisible shield termed the 'layer'. Changes in pressure, temperature and salinity as depth increases have a marked effect on sonar, creating 'interference' which prevents the surface ship from gaining an accurate fix on the submarine.

The submarine commander will initiate his attack sequence with a series of high-speed sprints at a depth of 400ft. Once close, the commander will come up to periscope depth to stalk visually his quarry, then adopt a firing position at right-angles to the target.

ing and cheering. The captain at the attack periscope was screaming out orders – 10 down, starboard 30, half ahead, 130 revs. Everyone was hysterical, stamping and cheering and it became quiet only after about two or three minutes.'

A few minutes after the attack, the sonar operators on *Conqueror* detected the sonar burst from the Argentinian escorts. One officer later wrote:

'We went deep there... and after about five minutes there was a loud bang – a depth charge. Everyone froze, but the skipper ordered shut off for counter-attack and we took evasive measures – hurtling down to... feet. There was silence throughout the boat – suddenly it was no longer fun to be doing what we were. We were at the receiving end.'

While *Conqueror* was evading the destroyer escorts, the *Belgrano* was beginning to sink. Each torpedo had been armed with a warhead containing 810lb of Torpex high explosive which, on detonation, tore through the decks of the cruiser destroying any possibility that damage-control measures could save the *Belgrano*. Out of a crew of 1138, Captain Hector Bonzo estimated that around 330 of his men had been killed by the initial explosions. Besides the high casualties, all power and light were lost, plung-

MARCONI

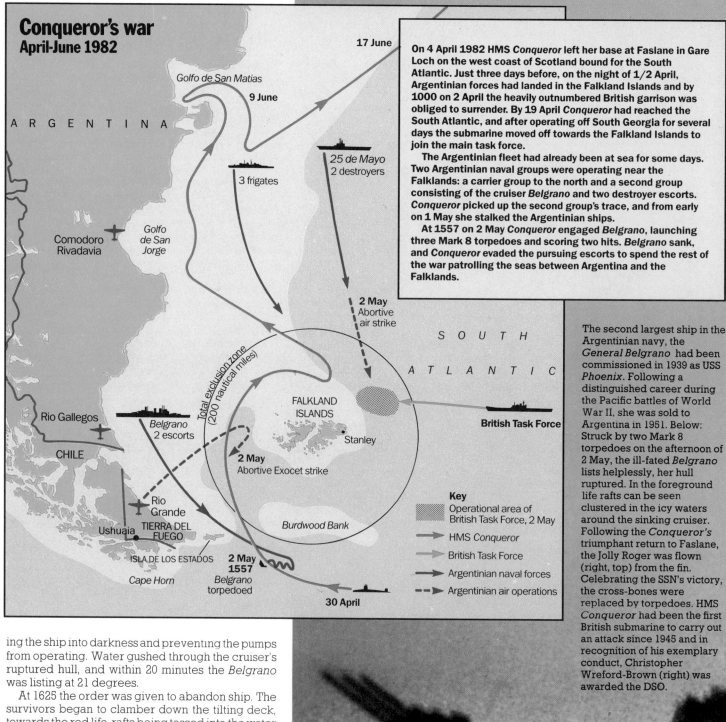

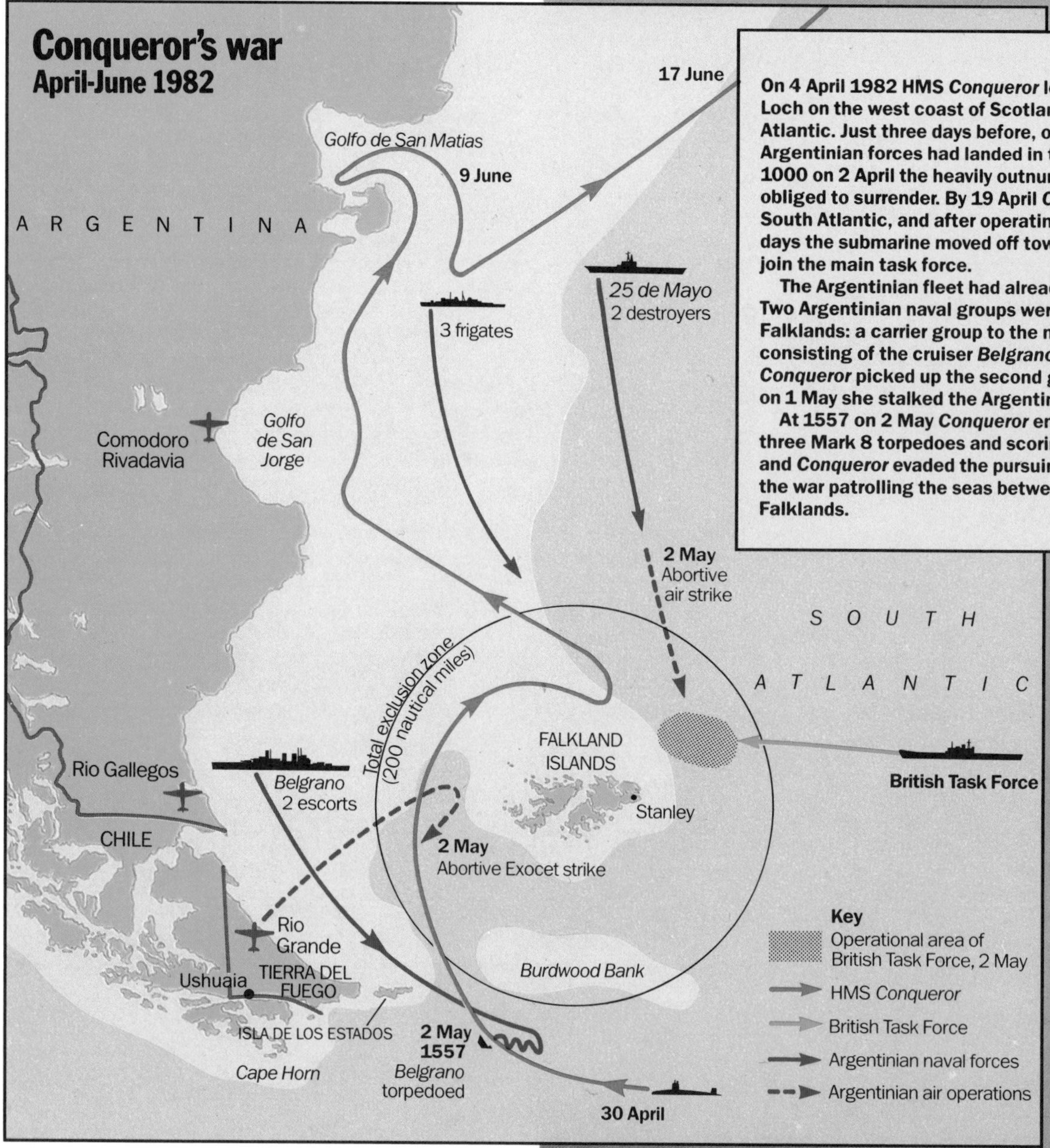
Conqueror's war
April-June 1982
17 June
Golfo de San Matias
9 June
ARGENTINA
25 de Mayo
2 destroyers
3 frigates
Comodoro Rivadavia
Golfo de San Jorge
2 May
Abortive air strike
SOUTH
ATLANTIC
Total exclusion zone (200 nautical miles)
FALKLAND ISLANDS
Stanley
British Task Force
Rio Gallegos
Belgrano
2 escorts
CHILE
2 May
Abortive Exocet strike
Rio Grande
Ushuaia
TIERRA DEL FUEGO
Burdwood Bank
ISLA DE LOS ESTADOS
2 May
1557
Belgrano torpedoed
Cape Horn
30 April
Key
Operational area of British Task Force, 2 May
HMS Conqueror
British Task Force
Argentinian naval forces
Argentinian air operations

On 4 April 1982 HMS *Conqueror* left her base at Faslane in Gare Loch on the west coast of Scotland bound for the South Atlantic. Just three days before, on the night of 1/2 April, Argentinian forces had landed in the Falkland Islands and by 1000 on 2 April the heavily outnumbered British garrison was obliged to surrender. By 19 April *Conqueror* had reached the South Atlantic, and after operating off South Georgia for several days the submarine moved off towards the Falkland Islands to join the main task force.

The Argentinian fleet had already been at sea for some days. Two Argentinian naval groups were operating near the Falklands: a carrier group to the north and a second group consisting of the cruiser *Belgrano* and two destroyer escorts. *Conqueror* picked up the second group's trace, and from early on 1 May she stalked the Argentinian ships.

At 1557 on 2 May *Conqueror* engaged *Belgrano*, launching three Mark 8 torpedoes and scoring two hits. *Belgrano* sank, and *Conqueror* evaded the pursuing escorts to spend the rest of the war patrolling the seas between Argentina and the Falklands.

ing the ship into darkness and preventing the pumps from operating. Water gushed through the cruiser's ruptured hull, and within 20 minutes the *Belgrano* was listing at 21 degrees.

At 1625 the order was given to abandon ship. The survivors began to clamber down the tilting deck, towards the red life-rafts being tossed into the water alongside the ship. Conditions were not good, with a choppy sea, a temperature near freezing and a 30 mile per hour wind, which was increasing steadily. As the rafts bobbed up and down in the sea, survivors watched their ship slowly keel over, and at 1700 hours she went under. At a later press conference Captain Bonzo recalled the survivors' ordeal:

> 'Over 50 rafts started drifting south, blown along by the wind. The temperature of the water was 2°C but the thermal sensation [chill factor] was about minus 20°C. The rafts carrying ten or more people managed to overcome the hazards, but there were some – one carrying four men and another three – in which the crews were frozen to death.'

Only by huddling together en masse could the men survive. Rescue craft were slow in coming and only on the afternoon of the following day were the

The second largest ship in the Argentinian navy, the *General Belgrano* had been commissioned in 1939 as USS *Phoenix*. Following a distinguished career during the Pacific battles of World War II, she was sold to Argentina in 1951. Below: Struck by two Mark 8 torpedoes on the afternoon of 2 May, the ill-fated *Belgrano* lists helplessly, her hull ruptured. In the foreground life rafts can be seen clustered in the icy waters around the sinking cruiser. Following the *Conqueror's* triumphant return to Faslane, the Jolly Roger was flown (right, top) from the fin. Celebrating the SSN's victory, the cross-bones were replaced by torpedoes. HMS *Conqueror* had been the first British submarine to carry out an attack since 1945 and in recognition of his exemplary conduct, Christopher Wreford-Brown (right) was awarded the DSO.

exhausted and frozen survivors picked up. Altogether, 368 crewmen from the *Belgrano* died.

After giving her pursuers the slip, *Conqueror* sailed north around the Falklands and took up a position northeast of the islands. There, repairs were made to the submarine, which included a diver from the ship's company freeing a wire fouling her propeller. Towards the end of May, intelligence reports indicated signs of Argentinian naval activity within their 12-mile national limit. The *Conqueror* was swiftly despatched westwards to deal with any incursions outside Argentina's coastal waters. On 9 June she crept inside the limit, to within six miles from land, and probed the Gulf of San Matias for any signs of a build-up of an Argentinian naval force. But the waters were clear; the enemy's warships were confined to port following the *Conqueror*'s deadly strike – they did not venture out to sea again. Five days later the Argentinians in the Falklands surrendered and *Conqueror* set off for Britain, arriving at Faslane on 3 July after a 25,000-mile round trip. Cheering crowds greeted the submarine as she sailed up the Clyde and Commander Wreford-Brown received a DSO for his services.

The sinking of the *Belgrano* aroused great controversy and the full story may never be revealed. Nonetheless, the Royal Navy considered it was the right decision, and one which played a significant part in Britain's victory in the Falklands. Commander-in-Chief, Fleet Admiral Sir John Fieldhouse, bluntly summed up the importance of the sinking of the *General Belgrano* by HMS *Conqueror*:

'I have no doubt that it was the best thing we ever did. It cut the heart out of the Argentinian Navy and we only had their Air Force to deal with then.'

THE AUTHOR Adrian Gilbert has edited and contributed to a number of military and naval publications including *Vietnam: The History and the Tactics.*

TASK FORCE PROTECTION

In advance of the British Task Force, the Royal Navy's five hunter-killer submarines (SSNs) sped towards the Falklands. En route they received their orders: to secure the 200-mile Total Exclusion Zone which had been imposed on 12 April. Composed of 44 fighting ships, 24 auxiliaries and 45 merchantmen, the Task Force only included two aircraft carriers: HMS *Hermes* and *Invincible*. Normally, three were considered essential for a force of this size, particularly one so far from home.

The Argentinian fleet, Task Force 79, put out to sea between 15 and 17 April from Puerto Belgrano. The northern group comprised the aircraft carrier *25 de Mayo* with her complement of 18 A-4Q Skyhawks. Three corvettes made up the central group while the Belgrano and her two escorts sailed south, operating in a surveillance capacity.

No threat to the British Task Force, however small, could be tolerated, and it was the responsibility of *Conqueror* to seek out and destroy any such threat. Admiral Lewin (Chief of Staff) and Admiral Woodward (Task Force commander) were gravely concerned about the position of Task Force 79, particularly when HMS *Spartan*, tracking *25 de Mayo*, lost her quarry. There was a possibility that the *Belgrano* could be intending to use her long-range surveillance equipment to direct Argentinian aircraft to the Task Force. This risk could not, in the opinion of Lewin and the Prime Minister, be tolerated. As Lewin later commented: 'she was still at sea, she was still a warship, and she was still capable of attacking our forces....' Responsible for the lives of thousands of servicemen, Lewin felt he had no choice but to recommend that *Conqueror* be used to eliminate the *Belgrano*, and his political masters, aware of the Task Force's vulnerability, gave the order to attack.

Hunted by Japanese patrols, the coastwatchers provided a crucial intelligence network during the height of the Pacific War

COAST

THE CONCEPT of an Australian 'Coastwatching Service' originated in 1919, when Captain C.J. Clare, the District Naval Officer for Fremantle, Western Australia, suggested the creation of an organisation whose unpaid civilian members would, in time of war, report on any 'suspicious happenings' along Australia's 23,000 miles of mostly isolated coast.

Clare's idea was agreed to in principle by an Inter-Services Committee in 1922, but it was left to the Australian Naval Headquarters in Melbourne to evolve a detailed scheme. The task of organising and operating the service was the responsibility of the Naval Intelligence Division (NID), also based in Melbourne.

Gradually, the ranks of the 'coastwatchers' swelled and came to include men from all walks of life – ranging from outback policemen to men working on remote cattle and sheep stations. The service was initially confined to the Australian mainland, but was later extended to those islands to the northeast that came under Australian control – eastern New Guinea, New Britain, New Ireland, Bougainville, the Admiralties, the Trobriands, and others, by arrangement with the British Solomon Islands Protectorate. At the outbreak of war in 1939, therefore, there were 700 coastwatchers stationed along the Australian coastline and in the islands to the north and northeast.

The threat of Japanese encroachment had acted as a tremendous stimulus to the service. Consequently, after the attack on Pearl Harbor in December 1941, when Japanese forces thrust with lightning speed into Southeast Asia and the Pacific, the coastwatching service was well prepared. In the South Pacific, this feat of organisation owed much to the efforts of Lieutenant-Commander Eric Feldt, Royal Australian Navy (RAN). Feldt had left the navy in 1923 to join the New Guinea administration as a district officer, and had acquired an expert knowledge of both the islands and their inhabitants. In 1939, however, Feldt was recalled to the navy by Commander R. B. Long, the director of NID. Feldt was to be responsible for the recruitment of coastwatchers, in addition to directing and administering the service throughout the islands. The speed with which Feldt proceeded to plug the gaps in Australia's northern 'intelligence screen' and ensure the delivery of essential communications equipment proved that he had been an inspired selection for the job.

As on the Australian mainland, the coastwatchers on the islands came from all walks of life. However, in the hope that military rank might ease their plight if captured by the Japanese, the coastwatchers were commissioned into the navy, or occasionally the army, air force or the British Solomon Islands Protectorate Defence Force. The information they provided was filtered through the Naval Intelligence Division and then relayed to the Central War Room. Aware of their strategic position, many coastwatchers elected, contrary to Long's advice, to continue reporting despite their territory being occupied by the Japanese. Staffing a predominantly civilian service, these gallant men possessed no distinguishing badge or insignia. They were known simply as – 'the coastwatchers'.

When war came to the South Pacific, Cornelius Page was a plantation manager and coastwatcher on Tabar Island, 20 miles north of New Ireland. On 9 December 1941, Page observed and duly reported an enemy aircraft on its way to reconnoitre Rabaul, on the island of New Britain. Further reports followed during the next two months, but because of Page's early warnings the Australian garrison at Rabaul was able to keep casualties to a minimum. On 20 January Rabaul was subjected to a raid by over 100 enemy aircraft – once again, a timely coastwatcher warning proved invaluable to the defenders and little damage was suffered.

On 23 January Kavieng, at the northern tip of New Ireland, fell to Japanese marines and Page's position became increasingly untenable. New Britain was invaded soon after, and a number of coastwatchers were captured. Page was ordered by Feldt to effect

Right: A Japanese supply ship finds itself the target of a low-altitude surprise attack by American bombers. By acting on information received from the coastwatchers (far right), Allied aircraft were able to deal a series of crippling blows to enemy supply lines.

WATCHERS

his escape immediately, but the plantation manager refused to leave. The islands were his life, and Page continued to transmit information to NID via his teleradio, keeping naval intelligence abreast of enemy naval and air acitivites, defensive positions, the names of Europeans captured and other developments. Together with a planter called Jack Talmadge, Page organised a group of loyal natives into a rudimentary – but effective – 'spy' network.

In the hope that it might save his life if caught, Feldt commissioned Page as a sub-lieutenant in the Royal Australian Navy Volunteer Reserve (RANVR) and arranged for supplies to be dropped to him. Among these were a naval officer's cap and the badges of his rank. Meanwhile, Page and Talmadge were on the move – hiding in the jungle and using hillside caves as refuge from the enemy forces that hunted them. A Catalina transport flew in to attempt a rescue, but it was too late; Page and Talmadge were captured in the middle of June 1942, after five months in enemy territory. Both men were executed, as indeed were many of the coastwatchers who were unfortunate enough to fall into enemy hands.

Japanese naval forces had occupied Rabaul on 24 January 1942, and they immediately began to strengthen the port's defences. Setting up bases on strategic islands, the Japanese swept through Buka Island and Bougainville, and in May captured Tulagi, the island capital of the British Solomon Islands Protectorate – 50 miles north of Guadalcanal. To the chiefs of staff in Australia, the enemy's intention was clear – to use Rabaul as a base from which to attack Port Moresby on New Guinea, and infiltrate onto the islands further south. If the Japanese then launched a massive thrust towards New Zealand, they would be effectively cutting the sea lanes between the United States and Australia. It was decided to mount a massive assault on Guadalcanal, the eventual success of which owed much to the unstinting efforts of a small band of coastwatchers.

Among the officials, missionaries, planters, traders and Australian soldiers who stayed on the islands in the wake of the Japanese advance were a number of coastwatchers. Stationed on the northern tip of Bougainville, overlooking Buka Passage, was Assistant District Officer Jack Read, later commissioned as a lieutenant in the RANVR. Read was sending a continuous stream of information on Japanese activities in the passage and harbour, as well as monitoring the construction work on a fighter airstrip. Acting on intelligence passed on by Read, the Royal Australian Air Force (RAAF) bombed enemy supply dumps, barracks and camps wherever possible and then relied on Read to signal the result of each raid. As the flow of information increased, an army signaller, Corporal D.L. Sly, was inserted onto the island to assist Read. One hundred miles further south at Buin, on the southern tip of Bougainville, Paul Mason manned a mountain-side observation post overlooking the Shortage Islands – an anchorage site for a significant proportion of the Japanese fleet deployed in this area. A planter by trade, Mason was commissioned as a petty officer within the RANVR and later promoted to the rank of lieutenant. Both Read and Mason formed part of a chain of coastwatchers stationed along the southbound enemy flight paths from Rabaul to Kavieng, and complete radio silence was observed in the run up to the Allied assault on Guadalcanal.

On 7 August 1942 the combined guns of American and Australian warships bombarded Tulagi and Guadalcanal. Soon after, marines from the US 1st Marine Division hit the beaches. The force that came ashore at Tulagi was 6000-strong, and the task of guiding the marines into the hinterland was the responsibility of two coastwatchers – H.E. Josselyn and Dick Horton. Both men had been district officers of the Solomon Islands, and were later commissioned as sub-lieutenants in the RANVR. Josselyn and Horton came ashore in the first wave, and the Japanese garrison was wiped out after two days of vicious fighting. One hour after the first landings at Tulagi, 10,000 marines came ashore on Guadalcanal between Lunga Point and Tenaru. Japanese forces on the island, composed largely of construction units, retreated to the west of Guadalcanal, leaving the marines to occupy the partially completed airbase southwest of Tenaru.

At 1315 the Allied ships heard the 'Tally Ho' on the fighter radio net

Two days before the landings, coastwatcher Mason, stationed at Buin in southern Bougainville, had been told cryptically by radio to use as his call sign the first three letters of his married sister's surname. At 1137 hours on 7 August the Allied ships off Tulagi and Guadalcanal received the following warning: 'From STO. Twenty-four bombers headed yours.' The enemy aircraft were still 320 miles away – over two hours flying time – and Mason's timely message allowed the ships to take evasive action, backing away from the landing beaches and dispersing. As the ships' guns were being made ready, fighters took to the air from their carriers with plenty of time to spare. At 1315 the Allied ships heard the 'Tally Ho' on the fighter radio net, and in the action that followed only one enemy torpedo bomber survived to make it back to Rabaul. Another bomber assault, one and a half hours later, cost the Japanese a further nine aircraft.

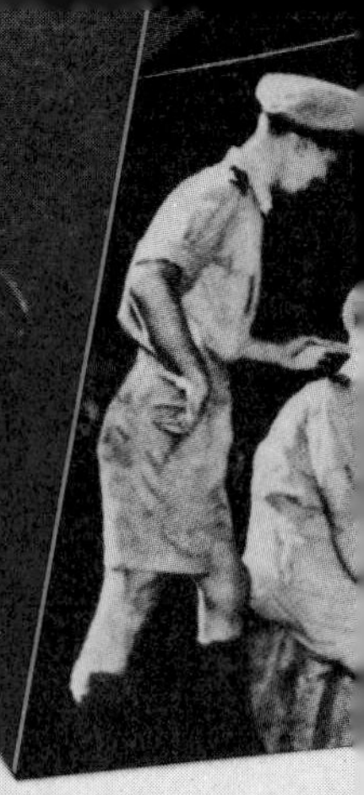

Inset right, clockwise from left: Lieutenant-Commander Hugh Mackenzie (seated) holds a conference with other coastwatchers at operational headquarters on Guadalcanal. Among the officers assembled for this photograph is Lieutenant 'Snowy' Rhoades (fourth from right); Lieutenant-Commander Eric Feldt – the architect of the coastwatching service in the Pacific islands; Lieutenant Paul Mason; Commander R.B. Long, the Director of Naval Intelligence; and Lieutenant Jack Read.

Right: Having delivered its pay-load, a B-24 Liberator flies over Salamaua, a major Japanese base 170 miles north of Port Moresby.

The next morning Jack Read reported that 45 dive-bombers were passing overhead at Buka Passage on their way to Guadalcanal. Again forewarned, the Allied fighters were airborne and awaiting the enemy's arrival. The Japanese later admitted to the loss of 17 torpedo bombers. Once again, a coastwatcher's report had proved its weight in gold. However, Japanese naval activity in the area gradually increased and the Allied landing ships were forced to retire, leaving the marines short of equipment and supplies. The battle for Guadalcanal was beginning in earnest.

One week after the marine landings, four coastwatchers arrived to organise an effective intelligence system in preparation for what was expected to be a prolonged and bitter battle. Lieutenant-Commander Hugh Mackenzie, who had spent many years in the islands, took command of operations. With him were H.G.C. Train, a government official, Rayman, a New Ireland native trained by the coast-

PACIFIC RESCUE

Another very important aspect of the coastwatcher's work was the rescue of downed aircrews and the survivors of naval actions. On 6 August 1943 the port of Munda, on the east coast of New Georgia, was finally captured by the US Marines after a month of heavy fighting. However, ground fighting on the island of New Georgia itself did not end until 23 August.

The land battles had been accompanied by clashes at sea between 'Tokyo Express' groups (Japanese supply ships) and American destroyers and PT boats. In the early hours of 1 August 1943 a Tokyo Express destroyer group successfully ran supplies through to the Japanese base on Vila, on the island of Kolombangara, despite the presence of PT boats in the area. As the enemy ships retired, the destroyer *Amagiri* came out of the darkness at high speed and sliced PT 109 in half. The fuel tank exploded, but the commanding lieutenant and his nine crew members managed to swim the three miles to a small island west of Kolombangara. Badly injured in the back, the lieutenant employed the help of friendly natives to send a message, scratched on the back of a coconut shell, to the nearby island of Wana Wana.

Coastwatcher Evans intercepted the message and organised transport for the young lieutenant, who later arrived on Wana Wana hidden under ferns in the bottom of a native canoe. Evans then made arrangements with a PT boat for the rescue of the remaining crew members. Eighteen years later, ex-coastwatcher Evans was invited to an inauguration ceremony in Washington to see the young lieutenant, John F. Kennedy (below), become the 35th President of the United States.

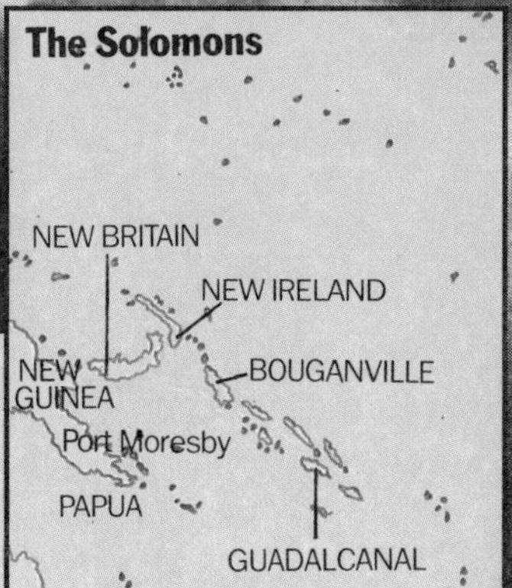

The Solomons
NEW BRITAIN
NEW IRELAND
NEW GUINEA
BOUGANVILLE
Port Moresby
PAPUA
GUADALCANAL
AUSTRALIA
Brisbane

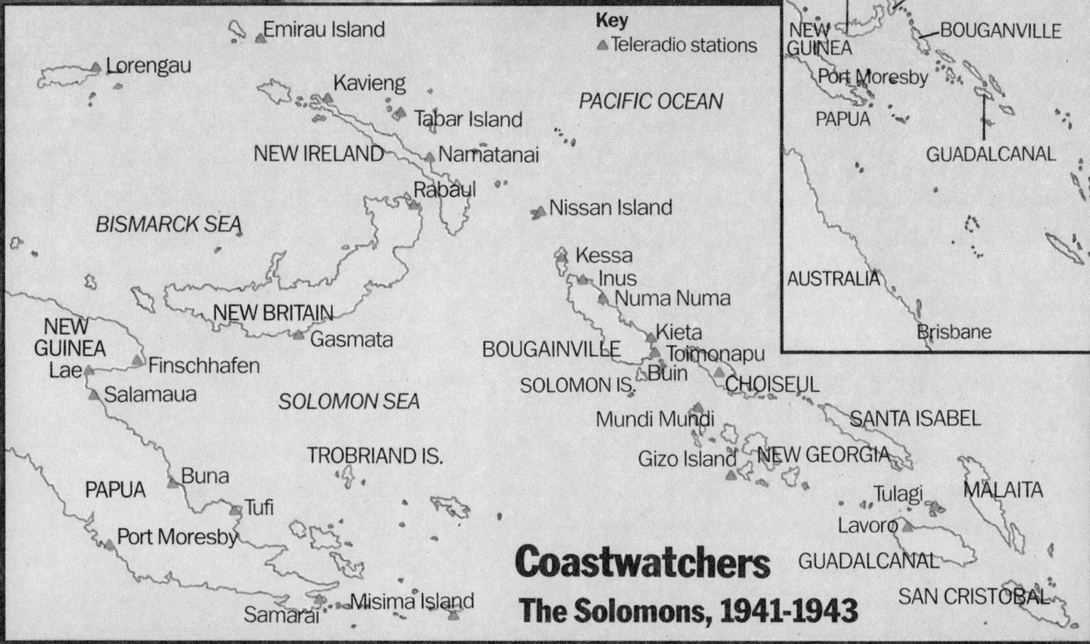

Key
Teleradio stations
Emirau Island
Lorengau
Kavieng
Tabar Island
PACIFIC OCEAN
NEW IRELAND
Namatanai
Rabaul
Nissan Island
BISMARCK SEA
Kessa
Inus
Numa Numa
NEW BRITAIN
Kieta
Gasmata
BOUGAINVILLE
Toimonapu
NEW GUINEA
Lae
Finschhafen
Buin
SOLOMON IS.
CHOISEUL
Salamaua
SOLOMON SEA
Mundi Mundi
SANTA ISABEL
TROBRIAND IS.
Gizo Island
NEW GEORGIA
Buna
PAPUA
Tufi
Tulagi
MALAITA
Lavoro
Port Moresby
GUADALCANAL
SAN CRISTOBAL
Samarai
Misima Island

Coastwatchers
The Solomons, 1941-1943

watchers, and Mr. Eedie, a civilian radio expert who had volunteered his help. On 15 August, one day after their arrival, the four men were on the air and passing on vital air-raid warnings from the chain of coastwatchers in the islands to the marines working on the airbase – now known as Henderson Field. Mackenzie soon discovered that the Americans failed to heed warnings given too early of impending bomber attacks. Accordingly, a system was instituted whereby a warning of 'condition yellow' was given when the enemy was 30 minutes away, followed by 'conditioned red' 10 minutes before the bombers were expected to be overhead. Bombed by day and shelled by offshore Japanese warships by night, the four coastwatchers remained with the marines throughout the long war of attrition.

Dick Horton arrived at Henderson Field from Tulagi in late August. He learned that two coastwatchers – 'Snowy' Rhoades and L. Schroeder, a plantation manager and store owner respectively – had been cut off by the retreating Japanese forces and forced to go into hiding. Concern soon mounted as to their fate, and so Horton 'borrowed' a launch and set out to find his colleagues. Moving through waters infested with Japanese forces, Horton made contact with Rhoades and Schroeder and transported them back to safety – along with 13 missionaries and one American airman who had also been isolated in enemy territory.

Towards the end of October 1943, a large Japanese force of transports and warships assembled in the Caroline Islands, 900 miles north of Bougainville. The enemy were preparing for a major assault on Guadalcanal and, knowing that there were coastwatchers on Bougainville who would report their movements, they despatched patrols and tracker dogs to Buin to eliminate them. Mason quickly relayed this information and a Catalina flew over the island that night – by luck or good judgement its bombs killed all the dogs.

Read, Sly and Mason were hunted through the forested mountains until the patrols finally despaired of the rain and mud and gave up the chase. Wet and miserable, Read and Sly had reached the top of a mountain when the rain suddenly stopped and the sun broke through the clouds. Out to sea was a convoy of 12 large passenger ships heading southeast. Read set up his teleradio and reported an assault force heading – in all probability – for Guadalcanal. Meanwhile, returning to Buin on the heels of a patrol that had been hunting him, Mason found the harbour crammed with ships. He reported: 'At least 61 ships this area including 33 destroyers, 17 cargo, two tankers, one passenger liner of 8000 tons...'

Guadalcanal involved seven major naval engagements, several pitched battles and constant air activity. The Japanese reinforcements reported by Mason and Read landed west of Henderson Field in October 1942, but failed to breach the American defences. After suffering heavy losses, the Japanese were eventually evacuated from Guadalcanal in early February 1943. However, enemy aircraft continued to bomb the island's airfields for months after, and the coastwatchers maintained their vigilance. Feldt later commended the service on a system of 'streamlined coastwatching' that not only provided forewarning of Japanese attacks, but also enabled Allied aircraft to harass enemy bases.

Gradually, as the campaign in the Solomons neared its conclusion and the Allied forces moved inexorably northwards, most of the coastwatchers were withdrawn – having provided invaluable intelligence throughout the height of the Pacific War. Lieutenant-General Alexander Vandergrift, commander of the US 1st Marine Division, later paid tribute to 'our small band of devoted Allies who have contributed so vastly in proportion to their numbers.' In recognition of their work behind enemy lines, many coastwatchers were subsequently awarded American decorations.

THE AUTHOR John Brown is an Australian freelance writer who has a particular interest in Australia's contribution to the war in the Pacific.

When the tide began to turn after Guadalcanal and the Japanese defeats on New Guinea, the role of many coastwatchers changed dramatically. In March 1944, during the struggle to isolate and defeat the remaining enemy troop concentrations on New Guinea, a recce team, under the command of coastwatcher Captain 'Blue' Harris was inserted into Japanese territory prior to the Allied landings at Hollandia from April to July 1944. Its task was to reconnoitre the proposed landing sites and obtain information on Japanese positions in the area. However, after disembarking from the submarine USS Dace, the team was discovered by an enemy patrol and five men died during the fight to escape. The remaining members of the team had to survive starvation, sickness, wounds and the Japanese until the Americans landed one month later. It appears that Harris, mortally wounded, refused to answer the questions of his captors and was ruthlessly bayonetted. Below: On board USS Dace prior to the mission. Harris is pictured here third from the left.

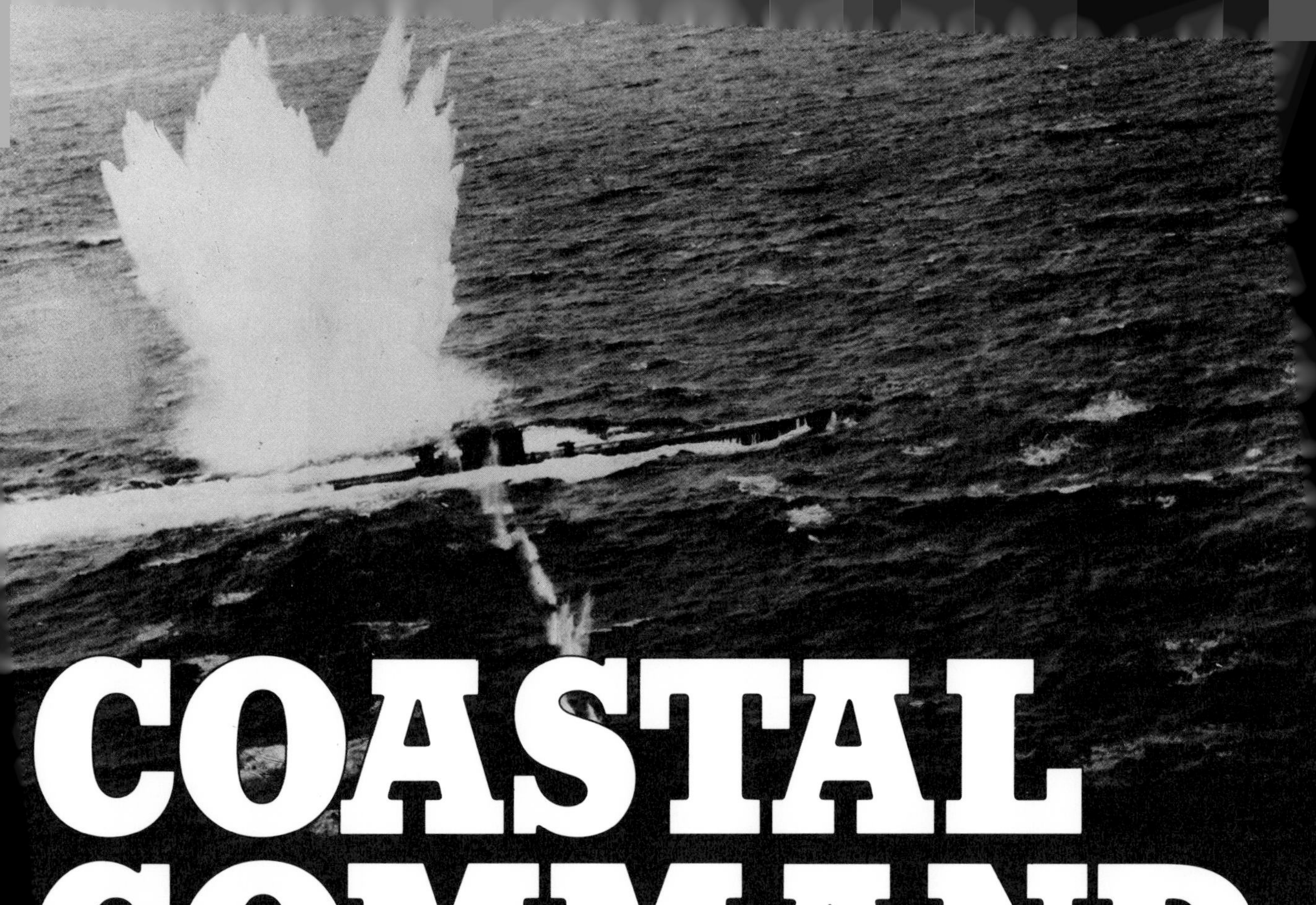

COASTAL COMMAND

SQUADRON
120
120
ROYAL AIR FORCE
ENDURANCE

NO.120 SQUADRON

Formed at Lympne in Kent on 1 January 1918, No.120 Squadron was equipped with Airco DH9s and DH9As for the day-bombing role, but as World War I drew to a close it was assigned the task of transporting mail between Britain and France. This seemingly mundane duty actually did much to educate the pilots in all-weather flying, a skill which was not usually demanded of bomber units, and after the Armistice it continued to supply mail to the Allied Army of Occupation. The squadron was disbanded in October 1919.

It was as a counter to the U-boat threat in the North Atlantic that No.120 Squadron was re-formed on 1 June 1941 at Nutts Corner, near Belfast in Northern Ireland. The first Consolidated Liberators arriving from the USA were being deployed by RAF Coastal Command in long-range patrols over the ocean, and the squadron remained in the anti-submarine role throughout the war. When the squadron was disbanded on 4 June 1945 it had 16 confirmed U-boats sunk to its credit, the highest score in Coastal Command.

No.120 Squadron reappeared on 1 October 1946 as a renumbering of No.160 Squadron. The unit's association with anti-submarine work was resumed in 1951 when it became the first squadron to fly the Avro Shackleton. Today, the squadron continues to patrol the Faroes Gap and the North Western Approaches, now flying British Aerospace Nimrod MR Mk 2s from its base at Kinloss on Moray Firth in Scotland.

Above: The badge of No.120 Squadron.

In the Battle of the Atlantic the Liberator pilots of No.120 Squadron, RAF Coastal Command took on the deadly U-boat wolf packs

THE CLOSING OF the mid-Atlantic 'air gap' was a crucial factor in the British defeat of the U-boats during the bitterly fought Battle of the Atlantic in World War II. So long as the German submarines could operate beyond the range of land-based Allied anti-submarine air patrols, they retained sufficient freedom of action to constitute a serious menace to the vital convoys from America. In spite of this, it was not until 1943 that RAF Coastal Command was able to assign more than a single squadron to the arduous duty of long-range patrols over the area, which at that time required over-water flights of 15 hours' duration or more. The prime cause was the critical shortage of the only maritime patrol aircraft then capable of such missions: the American-built Consolidated Liberator. The Liberator Mk I had an operational range of 2400 miles, compared with the 1300 miles of the Short Sunderland flying boat, which was the best of the British-built maritime patrol aircraft then in RAF service.

The pioneer Liberator unit in Coastal Command was No. 120 Squadron. However, such was the shortage of Liberators, that in August 1942, when U-boat activity in the mid-Atlantic intensified, only five very long range (VLR) Liberator Mk Is were on the unit's strength. They were equipped with ASV (air to surface vessel) radar and were armed with up to six 250lb depth-charges, plus four forward-firing 20mm cannon in a belly pack and a defensive armament of six .303in machine guns. The squadron was also flying Liberator Mk IIs during that period, but they were essentially bomber versions of the design and lacked the fuel capacity for VLR patrol work.

A Liberator spotted three U-boats in the vicinity of the convoy and forced them to crash-dive

Despite the shortage of aircraft, No. 120 Squadron's first year of operational service was an eventful one. After a short period of working up with the new Liberator, the unit began anti-submarine patrols in September 1941. Three months later came one of the decisive actions against the U-boats, when Convoy HG76 sailed from Gibraltar to Britain, accompanied by a strong naval submarine hunter-killer escort under the famous Commander F.J. Walker. After the loss in action of two merchantmen and the escort carrier HMS *Audacity*, the convoy was met 750 miles from base by a No. 120 Squadron Liberator on the morning of 22 December. The aircraft chased off a shadowing Fw 200 Condor and two hours later sighted and attacked a U-boat. A second Liberator spotted a further three U-boats in the vicinity of the convoy over a period of three hours and forced them to crash-dive. The enemy submarines then broke off their attack. The presence of air cover, combined with aggressive counter-action by the naval escort, had on this occasion cheated the U-boats of their prey, but it was to be many months before such a level of protection could be provided for all convoys in danger.

In May 1942 No. 120 Squadron was required

Page 79 , above: Caught in mid-Atlantic, and possibly prevented from diving by hull damage, a U-boat suffers an air attack from a Liberator. Page 1121, below: On 8 December 1942, two Liberators of No.120 Squadron succeeded in dispersing a wolf pack of 13 U-boats. The aircraft carried out 11 attacks, and once their depth-charges were released they had to rely on cannon and machine guns alone. Among those decorated for the action were Squadron Leader T.M. Bulloch (third from left), who received a bar to his DFC.

FIRE
EXTINGUISHER

Below: Two Liberators of No.120 Squadron return from a 16-hour anti-submarine patrol to their base in Reykjavik in Iceland. Bottom left: Squadron Leader Bulloch with the Liberator bearing his personal insignia. Bottom centre: Although the Liberator piloted by Flight Lieutenant A.W. Fraser (bottom right) was subjected to intense anti-aircraft fire from this U-boat, he succeeded in sinking it with an accurate depth-charge attack. He received a bar to his DFC for the action.

THE LIBERATOR

The Mk I and Mk II Consolidated Liberators first flown by No.120 Squadron over the North Atlantic were but a tiny fraction of the total production of Liberators in World War II. Manufacture began in September 1939, and by the close of war with Japan, 18,188 aircraft had been completed, giving a ratio of five to three with its closest rival, the Boeing B-17 Flying Fortress.

In October 1938 the Consolidated Aircraft Corporation was asked to open a second B-17 production line at San Diego in California. Instead, it proposed to develop a superior long-range bomber, and in January 1939 a prototype was ordered by the US Army Air Corps. Making its first flight from Lindburgh Field on 29 December, the prototype featured a radical new wing and tail unit, patented by David R. Davis, which effectively increased the aircraft's range by substantially reducing drag. The fuselage accommodated two bomb bays, each the full size of the B-17's single bay, and 8000lb of bombs could be carried. The power plant was that used on the Catalina flying boat.

The Liberator Mk I was a production model ordered by France before the Occupation, and the contract was transferred to the RAF. The Mk II was a better plane which had been tailored to British requirements. Though lacking some of the Mk I's fuel capacity, it had self-sealing tanks, better armour and an improved power plant. Its armament consisted of 11 .303in Brownings, eight of them mounted in Boulton Paul electric turrets in the mid-upper and tail.

In June 1941, the first examples of the famous B-24 Liberator (the B-24A) were delivered to the US Army Air Force.

The aircraft type underwent many further improvements during the war, and No.120 Squadron's relatively short-range Mk IIs were eventually replaced by B-24D Liberator IIIs and Liberator GR Vs.

to carry out two long-range reconnaissance missions to the Lofoten Islands, in support of the Arctic convoys. On the second of these flights, the squadron's Liberator was intercepted by Messerschmitt Bf 109 fighters. After a running fight, during which one of the attackers was claimed by the Liberator's gunners, the crippled RAF aircraft was forced to ditch in the sea off Norway. Four of the seven crew members survived the bitter cold in their dinghies for 48 hours, before they drifted ashore. They then evaded capture by German patrols and made their way overland to neutral Sweden, reaching safety a month after being shot down.

The anti-submarine patrols which constituted the squadron's main duty seldom produced much excitement, however. It was by no means uncommon for a crew to complete a full tour of duty without once sighting a U-boat. Yet one notable exception to the rule was provided by the career of Squadron Leader Terence Bulloch, who became No. 120 Squadron's most successful pilot and the ace U-boat hunter of Coastal Command during World War II. An Ulster man born in 1916 at Lisburn, County Antrim, Bulloch joined the RAF in 1936. His early war service, which earned him the Distinguished Flying Cross, was on Ansons and Hudsons. His first U-boat attack after joining No. 120 Squadron came on 22 October 1941, and by the following August he had made seven sightings and carried out three attacks, although none of them resulted in a kill. He was by that time a highly experienced airman, with a total of more than 2300 flying hours in his logbook, and he had received the official assessment of 'exceptional' as a pilot. The loss of a brother killed in action had made the war against Germany a matter of personal revenge for Bulloch. On 16 August, when patrolling off the Azores, he attacked and damaged *U-89* and two days later repeated the performance against *U-653*.

Bulloch's attack was a complete success and his victim, *U-597*, sank with all hands

In September 1942 a detachment of No. 120 Squadron began to operate from Reykjavik in Iceland, in order to help close the undefended area in the mid-Atlantic. Thereafter, until April the following year when the entire squadron moved to Iceland, it flew patrols from both Reykjavik and Aldergrove in Northern Ireland. The Icelandic base for operations provided the squadron with greater opportunities for action, and recent improvements in weapons and tactics further increased the chances of success. An improved depth-charge, set to explode at a depth of 25ft, had been issued to the squadron, following the discovery that the older weapons were exploding too far beneath a diving U-boat to achieve any worthwhile damage. Bulloch had also decided to abandon the standard method of attacking a U-boat by dropping widely-spaced depth-charges athwart the submarine; instead he determined to drop them in a closely bunched pattern right along the length of the target.

On 12 October Bulloch was given the chance to prove his ideas when he spotted a U-boat in the vicinity of Convoy ONS136. The attack was a complete success and his victim, *U-597*, sank with all hands. Three days later the Liberator, captained by Flying Officer S.E. 'Red' Esler, sank *U-661*. During the following three weeks, Bulloch's crew sighted four U-boats and was able to attack two of them, but all escaped unscathed. In early November, Convoy

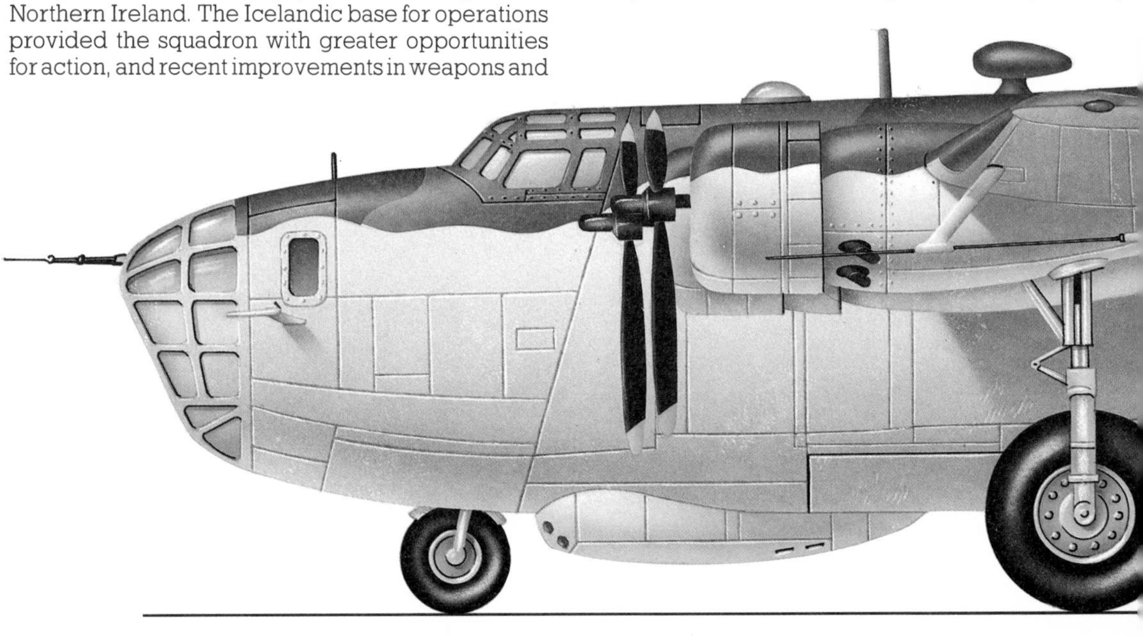

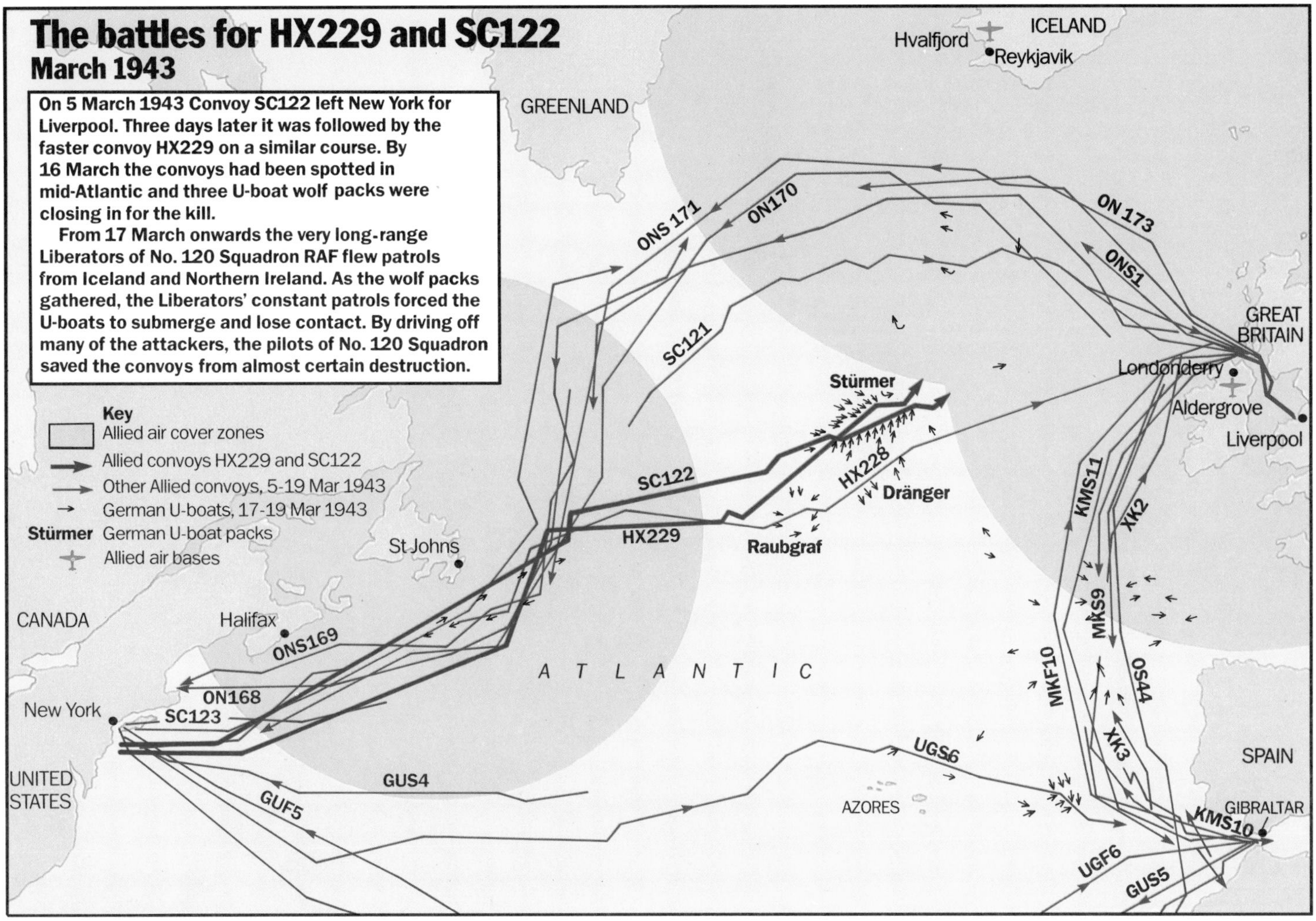
The battles for HX229 and SC122
March 1943
On 5 March 1943 Convoy SC122 left New York for Liverpool. Three days later it was followed by the faster convoy HX229 on a similar course. By 16 March the convoys had been spotted in mid-Atlantic and three U-boat wolf packs were closing in for the kill.
From 17 March onwards the very long-range Liberators of No. 120 Squadron RAF flew patrols from Iceland and Northern Ireland. As the wolf packs gathered, the Liberators' constant patrols forced the U-boats to submerge and lose contact. By driving off many of the attackers, the pilots of No. 120 Squadron saved the convoys from almost certain destruction.
Key
Allied air cover zones
Allied convoys HX229 and SC122
Other Allied convoys, 5-19 Mar 1943
German U-boats, 17-19 Mar 1943
Stürmer German U-boat packs
Allied air bases
ICELAND
Hvalfjord
Reykjavik
GREENLAND
ON 173
ONS1
ONS 171
ON170
SC121
GREAT BRITAIN
Londonderry
Aldergrove
Liverpool
Stürmer
HX228
Dränger
SC122
HX229
Raubgraf
St Johns
KMS11
XK2
MKS9
CANADA
Halifax
ONS169
ATLANTIC
MKF10
OS44
ON168
New York
SC123
XK3
UGS6
SPAIN
UNITED STATES
GUS4
GUF5
AZORES
GIBRALTAR
KMS10
UGF6
GUS5

Above left: A typical briefing of RAF Coastal Command aircrews. Below: This Liberator Mk 1 was one of a score delivered to Britain in 1941. It was fitted with forwards and sideways looking ASV Mk II radar, and armament was supplemented by a ventral pack of 20mm cannon. Its range with a full tank was an astonishing 2300 miles.

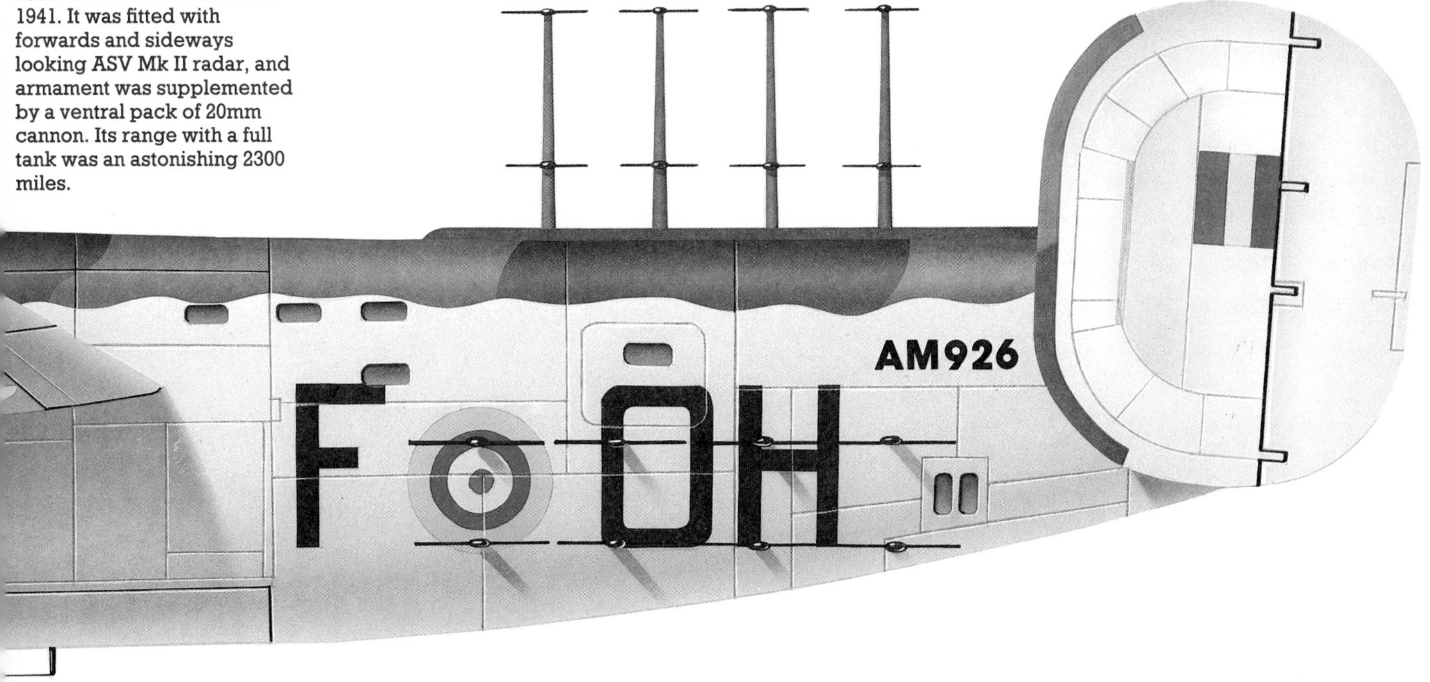
AM926
F OH

SC107 came under fierce attack from a German 'wolf pack' of 13 submarines, giving No. 120 Squadron a further opportunity of bringing the U-boats to task. Bulloch's Liberator was patrolling in the convoy's vicinity on 5 November when a submarine was spotted, but it crash-dived before he could attack. He then sighted and successfully attacked *U-132* for his second personal U-boat kill. With two depth-charges remaining, he ended an eventful patrol with an attack on a third enemy submarine, but this time without result.

The climax of Bulloch's career with No. 120 Squadron came on 8 December, when his Liberator provided air cover for the hard-pressed Convoy HX217. Bulloch recalled during conversations with the aviation historian Alfred Price that:

'"We arrived over the convoy just as it was beginning to get light. We knew that there were U-boats around and we were keeping our eyes skinned. The visibility wasn't too good. There was a sort of half-light and the hail storm didn't improve things. I started my patrol by making a wide sweep round the convoy and almost at once we struck lucky. Astern of the ships and on the Liberator's port beam I spotted a submarine travelling fast on the surface. It was going all out to catch the convoy." He attacked the U-boat with six out of his eight depth-charges and it disappeared from view.

'Just over an hour later, Bulloch sighted two submarines about 300yds apart "going like mad" for the convoy 20 miles away. He turned and attacked one of the boats with his two remaining depth-charges, but the submarine had submerged by the time the Liberator was in position to release, and there was no evidence of damage.

Bulloch swooped down onto the U-boat and strafed it with cannon and machine-gun fire, but it dived to the safety of deep water

'The Liberator's load of depth-charges was now expended, but Bulloch continued with the patrol. The crew settled to their routine tasks and one of the gunners cooked a lunch of steak and potatoes on the galley stove. Then, in Bulloch's words:

"I was sitting in the cockpit with a plate on my knee, with George [the automatic pilot] in charge. I was going to enjoy that steak, but another U-boat popped up. The plate with its steak and potatoes went spinning off my knee as I grabbed the controls and sounded the alarm and there was a clatter of plates back in the aircraft as the rest of the crew jumped to it, forgetting how hungry they were." '

Bulloch swooped down onto the U-boat and strafed it with cannon and machine-gun fire, but it dived to the safety of deep water.

All that the Liberator's captain could do without depth-charges was to strafe the U-boats and force them to crash-dive, thus effectively breaking off their contact with the threatened convoy. After more than seven hours over Convoy HX217, Bulloch's Liberator was relieved by a second No. 120 Squadron aircraft, captained by Squadron Leader D.J. Isted. Between them the two Liberators made no fewer than 13 U-boat sightings and carried out 11 attacks. This action fittingly marked the end of Bulloch's service with No. 120 Squadron, which had earned him a bar to his DFC and the Distinguished Service Order.

The new year was to see much fierce action against the U-boat wolf packs in mid-Atlantic, culminating in their final defeat. However, in January 194 No. 120 Squadron was still the sole operation Liberator squadron in RAF Coastal Command, ha ing five Liberator Mk Is and 12 Liberator Mk IIIs c strength. The latter had been manufactured as bor bers, and they had required extensive modificatic to turn them into effective VLR maritime patr aircraft, causing a delay which added to the proble of slow deliveries from the United States. Howeve two new Liberator units (No. 59 and 86 Squadron were shortly to become operational in Coastal Cor mand. Furthermore, better anti-submarine warfa equipment was in prospect, which would great improve the Liberators' ability to detect and attac enemy submarines. Centimetric ASV radar wi better range and resolution was to replace th

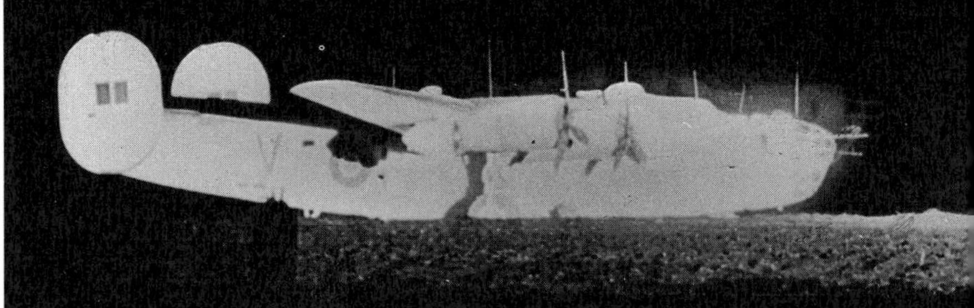

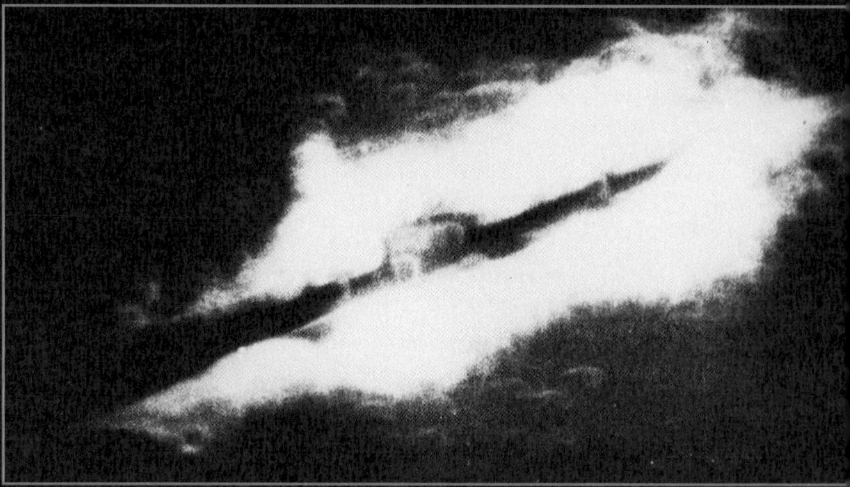

Below: By January 1943 the aircraft strength of No.120 Squadron had increased to five Liberator Mk Is and 12 Liberator Mk IIIs. The latter (seen below) were the British counterpart of the B-24D, the first major production version of the type. The chin radar of the third aircraft indicates that it is the fully updated Liberator GR.Mk V.

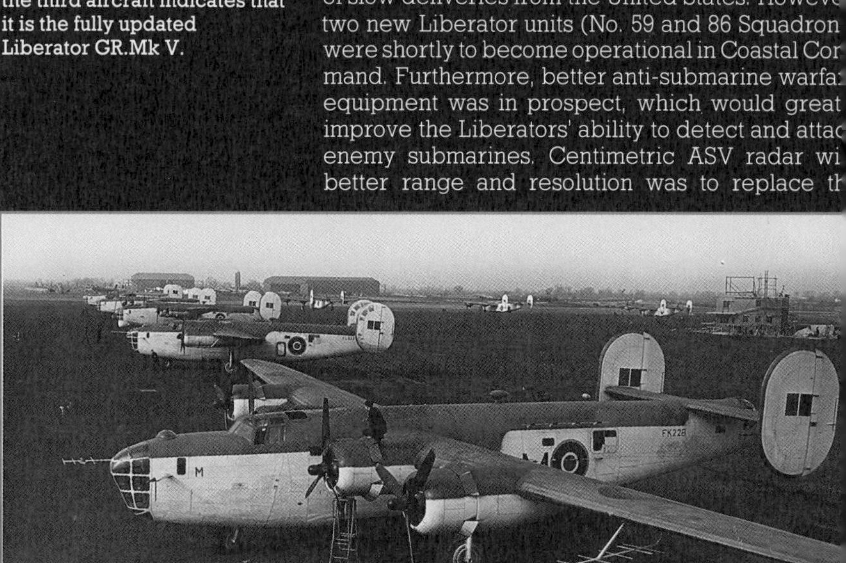

arlier millimetre-wavelength sets; the Leigh light airborne searchlight) was to enable attacks on U-oats which had been hitherto invulnerable in dark-ess, and the highly secret homing torpedo offered a emendous improvement in killing-power over the epth-charge.

The increased numbers and improved equipment the VLR patrol aircraft were soon to have a ramatic impact on the Battle of the Atlantic. In id-May, Convoy SC130 was beset by a wolf pack of U-boats, but despite the submarines' numerous tempts to go into the attack, all the ships reached afety in Britain. No. 120 Squadron was particularly ctive in the convoy's defence on 19 May. Four iberators made a total of 15 sightings, six of which ere followed by attacks. The only successful one as carried out by Flight Sergeant W. 'Smokey' toves, who launched two homing torpedoes at *-954*. The submarine vanished with all hands, one of s officers being the son of Grand Admiral Karl önitz.

Dismayed by the increasing losses of U-boats to atrol aircraft, the German High Command decided strengthen the submarines' anti-aircraft arma-ient to enable them to fight it out on the surface. On 4 June 1943 Pilot Officer A.W. Fraser encountered *-194* in mid-Atlantic and the U-boat threw up a eavy barrage of anti-aircraft fire. Undaunted, Fras-r dived into the attack at low level. The enemy's fire amaged the Liberator's hydraulic system and only wo depth-charges released properly, but these ere sufficient to send *U-194* to the bottom.

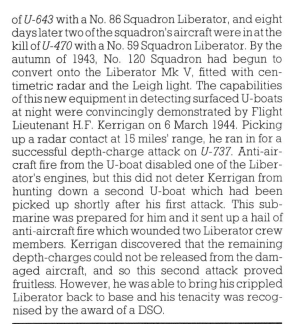

One result of the growing numbers of VLR patrol ircraft during the latter half of 1943 was the in-reased incidence of shared U-boat kills. On 8 October No. 120 Squadron shared in the destruction of *U-643* with a No. 86 Squadron Liberator, and eight days later two of the squadron's aircraft were in at the kill of *U-470* with a No. 59 Squadron Liberator. By the autumn of 1943, No. 120 Squadron had begun to convert onto the Liberator Mk V, fitted with centimetric radar and the Leigh light. The capabilities of this new equipment in detecting surfaced U-boats at night were convincingly demonstrated by Flight Lieutenant H.F. Kerrigan on 6 March 1944. Picking up a radar contact at 15 miles' range, he ran in for a successful depth-charge attack on *U-737*. Anti-aircraft fire from the U-boat disabled one of the Liberator's engines, but this did not deter Kerrigan from hunting down a second U-boat which had been picked up shortly after his first attack. This submarine was prepared for him and it sent up a hail of anti-aircraft fire which wounded two Liberator crew members. Kerrigan discovered that the remaining depth-charges could not be released from the damaged aircraft, and so this second attack proved fruitless. However, he was able to bring his crippled Liberator back to base and his tenacity was recognised by the award of a DSO.

Above: Until the introduction of the Leigh light, a British airborne anti-submarine searchlight, U-boats could not be pinpointed in darkness beyond the information given by radar, which became inadequate at very close range. Above right: A speeding British submarine illuminated on the surface during early trials of the installation. Top: The ghostly vision of a Liberator subjected to the full beam of a Leigh light.

On 22 March 1945, *U-296* was detected by a Liberator and despatched by a homing torpedo

By the spring of 1944 the character of anti-submarine operations had completely changed. After the defeat of the large ocean-going wolf packs, the main submarine threat came from schnorkel-equipped U-boats operating in offshore waters. Accordingly, No. 120 Squadron was withdrawn from Iceland in March and settled at Ballykelly in Northern Ireland. Operating from this airfield in support of Operation Overlord (the Normandy landings), a No. 120 Squadron Liberator succeeded in sinking *U-740* on 9 June. Because the new, schnorkel-equipped electric submarines did not need to surface in order to recharge their batteries, they proved to be especially elusive enemies. However, schnorkel tubes and periscopes could be visually sighted or picked up by radar, and sonobuoys (air-dropped miniature sonars, which transmitted data back to the parent aircraft) were able to detect submerged U-boats at short ranges. After many weeks of fruitless anti-submarine patrols, No. 120 Squadron aircraft obtained two sonobuoy contacts during December 1944 and were able to direct naval vessels into their vicinity. More positive results came in the new year, and on 22 March 1945 *U-296* was detected by a Liberator and despatched with a homing torpedo. A further kill was obtained on 29 April, when *U-1017* was the victim.

No. 120 Squadron ended World War II as the top-scoring anti-submarine unit of RAF Coastal Command. It had sunk a total of 16 U-boats, damaged as many again, and shared three kills with the Royal Navy. But beyond its tally of destruction, the squadron's ceaseless patrols had prevented the loss of countless merchantmen in the North Atlantic. Winston Churchill later claimed that only the U-boat peril had really frightened him during the war. To the stamping out of that peril, No. 120 Squadron made a handsome contribution.

THE AUTHOR Anthony Robinson was formerly on the staff of the RAF Museum, Hendon, and is now a freelance military aviation writer. He has edited the books *Aerial Warfare* and the *Dictionary of Aviation*.

COAST GUNS

The KA-bataljon m/80 forms the linchpin of Sweden's coastal defence against the threat of attack by the Soviet Red Navy

SWEDEN HAS LONG MAINTAINED a stance of strict defensive neutrality, and continues its attempts to remain aloof from the international power alignments that seem to bind almost every other nation around it. This defensive neutrality has to be purchased at a considerable economic price, a price that would make many other nations flinch at the taxes and costs involved. However, the Swedes value their neutral status so highly that these costs are accepted as a necessary part of its maintenance. To the monetary cost must be added the social cost of conscription and subsequent personal inconvenience – reserve and follow-up training duties have to be assumed by a large percentage of the population, sometimes for years after full-time national service has been completed.

The reasons behind this ready acceptance of military responsibility lie in Sweden's geographical position. The nation is perilously close to the Soviet Union (the two countries are separated only by the Baltic Sea) and history has taught Sweden the lessons of a Russian foreign policy that has been undeniably expansionist. Sweden therefore considers that to deter such an expansionist policy, she must convince the Soviet High Command that any attempt to stray into her territory would prove too expensive in terms of casualties and military material. Consequently, in an attempt to deter any attack on her borders, Sweden maintains strong defences of every kind.

Coastal defences are one type of defensive stance that very few nations outside Scandinavia and the Baltic region have chosen to retain. The usual counter argument is that the advent of the aircraft and the nuclear threat have made expensive coastal defences obsolete. However, the Swedes have rejected this view. The nation possesses a long coastline that is vulnerable to amphibious invasion in many places, and the Swedes are well aware that the Soviet Navy is only a short sailing distance away. Consequently, Sweden has installed formidable coastal defences to insure against an attack by the Red Navy.

These defences take many forms. An obvious element is static gun defence, comprising fixed batteries that fire out to sea from protected emplacements. A Swedish modernisation programme has up-dated these defences by installing a number of powerful Bofors 120mm ERSTA turret guns. Aug-

SWEDISH COAST ARTILLERY

The Royal Swedish Coast Artillery is largely organised into static protected batteries under the command of five brigades. The majority of the guns are 75mm and 120mm turret guns, although a few old 152mm guns still remain, along with a number of dual-role (anti-aircraft and coastal defence) 75mm mobile guns. These are now being joined by the 120mm KARIN mobile guns of the KA-bataljon m/80s. The 75mm turret guns were installed during the 1960s and have been followed by the powerful 120mm ERSTA turret guns, the first being installed in 1976.

The installations for these guns are usually dug deep into the surrounding rock, and feature protected living accommodation, communication and control centres. The entire installation is often four or five storeys below ground level. These ERSTA batteries can remain closed down for weeks on end.

When in action, their automatic-feed mechanisms can provide as many as 200 rounds through a single water-cooled barrel in 20 minutes. Radar and optronic fire-control centres allow pin-point accuracy on naval targets as far away as 30,000m.

These ERSTA guns are so complex and expensive that only two are produced each year at the AB Bofors factory.

Many of the gun installations are in remote areas, but their range enables them to defend long stretches of coastline. It is anticipated that the ERSTA guns will remain viable weapons for at least the next 40 years, thus off-setting their daunting initial costs.

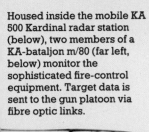

Housed inside the mobile KA 500 Kardinal radar station (below), two members of a KA-bataljon m/80 (far left, below) monitor the sophisticated fire-control equipment. Target data is sent to the gun platoon via fibre optic links.

menting these are specialised guided missiles, coastal ranger battalions, aircraft support and light coastal vessel flotillas. However, the degree of interest in coastal defence expressed by the Swedish military planners has led to the introduction of a new type of defence formation. These formations are unique to Sweden, and constitute one of the most important elements in the Swedish defensive network. They are known as the KA-bataljon m/80s, or Coast Artillery Battalions Type 80. The number of KA-bataljon m/80s that will eventually be involved in the defence of Sweden has not been disclosed. The concept of the unit was formulated on paper in 1980 (hence m/80), and the first fully trained and equipped battalion was incorporated into the Royal Swedish Coast Artillery as recently as June 1986. Further battalions are currently being raised as a mobile addition to the Coast Artillery, and they have been given specific defensive tasks.

Although most of the potential landing areas and approaches to important harbours and economic centres are already defended by static defences, there are several large stretches that remain open to possible invasion – the Stockholm archipelago alone has some 24,000 islands and reefs. The new mobile battalions are therefore based several kilometres back from the coast, ready for rapid deployment to any undefended area under threat of invasion. They would also be in a position to move to any area where existing local defence units had been overcome, or were in need of immediate reinforcement.

The total manpower strength of each battalion is approximately 750 officers and men. This is divided between a staff battery and two 12cm KA-batteri m/80s. The battalion commander and his immediate staff have direct access to a combat control data and overall command network known as STRIKA 85. This allows the commander to assess the overall coastal defence tactical situation. He is thus in a position to determine the main enemy attack lines, gauge the threat to each defended area and anticipate probable future moves by attacker and defender. He can thus deploy his available forces in the most advantageous position, and maintain finger-tip contact with the overall tactical picture. The STRIKA 85 network terminals, as with all other communication and control equipment in the battalion, are maintained in containerised shelters that are either towed or carried on trucks.

Each of the two 12cm KA-batteri m/80s that comprise the rest of the battalion has a strength of just over 300 officers and men, and constitutes the main striking power of the unit. The company commander and his staff have their own platoon, housed in four mobile containers. From here, he is in a position to direct a wide array of units, ranging from the fire-control platoon to the medical support platoon.

The fire-control platoon is divided into four units, two of them based on radar, and a third that uses optronics (television imaging and laser range-finding) for clear-weather firing against sea targets. The radar units use the highly mobile Philips 9 KA 500 KARDINAL, that employ a hydraulically raised mast mounting a radar head, together with optronic sensors. These fire-control units detect and

Below right: Ready to fire – a 120mm KARIN gun. Positioned over the barrel is a radar that measures muzzle velocity.

82805

THE KARIN COAST-DEFENCE GUN

During the early 1970s, the Swedish Army was looking for a new 155mm field howitzer at the same time as the Royal Swedish Coast Artillery was formulating plans for its new 120mm mobile coast defence gun. As a result, the 155mm FH-77 and the 120mm KARIN (designated CD-80) share the same split-trail carriage and many other components.

The first KARIN was issued to the Coast Artillery in 1978, and features an automatic feed system for the fixed ammunition, in addition to an onboard computer that lays the gun from a remote control station. The integral auxiliary power unit enables the main wheels to drive the gun over short distances, and can also be engaged to improve traction over difficult country. Two castor wheels underneath the trails add to the gun's manoeuvrability. In addition, the power unit provides hydraulic power to open and close the heavy trail legs.

The gun has a range of at least 30,000m and a new type of long-range ammunition is now being developed that will extend this to 40,000m. A special naval target shell is fuzed so that the shell will not explode until after it has penetrated its target's armour. This increases the shell's effectiveness.

The gun weighs 12,000kg in action, and has a crew of up to six – although fewer can serve the gun once in action. A complete round weighs 43kg, of which 24kg is the projectile.

Bofors is currently developing a new coastal defence gun, also based on the army's 155mm FH-77 howitzer. Known as the CD-77, the new gun will have a unique capability to combat moving targets at long range – with great precision.

track targets before sending their raw data to a central fire-control station, where all relevant fire-control information is processed. The radars use frequency-hopping to avoid jamming by the enemy, and if this should fail, they can still have recourse to the optronic sensors mounted above the radar aerials on the KARDINAL masts. The KOLIBRI, a new and much smaller form of optronic fire-control equipment, is currently under development.

The four 120mm KARIN guns of the gun platoon are the heart of the battery. These towed guns, produced by AB Bofors, are the most advanced of their type in the world, and can be moved to their firing positions at high speed. Once on station (usually between three and six kilometres from the coast), the guns can be manoeuvred into a firing position using their own integral auxiliary power units. Each gun has its own onboard fire-control computer that absorbs data from the fire-control centre, and then co-ordinates the necessary barrel movements required to lay the gun on its target. The gunner operating the computer simply has to monitor the procedure – the computer does the rest. The remaining members of the gun crew load the ammunition into the automatic feed mechanism, and the gun then fires at a rate of up to 15 rounds per minute to ranges of 30,000m. A trained KARIN battery can arrive at its firing position and open fire with its first salvo within five minutes.

Air defence is not neglected, and each battery has its own air-defence platoon

Supporting the gun platoon is the transport platoon. Using Scania SBA 4 × 4 and SBAT 6 × 6 towing trucks, this platoon acts as a 'rolling magazine', carrying palletised ammunition for the guns. The gun platoon goes into action with its own ready-use ammunition loads, but once fire has been opened these would soon need to be replenished – a four-gun KARIN battery can fire 200 rounds in less than 20 minutes. To assist with the ammunition handling, most of the platoon's trucks are equipped with their own hydraulic cranes. The transport platoon also carries spares and other supplies for the gun battery. In addition, there is a support platoon with an emergency medical aid facility resembling a small field hospital. This platoon also provides a field kitchen, and full field-repair facilities for all equipment in the battery. Air defence is not neglected, and each battery has its own air-defence platoon equipped with two 40mm L/70 Bofors guns with integral Type 75 optronic fire-control systems. These guns are provided with proximity-fuzed high-fragmentation ammunition that greatly increases the chances of bringing down an attacking aircraft.

To round off this impressive array of military investment, the battery is equipped with its own infantry defence platoon, tasked with the local defence of the battery. To fulfil this role, the unit's three sections are armed with the usual infantry smallarms plus an extra section of 84mm Karl Gustav anti-tank recoilless guns. The infantry travels in Volvo 4140 4×4 and 6×6 light trucks and on Husqvarna motor cycles. As the battery moves towards its position, the motorcyclists travel ahead of the column to survey and clear the route, check navigation and generally ensure that the battery keeps moving. Once on site, the platoon spreads out to defend the battery position perimeter.

Although the battery operates as a complete unit,

Bottom right: As the KARIN's onboard power unit moves the gun's trail legs into a firing position, the support units of the battalion go into action. A soldier from the infantry platoon guards the perimeter (bottom left), and a 40mm Bofors L/70 anti-aircraft gun performs an air-defence role (right). Below: Hidden from aircraft by camouflage, a KARIN battery awaits instructions from the fire-control platoon.

Main picture: The gun aimer's position, showing the gun sight and the onboard fire-control computer. Below: The rolling magazine. A Scania SBAT towing truck unloads a pallet of ammunition alongside the KARIN's position.

EXPLOSIV
VARA

it is always under the overall command of the battalion commander. The battery commander has a reasonable insight into the overall tactical situation, relying upon information provided by the STRIKA 85 data network. In addition, he is responsible for feeding fresh information into the network via his own terminal. However, the battalion commander alone can order the battalion into combat, oversee the subsequent action and then order the battalion to a fresh position for the next combat task.

The KA-bataljon m/80 can be called into action at any time of the day or night. This is no small demand, considering the extremes of temperature that are found in Sweden – varying from arctic winter to the heat of high summer. The greatest problem encountered by the men is the bitter cold, and all vehicles and shelters are therefore provided with extensive insulation and powerful heaters. Because many members of the battalion have to work in the open under all conditions, warm and waterproof clothing has to be provided and all weapons have to be maintained constantly to ensure their operation in sub-zero temperatures.

Being completely on wheels, the entire battalion is a flexible and powerful combat instrument. Its main tactical asset is that a potential enemy will never know exactly where it is, nor where it is likely to turn up. The arrival of two KARIN batteries at any stage of an amphibious landing could transform a well-plan-

ed operation into an immediate shambles. Salvoes f 120mm shells, each weighing 24kg, would come rashing down into the area at a time when the nvaders had not yet organised their forces or estab-shed their bridgehead defences. In addition, once n enemy attack had been neutralised, the entire battalion would be able to deploy to another landing ite to repeat the performance.

Since the KA-bataljon m/80 deals mainly with owed artillery, it comes as something of a surprise to earn that its personnel belong to the Royal Swedish Navy. The Royal Swedish Coast Artillery is part of the Navy, but the personnel of the coast artillery battalions are sailors who never go to sea. To the observer, they are uniformed and equipped in the same manner as Swedish Army personnel. The battalions have a small cadre of professional career officers and NCOs, but the bulk of the personnel come from every walk of life. In theory, the Swedish conscription system is universal, but only 40,000 men are selected each year for all three services. Once selected personnel have been allotted their duties, their terms of full-time training vary. All personnel carry out at least 300 days, but the more highly trained personnel can serve for up to 540 days.

After initial training, the KA-bataljon m/80 conscripts are prepared for their military role within the battalion. The substance of this specialised training varies enormously according to the role expected of each individual conscript. Having received instruction in the relevant skills, the trained conscripts are assigned to their position within the battalion. Following a series of full battalion exercises, they then join their KA-bataljon m/80. By this time, the conscripts' full-time national service period is usually over, and the men return to their normal civilian roles. However, they remain on the Swedish military reserve and, depending on their rank and function, they will return to their battalion every two years to maintain their high standards of training and military skills. Each battalion will join together as a full-strength unit at least every four years in order to carry out battalion-scale training and exercises. In this way, each KA-bataljon m/80 remains a viable combat unit. Although the conscripts return to civilian life, a full-time cadre will remain in the battalion – to keep everything at combat-readiness.

Since each battalion has a number of conscripts undergoing training at any one time, the work of the full-time cadre is very extensive. Ammunition, spare parts and all the other battalion requirements are kept permanently at an operational level, vehicles are regularly serviced, and every item in the battalion's armoury must be maintained at peak efficiency.

The methods, organisation and effectiveness of the Royal Swedish Coastal Artillery demand a high standard of training and an equally high level of dedication from all the personnel concerned. Both are present at all levels, for it seems that every Swede is fully determined to play his part. While Sweden continues to possess combat formations as powerful and as flexible as the KA-bataljon m/80, the nation can remain assured that no potential enemy will willingly take on such a ready and able opponent.

THE AUTHOR Terry Gander is a freelance military writer and is the author of the *Encyclopedia of the Modern British Army*, now in its third edition.

The defensive capability of the KA-bataljon m/80 is augmented by the firepower of vessels from the Royal Swedish Navy. Below: Armed with a 57mm gun and surface-to-air missiles, a Stockholm Class patrol boat conducts exercises in the Baltic. Below, inset: The shape of things to come. This picture shows an early prototype of the RBS 15 anti-shipping coastal defence missile system. Still under development, this system will soon take its place as the newest weapon in the arsenal of the coastal artillery. The RBS 15 has a range of 15 miles and is capable of sinking virtually any warship.

K11

PULVER

Inset left: The loading mechanism of the KARIN 120mm coastal defence gun. Ammunition is stored in the loading hopper on the right-hand trail leg (facing the muzzle). From here, rounds are automatically pushed into the ammunition loading tray (marked in black and yellow). Hydraulic pressure is then used to swing the tray towards the breech, seen here on the left of the picture. Once it comes into line, the shell is automatically rammed into the open breech.

THE SBS

In the aftermath of World War II, the plethora of special seaborne raiding forces that had been formed during the hostilities underwent a period of major reorganisation. Most were disbanded, but elements of three, the Royal Marine Boom Patrol Detachment (RMBPD), the Royal Navy's Combined Operation Assault Pilotage Parties (COPPs) and the Marines' School of Combined Operations Beach and Boat Section (SCOBBS), continued in service. The present-day SBS is the direct descendant of these units.

In the autumn of 1947, after the demobilisation of 'hostilities only' men, the RMBPD was transferred from its base at Appledore in Devon to the Amphibious School at Eastney in Hampshire. The RMBPD had already been joined by members of COPPs, and at Eastney it received recruits from SCOBBS.

COPPs had been formed in September 1942 from Royal Navy and Royal Engineer officers training for reconnaissance missions along the North African coast. Most of these men left at the end of the war, but one detachment joined the RMBPD in 1946.

The other unit to arrive at Eastney was SCOBBS, which had been formed at the School of Combined Operations at Instow in Devon in the summer of 1946 from Detachment '385' of the Royal Marines, and men from COPPs who had not been demobilised. The assembled forces were then forged into a single command known either as the Small Raids Wing (SRW) or the Small Boat Wing. Immediate control over the unit rested with the Royal Marines.

In 1957 the SRW was reorganised, with its headquarters, training cadre and Special Boat Sections becoming the Special Boat Unit.

A year later, the Unit was retitled the Special Boat Company. The Special Boat Company survived until 1975, when it was renamed the Special Boat Squadron of Special Boat Sections.

SBS

THE FALKLANDS CAMPAIGN

In recent years, the training and techniques of the SBS have been kept to the highest standards, as was shown in their success in the South Atlantic in 1982, pinpointing enemy positions in preparation for the main British landings

THE SILENT raiders of the Special Boat Squadron (SBS) began their 'invisible' war against the Argentinian forces occupying the Falkland Islands nearly a month before the main landings at San Carlos in late May 1982. On the bitterly cold evening of 22 April, 2 Section, SBS was flown by Wessex helicopter from HMS *Antrim* to a remote corner of South Georgia, an island some 1300km southeast of the Falklands. Their mission was to establish 'hides' (observation posts) on a headland jutting out into Cumberland Bay and report on the dispositions of the enemy at Grytviken, the island's main settlement.

After a difficult landing in the Sörling Valley, at a point over 200m above the chill waters of Hound Bay, the men, each burdened by over 30kg of food, spare clothing and ammunition, began humping the 180kg bags containing their Gemini inflatable boats towards Cumberland Bay, lying five kilometres away. Fit as they were, it took over eight hours to reach the water's edge. Once the Geminis had been inflated, the team members attempted to launch their craft; a gale force wind made the launch hazardous and, once at sea, sharp pieces of glacier ice threatened to puncture the boats' buoyancy chambers.

Despite the obvious dangers, the section set out for the pre-arranged destination. Paddling into a northwesterly wind, the teams struggled to keep their craft on the correct heading and fend off the

Below left: Riding the surf. The two-man crew of a Klepper canoe struggles against the power of the waves as they approach a beach on a training exercise. SBS training is highly demanding and recruits have to be able to handle their craft competently in hazardous conditions and in any weather. Above: On reconnaissance – an SBS man carries out a beach survey. Right: A team prepares to deploy from a submarine, in an inflatable boat. Below right: An SBS swimmer detachment stows gear under cover of rocks at the rear of a beach before heading inland on a reconnaissance probe.

dangerous pieces of ice stabbing against the sides of the Geminis. However, the ice proved to be too formidable an opponent, puncturing the boats' skins until they were beyond easy repair and forcing the raiders to withdraw. Reluctantly, at first light on the 23rd the section leader sent a message to *Antrim* giving details of the problems. By this stage it was clear that there would be no chance of establishing an observation post, and the team was ordered to hole up until a helicopter could land to take them off.

Although a frustrating start to SBS involvement in the retaking of the Falklands, the operation on South Georgia gives some indication of the wartime role performed by one of the British Navy's most secretive units. The swimmer-canoeist raiders of the SBS have always avoided publicity and decline to reveal the nature of their clandestine operations.

Despite this almost impenetrable veil of secrecy, it is known that SBS men are trained in intelligence-gathering skills and are also taught to mount highly destructive attacks behind enemy lines. However, both types of mission make it absolutely vital that neither the personal details nor the methods used by SBS men are communicated to potential enemies. Nevertheless, there are some aspects of the squadron's activities that can be disclosed without putting anyone's life at risk.

Entry into one of the sections that make up the SBS is no easy matter, and a serving Royal Marine Commando (all SBS recruits are drawn from the Commandos) must undergo a highly demanding and rigorous period of training before qualifying as an

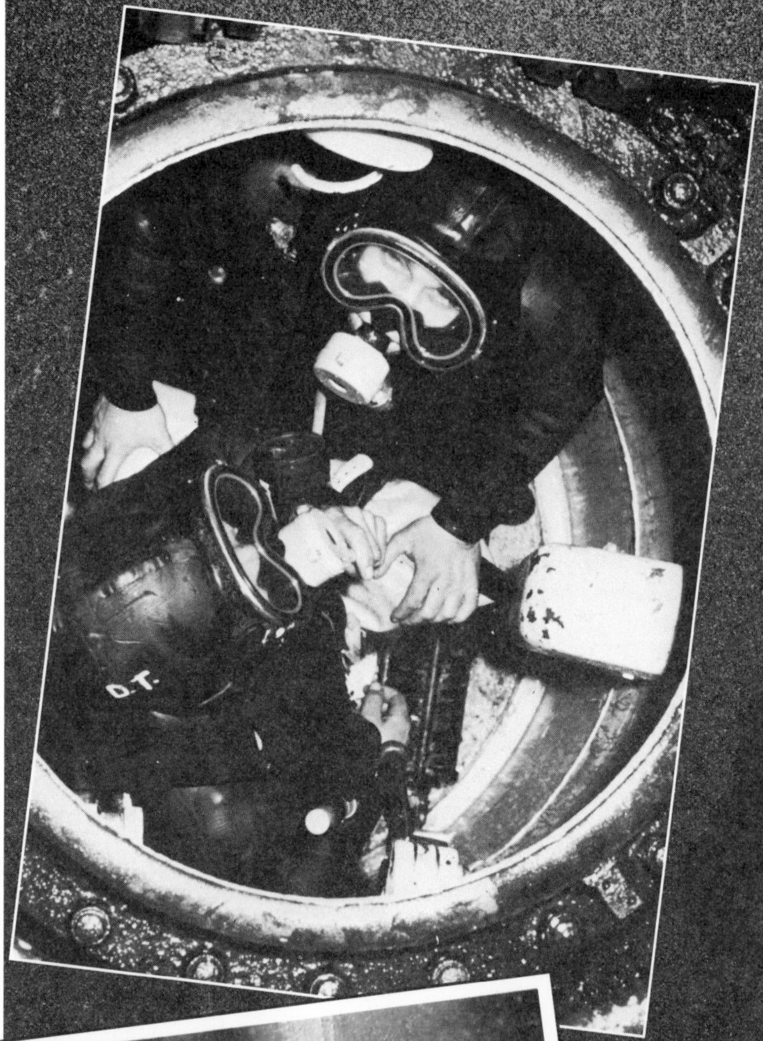

Proficiency in free diving is an essential element in the SBS repertoire. Recruits learn to operate from submerged submarines (right), to lay limpet mines against enemy shipping (far right) and to deal with any operational snags such as a fouled propeller (below).

SC3 swimmer-canoeist. Although many potential recruits come forward and are interviewed every year, very few are selected even for the initial training course. Many men are unsuited either physically or mentally to take part in one of the toughest induction programmes designed for the British armed forces.

SBS candidates have to be of above average intelligence since much of the unit's wartime work is likely to involve the use of complex electronic equipment and the compilation of detailed and accurate reports in a factual no-nonsense manner. Intellectual skills are also crucial to high quality and effective beach reconnaissance. During such operations, teams would be expected to identify suitable landing points for larger forces, take beach samples to test the load-bearing characteristics of the sand, and measure the beach profile. All of these activities would have to be carried out right under the noses of the enemy, and it is essential that the men leave no trace of their visit behind.

Much of their time in action will involve clandestine journeys deep into enemy-held territory

Swimmer-canoeists must never leave an injured man behind as he might, under pressure, reveal details of the operation to the enemy. Teams are warned that all casualties, whether dead or wounded, must be removed from the scene of an operation.

Swimmer-canoeists are trained to feel at home both on and under the water, as much of their time in action will involve clandestine journeys deep into enemy-held territory. Teams are inserted by a number of methods; on the surface the Gemini inflatable boat or the Klepper two-man canoe is used, but they are equally capable of deploying from submarines or making 'wet' jumps with parachutes. Recruits must be able to handle all craft in the most hazardous of conditions and be able to paddle their boats over long distances.

Another essential proficiency for all SBS members is free-diving. In their first exercises they train with compressed air and then progress to oxygen which requires the use of bulky tanks. Divers are taught to get in and out of a submerged submarine and to operate under water for considerable periods of time. Underwater swimming also allows SBS teams to engage in sabotage operations and recruits are shown how to attach limpet mines onto the hull of an enemy ship and set the fuse so that the explosion occurs when they are safely out of the immediate area.

Training for such work involves a great deal of physical stress and, although a number of recruits on the initial training course suffer injuries, most return to complete the SC3 programme at a later date. However, others fail to make the grade and are returned to their unit. Many are rejected because they are unable to cope with the strain of prolonged underwater work or cannot complete the intensive classroom studies which involve attaining a high level of proficiency in the sending of morse code, and learning to identify precisely details of enemy strength and equipment.

Weapons' proficiency is highly prized by the SBS, and although most recruits are usually skilled in the use of standard-issue smallarms when they arrive, they will have to learn the finer points of using the American Ingram and Heckler and Koch MP5 submachine guns and other equipment not regularly deployed by the Royal Marine Commandos. Particular attention is focussed on the development of sniping skills.

Because of the intensity of the training on the SC3 course, recruits have to learn to get by with little or no sleep. Their day begins at 0530 hours and 20 minutes later the men are expected to be in the gym, ready for an hour's physical exercises. Often the men will have only completed the previous day's activities at 0100, giving them just four-and-a-half hours' sleep. No details of the number of men who 'survive' this rigorous regime are published, but 30 years ago as few as 20 per cent regularly qualified.

If the recruit is not already a fully-trained parachutist, he is sent on a training course to develop the appropriate techniques.

Men are also taught procedures for rendezvousing with submarines at sea. After slipping free of his parachute harness a few metres above the water, the recruit has to wait for the submarine to reach him. There are a number of means by which the boat can home in on the swimmer, but the simplest, and most foolproof, is the 'bongle'. This is a sealed, 15cm-long tube containing a large ball-bearing which makes a distinctive underwater echo if the tube is turned over. Underwater this tapping sound can be detected by the submarine's sonar or other sound-location systems.

Having qualified, the SC3 will then serve with the squadron for a number of years. After this period, he may be posted for a tour of duty with another Commando unit. This system has two advantages: the Royal Marines do not wish the SBS to become a secret force within a force, and it also ensures that there will be a number of ex-SBS men serving outside the squadron who will be fully conversant with the needs and specialist methods of SBS teams. The qualified swimmer often returns to the squadron for further courses during his time with the Royal Marines, and many go on to gain further qualifications. In fact, there are two higher grades than SC3 – SC2 and SC1 – and each is progressively more difficult to attain than the initial training course. During these courses, men might learn an appropriate foreign language, while others are instructed in the finer points of Arctic warfare.

The full range of demanding skills developed in these extensive training programmes was utilised to the full during the battle for the Falklands and,

Below: Swimmer-canoeists paddle purposefully towards the shore in a Klepper canoe on a training exercise. The light-weight, 5.2m collapsible Klepper has replaced the Cockle types and is considerably more stable than its predecessors. The tough, rubber and polyester cord hull skin fits loosely over the wooden frame of the canoe and is tightened when buoyancy bags running under each gunwale are inflated.

despite the difficulties encountered on South Georgia on 22/23 April, the SBS played a key part in the preparations for the San Carlos landings on 21 May.

Three weeks before the main invasion force set foot on East Falkland, the first SBS teams, usually consisting of four men, were landed to carry out intelligence gathering operations. Their mission was threefold: they were to report on the strength and location of Argentinian defences, identify suitable landing sites for the main British force, and find a base where the Commandos could establish their Brigade Maintenance Area (forward supply base).

After detailed discussions aboard HMS *Fearless*, it was finally decided that San Carlos was the most suited to the requirements of the British and that detailed reconnaissances of the area should be undertaken by the SBS. In almost total darkness on the last day of April the first team lifted off the flight deck of *Hermes* in a Sea King helicopter that was to carry them the 300km to the Falklands.

The teams were dropped at landing zones (LZ) a safe distance from the coast and the main Argentinian bases, where the noise from the helicopter rotors, as they flew in low to avoid enemy radar, would not attract undue attention. The Sea Kings would hover over the LZs, giving the men inside just enough time to disembark and head for the nearest cover with their vital electronic equipment. Once the helicopters had departed, the teams began the difficult and strenuous night marches to their observation posts.

One team established a hide overlooking the Mutton Factory at Ajax Bay, where the Royal Marine Commandos intended to come ashore to establish the Brigade Maintenance Area. This team confirmed that no Argentinians occupied the factory and, after completing a night reconnaissance, reported that the site would be an ideal landing point. However, another team, operating a little way across the entrance to San Carlos water reported the worrying news that Fanning Head was held by an enemy observation post. If this position was not neutralised before the first landing craft headed into San Carlos, the Argentinians would be able to call up reinforcements and oppose the landings. It was essential that the post was knocked out.

Above left: Reconnaissance training. Armed with an L34A1, the silenced version of the 9mm L2A3 Sterling sub-machine gun, an SBS man creeps stealthily ashore from his Klepper on a clandestine intelligence-gathering mission. Once ashore (above), the SBS team takes up an observation position to monitor movements of enemy troops and equipment.

Marine, SBS, Falklands 1982

British specialist units were generally well-equipped for the cold-weather conditions of the Falklands and this SBS Marine is no exception. An arctic windproof smock in DPM is worn along with DPM trousers. Special features include a woollen cap, Norwegian Army shirt and civilian boots and gaiters. Field dressings are taped to his belt and onto the fore-guard of his 5.56mm AR-15 assault rifle. An SBS five-pocket magazine 'waistcoat' is worn across the chest. Rolled-up waterproof clothing is attached to his fully-packed bergen rucksack.

Above: The silenced Ingram sub-machine gun, a recent addition to the SBS armoury.

SBS ARMOURY

Because of the wide scope of modern SBS operations, the SBS has access to some of the most sophisticated military hardware currently available.
In recent years, the SBS's L34A1 silenced Sterling SMG has been replaced by the handier American Ingram sub-machine gun. Although a comparatively light-weight weapon, the Ingram is extremely compact (it is fitted with a retracting stock) and is ideally suited to close-quarters combat. When fitted with a flash and noise suppressor, it is particularly valuable on clandestine missions. The Heckler and Koch MP5 sub-machine gun, a weapon favoured by the SAS, is also available and, like the Ingram, is lighter and easier to conceal than the Sterling. In some instances, possibly reconnaissance work in built-up areas, the SBS team might be equipped with pump-action shotguns.
Incendiary devices are also an important component in the SBS armoury, and the main grenade is the 80WP. With a blast of phosphorus splashing everything within a radius of 15m of its detonation, it can start a fierce blaze while providing a 30-second screen of white smoke to enable the raider to escape undetected. The SBS also uses the stun grenade to provide a blinding flash and a loud report, sufficient to temporarily immobilise an enemy.
Although mortars have never been widely used by the SBS, teams have made use of grenade launchers. One of the more popular weapons is the US-built M79 which can fire a 40mm grenade to a distance of 400m.

On the evening of 20/21 May, as the leading ships of the assault group were steaming along the north coast of East Falkland, SBS teams were inserted by helicopter under cover of darkness. They landed on the high ground above Port San Carlos – ground they had patrolled in the earlier stages of their operations – and then set off to cover the 10km of rough moorland that lay between them and the Argentinians at Fanning Head. With the team was a naval gunfire support officer, who would direct the supporting fire from the 4.5in gun of HMS *Antrim*.

When the force was less than 600m from their objective, a Spanish-speaking marine went forward to demand that the Argentinians surrender. There was no reply to his request, so the naval officer called on *Antrim* to make the message clearer. As the first shells landed, the 11 Argentinians opened fire on the SBS party, who then added the fire of their own sidearms to the barrage of ordnance landing around the enemy's positions. Moments later, the Argentinians surrendered, having lost several men killed and three wounded. The SBS team had no time to search the area; they had to get back down to the beach to set up the landing lights that would guide the first wave ashore.

The SBS team ran back eastwards along Race Point and down through the dozen or so buildings and sheep sheds of Port San Carlos. There was no time to search these, but, if they had done so, they would have found the larger part of an enemy company that later in the day would shoot down two helicopters.

Although aware of this potential danger, the team reached the beaches and began setting up the landing lights. Everything went according to plan, and on the morning of 21 May, covered by its escorts, 3 Commando Brigade hit the beaches.

Undoubtedly, the SBS teams operating in advance of the main force had paved the way for the eventual retaking of the Falkland Islands.

THE AUTHOR James D. Ladd is one of Britain's acknowledged experts on the British Commandos. His previous works include *Inside the Commandos*.

Below: An SBS canoeist passes a mine to his swimmer colleague during an anti-shipping exercise.

SBS

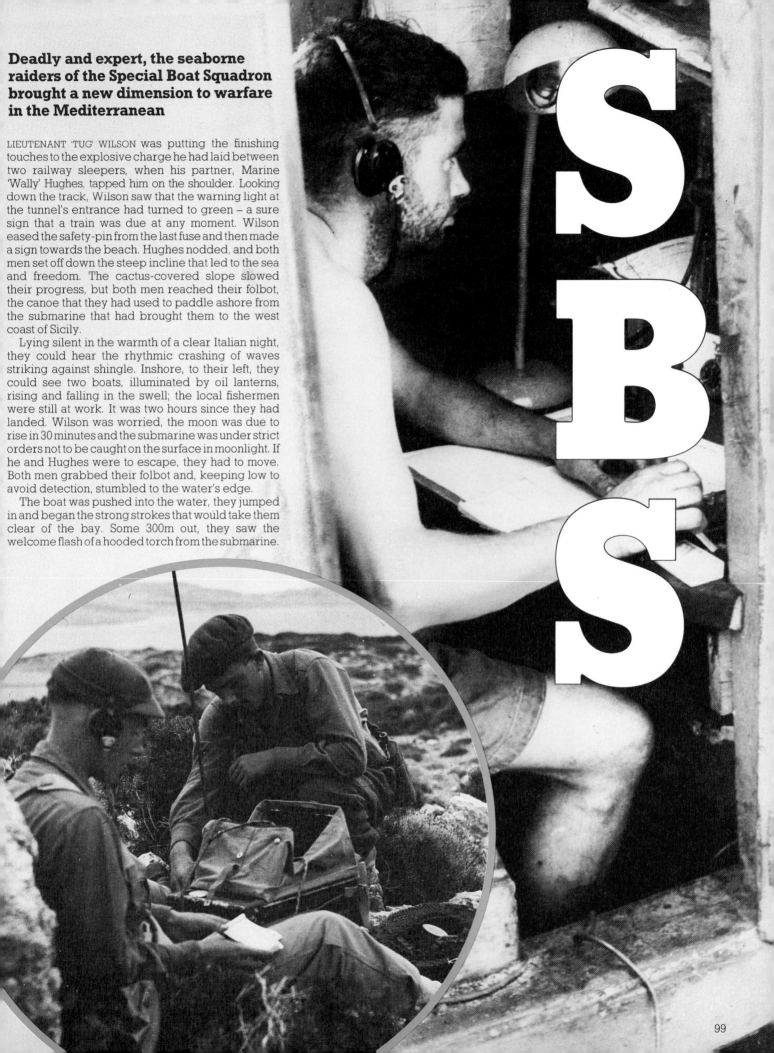

Deadly and expert, the seaborne raiders of the Special Boat Squadron brought a new dimension to warfare in the Mediterranean

LIEUTENANT 'TUG' WILSON was putting the finishing touches to the explosive charge he had laid between two railway sleepers, when his partner, Marine 'Wally' Hughes, tapped him on the shoulder. Looking down the track, Wilson saw that the warning light at the tunnel's entrance had turned to green – a sure sign that a train was due at any moment. Wilson eased the safety-pin from the last fuse and then made a sign towards the beach. Hughes nodded, and both men set off down the steep incline that led to the sea and freedom. The cactus-covered slope slowed their progress, but both men reached their folbot, the canoe that they had used to paddle ashore from the submarine that had brought them to the west coast of Sicily.

Lying silent in the warmth of a clear Italian night, they could hear the rhythmic crashing of waves striking against shingle. Inshore, to their left, they could see two boats, illuminated by oil lanterns, rising and falling in the swell; the local fishermen were still at work. It was two hours since they had landed. Wilson was worried, the moon was due to rise in 30 minutes and the submarine was under strict orders not to be caught on the surface in moonlight. If he and Hughes were to escape, they had to move. Both men grabbed their folbot and, keeping low to avoid detection, stumbled to the water's edge.

The boat was pushed into the water, they jumped in and began the strong strokes that would take them clear of the bay. Some 300m out, they saw the welcome flash of a hooded torch from the submarine.

Previous page: One of the most vital roles performed by the Special Boat Squadron was intelligence gathering. Small teams (below, inset) established observation posts on enemy-held islands to report on the location and movement of Axis troops and convoys. It was arduous and dangerous work; discovery or betrayal were ever-present threats. Main picture: Communication between raiding patrols and their base ships was maintained by wireless. Messages were usually sent in Morse code.

They had not been aboard for very long, just enough time to stow their craft and grab a very welcome ham sandwich, when the captain called them to the conning tower. Much to their delight, they heard the muffled whistle of a train from the direction of the tunnel, which was followed by a white flash and an almighty explosion. Their mission was an unqualified success.

The date of the raid, 22 June 1941, was to achieve a significance that neither Wilson nor Hughes was aware of. Later, when the war was over, they would be credited with carrying out the first mission of the unit that was to become known as the Special Boat Squadron (SBS). In the shorter term, the destruction of the tunnel provided more than ample justification for months of argument and persuasion by a few dedicated and far-sighted canoe enthusiasts.

Chief among these men was Roger Courtney, who, as a subaltern in No. 8 Commando in the summer of 1940, was given permission by his senior officer, Lieutenant-Colonel Robert Laycock, to recruit a small force expert in the use of canoes. As a result of their training on the Scottish island of Arran, six of these men were blooded in action during a raid on the Lofoten Islands off Norway in November 1940. The team landed and placed most of their charges before being withdrawn. It was a small but successful debut.

Although the raid was a taste of things to come, primarily hit-and-run raids in the heart of enemy-held territory, the scene of later actions switched to the Mediterranean, where recent British victories over the Italians in North Africa had raised hopes of an invasion against the Italian mainland. In response to these opportunities, Nos. 7, 8, and 11 Commando, collectively known as 'Layforce', left for the desert; packed deep in the hold of one of the convoy ships were the canoes of Courtney's Folbot Section, soon to be known as 'Z' Section. The arrival of the Afrika Korps in early 1941, however, put paid to any thoughts of an early invasion. Indeed, after the German occupation of Athens and the Peloponnese, the very role of Layforce was called into question, and the force began to disintegrate as men rejoined their original units, were posted to regiments decimated in the recent bout of fighting or were grouped into a new Middle East Commando. Courtney, however, rose to the occasion; he sought and was awarded an interview with Admiral Maund, Director of Combined Operations in Alexandria. Courtney put his case forcefully and Maund gave permission for further raids to be carried out in conjunction with the 1st Submarine Flotilla.

Courtney and his intrepid raiders were soon engaged in a variety of tasks; on the enemy-held coasts of Albania and Crete, they landed agents who carried out fact-finding missions in the heart of vital Axis positions. Despite the success and value of these operations, the most fruitful use of the canoeists remained the sabotage raids of the type carried out by Wilson and Hughes. In the following months, both carried out attacks against railways running along the coast of Italy. The second, against the main Brindisi-Milan line between Ancona and Senigallia, was successful, but it was becoming clear that the enemy were deploying a large part of their strength in defending these targets. Wilson's fertile mind reasoned that it would soon be too dangerous to carry out similar raids, and that it was time to seek out more vulnerable targets. Shipping was the obvious

Left: An SBS man armed with a captured German MP40 submachine gun. Right: Canoe training was essential to the raiders' art. Below: Defusing captured mines. Far right, clockwise from top: David Sutherland; Robert Laycock; and a two-man observation team.

choice; in harbour, vessels would be easy meat.

A few days before Christmas 1941, the first raid against enemy shipping was launched. In darkness, Lieutenant Wilson, clad in heavy 'Long Johns' and coated in Vaseline to protect his body from the icy waters of the Mediterranean, eased over the side of his folbot and, pushing a Limpet mine attached to a net-covered rubber tyre, headed towards his objective, an Italian destroyer anchored by the pier in Navarino Bay in south-west Greece. Wilson was soon in trouble; the water was so cold that he was in danger of hypothermia setting in. Hughes, his usual partner, was worried by the conditions and decided to pull Wilson back to the canoe by the lifeline. Their mission was a failure, but both men were able to recount their experiences when they returned to base – there would be no mistakes next time.

By this stage, Courtney's men had earned the right to exist as an independent unit and had been given an official title – the Special Boat Section (SBS). During this period the SBS underwent a transformation; many of the old faces, most notably Courtney, Wilson and Hughes left the unit for a variety of reasons and were replaced by officers and men from Layforce, chiefly Lieutenants David Sutherland and Eric Newby. Under their leadership the SBS carried out a new type of operation: attacks against enemy airfields on Crete and Rhodes. Both islands were a key part of the Axis war effort in the Mediterranean and their aircraft could interdict Allied shipping plying between British garrisons in the eastern Mediterranean and, most importantly, between Malta and North Africa.

The raid against Crete began on 6 June 1942, when three teams, under the command of Mike Kealy, left Alexandria. Their targets were the enemy bases at Maleme, Kastelli and Tymbaki. A fourth group, six SAS men escorted by Captain The Earl Jellicoe, were to attack the largest target at Heraklion. Four days later, the raiders were on Crete and on their way to the objectives. One group, 'S' Section, under Sutherland, discovered that Tymbaki lacked suitable targets, while another, under Kealy, was forced to accept that Maleme was too heavily defended to risk an attack. The base was surrounded by barbed wire and machine guns. Searchlights covered every possible approach route and, as Kealy remarked, 'there were so many police dogs about that the place sounded like Crufts on show-day'.

The team that headed for Kastelli, 'M' Section, was much more fortunate. Here, Captain Duncan and two men were able to sneak on to the airstrip and place charges against eight aircraft, six trucks, four ammunition stores and nine fuel dumps. Everything went according to plan and Duncan was able to watch the charges' effects. With a deafening explosion, the airfield erupted into a thin black cloud, and bright orange flames shot into the blue sky. Moments later, a series of smaller explosions indicated that the ammunition stocks had gone up as well. Over 70 enemy soldiers died in the attack.

Jellicoe and his men left the airfield through the main gate in the company of enemy officers

Jellicoe's team also scored a victory. After a hard march to Heraklion, made more difficult by heavy burdens that included weapons, maps and rucksacks containing at least 12 bombs and weighing over 22kg, they were in a position to observe the airfield on the 13th. At 2230 hours the group went in. Their entry into the complex was aided by a sudden, and totally unexpected, raid by British bombers that distracted the sentries. Once inside, charges were

THE SBS

The history of the Special Boat Squadron (SBS) began in the late summer of 1940 with the formation of a new raiding unit, the Folbot (canoe) Section under the command of a subaltern, Roger Courtney. The following February, Courtney and 15 men were sent to the Middle East with 'Layforce'. There, as 'Z' Section, the unit received reinforcements and then transferred to the 1st Submarine Flotilla in April 1941.

At the end of the year, after 'Z' Section and the Special Boat Section (Middle East) – a raiding unit formed in the spring of 1941 at Kabrit – had suffered heavy losses, they were absorbed into 'D' Squadron of the 1st Special Air Service Regiment, along with three groups of canoeists under the command of Earl Jellicoe. Jellicoe set about reorganising these different forces into three Special Boat Sections in the autumn of 1942. Each section, 'M', 'L' and 'S', was known by the first letter of its commander's surname.

In the spring of 1943, after the capture of David Stirling, the commanding officer of the SAS, the three sections were reorganised and retitled as squadrons with a full strength of 180 men of all ranks. Another group of SAS men became the 1st Special Raiding Squadron and, under the leadership of Major 'Paddy' Mayne, went on to play a key part in the invasion of Sicily in July 1943.

In November 1943 Jellicoe's Special Boat Squadron came under the command of Brigadier D.J.T. Turnbull's Raiding Forces Middle East and was rechristened the Special Boat Service. This unit then came under the control of Land Forces Adriatic, and conducted further operations during World War II in the Mediterranean, Adriatic and Aegean Seas.

OPERATION ALBUMEN, CRETE JUNE 1943

On 22 June 1943 two patrols of 'S' Squadron under the command of David Sutherland landed on the south coast of Crete, near Cape Kochinoxos. Their mission was to launch a series of raids against Axis airfields that could be used by the Luftwaffe to fly sorties against the Allied invasion of Sicily, planned for 10 July. On the following day, three groups were sent to the enemy bases at Kastelli, Heraklion and Tymbaki.

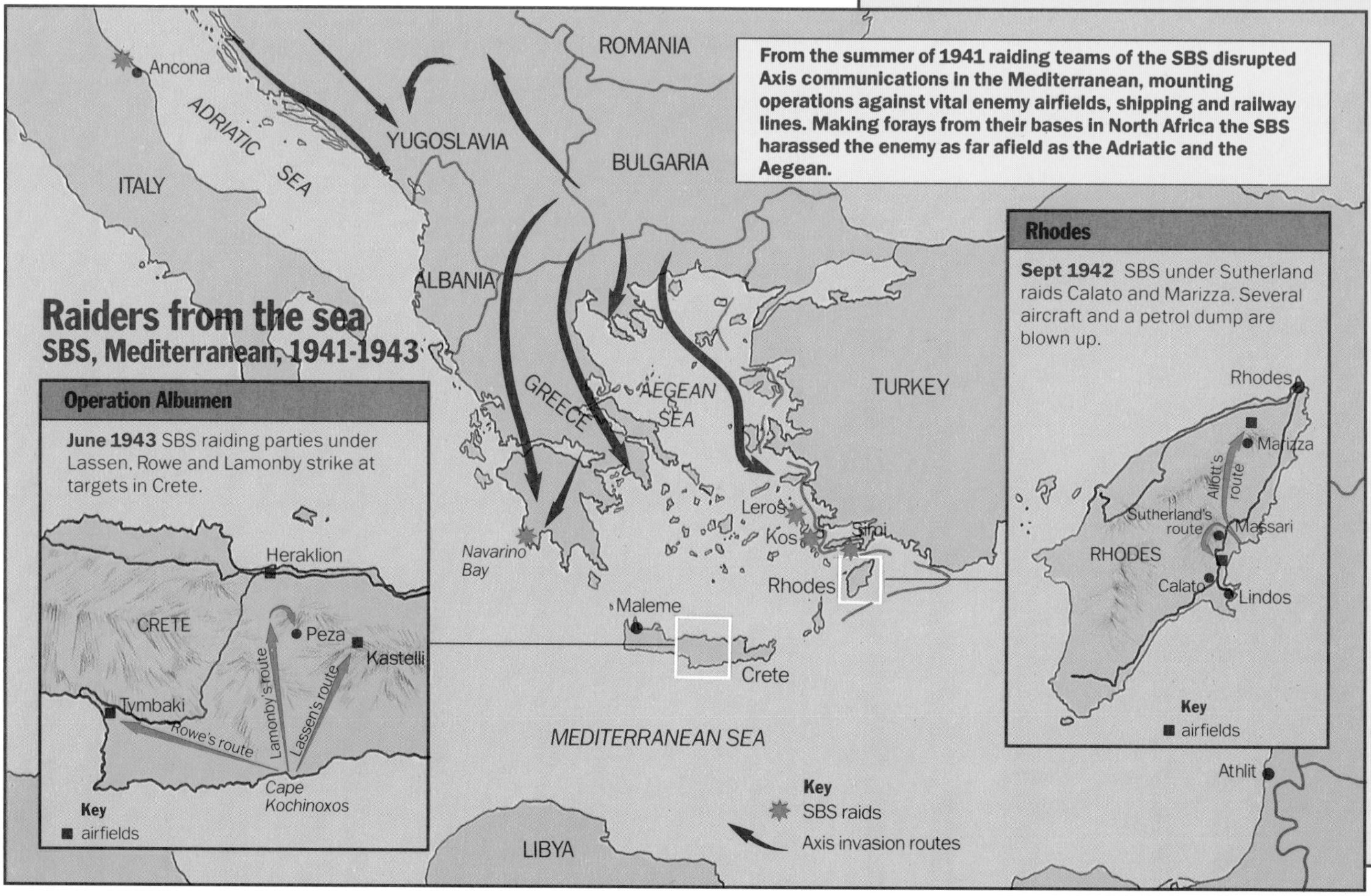
Raiders from the sea
SBS, Mediterranean, 1941-1943
From the summer of 1941 raiding teams of the SBS disrupted Axis communications in the Mediterranean, mounting operations against vital enemy airfields, shipping and railway lines. Making forays from their bases in North Africa the SBS harassed the enemy as far afield as the Adriatic and the Aegean.
ROMANIA
Ancona
ADRIATIC SEA
YUGOSLAVIA
BULGARIA
ITALY
ALBANIA
GREECE
AEGEAN SEA
TURKEY
Navarino Bay
Leros
Kos
Simi
Rhodes
Maleme
Crete
MEDITERRANEAN SEA
LIBYA
Athlit
Key
SBS raids
Axis invasion routes
Operation Albumen
June 1943 SBS raiding parties under Lassen, Rowe and Lamonby strike at targets in Crete.
Heraklion
CRETE
Peza
Kastelli
Tymbaki
Lamonby's route
Lassen's route
Rowe's route
Cape Kochinoxos
Key
airfields
Rhodes
Sept 1942 SBS under Sutherland raids Calato and Marizza. Several aircraft and a petrol dump are blown up.
Rhodes
Marizza
Allott's route
Sutherland's route
Massari
RHODES
Calato
Lindos
Key
airfields

placed against 16 Ju 88s and several other aircraft. Dawn, however, was only 30 minutes away and Jellicoe prudently ordered his men to withdraw; a move accomplished with surprising ease by 'mingling with the slightly harassed occupants' running around the barracks area and then slipping out through the main gate in the company of several unsuspecting enemy officers.

The four raids were a qualified success; between them they had destroyed 26 aircraft, some 20 trucks, large amounts of petrol, oil and ammunition, and caused the deaths of over 100 German and Italian troops. The raiders lost one Frenchman killed and three others taken prisoner.

The operation against Rhodes was scheduled for early September 1942, and, although the capture of Duncan and Newby in a raid on Sicily during the previous July threatened to jeopardise the mission, the operation was given the go-ahead. Under the command of Sutherland, the party boarded His Hellenic Majesty's Submarine *Papanikolis* anchored off Beirut on 31 August. Once under way, Sutherland briefed his men; their targets were the airfields near Marizza in the north and at Calato, halfway down the island's eastern coast. The force would be divided into two self-contained groups; Sutherland and five men would attack Calato while the other, four men led by Captain Allott, would strike out for Marizza. Sutherland found the going extremely tough:

'Due to frequent halts, the distance covered by 0400 hours [on 5 September] was little over a mile, then Captain Allott and myself decided that it was out of the question to cross the road that night. We therefore searched for a hideout and eventually found a grotto capable of accommodating the whole party.

'Once established there, the guides were sent to fill 12 water bottles from a source which they knew of near the road. They returned, however, just before dawn without water, reporting enemy activity in the neighbourhood of their destination. The next day was spent without water; during the day I observed enemy activity in the valley between Massari and Calato, on the aerodrome itself, and noted various positions and defences.

'Captain Allott and myself decided that for the sake of speed on his journey to Marizza, the parties should separate on the night of the 7th/8th. This meant he had five nights in which to reach his objective, and still had five nights clear to make his way back to the beach. I also advocated lightening the load by carrying minimum food and dumping all excess weight where we were lying up, to which he agreed.'

Fifteen separate fires illuminated the base in a ghostly glow. It was time to pull out

After Allott's departure, Sutherland divided his men into two groups for his attack; he and Marine Duggan formed one group, while the Greek Lieutenant Calambakidis, with Marines Barrow and Harris, formed the other. At dusk, the teams moved up to their pre-arranged targets. At midnight Sutherland penetrated the perimeter and then set about laying their charges against three aircraft and a petrol dump. The other group also laid explosives and then, like Sutherland, headed back to their mountain base. Minutes later, both groups had the satisfaction of hearing and then seeing the effects of their exploits; 15 separate fires illuminated the base in a ghostly glow. It was time to pull out.

It was during the following days that disaster struck. Although the raid by Allott was a success, he and his team were captured and a similar fate also befell Lieutenant Calambakidis' party.

Only Sutherland, Duggan and their Greek guide remained at large. Despite numerous brushes with Italian patrols, Sutherland was able to reach the pick-up point on 16 September. At about 2300 hours, he and Duggan (their guide had been captured) saw the welcome flash of a beacon offshore and both men began the exhausting swim to the waiting submarine. They were saved.

Between late 1942 and March 1943, the plethora of special forces units in North Africa underwent several changes in their organisation, training and deployment. David Stirling's Special Air Service (SAS) and the Long Range Desert Group (LRDG) were allowed to retain their identities, but the rest were faced with two options: either rejoin their own units or join the SAS. The SBS joined the SAS and although

By the 29th, one unit led by a Dane, Lieutenant Anders Lassen, had travelled over 25 km to reach its target and was in a position to make a recce of Kastelli, which lay in the centre of a wide valley. That night, the raiders planned their attack; Lassen and Gunner Jones were to cut their way through the perimeter fence to the west, while the other members of the force, Sergeant Nicholson and Corporal Graves, prepared to do the same from the east. Once inside the base, the two teams intended to lay explosives against several aircraft.

Both groups set off at 2230 hours. Lassen and Jones reached the airfield first and then began to edge along the perimeter road looking for a suitable entry point, pausing every few steps to listen for the enemy. After travelling about 70m, both men were forced to take cover to avoid a body of drunken Italian soldiers. Lassen, however, blundered into a more alert sentry and, although he bluffed his way past this and two other guards, a fourth levelled his weapon against the two men. Lassen faked drunkenness to draw the sentry nearer and then fired two shots. The Italian fell, but the firing alerted his companions. The two raiders threw a handful of grenades to delay their pursuers and then moved to a quieter spot to plan their next move.

The silence that followed their escape was deceptive; the Italians were closing in and once again Lassen was forced to shoot an over-inquisitive guard. Realising that any further attempts to reach the base was impracticable, both men withdrew. Nicholson and Graves, however, were able to make use of the alarm caused by Lassen and placed charges against four aircraft and a fuel dump, before making their escape.

Sutherland was able to evaluate the successes of the other raiding parties on 10 July: the group led by Lieutenant Rowe had had no luck at Tymbaki – it had been abandoned by the Germans – but Lieutenant Lamonby and Lance Corporal Holmes had destroyed over 200,000 litres of petrol at Peza, after discovering that their original target, Heraklion, was no longer a major base for enemy aircraft.

ANDERS LASSEN

Anders Lassen, a Dane, in London at the outbreak of World War II, enlisted in the British Army. After training as a commando, he took part in a raid against enemy ships near Dakar, on the west African coast; two merchantmen were sunk and a third was brought back to Britain. In the following months, Lassen was made an officer and spent some time training 50 of his fellow countrymen in commando techniques. Lassen then returned to his old unit, No. 62 Commando, and participated in raids against the French coast and the Channel Islands. At the end of 1942, the Commando was disbanded and Lassen joined the SBS training school at Athlit in the eastern Mediterranean, where he joined David Sutherland's 'S' Detachment. Lassen went on to have a distinguished career and fought with great skill, most notably during Operation Albumen, a raid against

Axis airfields on Crete, in June 1943, and on Simi a few months later. In 1944, he was promoted to captain, was given command of 'M' Squadron of the SBS and played a key role in the liberation of the Greek mainland. Lassen was killed on 8 April 1945, during a raid in Italy. He was 25 at the time of his death. In his brief career he won a Military Cross and two Bars, and was posthumously awarded the Victoria Cross for the action at Comacchio.

FOLBOT (COCKELL MK. 1)

The most urgent requirement of the SBS in the Mediterranean was for a light-weight canoe which could be used by small raiding parties to get ashore and back to their submarines as quietly as possible. The boat had to be easy to stow in cramped conditions and easily hidden on beaches. Although the army lacked a craft suitable for such clandestine operations, the Folbot Company produced a two-man collapsible sports canoe which readily fitted the bill. Several were used by Major 'Jumbo' Courtney's commando canoeists in 1940 and the craft was then adopted as the first SBS raider.

The 5m canoe was easy to assemble and consisted of a wooden frame within a rubberised canvas cover. When dismantled, it folded into a pack 1.4m by 0.3m by 0.3m with a weight of about 22kg. The joints between the wooden struts were usually bound up with heavy insulation tape to avoid accidental disconnection during operations.

The boat's two-man crew was equipped with double-bladed paddles which separated into two parts, and the craft was steered by lines running from the rudder to whichever man was guiding the craft.

As the SBS evolved its raiding techniques, it became common practice for the crew to have specific tasks; the basic distinction was between the canoeist and the swimmer, who attacked the target.

Although the folbot was a fairly seaworthy craft and was described as being very fast and silent in official reports, it did have several weaknesses. Most worrying was that it was very fragile and prone to turning turtle in all but the calmest seas. The canoe was also too lightly built to survive dragging across beaches when loaded with equipment.

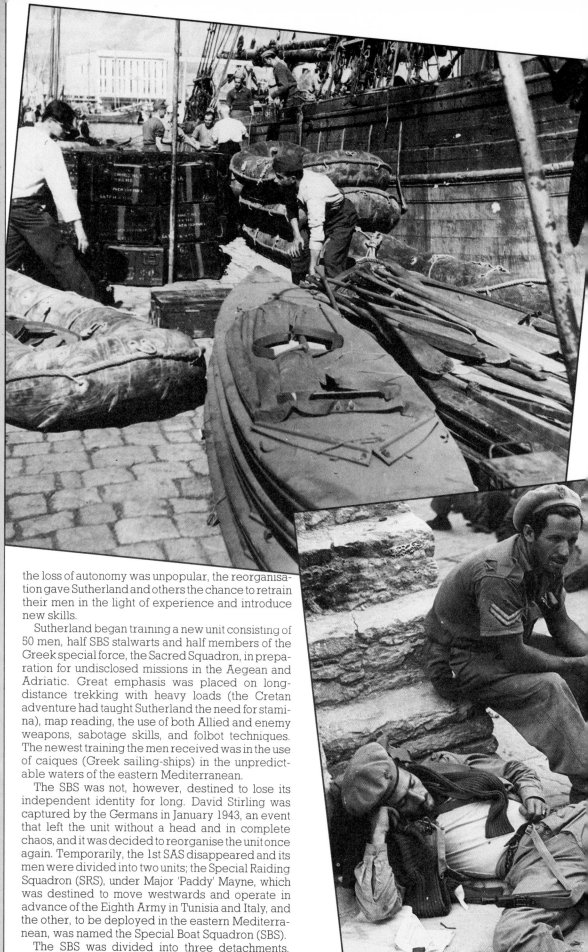

the loss of autonomy was unpopular, the reorganisation gave Sutherland and others the chance to retrain their men in the light of experience and introduce new skills.

Sutherland began training a new unit consisting of 50 men, half SBS stalwarts and half members of the Greek special force, the Sacred Squadron, in preparation for undisclosed missions in the Aegean and Adriatic. Great emphasis was placed on long-distance trekking with heavy loads (the Cretan adventure had taught Sutherland the need for stamina), map reading, the use of both Allied and enemy weapons, sabotage skills, and folbot techniques. The newest training the men received was in the use of caiques (Greek sailing-ships) in the unpredictable waters of the eastern Mediterranean.

The SBS was not, however, destined to lose its independent identity for long. David Stirling was captured by the Germans in January 1943, an event that left the unit without a head and in complete chaos, and it was decided to reorganise the unit once again. Temporarily, the 1st SAS disappeared and its men were divided into two units; the Special Raiding Squadron (SRS), under Major 'Paddy' Mayne, which was destined to move westwards and operate in advance of the Eighth Army in Tunisia and Italy, and the other, to be deployed in the eastern Mediterranean, was named the Special Boat Squadron (SBS).

The SBS was divided into three detachments, each with seven officers and 70 men: 'S' Detachment was given to Captain Sutherland, 'L' Detachment was led by Captain Langton and 'M' Detachment by Captain Maclean. Overall control of the squadron

Left: Tools of the trade. SBS men loading explosives, dinghies and collapsible canoes on to the SBS schooner *Tewfik* prior to a raid. The *Tewfik* was used to take teams to the general target area, but the last leg of the journey was usually by canoe or caique; a much less conspicuous craft. The canoe shown here, the Cockle Mark II, had a plywood deck and hull bottom, and canvas sides. The Mark II was a major improvement on the folbot as it could be collapsed to a compact depth of 15cm and was designed to withstand being dragged over rocky beaches. Below: Two weary members of the Greek Sacred Squadron take a break. Their intimate knowledge of the Aegean proved invaluable to the SBS.

LEROS, NOVEMBER 1943

After the Italian capitulation in September 1943, the SBS became involved in Allied attempts to gain control of enemy-held islands in the eastern Mediterranean. Although several fell to small raiding parties, the German response quickly gathered momentum. In early November they invaded Leros, a tiny speck of land less than 25 kilometres from the Turkish mainland. Bitter fighting lasted for five days before the British surrendered, having lost 400 men killed. Only a small SBS team escaped. Jeffrey Holland was one of those present:

'For a month we have been bombed. My gunpost comprised a stone revetment built about 50m above the beach on the south side of Gurna Bay. It was mid-afternoon (on 11 November) when I heard the roar of aircraft engines. Glancing out to sea, however, the source of the noise became apparent; 10 Ju 52 troop transports, followed by a second wave, flying in just above the crests of the waves. They were making straight for the bay, straight for us. Soon there were 500 or more parachutes floating down. We blazed away. Later, moving out to counter-attack, we observed that the German paras had quickly gathered their dead together – under parachute canopies. I estimated that we killed about 150 in the initial drop.'

In the days after the initial German landings, Holland was involved in heavy fighting for Mount Rachi, a feature that dominated much of the island:

'We moved out and started our climb to the ridge. I was in front, this was not intentional but, having started off, I could not stop. My sub-machine gun was set on full automatic. Then I saw the gun emplacements, I fired a burst and lobbed a grenade. Moments later, I threw two more, in quick succession, into an artillery emplacement. We formed a small group. There were about 20 dead Germans sprawled around looking like rag-dolls. Suddenly, the order to move was given.'

Despite the attack on Mount Rachi, the British garrison was forced to concede ground and was finally beaten into submission a few days later. Holland was one of the men captured:

'For two or three days, we were milling about. I visited the hospital which was crammed with wounded. There were beds in the corridors and stretchers under the beds. The Germans had patrols everywhere. Two of us tried to escape but it was a futile gesture. Ultimately, we were transported to Athens and then put on a prison train bound for Germany. After 15 days in a cattle truck we arrived at Stalag VIIA.'

Left: Jeffrey Holland, fought with the Royal West Kents and was a member of 21 SAS.

rested with Major The Earl Jellicoe, who received official confirmation of its establishment on 1 April 1943. The unit's base was to be at Athlit, a few kilometres south of Haifa in Palestine.

Although the SBS carried out a few small-scale raids during this period, Sutherland directed most of his attention to the training of the new recruits who were flocking to the unit. Chief among these new men was a Dane, Anders Lassen, who went on to have a highly-distinguished wartime career before his death in action in April 1945. However, as the spring gave way to summer, there were murmurings of discontent in the ranks; after training to fever pitch the men were ready for action, yet had no orders.

By May 1943 the operations in North Africa were drawing to a close and it was becoming clear that the next phase of the war would centre on the Italian mainland and the islands of the eastern Mediterranean. Later that month, Jellicoe received welcome news from Raiding Force HQ; he was ordered to prepare and brief teams for raids on Crete and Sicily.

Sutherland's 'S' Detachment with Lassen was the first to move; their operation, codenamed 'Albumen', had as its objectives the destruction of Axis aircraft at three airfields on Crete. The raids were to be a prelude to Operation Husky, the Allied invasion of Sicily, scheduled for 10 July 1943. The attack was carried out with great skill and helped to blunt Axis air raids against the Sicilian beach-heads.

The success of the Allied landings in Italy and the subsequent Italian surrender in September, left a power vacuum in the eastern Mediterranean; a situation that neither the Germans nor the Allies could allow.

As the main Allied armies were heavily committed in mainland Europe, it fell to SBS detachments to persuade the Italian garrisons in the area to surrender. For their part, the Germans believed that control of the Aegean would dissuade the Turks from throwing in their lot with the Allies.

At first the SBS had things much to themselves; Kos, Leros and Simi were captured between September and October 1943. The German response, however, was gathering momentum. On 3 October they landed on Kos, on 12 October the SBS was ordered to withdraw from Simi, albeit for a brief time, and, during early November, Leros fell to a combined assault by paratroopers and a sea-borne force.

Despite these setbacks, the SBS could look with a great deal of pride on its Mediterranean operations of the last three years. From often confused and haphazard beginnings the raiders had grown into a first-rate force able to operate with confidence in the hostile waters of the Mediterranean. Although they had suffered a few reverses, most of their operations had been successful, and with this record there grew a great deal of respect for those far-sighted men, who in 1940 had pressed for the creation of a select water-borne raiding force.

THE AUTHOR William Franklin is a military historian who has contributed to numerous publications. His particular interest is the history of elite forces of World War II.

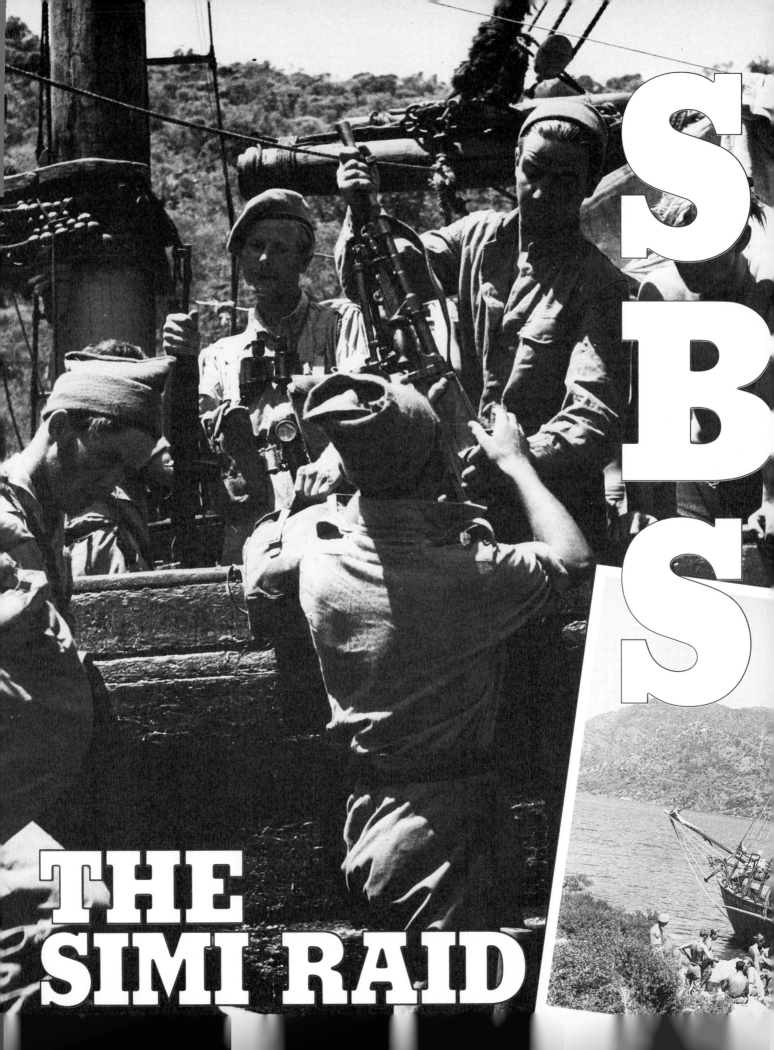

SBS
THE SIMI RAID

When the men of the Special Boat Squadron attacked the Axis base at Simi in 1943, they were looking for a quick victory – and also for revenge

THE SMALL Greek island of Simi lies in the eastern Aegean, north of Rhodes and some 30km from the Turkish coast. The Italians occupied Simi after the German conquest of Greece in the early summer of 1941 with men drawn from Rhodes, their principal garrison in the Dodecanese islands. The only major attempt to block the Axis advance through these islands was made by a force including Nos. 50 and 52 Commando, but their landings on two islands were driven off and a supporting destroyer was sunk.

When the Italians surrendered early in September 1943, the Allies again tried to seize control of the islands, by sending a small force to bolster the morale of the islands' Italian commanders against the pressure of German forces wanting them either to fight on in the Axis cause, or surrender their arms. The Allies had to mount their operations quickly and they had no major forces to spare from their operations at Salerno and in the 'toe' of Italy. Consequently, although the Allied High Command intended to bring the 8th Indian Division to the Aegean within a matter of weeks, Major The Earl Jellicoe's Special Boat Squadron (SBS) was the first unit sent to hold the ring, and was followed by Major 'Paddy' Mayne's Special Raiding Squadron (SRS) and men of the Long Range Desert Group (LRDG) who had taken to amphibious operations. Mayne's SRF had 250 all ranks, mainly drawn from 1st SAS, while Jellicoe's SBS consisted of SAS canoeists and former members of the Special Boat Sections of the Commandos. In all he had 250 men under his command.

Fifty men of Jellicoe's 'S' Squadron were landed on 9 September, the day after the formal announcement of the Italian surrender, on the island of Kastellorizon, some 100km east of Rhodes, and met little or no resistance from the 300-strong garrison. On the same night Lieutenant-Colonel D.J.T. Turnbull, who would command Raiding Forces Middle East when it was officially formed a few weeks later, flew to Simi in a captured Italian seaplane. From there he intended to join Major Jellicoe who had parachuted with two others onto Rhodes. After Jellicoe had survived the Italian garrison's attempts to shoot him as he floated down, and then established his credentials with their commander, Admiral Campioni, he was received courteously. But the admiral, like many Italian officers with families in German-occupied towns, was under the threat of retribution if he did not co-operate with the Germans and, since Jellicoe could not promise that a major British force would arrive for some time, the negotiations came to nothing.

As cannon fire cracked over his head, Lassen swore so loudly that the gunners ceased firing

Nevertheless, SBS units occupied several other islands and one, Major J.M. 'Jock' Lapraik's 'M' Squadron, reached Simi on 17 September in a fleet of caiques, the local Aegean fishing and trading vessels. This island would become very much the squadron's stamping ground in the future but on that first landing they were met by bursts of 20mm cannon fire. One of Lapraik's men, Anders Lassen, had been sent inshore in his canoe to recce the landing point and, as the cannon fire cracked over his head, he swore so loudly in his native Danish that the gunners ceased firing. Once the force was ashore, Lapraik needed all his lawyer's patience not only to negotiate the surrender of the 140 men in the garrison (nearly three times the size of his own force) with their commander, Lieutenant Andrea Occhipinti, but also

Above: Major 'Jock' Lapraik, the leader of the SBS raid against the Axis garrison on the Greek island of Simi in November 1943. Left: Pre-raid preparations. Two men load a Bren-gun onto the deck of the schooner *Tewfik,* while a comrade stands watch, armed with a US M1 carbine. The .303in Bren proved invaluable during the Simi raid; its accuracy enabled the SBS to silence fire from enemy machine-gun positions. Below left: The *Tewfik* was used as a floating headquarters by the SBS. Wireless equipment, stored in the ship's cabins, was used to keep raiding teams in touch. Below right: The Earl Jellicoe, leader of the SBS, (sitting, centre left), briefing Lapraik's party.

THE EARL JELLICOE

George Jellicoe was in his mid-20s and studying at Cambridge University when World War II began. Coming from a military and naval background, he followed in his family's footsteps and enlisted in the British Army.

His rise to prominence began when he joined David Stirlings 1 SAS, fighting in North Africa. He was quickly recognised as a fine officer, and, after taking part in several raids, he took control of 'D' Squadron, 1 SAS in March 1943.

His first task was to prepare for operations in the eastern Mediterranean and, to this end, he established a training camp at Athlit in Palestine.

Following the Italian Armistice in September 1943, Jellicoe took part in operations on the islands of Rhodes, Cos and Leros, The raids met with some success but the SBS suffered losses, and Jellicoe was forced to reorganise his command.

During 1944, the SBS mounted operations against the Greek mainland and, on 13 October, Jellicoe was one of the first men to enter Athens after the German withdrawal. In the following weeks, he was given control of 'Pomp Force', a mixed, all-arms outfit used to harass the retreating German forces.

Jellicoe's success had not gone unnoticed: he had already been promoted to lieutenant-colonel, and in December 1944 he left the SBS to take up a senior post at the Staff College at Haifa in Palestine.

Raid on Simi
SBS, November 1943

On 20 November 1943 two SBS patrols under Major Lapraik and Lieutenant Bury landed on the Aegean island of Simi. Bury's group attacked the German garrison in the castle while Lapraik and his men set incendiary devices in the island's boatyard.

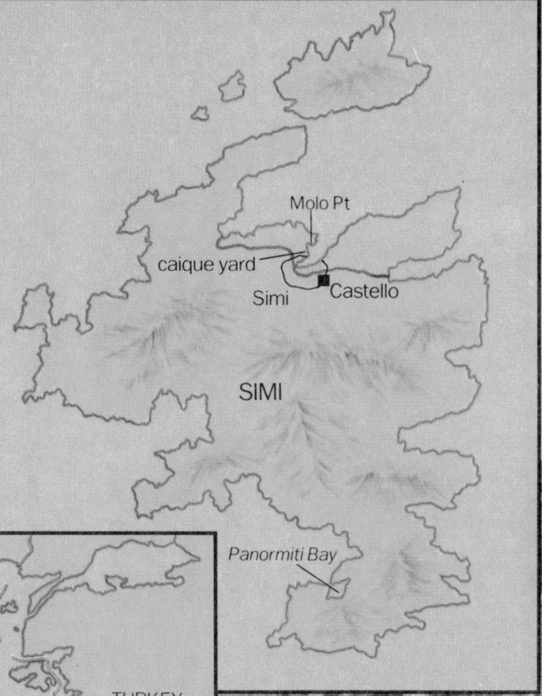

Molo Pt
caique yard
Simi
Castello
SIMI
Panormiti Bay

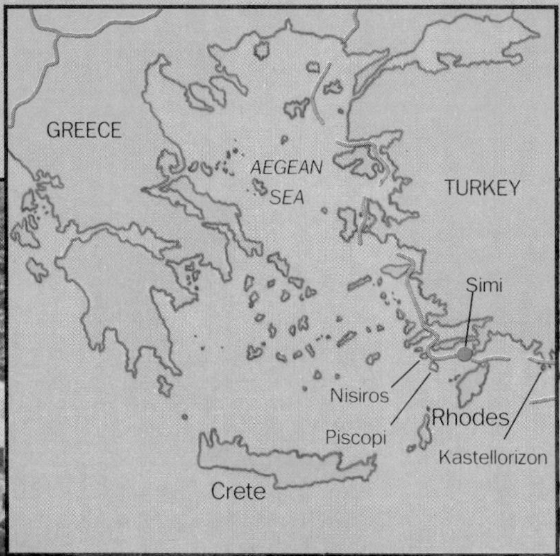

GREECE
AEGEAN SEA
TURKEY
Simi
Nisiros
Piscopi
Rhodes
Kastellorizon
Crete

Main picture: The peaceful harbour of Simi before the attack. The commander of the German garrison had established a heavy machine-gun position on Molo Point, above the town, and in the governor's house. Although every section of the bay was covered, the SBS were able to sneak in undetected. Below right: Five SBS men grabbing a quick meal before the raid. Bottom: Two heavily laden members of Lapraik's team disembarking from one of the caiques used to reach Simi.

to keep the peace between the Italians and the local Greeks. Aside from the garrison, nine 8mm and two 20mm cannon fell into British hands.

In the next few weeks Lapraik's men made recces of Rhodes and the neighbouring islands. However, the plans were thrown into confusion when the Germans, engaged in the systematic recapture of the Dodecanese, reached Simi. On the morning of 7 October their first attack at Pethi Bay was repulsed by accurate fire, particularly from SBS Bren guns, but their second was more successful. However, the Germans were forced to withdraw after they had lost over 50 men to 'M' Squadron's one killed and two wounded. As the Germans possessed air superiority, they were able to bomb Lapraik's remaining defence positions over the next few days and, as SBS casualties rose, the squadron was withdrawn on the 12th. Having cleared the island of British forces, the Germans also withdrew.

By November, however, there were sufficient German troops in the islands to put a permanent garrison, under a major, on Simi. He had 18 of his own troops, two Italian officers and 60 men from the Fascist Militia, 10 'cooks and bottle-washers' and a few Italian *carabinieri* who policed the island under his command. Posts were established at Malo Point, Panormiti and in the governor's house – adequate defences against most seaborne raiders, but not against 'M' Squadron who were familiar with the island and determined to succeed.

In late October 1943, the Raiding Forces' staff at GHQ Middle East began planning a raid that would become recognised as a minor classic in the use of seaborne forces for small-scale raids that have effects far beyond the mere destruction of enemy defences. If the planned raid was successful, the Germans would have to reinforce their island garri-

ATHLIT

In A43 the commanding officer of the SBS, Major The Earl Jellicoe, established a new specialist training base at Athlit, a few kilometres south of Haifa in Palestine. Here SBS men were subjected to a gruelling regime designed to improve their combat skills and teach them the rudiments of survival and evasion behind enemy lines.

Conditions at Athlit were, to some extent, unorthodox; little attention was paid to parade-ground discipline and the men were allowed to wander around in less than military attire. But, despite outward appearances, there was a self-imposed code. Men who failed the basic course knew that they would be RTU'd (returned to unit) and most threw themselves into the daily routine as if their very lives depended on it.

Every day, small groups of recruits could be seen tramping over the rugged slopes of Mount Carmel or paddling folbots in the deep blue sea of the eastern Mediterranean.

Others were familiarised with the handling problems of Greek caiques, under the critical gaze of an often bemused instructor. There was also ample time for those men who needed coaching in the finer points of handling the ubiquitous Tommy-gun to improve their accuracy. Much time was given over to the teaching of demolition and sabotage techniques under a variety of conditions with an assortment of explosives.

Not all of the training exercises, however, were an unqualified success. On one occasion the suggestion that the men should be taught the finer points of living off the land resulted in the creation of an inedible mess which the men christened 'Palestine Soup'. Only Jellicoe spent the night without having to visit the latrines. Despite such occasional upsets, the SBS recruits at Athlit gained the training and expertise that would serve them well in their raids and clandestine operations.

sons at the expense of their strength on the main front, since Hitler believed they had to retain their hold in the Aegean. Not only had the garrisons to be supplied, but in doing so their supply convoys had to run the risk of Allied air attack, and any losses incurred would be a major drain on Germany's scarce naval resources.

The chief planners, Turnbull and Lapraik, knew all this, but they also intended to inflict damage and casualties on the garrison on Simi. To facilitate their plans, recce teams had been landed on the island during the second week in September to gain specific intelligence on the strength and location of the enemy's defences and the state of the island's boatyards and other resources.

A second patrol crept into the boatyards to destroy the caiques being built there

Lapraik planned to land part of his squadron, a patrol led by 23-year-old Lieutenant R. 'Bob' Bury, to attack the garrison's headquarters in the town's old castle-palace which was defended by Germans. This patrol was to cause as many casualties as possible to the garrison, while a second patrol consisting of Lapraik and three others crept into the boatyards to destroy the caiques being built there. These craft weighed up to 20 tons and were regularly used by the Germans to resupply the islands; their destruction would hamper this resupply. A third party, mainly of Bren-gunners, was to be landed to cover the withdrawal of the first two.

In addition to Brens, the squadron had a variety of smallarms including captured German Schmeisser machine pistols. With a rate of fire of 500 rounds a minute and a reliability far greater than any British sub-machine gun of the time, they were prized possessions. The men had also been trained in SAS-type demolition methods and were familiar with the Lewis bomb (a .45kg mix of plastic explosive and thermite incendiary material, looking not unlike a Christmas pudding) and other destructive charges that were set to explode after a delay. Many of Lapraik's men had seen service in the desert before

they became canoeists and others had fought with the Commando Special Boat Sections. All were hardened professionals.

On 20 November the patrols arrived off Simi in two caiques and were put ashore some way from the harbour. Bob Bury, who possessed the courage and aggressive initiative demanded of all SBS men, led his force towards the enemy's headquarters. In bright moonlight, they picked their way carefully through the rubble and debris left over from previous bombings, at pains to avoid the broken glass that littered the narrow pathways leading to the governor's house. Although they could find no signs of sentries, they must have been heard by an enemy soldier because Bury caught the sound of whispered voices giving an urgent warning. Bury reacted quickly; he flung a grenade into the opening of what was a light machine-gun position sited in the damaged corner of a ground-floor room of the German HQ. After it exploded, Bury and his men heard the groans of several wounded men. Other Germans approached along the road leading from the harbour and were caught by two bursts from Sergeant 'Tanky' Geary's Schmeisser which killed all seven of them. Another German who appeared fleetingly at a window was shot by Bury.

For a few minutes after this burst of activity, an eerie quiet descended on the town. The German major was organising a counter-attack and the rest of the garrison's attention was drawn away from the boatyards. where Lapraik's team were busy. Bury took the opportunity of the lull to set at 10kg charge against the side of the building and, having set the fuse, withdrew towards a rendezvous with Lapraik's demolition team. As Bury made his way clear of the buildings, he took the precaution of delaying any pursuers by dropping a booby-trapped charge where it might be seen in the moonlight. Moments later, it exploded, causing more casualties to the garrison.

Left: A key factor in the success of the Simi raid was good intelligence on the location and strength of the enemy. Here, two men are working with a wireless whilst another pair keep a careful watch for signs of an Axis patrol. Below right: Dehydration was an ever-present danger in the eastern Mediterranean, and this man is taking care to drink as much water as possible. Wary of sudden attack, he has his weapons, an M1 carbine and a German sub-machine gun, close to hand. Below centre: During their return visit to Simi a few days after the first landing, Lapraik's men destroyed the enemy's deserted weapon's pits. Below left: With their Tommy-guns at the ready, two SBS men search the horizon for any signs of the remaining garrison.

Meanwhile, Lapraik's team had worked their way unseen into the boatyards and, although there was a series of machine-gun positions manned by the Fascist Militia on Molo Point above the harbour, their approach was undetected. The raiders laid incendiary devices on the skeletal frames of several caiques being built on the slipways, and then set charges on the generators they found in a small power station and in a rations store. When the time-delay pencil-fuses of these devices set them off, the Italian gunners began firing indiscriminately towards the harbour, no doubt under the impression that the raiders had boats there ready to take them off the quays. This gunfire was not only misdirected but it also revealed the exact location of each defensive position and Sergeant Whittle's team silenced them with their Brens as the other groups withdrew.

With the SBS men safely back aboard their two caiques, Lapraik decided that they should next raid Nisiros; whether this move was part of the original plan is not certain but it seems likely. Nisiros lay 40km west of Simi and the caiques would have to lie up at some stage during daylight to avoid enemy aircraft. This was done by mooring the boats close-in to the bare, bleached rocks of a deserted cove and then covering them with a fine-mesh camouflage net so that they blended in with the background. Resting places were not always found on the coast of a Greek island, and on some occasions the SBS caiques hid along the neutral Turkish coast. Their skippers carried gold coins to buy the silence of any inquisitive passerby; a quieter method, less likely to have diplomatic repercussions, than shooting him or her.

As the two caiques reached Nisiros, the SBS men saw that it had two small harbours and, being an extinct volcano, rose to over 750m. It would be the scene of the SBS's capture of two large supply lighters in March 1944, but during this raid a patrol led by Lieutenant Bimrose found only a few caiques being used by the Germans. These were set on fire and the island's submarine telephone cable was also destroyed. The cable's destruction would prevent the Germans from using the only means they had of sending messages between garrisons which could not be intercepted by radio or capturing the vessels carrying such orders. Indeed, the inter-island telephone system became one of the squadrons' main targets, during this phase of their operations in the eastern Mediterranean.

The men who had landed on Nisiros rejoined the caiques which then visited the island of Piscopi where the defenders, a handful of *carabinieri* were disarmed, and a telephone station was destroyed. The raiders then sailed back to Simi to ascertain the extent of the damage they had caused.

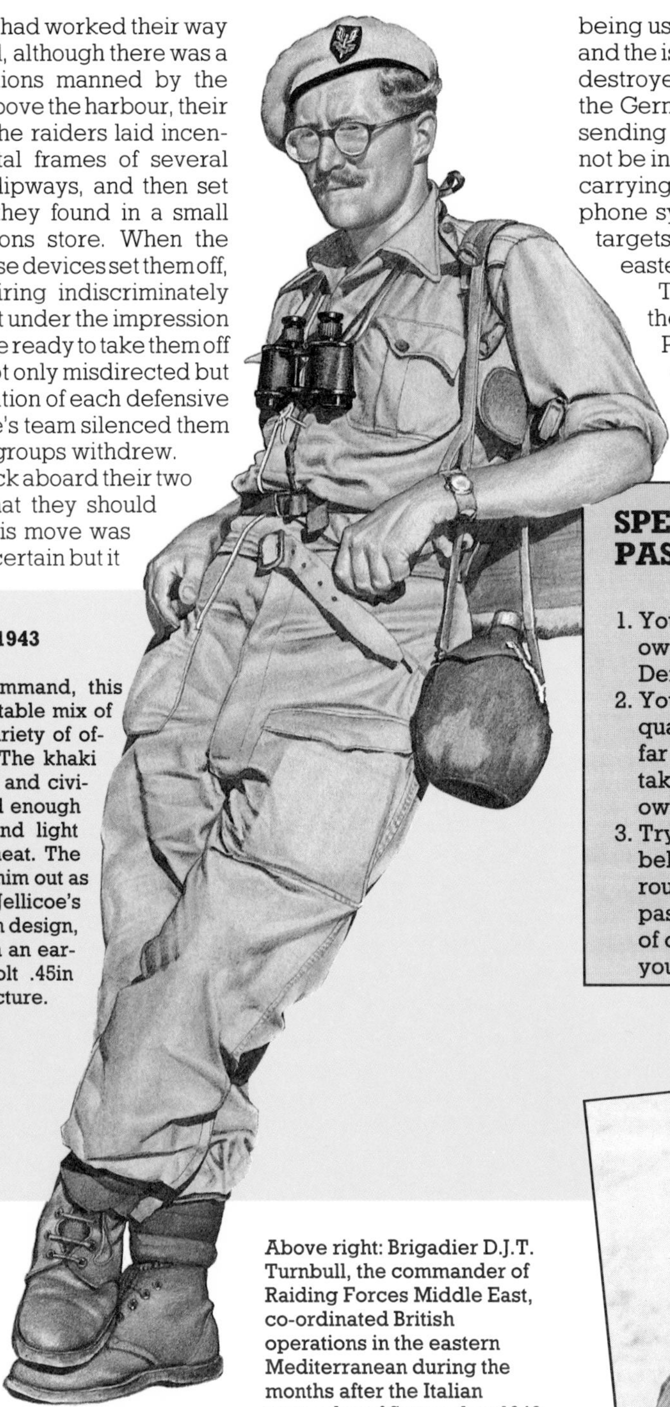

SBS officer, Simi, November 1943

Like the men under his command, this officer wears a loose, comfortable mix of clothing picked up from a variety of official and unofficial sources. The khaki denim overalls, short puttees and civilian suede boots were rugged enough to withstand hard knocks and light enough to wear in extreme heat. The beige beret and badge mark him out as one of the SAS men who joined Jellicoe's SBS. The waterbottle, an Italian design, is probably booty captured in an earlier raid. His side-arm, a Colt .45in calibre pistol, is of US manufacture.

SPECIAL BOAT SECTION PASSING OUT INSTRUCTIONS

1. You are now considered fit to operate on your own, and should be proficient in Navigation, Demolition and Scoutcraft.
2. You have been selected on your character qualifications as much as anything else and as far as we can judge, you can be trusted to take responsibility and can be trusted on your own.
3. Try and be 'world minded', remember you belong to an organisation which stretches round the globe, your SBS badge should be a passport into any Naval Mess. We are jealous of our good name, and our reputation is in your hands.

Above right: Brigadier D.J.T. Turnbull, the commander of Raiding Forces Middle East, co-ordinated British operations in the eastern Mediterranean during the months after the Italian surrender of September 1943. Right: Many of the Italian troops garrisoning the Greek islands had little desire to continue the struggle and only the threats of their German masters prevented them from surrendering. Few viewed the prospect of being a prisoner of war with regret. Far right: The SBS made heavy use of both Brens and German MP38/40s ('Schmeisser') during the raid and most, like the weapons shown here, needed to be throughly checked.

Once ashore, they also destroyed an outlying machine-gun position, pointed out to them by some of the Greek islanders. An Italian patrol attempted to prevent them withdrawing after this attack but was successfully driven off with fire from the squadron's Brens.

The raids on the three islands had been so successful that the Germans suppressed any news of them; many of the Simi garrison were casualties and 19 of the survivors deserted to Turkey rather than face the brunt of any further SBS raids. But this policy proved counter-productive as other German garrisons were not as prepared as they should have been to repel later SBS raids. Early in 1944, however, the island garrisons were strengthened with seasoned troops from the XXI Mountain Corps. The garrison on Simi consisted of a reinforced company of 210 officers and men, while larger islands like Leros had garrisons of over 4000. These reinforcements meant that fewer men were available to stem the Russians' drive into the Balkans.

The Raiding Forces Middle East maintained the pressure on these garrisons, and in July 1944 Colonel Turnbull led a force of 210 men, mainly Greeks of the Sacred Squadron but including 81 from the SBS, in an attack on Simi. The much-improved defences held out for five hours before the headquarters surrendered. The raiders then left the island.

This was the last major operation of the SBS in the Aegean; in eight months of aggressive raiding, they had forced the Germans to commit over 18,000 men to the defence of the islands. The Allies never had more than 3000 deployed in this island war, including aircrews and naval forces and the 250 men of the SBS. It was to the great credit of the SBS's commanders, men like Jock Lapraik who added a Bar to the MC he had won in Africa, and was to win a DSO and an OBE, that the Germans had to deploy such a large force in the theatre. Some measure of Lapraik's character was perhaps to be seen in his childhood; he was crippled at seven with tuberculosis of the knee, yet had become a successful middle-distance runner. He, like his men and others in the SBS, was tough.

4. If you go abroad you will very largely have to administer yourselves. People are usually helpful, but remember if you have to deal with military establishments ashore, that the personal touch will get you more than a mass of paper work would.
5. Give of your best at all times, first for the War Effort, secondly for the SBS, and lastly for yourself.
6. If you find any way that our system can be improved, put it into practice and let us know the results, and we will do the same for you.
7. The SBS Depot is your servant, let us know what you want and we will let you have it by the quickest possible means.
8. Keep in touch, and let us have regular progress reports.
9. Good luck and good hunting.

THE AUTHOR James D Ladd is one of Britain's acknowledged experts on the British Commandos. His previous works include *Inside the Commandos.*

ASSAULT SQUADRON

Although one of the youngest units in the British order of battle, 539 Assault Squadron has already amassed unrivalled expertise in the art of amphibious warfare

AS THE LONE SEA KING helicopter rose into the night air from the flight deck of a Royal Navy frigate, a long flat package dangled beneath it. After setting course, the pilot headed towards the enemy shore and dropped the inflatable boat into the water 50 miles from the target. One man left the security of the helicopter and abseiled down into the waiting vessel below. Protected from the numbing cold by several layers of clothing and a waterproof immersion suit, he wore a balaclava helmet and a pair of ski goggles to mask his face from the icy spray. Once he had motioned to the helicopter above, a further six men, laden with arms and ammunition, followed him into the boat. Seconds after their arrival, the Gemini's outboard motor sprang into life and the assault force was en route to its target.

This mission was one of many carried out by the Royal Marine assault and raiding squadrons during the Falklands conflict of 1982. As the forerunners of 539 Assault Squadron, these units demonstrated that well-practised techniques and seamanship have an essential role to play in the successful execution of amphibious operations.

From the initial Argentinian invasion on 2 April 1982, to the surrender of Argentinian forces on 14 June, the campaign to regain the Falkland Islands lasted a total of 74 days. Operation Corporate, as it was known, owed much of its success to the skill and experience of the Royal Marine amphibious units of 3 Commando Brigade.

The brigade's new role also resulted in the rationalisation of the raiding squadrons

Prior to April 1982, the Royal Marines possessed two distinct types of unit responsible for conducting amphibious landings; the assault squadrons and the raiding squadrons. The former comprised marines from the Landing Craft (LC) branch of the Royal Marines (responsible for manning the Royal Navy's assault craft since 1943), and retained their predecessors' considerable expertise in the tasks necessary for amphibious operations. It was not until the early 1970s, however, when 3 Commando Brigade became committed to the defence of NATO's northern flank, that the importance of a strong amphibious capability was finally recognised. The LC branch therefore underwent a period of expansion, with the newly formed elements beginning a series of arctic trials. The brigade's new role also resulted in the rationalisation of the raiding squadrons. 1 and 2 Raiding Squadrons had previously been an integral part of the LC branch, but in 1972 1 Raiding Squadron came under the command of the Commando Logistic Regiment. 2 Raiding Squadron was disbanded, only to be reformed in 1979 as part of the Royal Marine Reserve (RMR). An additional unit, 3 Raiding Squadron, Royal Marines, was formed in 1980 to provide amphibious support to British forces in Hong Kong.

The Royal Navy has two assault ships, known as

539 ASSAULT SQUADRON

539 Assault Squadron, Royal Marines, is an independent amphibious unit comprising 103 men all ranks, divided into four troops. Its present commander is Major Ewen Southby-Tailyour.
The Landing Craft Troop is commanded by a lieutenant and comprises three sections: an LCU section equipped with two Landing Craft Utility; an LCVP section equipped with four Landing Craft Vehicle Personnel; and an Assault Beach Unit (ABU) section. The latter is responsible for setting up beachhead communications.
The Raiding Troop comprises three raiding sections, each equipped with five Rigid Raiders. This unit possesses an integral maintenance section that is responsible for the service and repair of its craft.
The Headquarters Troop provides 539 Assault Squadron with its motor transport, communications, logistical support and administration. This unit is commanded by a lieutenant who has come up through the ranks.
The Support Troop comprises personnel from the Royal Navy, and provides the squadron with its mechanical and engineering back-up.
The men of 539 Assault Squadron, with the exception of the Royal Navy personnel, are all fully trained commandos in addition to their individual specialisations.

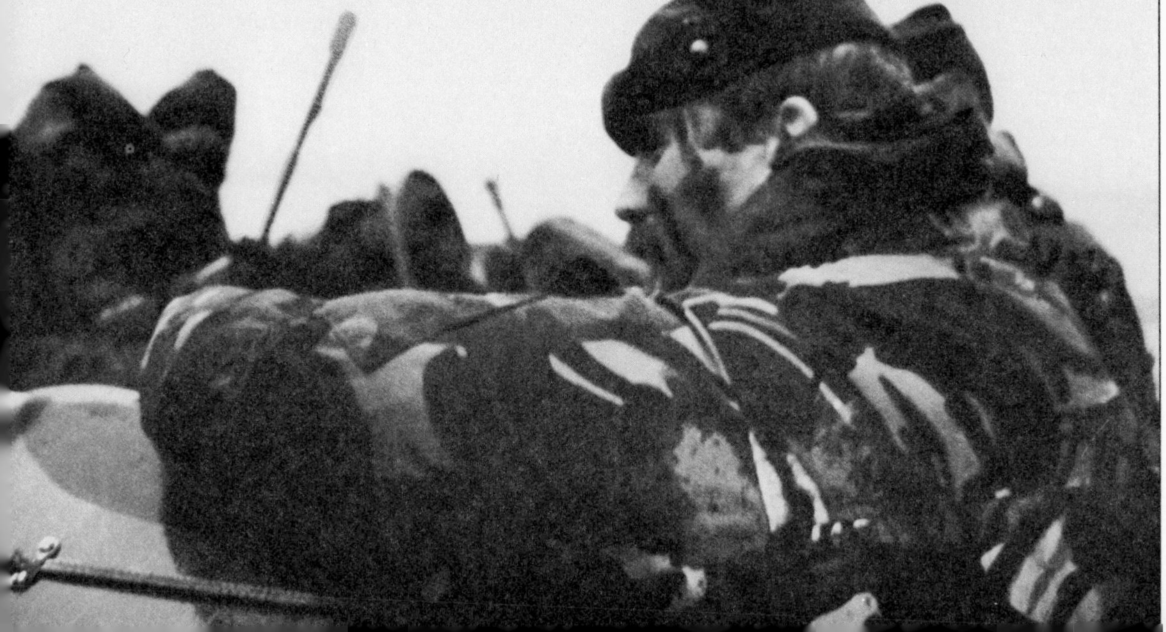

Above left: Hovering over the water, a Sea King helicopter carries out a winching drill with one of the Rigid Raiders from 539 Assault Squadron. Far left: Royal Marines from Raiding Troop disembark from a Rigid Raider during one of many exercises designed to test the operational capability of Britain's elite amphibious unit. Left: As dawn breaks, camouflaged marines complete an extraction exercise.

ASSAULT CRAFT

539 Assault Squadron is equipped with three main types of vessel with which to carry out its enormous variety of tasks. The Rigid Raider is the smallest of the craft normally operated by the squadron. Designed primarily for conducting small-scale amphibious commando raids, this 17ft craft is one of the best of its type available. The older Johnson 140 horsepower outboard engines are currently being replaced by Suzuki single engines. These have been modified to replace the noisy mechanical tilt with a manual one that is more suitable for covert operations. The 'raider' can carry nine fully equipped men, and is capable of a top speed of 40 knots. The squadron also has four Landing Craft Vehicle Personnel (LCVPs), although it is capable of operating a total of eight in war time conditions. The LCVP is fitted with an arctic canopy over the cargo deck, and the vessel has a range of 90 nautical miles at a speed of 9.5 knots. Until recently, 539 Assault Squadron operated two elderly Landing Craft Utility (LCUs), affectionately known as 'Black Pig' and 'Brown Sow'. These have now been replaced by two new LCUs (as yet unnamed) that have been specially constructed using the data compiled by the squadron during numerous trials. Controllable pitch propellers make these craft more manoeuvrable than their predecessors. Fitted with purpose-built stacking canopies known as 'igloos', the LCUs can carry up to 70 passengers and their equipment in relative comfort. Another welcome addition has been the installation of sleeping accommodation for the crew, and cooking facilities. These and other modifications make the LCUs capable of extended operations in the icy waters of northern Norway. 539 Assault Squadron also operates a number of inflatable Geminis. These small craft are more suited to warmer waters, but can be very useful for floating off submarines – a technique sometimes employed by the squadron when working in conjunction with the SBS.

Landing Platform Docks (LPDs) – HMS *Fearless* and HMS *Intrepid*. Both vessels were built specifically for amphibious operations and are capable of transporting an entire military formation, together with its supporting arms and equipment. In addition, each ship has its own assault squadron, complete with four Landing Craft Mechanised (LCMs) and four Landing Craft Vehicle Personnel (LCVPs).

Measuring 85ft and weighing 100 tons, the LCM Mk 9s are the larger of the two craft and are capable of carrying two main battle tanks or anything up to their own weight in cargo. They are transported in the LPD's docking well, allowing them to be floated out through the open stern once the assault ship has been lowered in the water by controlled flooding. The second type of craft carried by the Landing Platform Docks, the LCVPs, are transported beneath heavy davits and are capable of carrying up to 36 fully equipped troops. Both the LCMs and the LCVPs are crewed by Royal Marines, with senior NCOs commanding the LCMs, and either junior NCOs or marines commanding the LCVPs.

A third type of landing craft is also available to the Royal Marines. Known as Rigid Raiders, these vessels are 17ft in length and are capable of carrying nine fully equipped men in addition to the coxswain. When operating in arctic waters, however, only five or six men are carried. Designed specifically for use by commando units conducting amphibious operations, the 'raiders' can also be used as dive-support vessels, or to transport stores and equipment ashore.

The LCVP crews had to rely on their stealth and skill rather than heavy firepower

When the British Task Force reached the Falkland Islands in early May 1982, it was fortunate to have at its disposal the assault squadrons from both *Intrepid* and *Fearless*, in addition to 1 Raiding Squadron. Both the assault and raiding squadrons had considerable operational experience in adverse weather conditions, a factor that would weigh heavily in their favour in the South Atlantic. *Intrepid*'s assault squadron had completed exercises in northern Norway as recently as 1980, and by 1981 both assault squadrons had developed a forward base element that was capable of conducting operations without the support of their parent LPD. The credentials of 1 Raiding Squadron were equally impressive. The unit had been developing techniques for arctic operations since the early 1970s, and had completed its annual winter deployment to Norway only days before embarking on the long voyage to the South Atlantic.

The high speed of the Rigid Raider (below) is a valuable asset during patrols. In addition, a composite glass-reinforced plastic (GRP) and foam hull makes the craft virtually unsinkable, even when extensively damaged. Above: Ploughing through the water at a speed of 10 knots, a Landing Craft Vehicle Personnel Mk 4 takes part in Arctic Warfare Training exercise off the coast of Norway.

Within three days of the first British landings in the Falklands, the two assault squadrons and the raiding squadron had been formed into the Task Force Landing Craft Squadron (TFLCS), under the command of Major Ewen Southby-Tailyour, a Royal Marine officer who had been responsible for amphibious warfare trials in the Arctic. From his command post at San Carlos, Major Southby-Tailyour co-ordinated the landing craft that operated in the waters

surrounding the Falkland Islands. He knew these waters intimately, having charted the various channels, inlets and coves around the islands some five years previously, while in command of the Falklands Royal Marine detachment (NP8901).

The TFLCS carried out a wide range of tasks during Operation Corporate. It was responsible for transporting troops, vehicles, equipment and supplies ashore, and its LCMs towed HMS *Argonaut* out of the danger area after she had been bombed by Argentinian aircraft. The LCVPs also carried out numerous minesweeping missions in the surrounds of Salvador Waters and the north coast of East Falkland, trawling for acoustic and magnetic mines.

Operating a unique taxi service, the squadron moved the 1st Battalion, Scots Guards, around the south coast, and was also responsible for SAS/SBS patrol insertions and extractions. The latter, conducted under the cover of darkness, were usually carried out by a single landing craft under the command of one of the squadron's NCOs. Armed with no more than one or two General Purpose Machine Guns (GPMGs), together with the personal weapons of their passengers, the crews had to rely on their stealth and skill rather than heavy firepower. During the Falklands campaign, the TFLCS took part in every sea-launched operation undertaken by 5 Infantry Brigade and 3 Commando Brigade. The skill and experience level of the LCM, LCVP and Rigid Raider crews was put to the test, and they passed their ordeal by fire with flying colours, playing a crucial role in the eventual British victory. The unit lost only six men, with 11 awards being made for gallant and distinguished service.

Below: A Rigid Raider sets out for shore from 'Black Pig', one of the squadron's Landing Craft Utility (LCUs). Being spacious and self-contained (left), the LCUs can operate independently, staying away from their parent vessel for extended periods and acting as a base for the smaller LCVPs and Rigid Raiders. They are capable of breaking through ice up to 12in thick, and can land oversnow vehicles such as the BV 202 directly onto the ice.

The Rigid Raiders usually operate at night, arriving at the drop-off point at last light

After the Task Force returned from operations in the South Atlantic, the case for an independent squadron was put forward and accepted – 539 Assault Squadron was officially formed in April 1984. The new squadron's first, and present, commander is Major Southby-Tailyour, who was awarded the OBE for his service during the Falklands campaign. During the reorganisation, 1 Raiding Squadron was amalgamated into the 539 Assault Squadron and became Raiding Troop. Today, the squadron comprises a headquarters troop, a support troop, one landing craft troop and one raiding troop. The raiding troop is divided into three raiding sections (including an integral maintenance section), and is equipped with a total of 23 Rigid Raiders.

Various tactics are practised by the squadron, providing it with a variety of options that can be employed according to each situation and mission objective. The Rigid Raiders usually operate at night, arriving at the drop-off point (DOP) at last light

to deliver their passengers on a beach within striking distance of the target. Secure beaches are preferred, and the squadron will seek to ensure that there is a patrol already in position to direct the raiders ashore either by torch signals or radio. Each raiding section has five boats, capable of carrying one commando rifle troop between them. For defence, they rely on speed and stealth, having only the personal weapons of their passengers to protect them should they encounter enemy fire.

During the Falklands campaign, the commandos of 1 Raiding Squadron conducted a diversionary raid on Wireless Ridge, just outside Port Stanley. Carrying a combined SAS/SBS force, the raiders came under intense fire from Argentinian defenders. They were able to extract themselves from a potentially disastrous situation by the skill of their coxswains and the high performance of their craft. Many of the coxswains who today serve with 539 Assault Squadron saw action with the Task Force Landing Craft Squadron, and their expertise is renowned throughout the Royal Marines.

For large lifts, the squadron would employ its LCVPs. These have been fitted with arctic canopies; special fibreglass constructions beneath which the passengers are protected from the hostile weather outside. Temperatures can drop to below -70 degrees centigrade in the Arctic, and protection from the elements plays a vital part in the planning of amphibious operations – particularly when Rigid Raiders are used. However, this does not restrict operations, as exercise 'Cold Winter '75' proved. Here, the Arctic Warfare Section of raiders covered over 250km in under 10 hours to carry out a behind-the-lines attack on the positions of 'enemy' Norwegian forces.

In addition to the Rigid Raiders and LCVPs, the

squadron has two Landing Craft Utility (LCUs). These are the largest landing craft operated by 539 Assault Squadron, and they are also fitted with removable stacking canopies for use in arctic conditions. Each is capable of housing up to 70 troops in relative comfort – allowing them to feed, wash and dry out while being transported through the fjords to their drop-off point.

However, it is not the craft that make 539 Assault Squadron such a formidable unit, but the men that operate them. The unit's annual training cycle begins in January when the squadron deploys to Harstad, in northern Norway. For three months, the men undergo an arduous Arctic Warfare Training schedule designed to test them to the limit of their endurance. This constitutes the squadron's principal training task of the year. Between May and July, the various troops undergo three two-week training courses during which each man's basic military skills are evaluated. These exercises also provide an opportunity to put the squadron's landing craft and crew through their paces in a variety of combat scenarios. This 'raiding training' is carried out in conjunction with 40 and 42 Commando, Royal Marines, either in the Plymouth area or off the coasts of Wales or North Devon.

The 3 Commando Brigade exercise is held in Scotland or northwest Europe between September and November. For one month, the whole squadron conducts a wide range of amphibious operations, ranging from the transport of men, equipment and supplies ashore from large vessels, to the co-ordination of small raiding parties during 'attacks' on specific targets. Towards the end of each year, in a training programme known as 'black shod', each troop prepares itself for the forthcoming winter deployment to Norway. This acclimatisation

The marines of 539 Assault Squadron must be prepared to fight by land and by sea, and their annual deployment to Norway provides an opportunity to put their combat skills to the test. Far left: Marines loose off a few rounds from a General Purpose Machine Gun during live weapons training. Right: Taken with a night-vision lens, this photograph shows Raiding Troop covering a 'beachhead' during an exercise conducted under the cover of darkness. Below right: Having deposited its cargo on the shore, an LCU returns to the stern docking well of HMS *Intrepid*. Main picture: Three Rigid Raiders head out towards *Intrepid* in line abreast following manoeuvres in Norway.

Left: Abseiling, usually with full equipment, is an essential part of 539 Assault Squadron's training.

programme usually takes the form of one week in Wales or Scotland, where the men practise night navigation across country, rock climbing and river crossings. They also carry out a series of endurance marches, or 'yomps'. Throughout the year, each troop also carries out a series of minor tasks and training periods that include nuclear, biological and chemical (NBC) exercises. The squadron's training never ceases, a factor that ensures unrivalled expertise in the techniques of amphibious operations.

The squadron currently has a standing strength of 103 all ranks. The crew of the landing craft and Rigid Raiders are all fully trained commandos who have seen service with rifle companies before specialising in amphibious warfare.

There are three grades of coxswain in the squadron. The lowest grade is LC 3, a standard that all marines joining the unit must attain, allowing them to crew an LCVP or LCU. The LC 3 course lasts for four weeks and teaches basic seamanship. The next level is LC 2, which can only be reached after passing an intensive course that lasts 10 weeks. This qualification allows the marine or junior NCO to cox an LCVP, Rigid Raider or Gemini inflatable or, alternatively, to be the second coxswain of an LCU. The highest grade is LC 1, attained only after passing a demanding 12-week course. The LC 1 course requires a high standard of navigation as well as seamanship and boat handling. The squadron's LC 1s are senior NCOs with years of experience in amphibious operations behind them. In addition to these qualifications, Royal Marine NCOs may be awarded the Bridge Book-keeping Certificate when serving with one of the assault squadrons aboard a Landing Platform Dock.

There can be no substitute for a wealth of practical and operational experience

To maintain the skill in amphibious operations for which it is famous, 539 Assault Squadron relies heavily upon realistic training – seamanship cannot be taught on a simulator. Even when it is cold, wet and miserable, and the boat is bucking around, the coxswains must be capable of looking after their passengers and payload before delivering them safely to their destination.

Although 539 Assault Squadron, Royal Marines, is barely three years old, the unit has already developed a tremendous esprit de corps. Among its personnel are some of the most experienced NCOs in the Royal Marines, men highly skilled in the art of amphibious warfare. Many of their officers have turned down promotion in order to stay with this small but outstanding unit.

Amphibious operations, particularly in the Arctic region, demand a great deal of skill and practise for them to be effective. The expertise of 539 Assault Squadron is therefore seen as a vital element in NATO's defence of its northern flank. There can be no substitute for a wealth of practical and operational experience, and the men of 539 Assault Squadron possess an abundance of both.

THE AUTHOR Peter Macdonald is a freelance defence photo-journalist and served with the British Army and Rhodesian Security Forces between 1974-80.

UNDERWATER SOLDIERS

OPS

True to their motto 'Ubique', the divers of the Royal Engineers are equipped to operate in every type of hazardous underwater environment

THE MOTTO of the Royal Engineers is 'Ubique', (Everywhere), and this includes engineering work under the water as well as on land. The Royal Engineers have been diving since 1838, and were the first military or naval unit in the world to recognise the importance and potential of being able to work underneath the water. Today, they select, train and administer the divers of the British Army; the amphibious operations teams of 148 Commando Forward Observation Battery, Royal Artillery, a small number of Royal Electrical and Mechanical Engineers (REME) soldiers who attend tank river-crossing sites in case of breakdowns, and their own expert underwater engineering and reconnaissance teams.

Royal Engineer divers carry out combat engineer and artisan tasks, and are also responsible for underwater bomb disposal. On operations, they would use mines to create underwater obstacles at vehicle crossing points, demolish bridge piers, abutments and lock gates, detect and clear mines and obstacles, and recce beach, river and canal bottoms to assess currents, hazards and profiles for landing and crossing sites. Sapper bridging equipment requires the presence of divers to help with emplacement and removal. The danger of enemy sabotage to quay walls, locks, sluices and dams, requires the divers to spend very long periods submerged, searching for these underwater hazards. Artisan tasks include repairs to ships and harbour equipment, the construction of jetties, and the provision of offshore fuel and water-handling pipeline equipment. In peacetime, sapper divers help the police and public authorities in a wide range of tasks; from searches for murder weapons and victims, to the demolition of wrecks and the location and recovery of crashed aircraft and stolen vehicles. Sapper diving teams also operate in Northern Ireland, their primary role being to search for explosives, bodies and weapons. They played an active part in the Falklands conflict in 1982, and have been busy in the islands since, repairing jetties and port installations damaged in the fighting. Sapper divers recently located the sunk Argentinian submarine, *Santa Fé*, in Grytviken Harbour, South Georgia.

Diving is a cold, dirty and dangerous job that demands fitness and determination. Not everyone has the physical or mental aptitude. Military diving invariably takes place in conditions where the diver's vision is extremely restricted. His hand in front of his face-mask will be lost in a brownish-green swirl of mud, stirred up as he works. The cold and the pressure of the water at depth make the use of tools very hard labour. The operations of 'sandbagging' (filling and placing sand-bags underwater), and operating the hydraulic heavy breaker (a form of rock drill), are several times more difficult underwater than on land. What is more, they require completely different techniques that can only be learned by hard experience.

When underwater, divers rely utterly upon their colleagues on the surface. Any lapse of attention or slight error could be fatal. The combination of intelligence, reliability, patience, determination and toughness is rare, and selecting the right men to train for this work has to be done with great care. Warrant Officer 2 Bill Wallace, formerly of 148 Commando Forward Observation Battery, now transferred to the Royal Army Physical Training Corps, is responsible for the three-day diving aptitude courses that all prospective army divers must pass before

AIR

Trainee divers practise an 'Awkward', a naval operation in response to frogman attack. Clockwise from bottom left: A routine exercise run is suddenly interrupted by the instructor's shout of 'Awkward' and the divers have three minutes to change into their full diving rig and form up, ready to dive (left).

being allowed to start basic diver training. The process begins with a medical examination of the parts that no amount of lager ever reaches. This includes a dental check of each filling – at depth, compressed air can get between nerve and tooth causing agony as the diver ascends and the air expands. 'We are not looking for supermen,' explains 'Q' Wallace, 'Just the sort of bloke who can react intelligently under pressure. Obviously, if he hasn't got the brainpower to start with we can't train him.'

The pressure is constant, starting with PT and moving on to the frantic pace of an 'Awkward' – the name of the operation in which Royal Navy divers prepare to search their ship's hull for limpet mines or enemy frogmen. At the single shout of 'Awkward' by one of the instructors, the candidates dash to the diving changing shed. They have three minutes to change from their combat clothing into full diving rig ready to dive. This procedure will become all too familiar to the men in their basic diver training.

'It scares me a bit, actually – you can never be certain that they've fully understood the physics of diving'

The heavy rubber suits are hot and unpleasant, and anyone who is unable to work hard while wearing the equipment ashore will not be able to survive underwater; this heat will be accompanied by very cold water trickling into the cuffs and neck seal, and body squeeze at depths over 15m. Runs through river mud at low tide, combined with swimming, test the candidates' ability to endure the constant discomfort of diving. Bill Wallace takes this initial selection procedure very seriously indeed:

> 'In the aptitude course we want to see determination rather than a high standard of physical fitness. We teach them the physics of diving and how the equipment works before we put them into cold, muddy water. It scares me a bit, actually – you can never be certain they've fully understood the physics of diving. It's a bloody dangerous game. Anyone who looks uncertain or we are not happy about we pull out early.'

About half of those candidates who start aptitude courses fail to last the distance.

For those who pass the course, there are three levels of diver training in the army: the basic Army Compressed Air Diver (ACAD); the experienced professional diver – the Army Advanced Diver (AAD); and the Army Diving Supervisor (ADS). Army divers use compressed air to its maximum limitations – down to 55m, with a usual working depth of 35m. The training combines physical effort, intensive classroom work and long cold hours underwater practising everything that has been taught during the course. Divers need to develop efficient cardiovascular systems that can make maximum use of the air available. Hearts and lungs grow larger as the students spend more and more time diving. The usual PT on land is accompanied by 'wet PT' in the water. Here, the divers gain confidence and familiarity with their equipment, finning long distances and leaping from jetties and the bows of ships.

The basic course lasts six weeks, after which the diver is able to use a wide range of tools at depths of 18m and wears a diving helmet badge with the initials 'SW', denoting 'shallow water' diver. In fact, every army diver knows that this stands for 'shark wrestler'. The advanced course lasts a further eight weeks, after which he is able to dive and work deeper (35m as normal, and up to the absolute maximum of 55m with special permission). By this stage, the level of diving skills and use of more sophisticated tools has increased greatly. Advanced Divers are the army's professional artisan divers, able to use several different types of dive set; the usual two-cylinder Aquarius, the Aga Divator for use in very confined spaces in noxious waters, the surface-supplied Kirby Morgan Bandmask, as well as the standard diver equipment.

Right: The dry-land weight of the two-cylinder Aquarius compressed air unit is around 40lb, and help is required to strap it on. Above right: W.O. Bill Wallace teaches the pre-dive procedures and equipment checks on which his trainees' lives may depend. Far right: Underwater exploration is made easier by a video camera with a fitted searchlight. Below right: A mobile decompression chamber is available should a diver suffer an attack of the bends. Below: Sparks fly as a thermal lance slices through a metal girder.

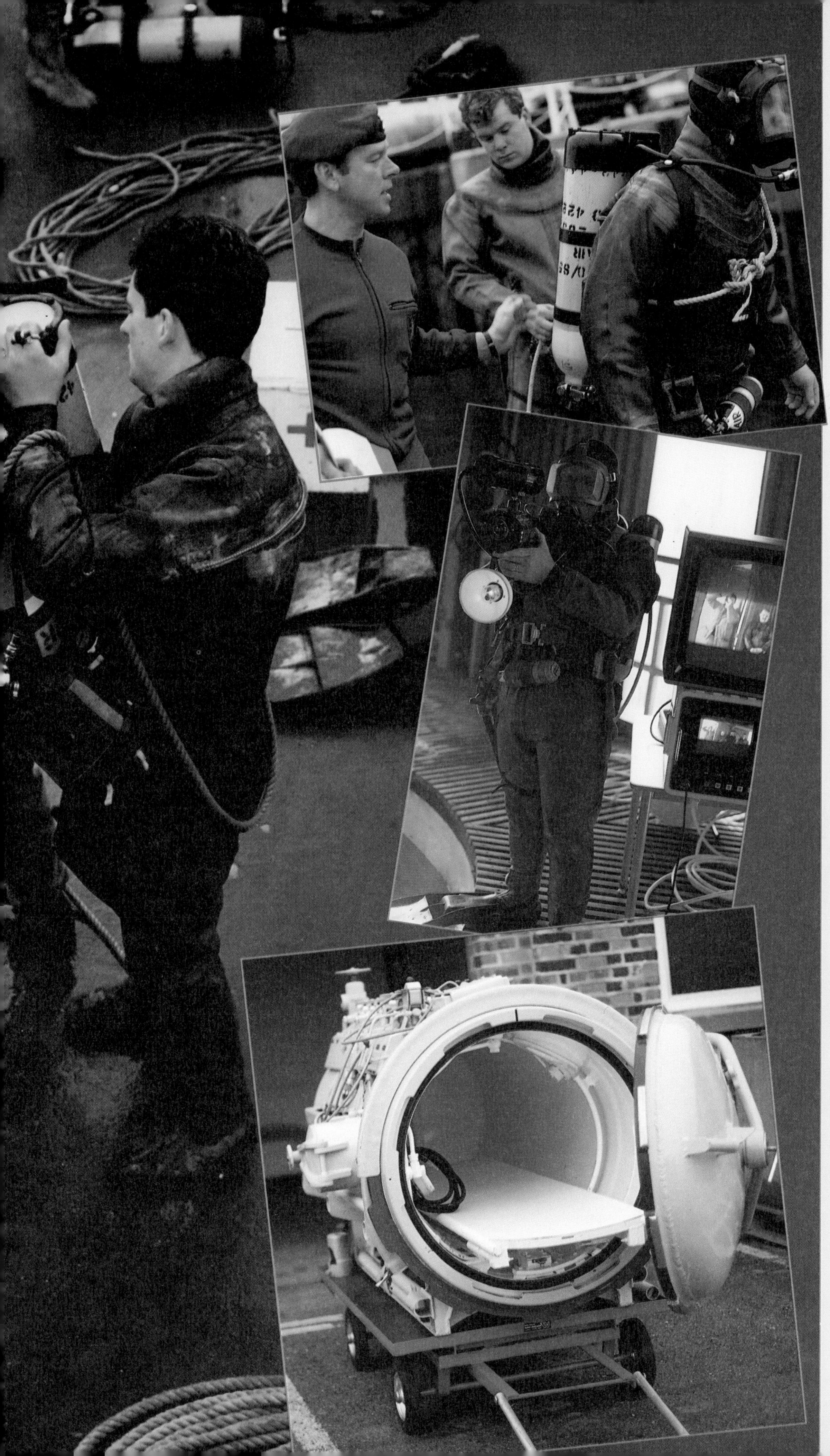

THE ROYAL ENGINEERS DIVING ESTABLISHMENT

Members of the Corps of Royal Engineers have been diving since 1838, when Colonel Pasley, who was Commandant of the Military Academy, Woolwich, and inventor of the electric detonator, experimented with the Seibe and Gorman diving apparatus and became the world's first military diver. In 1839 Pasley's divers carried out underwater explosive clearance of wrecks in Portsmouth harbour and Chatham dockyard. During operations on the wreck of the *Royal George* in Portsmouth, they accidently destroyed part of the remains of Henry VIII's warship, the *Mary Rose*, which more than a century later was to be raised by a new generation of sapper divers.

The Royal Engineers Submarine Mining Service was created in 1871 for work in dockyards throughout the world. Many lives were lost through decompression sickness and malfunctions in the early versions of Standard Diving Apparatus, with its huge copper helmet, lead boots, chest weights and heavy rubberised suit. In 1905 the Royal Navy took over many of the dockyard diving tasks and the Royal Engineers extended their operations to include inland waterways.

During World War II, sapper divers provided beach clearance teams for the Normandy landings and helped in the construction of the Mulberry harbours and the repair of bomb-damaged docks. The Royal Engineers Diving Unit was formed at Marchwood in 1963 with a wing at Kiel in Germany. The Royal Engineers Diving Establishment (REDE) was formed in 1977 and has since moved from Marchwood to HMS *Vernon*.

Royal Engineers' unit diving teams have a vast array of equipment at their disposal, including air compressors to recharge cylinders and underwater cutting gear. The latter includes the Vixen portable oxygen/hydrogen sets, the Boco electric cutting lance ('the perfect safe-crackers' kit') and the volatile Kerry cable. Hydraulic tools are powered by a Hopkins engine that produces a variable flow of hydraulic oil in a closed circuit, and include concrete breakers, rock drills, wood augers, chain saws and angle grinders. Explosive rivet guns are able to punch holes through inch-thick steel plate or drive heavy-duty bolts deep into ships' hulls to allow patch plates to be screwed on and welded.

The final level of expertise is provided by the Supervisors' course; three weeks of classroom work, evening study and the successful completion of several complicated diving tasks. Continuous diving makes necessary the intricate timetabling of decompression. Any mistake by the supervisor in the mathematics of the dive will lead to a diver suffering the agony of a serious bend which, without instant treatment, will leave him paralysed or dead.

In service, diving bends are rare. However, most weekends during the summer, the standby supervisor at HMS *Vernon* will have to treat amateur civilian divers – by 'blowing them down' to 18m in the chamber and giving neat oxygen until the nitrogen bubbles that cause the bends are removed from the body. In 1981, Staff Sergeant Tony Liddicoat saved the life of a former professional diver from New Orleans who was struck by a severe bend when on holiday in Belize – where there is no decompression chamber. The local hospital had already administered Last Rites. The patient was flown out to St George's Cay, taken two miles out to sea in an inflatable boat, and then lowered in a chair down to 30m for two hours. Staff Sergeant Liddicoat remained

with him, changing his air cylinders – despite the constant presence of sharks. It became necessary to repeat the treatment when the symptoms returned. This time, they had to brave a tropical storm, remaining submerged for over seven hours.

Hands quickly become numb and masks mist up, having to be kept half-filled with water to remain clear.

Sapper diving takes place in extremes of temperature; from the heat of the tropics to the harsh arctic winter of Norway. Being accustomed to the different types of diving gear after the exertions of wet PT during selection and training pays dividends to divers forced to work hard in tropical waters too dirty to permit the wearing of more comfortable wet suits. Diving in arctic waters poses the problem of keeping warm – not when diving, but when out of the water. Air temperatures can be 15 or 20 degrees lower than the water temperature, and the wind-chill factor increases this difference still further. Hands quickly become numb and masks mist up, having to be kept half-filled with water in order to remain clear. Senior Instructor Captain Henry Morgan compares the constant 'swooshing' around of this water to clear the condensation on the inside of the mask to 'being slapped constantly across the face with a frozen kipper.'

Sapper divers search snow-edged shorelines and bitterly cold anchorages for mines and booby traps, or lay such devices themselves as a hidden defence barrier. Diving through the ice, linked to the hole only by lifeline is, in Morgan's words: 'an eerie, quiet experience.' In amphibious operations, sapper divers are an essential part of the bustle of a busy anchorage. They install ship-to-shore refuelling supply lines, mooring the platforms and flexible hose securely to the sea bottom. In particular, the huge floating cylindrical fuel dracones impose a great strain upon their moorings. Each has to be given five separate anchorages, 'starred out' from the centre.

The underwater bomb disposal experts of the Royal Engineers are the men of 33 (EOD) Regiment, RE, stationed at Chattendene. The regiment specialises in neutralising World War II bombs found in lakes, flooded quarries and other water sites. In December 1986 it was called out to investigate an obstruction to a water sump 40ft down, at the base of No. 4 gas holder, Beckton Gas Works, East Ham. The divers discovered a German 1000-pounder that was accessible only through the airlock at the top of the gasometer. Using a bosun's chair and winch, they had to be lowered through darkness down to the surface of the water – inside the pressure tower. Samples taken from the nose section of the bomb were sent away for analysis. The results showed that the TNT was still volatile. After local police had evacuated the area, Major Robbie Hall and his team dived again into the pitch-black waters of the gas holder, winching out the bomb and extricating it with some difficulty through the narrow entrance of the airlock at the top of the gas holder. Almost 12 hours later, the bomb, its explosive filling carefully steamed out, was declared safe.

During the Falklands conflict, sapper divers from 59 Independent Commando Squadron, RE, started working at Ascension Island before the Task Force sailed for the South Atlantic. The threat of Argentinian sabotage to warships in the anchorage led to Operation Awkward, in which all the ships' hulls were searched for limpet mines and explosives. By day and night, the water was very clear and visibility good. But waste pipes and garbage disposal had made the ships a major attraction to large shoals of

The old-fashioned diving suit (top left), which is supplied with air via a tube from the surface, is still in constant use at the Royal Engineers Diving Establishment. A modern version of this type of suit is used during lengthy dives when frequent surfacing to change air cylinders may interfere with the task in hand. Several methods are used to clear underwater obstructions; beams and spars are cut through with a chain saw (below left) while more substantial obstacles have to be destroyed with explosives (below right). The ropes attached to the divers are not only a safety measure to enable them to be pulled up quickly in an emergency, but are also a means of communication with the surface. A code of signals made up of 'bells' (a short tug) and 'pulls' (a sustained pull) enables complicated messages to be transmitted.

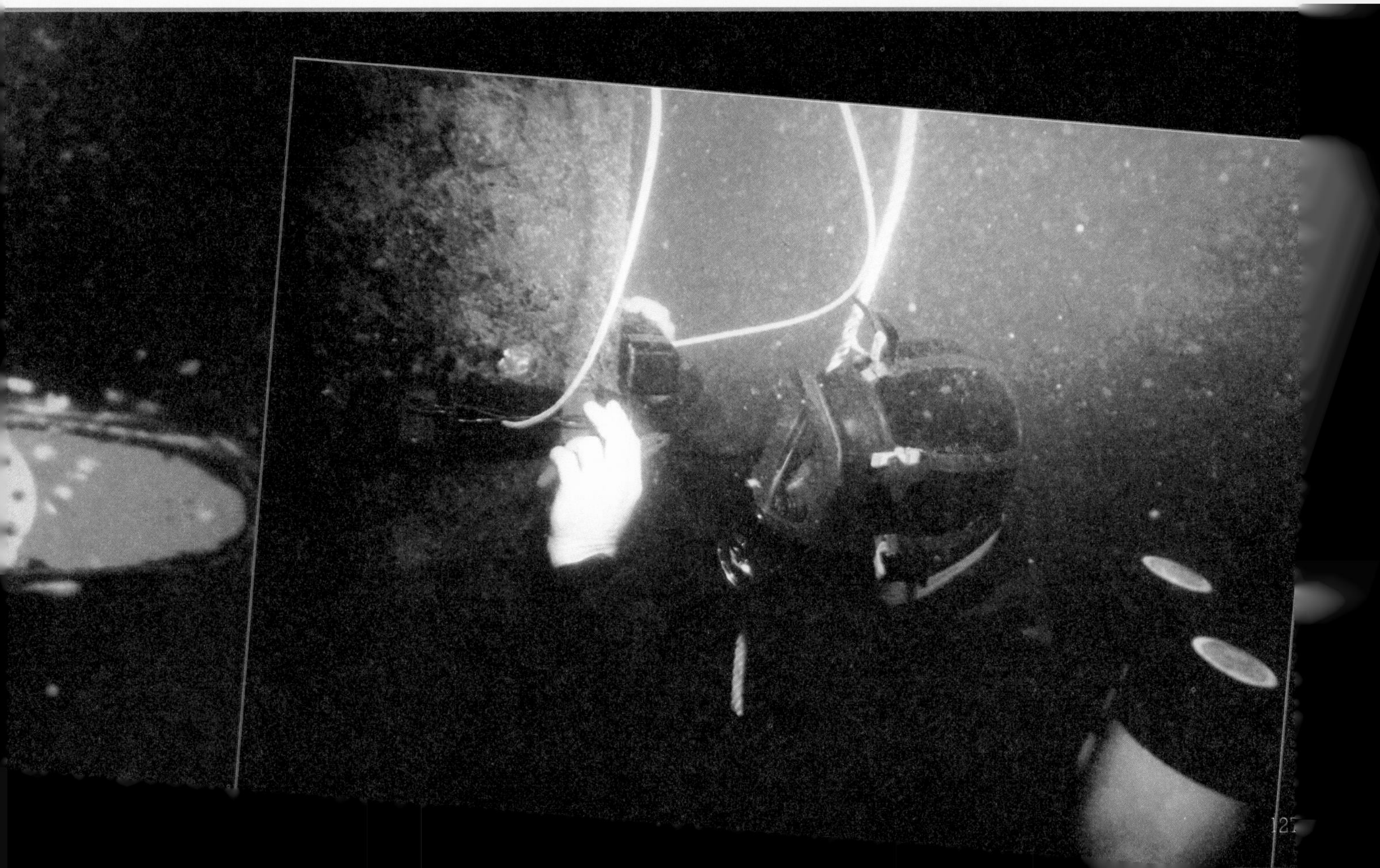

SAPPER TRAINING

All Royal Engineers are trained as infantry soldiers and can be called upon in time of war to form extra infantry units for reinforcement and reserve duties. Their main work, however, is combat engineering, including the laying and clearance of minefields, trench digging and the construction of defensive bunds around artillery pieces and Harrier launch pads, the creation and clearance of obstacles, and the repair or destruction of roads, bridges and airfields. In addition to these infantry and combat engineer roles, all sappers possess at least one artisan skill – for example as welder, bricklayer, carpenter, plant operator, mechanic, pipe fitter, electrician or blacksmith. These skills are developed to a very high level and require a great deal of time to maintain. Sappers may volunteer to undergo specialist training, for example, as commandos and paratroopers. Their basic infantry and combat engineer training must still continue, in spite of the demanding nature of these particularly arduous additional skills. Sappers also circulate from one unit to another every three years in order to acquire the maximum engineer experience. Many men rotate from the sapper parachute squadron (9 Squadron) to the commando squadron (59 Squadron). Diving is a particularly demanding specialist qualification. The careful training is designed to enable the normal engineering skills already mastered by each combat engineer to be used in all types of underwater environment. The maintenance of diving skills takes much effort on the part of each soldier and a lot of training time. It is not surprising, therefore, that red and green berets are often seen around the Royal Engineers Diving Establishment.

trigger fish (nicknamed 'shit fish'). Divers with cuts or open abrasions would be swiftly surrounded by a swirling black cloud. Over 19 hours were logged at depths down to 30m. On 24 May, after the landings at San Carlos, Lieutenant Richard Hendicott and his team from 59 Commando Squadron, RE, installed vital emergency fuel-handling equipment (EFHE) anchorages and carried out recces for landing sites at Port San Carlos.

At the time of 2 Para's attack on Darwin and Goose Green, a 70ft coastal craft crewed by Argentinians was unable to sail, having fouled its propeller. As the vessel had become an obstruction, Corporal Speak and Lance-Corporal Smith flew down immediately after the battle to clear the fouling. Their task, complicated by bad weather, took them three hours. They also checked the foot of a jetty (where Argentinians had dumped large quantities of weapons and ammunition to ensure that they were safe), recovering some abandoned radio equipment in the process. Even after the end of hostilities, sapper divers were still very active in the Falklands: siting underwater cables and slipways, searching ships' hulls, carrying out basic repairs, clearing fouled propellers, searching for weapons, radios and sunken vessels, and performing general tasks in connection with harbour construction and maintenance.

Less well known is the recovery of a crashed Soviet military aircraft from the Harvel river in 1971. Following the accident, on the border between East and West Berlin, the race to recover the wreckage was won by the Royal Engineers, who recovered the plane – the engine of which was of particular interest

The divers of the Royal Engineers Diving Unit are used to working in extremes of temperature, from the sub-zero conditions of arctic waters (bottom left) to the warmer and more hospitable Solent, where they were recently involved in the successful task of raising the Tudor warship *Mary Rose*.

When the decision was taken in 1980 to recover the warship *Mary Rose* from the seabed, the Royal Engineers were called in to assist. Lieutenant-Colonel Peter Chitty, Superintendant of Army Diving, planned the delicate lifting operation and Captain Jon Branham, the Inspector of Army Diving, was appointed Project Officer. He played a vital part in the design and development of the lifting frame and cradle in which the ship was raised (above). Fifty-two sapper divers worked for six months to suspend the wooden ship in a network of wires and move it into the tubular metal cradle constructed under water to receive it (top left, below).

to the military experts.

The worst jobs, in the eyes of sapper divers themselves, are sewer searches – a constant requirement in Northern Ireland. The compact Aga Divator equipment allows divers to squeeze through narrow spaces, and provides air at slightly over the surrounding water pressure to prevent sewer water poisoning. These searches, for weapons, explosives and bodies, are cold, laborious and tedious.

The Royal Engineers divers have an enviable safety record. In spite of the hazardous nature of the work, and of the environment in which it takes place, since the last war there have been only three deaths attributable to diving over that period. Commanding officer Lieutenant-Colonel Roger Mundy always encourages visiting senior officers to try on the divers' equipment and have a short dive. His reason is simple: 'Because otherwise it is impossible for anyone to understand what it is like for the working diver.' He justifies the careful psychological, physical and educational preparation of army divers not in terms of the heavy manual work that they perform, but of the circumstances in which they have to operate. 'They work,' he says, with some understatement, 'in a very unforgiving environment.'

THE AUTHOR Major Hugh McManners, an Army Unit Diving Supervisor, was one of the Naval Gunfire Forward Observers of 148 Commando Forward Observation Battery during the Falklands campaign of 1982. His book, *Falklands Commando*, has recently been published in paperback. The author and publishers would like to thank Lieutenant-Colonel Roger Mundy, Captain Henry Morgan, SMI Les Rutherford, WO2 Bill Wallace and Major Leslie Richmond, without whose help this article would not have been possible.

As Viet Cong operations in South Vietnam increased in scale, the US developed a riverine force to attack and sever enemy supply lines

AS THE UNITED States began to commit its ground forces to combat in Vietnam in 1965, so too it began a campaign in that country's 'brown waters' (those of rivers and coasts as opposed to the 'blue water' of the oceans in naval terminology). The unique requirements of riverine and inshore operations spawned a new group of weaponry, fashioned specifically for warfare in this environment.

The armed forces of the United States were by no means breaking new ground. During the early stages of the Indochina War, both France and the Republic of Vietnam had developed small flotillas of vessels designed to patrol and operate along the rivers and coasts. The experience of these operations, during the 1940s, 1950s and 1960s, was utilised by the US Military Assistance Command, Vietnam (MACV) when it began to approach the problem of military missions on brown waters. However, MACV planned from the outset to take a deliberate, even slow, approach to the formation of its inshore and riverine force. The first step was to obtain the authorisation of the Joint Chiefs of Staff in Washington for stop-and-search missions against the coastal shipping of Vietnam, since it was obvious that the Viet Cong (VC) and North Vietnamese Army (NVA) were receiving substantial supplies of weapons, ammunition and medical equipment from this route. The US Navy established Task Force 71 (TF 71) to undertake Operation Market Time, beginning on 11 May 1965. This force later became Task Force 115 and, to better integrate its operations in the broad scope of US intervention, it came under the direct command of MACV.

The only vessels actually engaged in stopping the coastal traffic were the Coast Guard cutters

At the outset of its operations, in August 1965, TF 115 consisted of seven destroyer escorts equipped with radar, two ocean-going minesweepers, two (later three) Landing Ships, Tank (LSTs) also equipped with radar, 17 Coast Guard cutters, plus several squadrons of maritime reconnaissance aircraft. Of these, the only vessels actually engaged in stopping the coastal traffic were the Coast Guard cutters. These 65-tonne boats possessed a top speed of 20 knots and were armed with a 0.5in machine gun and an 81mm mortar in a dual mounting in the bow, with a pair of 20mm guns mounted in the stern.

When Market Time began, the navy was well aware that the Task Force possessed insufficient numbers of the Coast Guard cutters to ensure an adequate patrol of the coast. To supplement them in their duties, a new craft was ordered from Sewart Seacraft of Louisiana, based on a boat which had been designed to service the oil-drilling rigs in the Gulf of Mexico, off the coasts of Louisiana and Texas. Called 'Swifts', these boats were 50ft long and could

Right: Stop-and-search patrol for a PBR. Above right: A Swift cruises up the Mekong Delta. The oversized helmet of its rear gunner (far right) contains communication equipment linked to the bridge, allowing the commander to direct fire against enemy positions.

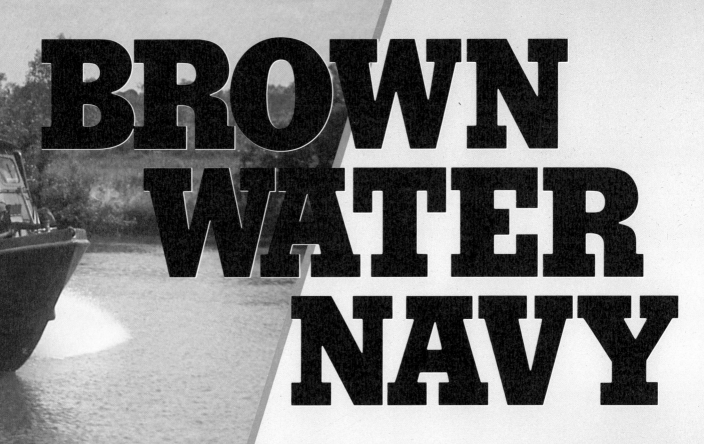

BROWN WATER NAVY

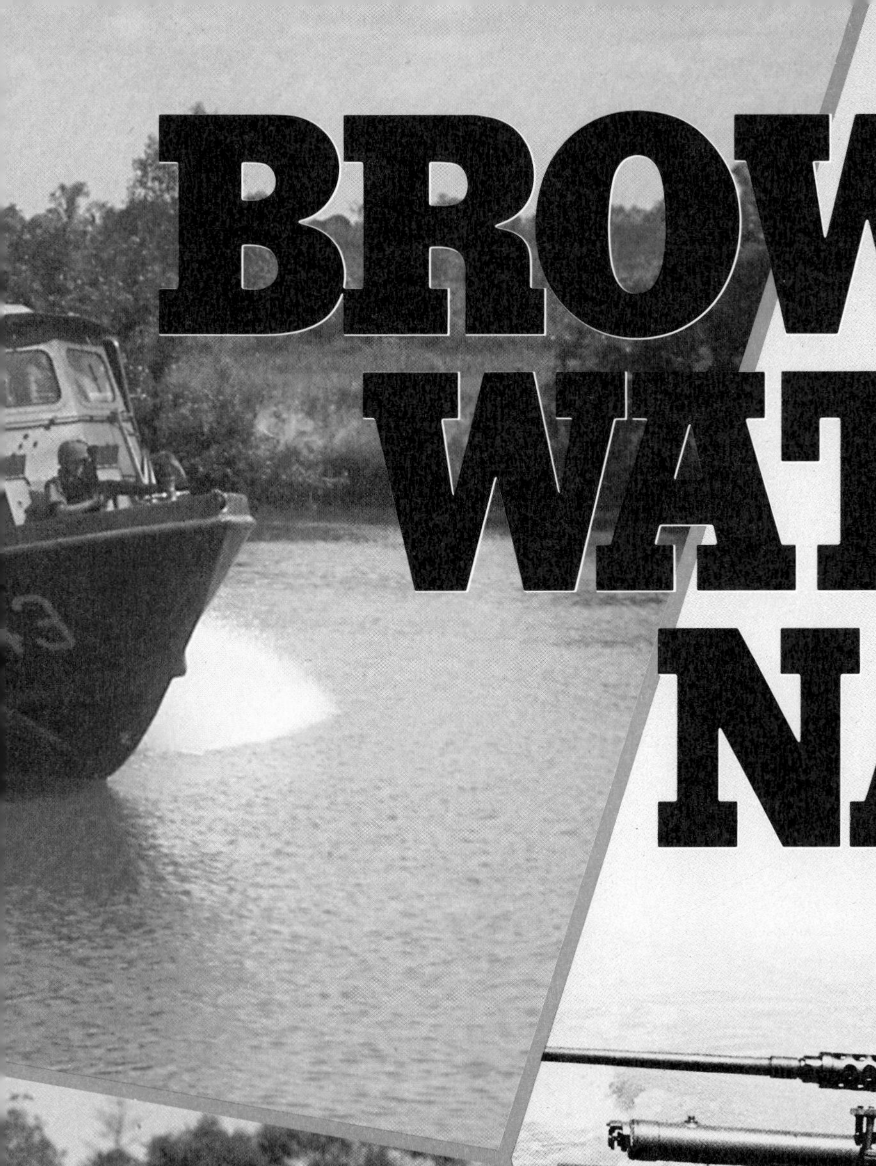

EARLY RIVERINE FORCES

During the Indochina War of 1946-54, French forces created the *Dinassaut*, a combat organisation capable of operating in the hostile environment of Vietnam's waterways. Each *Dinassaut* comprised a variety of modified landing craft. Some were deployed in a fire support role, mounting a multitude of weapons that included 0.3in and 0.5in machine guns and 20mm, 40mm or 57mm cannon. Other craft such as the French River Patrol Boat (FOM), were only lightly armoured and could not stand up to the heavy fire of an ambush. However, their 20mm cannon and high speed made them invaluable as stop-and-search craft.

Landing Craft, Vehicle and Personnel (LCVP) vessels were armed with 20mm cannon and a number of 0.3in and 0.5in machine guns. They were used as escorts for river convoys and in search-and-destroy missions against guerrilla forces.

In 1953 the first Vietnamese naval units were established, coming under South Vietnamese control two years later. The main equipment of the Vietnamese *Dinassauts* was the French Vedette patrol boat, until it was replaced by newer American equipment in the 1960s. By 1964, the Vietnamese river forces, now known as River Assault Groups (RAGs) possessed over 200 craft.

attain speeds in excess of 25 knots. Armament usually comprised twin 0.5in machine guns mounted over the pilothouse, with a dual 0.5in and 81mm mounting in the stern. The crew of the boat also had available M79 40mm grenade launchers and M60 7.62mm light machine guns to supplement their firepower. The official designation of the Swift was Patrol Craft, Fast (PCF) and two variants were built: the Mark I and the Mark II, the latter distinguished by its pilothouse set further astern. The US Navy took delivery of 104 Mark Is and about 95 Mark IIs.

The largest craft deployed by the navy for preventing seaborne infiltration were the gunboats of the 'Asheville' class. These began to enter service in early 1966 and were armed with a single 3in gun in a forward turret, two twin 0.5in machine guns mounted on the superstructure, and a 40mm anti-aircraft gun astern. They could reach speeds of up to 40 knots with their gas turbine engines, but for longer cruising they would use a diesel engine. Although their length of 161ft and 225-tonne displacement made them much larger than the Swifts and Coast Guard cutters, the lightly-armoured hull of the Asheville gunboat made it extremely vulnerable to rocket attack.

The tactics employed in Market Time operations were based on radar. Contact with a target would be established by picket destroyer, minesweeper or aircraft, and this position would be radioed to a Swift, cutter or gunboat waiting in port. The intercepting

One of the main tasks of the PBR (left) was to patrol the waterways of Vietnam, searching the numerous junks and sampans that were suspected of ferrying weapons and supplies to the Viet Cong. Bottom left: A PBR Mark II hugs the shoreline, on the lookout for VC. Atop the mast is a radar unit used to locate the enemy during night patrols. Inset left: A French-built LCM, modified by the South Vietnamese Navy into a Command and Communications Boat. Below: Reconnaissance by fire.

vessel would then attempt to intersect the course of the target by means of a vector on the target's compass heading, supplemented by updated information radioed from the contact ship or aircraft.

The US Navy also established a complementary force to conduct similar operations on the rivers of southern Vietnam. Task Force 116, codenamed Game Warden, was set up in September 1965 to assist Vietnamese river forces in denying the VC the use of the inland waterways. Requiring a type of craft not present on the navy's inventory, once again the appropriate vessel was adapted from a civilian design. In November 1965, United Boatbuilders, a pleasure craft manufacturer located in Washington State, received an order for 120 small boats based on one of its designs. The result was the Patrol Boat, River (PBR), a 31ft vessel that was to form the backbone of Task Force 116. The hull was made of fibreglass, lined with plastic foam, and the craft was propelled and steered by two pumped water jets to a top speed of 25 knots. Armament, as with the Swifts, could vary, but the most common layout was a twin 0.5in forward mounting, and a 0.3in machine gun mounted behind a shield in the stern. The crew also had an M79 grenade launcher at its disposal. The engine compartment was protected by thin armour, capable of stopping small calibre rounds. Operational experience led to an improved PBR, the Mark II, being ordered from United Boatbuilders in March 1967. This model was slightly larger, with armament upgraded to a third 0.5in in place of the 0.3in machine gun, plus a 60mm mortar.

Game Warden, as its name implies, was a policing operation similar to Market Time. The PBRs cruised the rivers and waterways of southern Vietnam, hoping to cover up to 30 miles during 12-hour patrols. At night, patrols were more frequent – any Vietnamese craft underway at that time was in violation of the curfew, and constituted fair game.

Its basic unit was the river assault squadron, made up of a wide variety of ships and boats

Neither Market Time nor Game Warden was capable of conducting assault operations, yet the inability of the Republic of Vietnam to contain the activities of large Viet Cong forces active in the Mekong Delta, and on the river approaches to Saigon, created a demand for a riverine combat force. MACV chose to deploy US ground forces in Corps Tactical Zone IV, covering the Mekong area. However, there seemed no easy method of basing them in such a densely populated area with scarcely any unused land available. As most of their operations would be conducted on inland waterways, the staff at MACV opted to base this new force on water. This decision led to the creation of the Mobile Riverine Force (MRF).

The Mobile Riverine Force was composed of two elements: the 2nd Brigade, 9th Infantry Division, and the US Navy's Task Force 117. All shipping elements were to be controlled by TF 117. Its basic unit was the river assault squadron, made up of a wide variety of ships and boats. Most of these were modelled on the Landing Craft, Mechanized (LCM) 6 – a basic vessel in the US Navy's postwar amphibious fleet. These craft were 55ft long, and were designed to carry up to 12 troops, or one tank. To adapt them for riverine operations, it was necessary to arm and armour them.

The most common boat in the river assault squadrons was the Armoured Troop Carrier (ATC), which was capable of carrying a full infantry platoon. A framework of steel slats, resembling Venetian blinds, was placed on the sides of the hull and superstructure, affording protection against RPG or recoilless-rifle rounds. The superstructure was redesigned to carry a 20mm cannon in a barbette at the rear, while just in front of the 20mm position were two 0.5in machine guns in barbettes, one on either side of the superstructure. The attachment of a large steel plate over the cargo well on ATC (H)s could be used as a helicopter pad, and these craft were used as first aid stations, with operating facilities below deck. Later models of ATCs had, in addition to the normal armament, two Mk 18 40mm grenade launchers. Each river assault squadron had 26 ATCs, one of which was fitted out as a refueller – indispensable during prolonged operations.

The LCM(6) hull also provided the basis for two further ships of the MRF: Monitors and Command and Control Boats (CCBs). Both of these types had

SHARKMOUTHED RAIDER

One of the most unique craft employed by the US Army and Navy on missions in the Mekong Delta was the Patrol Air Cushion Vehicle (PACV), or hovercraft. Produced by Bell Aerosystems, the PACV (above) was designed to operate over both land and water and had the ability to move over low obstacles and clear 5ft waves. The navy hoped to use the PACVs to replace the helicopters of TF 116, while the army sought to improve the mobility of the MRF. The craft were 39ft long and weighed five tonnes, with a General Electric LM-100 gas turbine engine that provided a top speed of 60 knots over water. Armament was limited to twin 0.5in machine guns mounted above the pilot's cockpit. In May 1966, three PACVs were deployed to Vietnam for evaluation by the Market Time and Game Warden forces, operating on the inland waterways and coastal waters respectively. During Operation Quai Vat, in the region known as the 'Plain of Reeds', the PACVs showed that they were effective in combat conditions. Their massive shape, noise and the dust they kicked up had a huge psychological effect on the Vietnamese. PACV crews began to use 'monster' as their call sign and painted large shark mouths and slanted eyes on the front skirts of the hovercraft. However, in 1969 the PACVs were withdrawn from the I Corps area after three years of continuous operation and taken out of service.

similar armament. The ramp of the LCM(6) was removed, and replaced with a rounded bow, on which was mounted a 40mm cannon, capable of a high volume of fire during landing operations. In a well between the superstructure and the 40mm gun turret, the Monitor carried an 81mm mortar along with two 0.3in machine guns. In addition, at least two Mark 18 grenade launchers were carried. The CCBs replaced the mortar with a shed-like structure that contained the communications equipment essential to battalion and task force commanders during operations. On some of the Monitors, the 40mm cannon was replaced by a flamethrower. Each river assault squadron had 3 CCBs and 5 Monitors.

The Mobile Riverine Force had at its disposal only one boat specifically designed for its operations: the Assault Support Patrol Boat (ASPB). These were 50ft long with a crew of five, and were designed to provide fire support in addition to minesweeping duties. The hull was made of steel, while the superstructure was made of aluminium to save weight. A 20mm cannon was carried in a bow turret, while a turret on top of the superstructure carried the ubiquitous 0.5in machine gun in a twin mounting. An 81mm mortar was carried aft, plus two Mk 18 grenade launchers. Although designed to attain a top speed of 16 knots, in service these vessels could only manage 14. To reduce engine noise, a unique underwater exhaust system was used. There were 16 of these boats in a river assault squadron and they were employed in a wide variety of roles: ambushes, patrols, reconnaissance and escort missions.

Much of the heavy weaponry of the battalions which comprised the Mobile Riverine Force was deleted from their table of organisation and equipment. It was hoped that the heavily-armed ASPBs and Monitors would provide the compensatory firepower. However, a battalion of artillery was attached to the 2nd Brigade and it was planned to deploy its 105mm howitzers in support of operations. An ATC would carry the gun and its towing vehicle to the site of a firebase on the river bank. The ATC would then beach, allowing the howitzer and its tow to drive onto the shore. The terrain of the Delta, however, gave rise to doubts as to whether such a plan was feasible. Tidal pull on the Mekong is very strong, and the difference in water level can be as much as 13ft; in addition, the river banks themselves are very steep. Lieutenant-Colonel Carroll Meek, the commander of the 3rd Battalion, 34th Artillery, began experiments on a novel way of basing the howitzers. Placing the 105mm on a barge and finding that it could be fired safely, Meek asked to have a barge specifically designed for the purpose of basing the 105mms.

A preliminary design was made at Cam Ranh Bay, tested, modified slightly, and then brought into service. It consisted of 15 small pontoons welded together into a platform. A shelter to provide the crews' quarters divided the barge into two, and an M102 105mm howitzer was placed on either side, with ammunition for the artillery being carried in armoured superstructures at the bow and stern of the barge. The barges were towed into action by an LCM(8), modified to carry the battery command post and armed with two 0.5in machine guns. General William B. Fulton, who commanded the Mobile Riverine Force at the outset of its operations, said of these barges: 'The decision to develop the artillery barges was the most important equipment decision

Tasked to provide fire support, an ASPB (inset left) heads an MRF column in pursuit of the enemy. Left: Its armoured hull breached by a Viet Cong rocket attack, an ASPB is run aground to prevent it sinking. Returning heavy VC fire, the crew struggles to repair the damage. Below: A monitor 'Zippo' uses its flamethrower to burn away riverside foliage, denying the VC the cover from which to launch an ambush. Bottom right: Mission completed, a river minesweeper enters Nha Be harbour. Bottom left: Maintaining weapons back at a PBR base.

made by the army for the Mobile Riverine Force because the barges provided effective artillery support at all times.'

In a further attempt to improve the mobility of artillery, airmobile platforms were developed and used for the first time in November 1967. These were equipped with legs that rested on the river bed and their height could be adjusted to accommodate deep or shallow waters. They were carried into action by CH-47 Chinook helicopters. As a result, the Mobile Riverine Force did not suffer from a lack of artillery or helicopter support.

On the smaller waterways, the convoys would employ reconnaissance by fire

Task Force 117 and the Mobile Riverine Force developed a standard procedure for most operations. The boats would move along the waterway in a column formation with ASPBs leading, flanked by minesweepers. They were followed by a CCB, with the river assault squadron's naval commander aboard. A Monitor was usually the next craft, followed by three ATCs carrying the battalion's first company. The company commander's ATC would appear at varying points along this convoy according to the scale of the operation.

For landing, each company would be assigned its own section of the river bank, usually at intervals of between 150 to 300yds. To soften up enemy defences, preparatory fire from artillery, ASPBs, or Monitors was an option available to the battalion commander. He would travel in the CCB of the assault squadron commander or, alternatively, fly aloft in a helicopter. On the smaller waterways, the convoys would employ reconnaissance by fire in the hope of smoking out any possible VC ambushers. However, as the Mobile Riverine Force's methods became familiar to the VC, it became a favourite tactic of theirs to open fire from concealed positions at the ATCs and CCBs with RPG-2s and -7s, or recoilless rifles. When the convoy arrived at an operational area, the beach was marked with coloured smoke – a tactic also used in airmobile landing zones. Troops re-embarked in the same vessel that had brought them into action, identifying their craft by means of a distinctive pennant flown from the mast, as well as varying colour combinations of the three running lights, also carried on each ATC's mast.

When discussions first began on the formation of TF 117, it was accepted by MACV that the force's mobility would be greatly enhanced by the possession of its own base facilities afloat. To this end, two self-propelled barracks ships (APBs) – the USS *Benewah* and the USS *Colleton* – were allocated to provide accommodation for the men of the riverine force. Although each could accommodate 800 troops, in practice it was found that additional barracks space was required, and a towed barracks ship, with space for a further 625, was also provided. Two repair ships kept the boats of the Mobile Riverine Force in good order; their cranes could winch the ATCs, Monitors or ASPBs out of the water and deposit them on pontoons moored alongside for drydock work. Tugboats, salvage craft and other support vessels were also provided.

Since the base was an extremely valuable asset, it was kept well-protected. A rifle company normally deployed two platoons, one on each bank, guarding against VC attack, while the remainder of the company was held in reserve on one of the barracks ships. The platoons ashore secured their area by means of frequent patrols, hoping to gain foreknowledge of any enemy movements towards the base. The base was never further than 30 miles from the zone of operations and, for their own self-protection, the *Benewah* and *Colleton* were equipped with two 3in guns, two quadruple 40mm mountings, eight, 0.5in and 10, 0.3in machine guns. No attacks on the base were launched until 1968, when several attempts were made with recoilless rifles which caused only superficial damage. A more dangerous threat appeared in November that year, when VC or NVA divers began to place mines against the hulls of MRF craft. One salvage vessel was sunk, and the USS *Westchester County*, an LST, was damaged in these attacks. However, anti-swimmer nets and increased vigilance by the watches enabled the Mobile Riverine Force to overcome this threat.

THE AUTHOR P.M. Szuscikiewicz is an American writer, based in London, who has published several articles on naval and military affairs.

RIVER PATROL FORCE
TF-116

T-111-6

By the end of 1968, the three main US Navy task forces in Vietnam – TF 115, 116 (whose insignia is shown above) and 117 – had achieved their respective objectives. However, although the infiltration of supplies through the Mekong Delta and via the sea had been reduced to a trickle, the VC had begun to exploit an alternative route – across the Cambodian border. To counteract enemy activity in this area, various units of Market Time, Game Warden and the MRF were moulded into a combined force under the codename 'Sealords'. As PBRs, exploiting their shallow draught, pushed upriver, their patrol areas were taken over by the Swifts. Operations continued, with the South Vietnamese Navy gradually assuming greater responsibility as US forces in Vietnam were progressively withdrawn. By the spring of 1972, only liaison officers remained to assist the Vietnamese units. Below: An ATC, modified to carry a high velocity spray system, unleashes a jet of water against VC fortifications near the shoreline.

BRILLIANT

ACTION LYNX!

The two Lynx helicopters aboard HMS *Brilliant* were to play a major role in neutralising the threat of the Argentinian submarine *Santa Fé* during the 1982 Falklands campaign

EIGHT SLEEK, sharp-prowed ships knifed their way through the sunny waters, heading south for the dreary wastes of the South Atlantic. The day before, 2 April 1982, a signal had been received directing the FOF1 (Flag Officer First Flotilla) to race south from the North Atlantic – Argentina had invaded the Falkland Islands. The spearhead group comprised HMS *Glamorgan,* the flagship, and five other destroyers, HMS *Antrim, Glasgow, Coventry, Sheffield* and *Plymouth,* with the Type 22 frigate HMS *Brilliant* and the Type 21 frigate HMS *Arrow.* Altogether they made a fast, hard-hitting, Exocet-armed task force.

The final stages of Exercise Springtrain, based on Gibraltar, had been abandoned, and the spearhead group paired up with ships returning to Britain in order to swap stores. Positioned alongside her sister ship HMS *Battleaxe, Brilliant* began the first of the 'vertreps' (vertical replenishments by helicopter) which were eventually to become commonplace during Operation Corporate. For 12 hectic hours she took aboard, via jackstay, boat and vertrep, *Battleaxe's* stores of Sea Wolf missiles, torpedoes, machine guns, internal security gear, ammunition, and all manner of naval and victualling items, steadily sinking into the water as *Battleaxe* rose. Both her Lynx helicopters (commonly abbreviated to 'helos') flew continually in support of *Brilliant* and the other ships, landing cross-deck with underslung loads.

The helicopters acted as the eyes of the task force, beyond the range of its radar

Then, in high frequency (HF) radio and radar silence, sailing between 25 and 50 miles apart, they headed at up to 25 knots through 'absolutely gin clear' air towards Ascension Island. As the Anglo-Argentinian diplomatic efforts continued to founder, the speeding ships practised operational techniques, honing themselves for battle should hostilities actually arise. The main Argentinian threat was seen as a surface one, and emphasis was laid on surface reporting and OTHT (over the horizon targeting), in which the helicopters acted as the eyes of the task force, beyond the range of its radar. In the absence of an aircraft carrier, however, air defence exercises could not be conducted at task-force level: that was to come later when HMS *Hermes* and *Invincible* arrived on the scene. During the voyage, the aircraft and the Royal Marines practised attacks against Sheffield-class Type 42 destroyers (similar to those deployed by the Argentinians). Pacific Seariders (inflatable assault boats) were successfully mounted with Carl Gustav anti-tank weapons, and the all-purpose Lynxes made dummy sorties using the limited weapons available to them.

Although their potential role as gunships was appreciated, neither of *Brilliant's* helos had been fitted with the standard mounting for the GPMG (7.62mm General Purpose Machine Gun), and the first of many clever improvisations was devised. The metal section of a typist's swivel chair was upturned and bolted to the deck, and a brass mounting constructed to carry the GPMG. It was then operated by two Royal Marine gunners to great effect, and an oil drum was sunk first time on a practice shoot.

Although the men were prepared for the worst, the atmosphere aboard *Brilliant* was one of excitement, almost a holiday spirit, and there was no appreciation of threat. As one crew member put it, they were off to 'shake a gunboat at those dagoes'. This feeling transmitted itself to the helo aircrews. The flight commander, Lieutenant Commander Barry Bryant, and his pilot, Lieutenant Nick Butler, with the crew of the second Lynx, Lieutenant Commander Clark and Lieutenant McKay, threw themselves into the exercises with great determination.

Practising surface actions and other OTHT procedures, the spearhead group arrived at Ascension, where *Antrim, Plymouth* and *Tidespring,* a fleet tanker, were diverted to South Georgia. There, in Operation Paraquet, they were to land some 60 men, drawn from the 22nd Special Air Service Regiment, the Special Boat Squadron, and the Royal Marines, to retake the island from the Argentinians. The remainder of the force kept out of sight of Ascension Island for security reasons, and the helicopters plied between them, replenishing vital stores. *Brilliant* also exchanged her basic type of Lynx for a more advanced model that was capable of firing Sea Skua missiles. This helicopter had been dismantled, and it arrived in bits at Ascension after a 12-hour flight in a Hercules. It was assembled in less

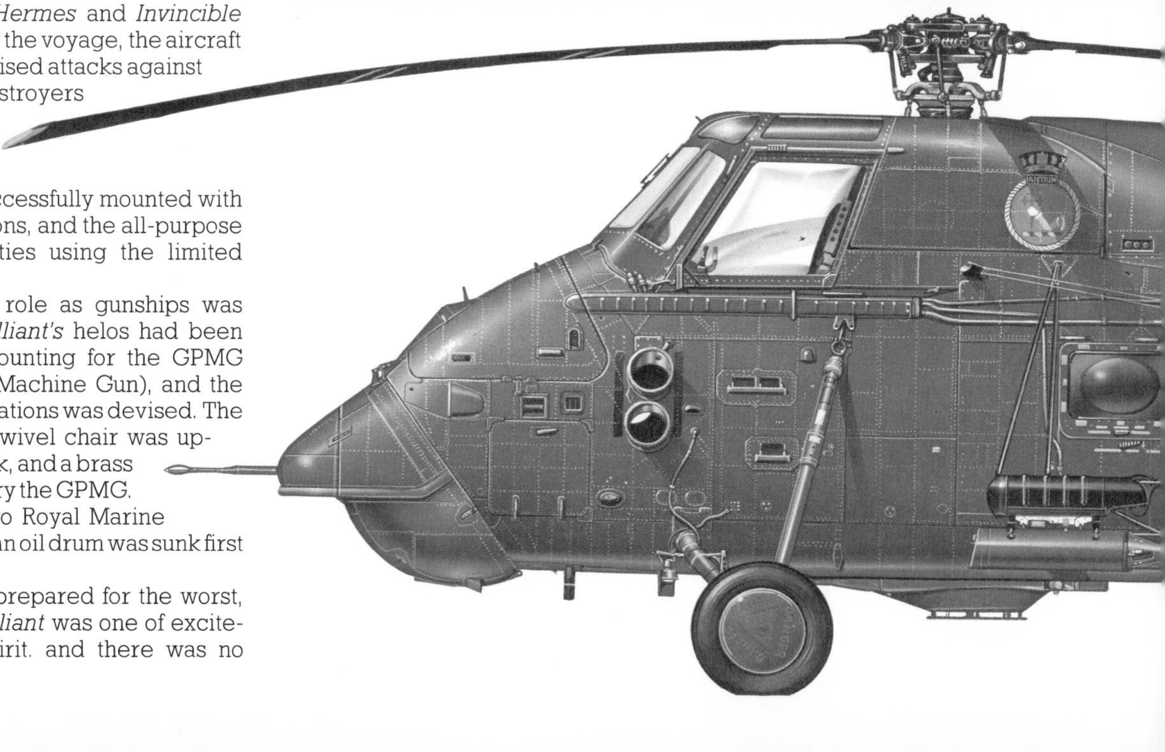

ANTI-SUBMARINE OPERATIONS

The Type 22 Broadsword-class frigates were the first vessels of the Royal Navy to exchange primary gun armament for extensive anti-submarine warfare (ASW) weaponry, in addition to their Exocet anti-ship missiles and Seawolf point-air-defence system. The two Lynx helicopters carried by each frigate perform a vital role in ASW operations. Their initial task is submarine detection, for which they use sonar, which is dipped in the water ('dunking sonar'), search radar and a passive radar receiver, and MAD (magnetic anomaly detectors), which locate an underwater metal hull by identifying the disturbance it creates in the earth's magnetic field. Following contact with the submarine, the Lynx will often act as the frigate's primary weapon delivery system, although it may carry out mid-course correction of surface-to-surface missiles from the parent ship by employing its radar. The Lynx's own armament comprises two Mk 44, Mk 46 or Stingray torpedoes, or two Mk 11 depth-charges, or four Sea Skua semi-active homing anti-ship missiles. The Sea Skua is designed to be guided by target reflections of signals from the Lynx's Ferranti Seaspray radar.

Page 137: The Westland Lynx, armed with Sea Skua missiles, and the Type 22 frigate *Brilliant,* with its badge.
Above: A Lynx circles over *Sheffield.* Left: The ships set sail. Right: One of *Brilliant's* Lynxes supplies smallarms ammunition to *Hermes.* Bottom: Nicknamed 'Humphrey', *Antrim's* Wessex Mk3 helicopter was to play a vital role in Operation Paraquet.

ROYAL NAVY
XP 142

THE LYNX HAS.MK2

In 1967, Westland Helicopters and Aérospatiale in France agreed to co-produce three helicopter types. The French assumed design responsibility for two, the Puma and the Gazelle, while a British project, begun by Fairey in the 1950s and then known as the WG.13, went ahead to become the versatile Lynx.
In all, 13 prototypes were built, each intended for a specialised role, and the first flew on 21 March 1971. The Royal Navy prototype, tailored for anti-submarine work and known as the Lynx HAS.Mk2, first flew on 25 May 1972 and entered service with No.702 Squadron for aircrew training in 1977.
The Lynx incorporates several important design innovations, including a new kind of gearwheel, the Wiktor/Novikov conformal gear, and a one-piece rotor hub forged in titanium which has enabled rotor diameter to be cut down to only 42ft. The Lynx HAS.MK2 is powered by two 900shp Rolls-Royce Gem 2 turboshafts, while the uprated Lynx HAS.Mk3 has 1120shp Gem 41-1s. The former aircraft has a cruising speed of 144mph at maximum weight, and its range is 369 miles.
The Lynx normally has a crew of two, or a pilot (whose Naval Air Arm wings are shown above) and up to 10 troops. Torpedoes or depth-charges fired from the pylons can be replenished from the cabin.

than 24 hours in primitive conditions under a canvas awning.

At 1635 hours on 14 April, *Brilliant's* commander, Captain John Coward, was ordered to lead a group of ships far into the South Atlantic towards the Falklands, in an attempt to escape the attention of Argentinian aircraft and 'become lost'. Led by *Brilliant,* the ships *Arrow, Coventry, Glasgow* and *Sheffield* headed south at 25 knots. A freight tanker, *Appleleaf,* and an afloat support ship, *Fort Austin,* were to follow and rendezvous.

Brilliant's Lynxes continued to vertrep stores even as the ships headed south, the last trip being made from Ascension in pitch darkness. Around midnight, Nick Butler brought his helo in with just 12 minutes of fuel left, well below the acceptable safety margin. The deck was pitching wildly and the flightdeck crew was 'invited' to unload very quickly indeed. The pilot had identified the ship by her 'red head', a flashing red light at the top of her mast. As he brought the aircraft in, hovering at 25ft to lower the load, his only guide a horizontal bar of light, two men made their way over a deck 'goffered' with spume, harnessed the load and unhooked it in 30 seconds flat. As the Lynx came in to touch down, the ship lurched, and one of the aircraft's main wheels struck Air Engineer and Mechanic House a glancing blow on the head, sending him sprawling on the deck. More shaken than hurt, he was able to stagger to the comparative shelter of the open hangar.

'Wolf! Wolf!' came clearly over the radio, and the Wessex went into a depth-charge attack

On 22 April, *Brilliant* detached from the group at maximum speed to offer support to *Antrim's* group off South Georgia. This group had had only three Wessex helicopters at its disposal, and two of them had crashed on a glacier, forcing on *Brilliant's* two Lynxes a vital role in implementing the landings. Smashing through mountainous seas in the teeth of a howling gale, her stern rising and falling 30ft, *Brilliant* joined *Antrim* and *Plymouth* 150 miles north of South Georgia. The invasion of South Georgia had been scheduled for 25 April, but an additional complication had arisen: the Argentinian submarine *Santa Fé* had been spotted off Grytviken. *Antrim,* now acting as flagship, decided that the landing must be deferred until the submarine was eliminated. At 0855 hours on 25 April , *Antrim's* surviving Wessex 3 sighted her coming out of the harbour. She had landed troops and was preparing to dive to clear the area. 'Wolf! Wolf!' – the signal for submarine on the surface – came clearly over the radio, and the Wessex went into a depth-charge attack.

Aboard *Brilliant,* Lynx 341, at alert five, was directed to join in the attack. (Alert 45 meant a helo at 45 minutes' readiness; alert 15 at 15 minutes' readiness, and alert five , at five minutes' readiness for immediate take-off. Usually take-off took only three and a half minutes.) Lynx 341's pilot and observer were aboard, and an MK 46 torpedo had been loaded. As the Lynx strained at her 'harpoon' decklock system, four members of the flightdeck crew undid the aircraft lashings, under the watchful eye of the SMR (Senior Maintenance Rating) Chief Petty Officer O'Hara. Spray, driven by a fierce wind off the glaciers, lashed across the violently pitching deck as the order came from the ops room: 'Action Lynx!' Nick Butler pressed the starter button, both engines roared into life, the rotors were engaged, and Barry Bryant punched in the computer sequence. Lieutenant Commander Morris, the FDO (flight deck officer), cleared the flightdeck. 'Launch!' came over the intercom. The pilot released the harpoon and the Lynx lifted off, making for the *Santa Fé.*

Ahead, the Wessex hovered, having dropped two depth-charges, waiting for Lynx 341 to arrive before returning to *Antrim* to re-arm. The Argentinian submarine was heading for Cumberland Bay and Grytviken harbour, and the Lynx crew could see that her fin was damaged and she was weeping oil from the stern. They made a classic visual torpedo attack, but the submarine captain, seeing the Mk 46 on its parachute landing in the water alongside him,

341
RESCUE

744
ROYAL NAVY

PB

Above: For maximum stability on pitching decks, the landing gear of the naval Lynx can be angled away from the fuselage. Left: A Lynx receives its anti-submarine missile armament.

ROYAL NAVY
XZ697
DANGER

decided to remain on the surface. He was fully aware that the MK 46 was strictly an underwater weapon, only able to operate at a minimum depth of 30ft. There he was, resting on the surface, with enough high explosive circling beneath him to blow the *Santa Fé* out of the water.

The Lynx was determined to keep him on the surface, and after the observer had scrambled into the back to man the GPMG, the pilot took the helo in, making a low pass 'to sharpen him up', gun chattering. The submarine crew scattered on the conning tower, and it was not until the third pass that they replied with their own GPMG. A 7.62mm bullet would have little effect on a submarine's fin, but it could smash a periscope or radar antenna and it certainly kept the crew on their toes. The helo swept in again and again to strafe the fin at 100yds range and at a height of 30ft.

The Lynx had joined the Wessex at 0905 hours, 50 or 60 miles from *Brilliant,* too far for low frequency transmission, so they used HF radio, on the frequency common to the whole of the task force. Over 300 miles away, the pilots of *Hermes* and *Invincible* sat in their aircraft on the flightdecks, listening incredulously over their radios to Nick Butler's blow by blow commentary on the machine-gun action with the *Santa Fé*. They could hardly believe that he was being fired at by an enemy. Over the radio came, 'Do not strafe survivors with GPMG,' much to the chagrin of the aircrew, who had not the slightest intention of doing so. They hung about 'causing vexation', using their height advantage to fire on the *Santa Fé*, hoping for a hit on either the periscope or the radar.

Suddenly, at 0930 hours, the trail of an AS. 12 wire-guided missile, fired from a Wasp, flashed beneath the Lynx, now flying at 800ft, to crash into the fin of the submarine, causing more oil to weep. A second AS. 12 went up in the water ahead of the *Santa Fé. Brilliant's* other Lynx, 342, arrived on the scene, supplementing the machine-gun attack. Another Wasp came in to fire more AS. 12s at the damaged submarine, which was still limping towards Grytviken, leaking even more oil and streaming smoke. As the *Santa Fé* reached King Edward Point in Grytviken itself, groundfire from machine guns ashore caused the aerial attack to break off. The decision was then taken to send in the ground troops.

The three close-flying helos went straight into the bay, very fast and very low, 15ft above the water

Lynx 341 refuelled and searched the indented north coast of South Georgia on the look-out for lurking Argentinian FPBs (fast patrol boats), even though there was not much likelihood of them having reached the island in the time available. As bad weather closed in, and in that latitude it could happen in a very few minutes, visibility was reduced to a quarter of a mile and flying became very hazardous. The Lynx, 'flogging around' the hostile cliffs, was surrounded by 'millions of enormous sea birds', mainly albatross. Not being used to aircraft, the birds constituted one of the biggest menaces the crew encountered at South Georgia, and at Bird Island the number of birds increased to the point of becoming positively lethal.

Following its patrol, Lynx 341, after refuelling and food, launched from *Brilliant* at 1430 to begin landing the SAS. Foiled by the increasing deterioration in the weather from going into Cumberland Bay via a devious route, the three close-flying helos went straight into the bay, very fast and very low, 15ft above the water, to take the enemy by surprise. At 1715, the Argentinians surrendered and a white flag appeared. The SAS landings were halted, despite the troops 'bickering and wingeing' in their anxiety to get ashore. About 10 minutes later, the commander of the *Santa Fé* handed Barry Bryant and Nick Butler a certificate, announcing that a Lynx helicopter of the British Navy had attacked and captured his submarine, and signed 'the submarine captain'. He thought depth-charging was fair enough, but machine gunning was just 'not cricket'!

Next day, the commander of *Brilliant*, Captain John Coward, himself an ex-submariner, flew into Grytviken to inspect the *Santa Fé*, now at the jetty and slowly sinking. She was listing to port and down by the head, her fin and casing riddled by bullet holes and part of her bridge area blown away by the AS. 12 missile attack. Most of the AS. 12s had punched straight through before exploding. Apart from surface damage and innumerable bullet holes, there was little evidence that the submarine had suffered harm. Inside, it was another story. *Santa Fé* was a total shambles, she was slowly taking water into the bilges and probably also into the battery tanks, the tankside valves were passing almost as much air shut as open, and there was only emergency lighting.

After attempts to restore full buoyancy had failed, it was decided to move the submarine away from the jetty. Rather than sink her in deep water, she was to be towed alongside a shallow berth at the old whaling station where she could settle on the bottom. A small number of the Argentinian crew were to man the switchboard in the control room, under the supervision of a British officer and guarded by Royal Marines; the commander of the *Santa Fé* would be on the bridge with Captain Coward. Blowing tanks throughout, the submarine was limping slowly towards its new berth when suddenly it listed and showed signs of losing buoyancy. The Argentinian commander issued a stream of orders in Spanish, trying to get the crew to blow all ballast, but the men

ROYAL NAVY
506

Top left: The South Georgia task group possessed three Westland HAS. Mk 1 Wasps, two on *Endurance* and one on *Plymouth.* Attacking in support of the Wessex and Lynxes, they fired AS.12 missiles which shot through the submarine's glass-reinforced plastic conning tower without exploding.

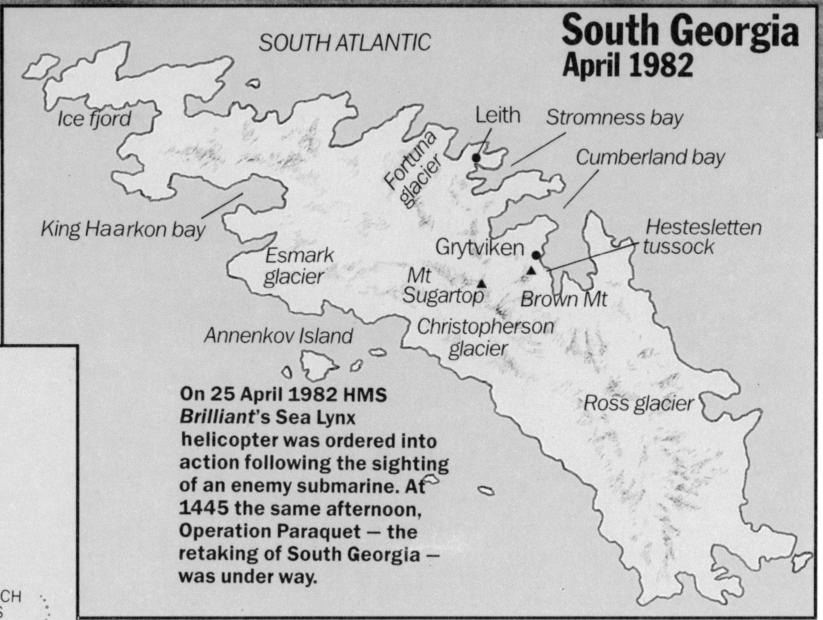
South Georgia
April 1982
SOUTH ATLANTIC
Ice fjord
Leith
Stromness bay
Cumberland bay
Fortuna glacier
King Haarkon bay
Hestesletten tussock
Grytviken
Esmark glacier
Mt Sugartop
Brown Mt
Annenkov Island
Christopherson glacier
Ross glacier
On 25 April 1982 HMS *Brilliant*'s Sea Lynx helicopter was ordered into action following the sighting of an enemy submarine. At 1445 the same afternoon, Operation Paraquet – the retaking of South Georgia – was under way.

ARGENTINA
SOUTH ATLANTIC
FALKLAND ISLANDS
SOUTH GEORGIA
SANDWICH ISLANDS
CHILE

Top right: Captain Coward (right) and Lieutenant-Commander Bocain inspect the damage on *Santa Fé*. Background: The Argentinian submarine, listing heavily to port, in the shelter of Grytviken. Above: The shattered conning tower, showing the holes made by the AS.12 missiles.

in the control room panicked, thinking the boat was going down. A petty officer, presumably rushing to carry out his orders, was shot dead in the belief that he intended to scuttle the submarine. Despite this tragic incident, the *Santa Fé* was finally berthed.

Experiencing surface attack and hazardous night flights, dicing with icebergs, Lynx 341 and her crew flew a total of 56 hours in support of Operation Paraquet. They were deployed from 25 to 28 April, in often appalling conditions, without missing a single sortie or take-off, and no man who was present would deny the enormous contribution they made to the successful action in South Georgia.

THE AUTHOR Bernard Brett left the Royal Navy at the end of World War II, and has since written several books on ships, sea power and naval warfare. He is currently preparing a history of modern sea power.

MORSKAYA PEKHOTA

The foundations of the Soviet Naval Infantry were laid by Peter the Great, the father of the Russian navy. In 1705 the marines had a strength of 45 officers and 1320 men, and their first victory was chalked up one year later when a boarding party captured the Swedish ship *Espern*.

The 'sea regiments', as the marines were called, played a crucial part in the eventual Russian victory in the Great Northern War; their amphibious raids helped to grind down the Swedish resistance.

Using galleys that were the fastest and most manoeuvrable vessels of their day, the naval infantry added to their colours during Catherine the Great's war against the Turks five decades later. With a string of battle honours already to their name, the marines extended their operations into the Mediterranean, capturing the fortress of Beirut in 1773. (More than two centuries later the Soviet Naval Infantry is back in the area, conducting exercises with their Syrian allies.)

Over the next few decades the marines fought in a succession of wars and campaigns, mostly centred around the Baltic.

The naval infantry saw action in the Crimean War (1854-56), and the Russo-Japanese War of 1904-05, and by the end of World War II there were two divisions of marines in the Baltic and Black Sea.

Above: Soviet Naval Infantry sleeve badge.

In the event of conflict, highly trained naval infantry would form the spearhead of Soviet amphibious assault strategy

THE SOVIET NAVY comprises four major fleets: the Northern, based at Severomorsk; the Baltic, based at Kaliningrad; the Black Sea, based at Sevastopol; and the Pacific, based at Vladivostok. Under each fleet commander there are several main operational elements, including surface and submarine forces, naval base commands, naval aviation and naval infantry. The latter component, an amphibious assault force known as the Soviet Naval Infantry (SNI), has been considerably developed during recent years, an indication of the Soviet effort to expand its theatre of operations.

In the event of war, the Soviet marines would be tasked with a key mission – to seize vital Western installations in each of the four theatres, allowing the Red Banner Fleets (particularly the nuclear-missile armed submarine groups) to break out into the high seas and engage the enemy. The 16,000-man naval infantry, or Morskaya Pekhota as the Soviet marines are called, would also be responsible for capturing NATO positions in Norway and Denmark. In joint operations with the Soviet Army, the SNI would seek to encircle the Western Alliance's northern flank.

In preparation for these roles, the naval infantry trains to launch amphibious assaults amid nuclear strikes, swooping in from the sea to storm ports, airfields, and submarine and tactical missile bases, and other important coastal targets. These contingency missions are facilitated by the routine deployment of Soviet amphibious forces in exercises as far afield as Vietnam, where there is a large base at Cam Ranh Bay, and Socrata Island near the strategic Gulf of Aden. Gradually, the SNI has evolved into an elite force whose wartime role would be crucial to the Soviet strategy of a short but incisive conflict.

Under the watchful eye of Admiral Sergei Gor-

shkov, the marines have been equipped with upgraded weapons such as T-72 battle tanks, 122mm artillery and assault hovercraft. Although considerably smaller than the 198,000-strong US Marine Corps, the Soviet Naval Infantry should not be underestimated. Its training is more rigorous than that of the army, and observers of amphibious exercises along the Baltic coast have noted that a regiment of SNI is equivalent in effectiveness to an entire division of motorised land troops.

By the end of World War I the Russians had two divisions of naval infantry in the Baltic and the Black Sea. However, following its involvement in the 1921 anti-Bolshevik uprising at Kronstadt, the naval infantry was disbanded, one of several demobilisations in its long history. Reformed for the Winter War against Finland in 1939, the SNI had been expanded to 25 rifle brigades by the time that Germany invaded the Soviet Union in 1941. At the end of World War II, the marines' strength exceeded 100,000 men, divided into 40 brigades and six independent regiments. Thousands of Soviet sailors, their warships bottled up in the Baltic or Black Seas by the German Blitzkrieg, had been formed into infantry rifle brigades, and deployed in the critical defensive battles around Moscow, Leningrad and Stalingrad. Initially, the naval infantry was chiefly used for amphibious landings along the Baltic coast in a desperate effort to halt the progress of the Wehrmacht juggernaut. The assaults were spearheaded by the naval infantry and supported by ground forces landed by boat.

At first, these operations were hastily organised and clumsily executed. Indeed, naval records show that many were planned and carried out within 24 hours – a pathetically brief period by any military standards. The landings were generally on a small scale, often comprising less than three platoons using rusty landing craft or shallow draught coasters. However, by 1943 the Soviets had refined their tactics and amphibious techniques had developed accordingly. Landings became more ambitious in their conception and benefited from the co-ordination of naval gunfire, air strikes and paratrooper support. Four out of the 114 landings by the naval infantry during World War II involved several thousand troops. Three of these were in the Baltic, while the fourth was in the Black Sea.

Included in the ranks of the SNI during World War II were several officers destined for top naval, military and political command. The most prominent of these was Captain Sergei G. Gorshkov, one of the few effective flag officers serving in the Soviet Navy during the conflict. Gorshkov commanded a number of amphibious landings in the Black Sea, including

Below right: Amphibious BTR-60Ps bring Soviet Naval Infantry (SNI) ashore during an operation designed to test their rapid deployment capability. Like most elite units, the SNI has its own battlecry – '*Polundra*' – meaning 'Watch out below'. Below left: A T-54 main battle tank provides transport for three naval infantrymen. Below centre: A Soviet naval guard on duty, armed with a 7.62mm AKM assault rifle.

RED SEA ARMY

ASSAULT VESSELS

The Soviet Navy's amphibious capability has been greatly enhanced by the development of larger and faster vessels such as the Ivan Rogov class of landing ship. Although only two of this type have so far been built, they represent the biggest and most versatile addition to the Soviet Navy.

They are capable of carrying a full battalion of naval infantry, along with 10 PT-76 combat tanks, 30 armoured personnel carriers, four KA-27 Hormone helicopters and three Lebed class air cushion vehicles (ACVs). These 86-ton combat hovercraft can carry 120 troops at speeds up to 65 knots, far faster than more conventional craft.

The Soviet Navy now possesses the world's largest force of ACVs, and according to the Pentagon, the new Pelikan and Pomornik classes were incorporated into the Baltic Fleet in 1985. The naval infantry are increasingly using ACVs in their exercises, and the speed with which Soviet assault forces can now land is seen by Western experts as posing a considerable threat to NATO security.

The 250-ton Aist class ACVs, the world's largest military hovercraft, can each carry 200 troops in addition to four PT-76 amphibious tanks. The Aist class increases the Soviet capability of deploying the naval infantry in short-range coastal strikes against NATO targets in the Baltic and Scandinavia.

the insertion of 2000 naval infantrymen behind the Romanian Army encircling Odessa. Gorshkov later landed several thousand troops near the besieged naval base of Sevastopol in the Crimea, delaying its fall for six vital months.

Following the end of the war, in 1947 the naval infantry was again disbanded. In 1956 Admiral Gorshkov became Commander-in-Chief of the Soviet Navy, and a modernisation programme was launched that would transform the fleet into a formation which today constitutes a major challenge to the long-dominant US Navy. Analysing the methods of the US and Royal Marines, Gorshkov and the Soviet military planners decided that the expanding Soviet Navy required a hard-hitting amphibious force as an integral part of their strategic plans for wide-ranging fleets. As a result, in 1964 the marine force was reactivated. In the last few years the naval infantry's strength has reached 16,000, and the three regiments serving with the Northern, Baltic and Black Sea fleets have been upgraded to brigades of more than 3000 men each. Admiral Gorshkov retired in 1985, having presided over a remarkable transformation in the fortunes of the Soviet Navy. His 30-year tenure is even more remarkable given the vagaries of the purge-prone Soviet political system.

The naval infantry component of the Pacific Fleet comprises a division of two regiments, totalling 7000 men. This force is divided into two tank and five motorised infantry battalions, backed by self-propelled artillery. Each brigade has three rifle battalions of around 400 men. One of the tank battalions has three companies, equipped with 10 amphibious PT-76 light tanks, while the other has 10 snorkel-fitted T-54 and T-55 battle tanks. Unlike the US Marines, who are not equipped with armoured vehicles to ferry them into combat after landing, the Soviet assault troops are carried ashore by amphibious BTR-60P armoured personnel carriers (APCs); each battalion has five of these at its disposal.

The brigades also possess integrated combat units, comprising five elements. A reconnaissance company is equipped with three PT-76s and nine BRDM-2 heavy armoured vehicles; a rocket battery with six BM-21 rocket launchers for fire support and counter-battery fire; an anti-tank battery with Sagger guided missiles and SPG-9 73mm recoilless rifles; an air-defence battery armed with self-propelled ZSU-23-4 gun systems and SA-9 infra-red homing missiles mounted in packs of four; and a mortar platoon equipped with 82mm and 120mm weapons.

Supporting each unit are supply, medical and signal platoons and a 35-man chemical warfare defence company. In addition, the brigades may also possess a helicopter company, whose Mi-8 Hip Es would carry the assault troops, including the

A wide range of purpose-built craft has been developed by the Soviets in an effort to further enhance the effectiveness of their marine force. Main picture: After disembarking from three Polnocny-class landing ships and being ferried ashore by BTR-60P amphibious armoured personnel carriers (APCs), Soviet Naval Infantry storm a beachhead in full battledress. The growing scale of such exercises has convinced Western experts that the SNI would pose a major threat in the event of a conflict. Far left: The SNI's rigorous training programme incorporates realistic assaults on enemy positions.

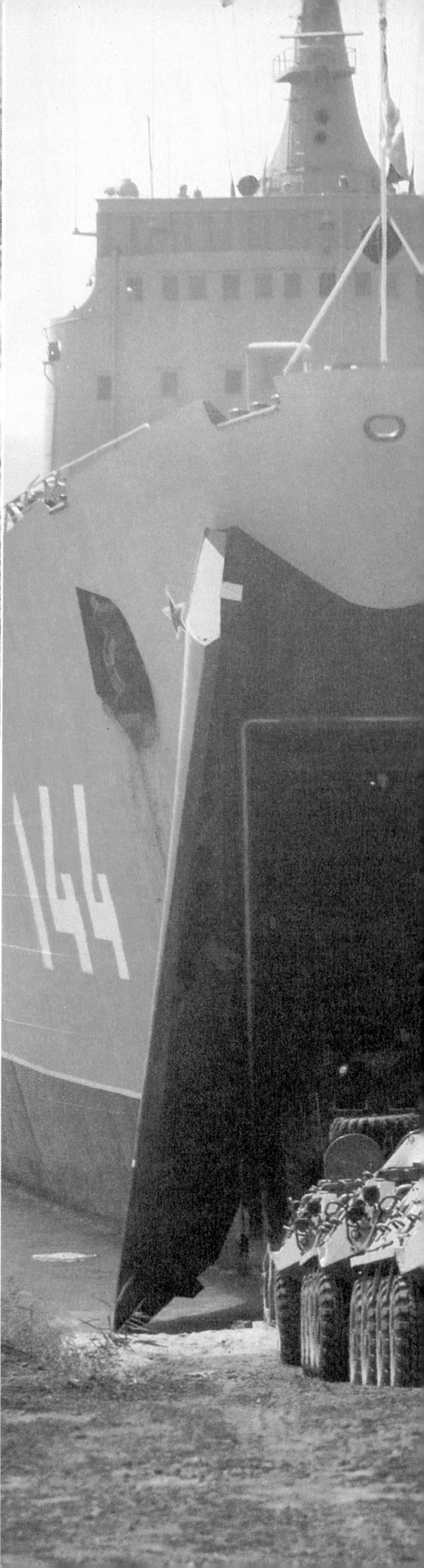
144

Below: As the bow doors of a Polnocny are opened, the cargo of the landing ship is revealed – a column of BTR-60Ps. Far left: Trim vanes extended to provide stability, a flotilla of PT-76 tanks demonstrate their amphibious capability. A periscope mounted in the forward section enables each commander to see over the spray, and two extra fuel tanks mounted at the rear provide greater range.

sappers, into combat ahead of the main force. This advance party would be responsible for clearing underwater obstacles such as mines and tank traps, and is also equipped with BTR-60P armoured personnel carriers in order to launch surprise attacks on beachhead targets.

Unlike their American counterparts, the Soviet amphibious forces are not tasked to fight on after they have secured a beachhead. Instead, follow-up ground troops would be landed from the sea or air, enabling the naval infantry to be withdrawn. Such a restricted use of the SNI underlines the basic Soviet doctrine of short-range amphibious operations, supported by the 6in guns of Sverdlov-class cruisers and a barrage of 122mm shells and surface-to-air missiles (SA-N-4 and SA-N-9) from the naval infantry's assault ships.

For this type of complex landing operation, a precise co-ordination of the assault, naval and air forces is required if the element of surprise is to be retained. With this in mind, the Soviet marine force is far more versatile than Britain's Royal Marines, despite being double the size and not so well equipped. Victor Suvorov, a former army intelligence officer who defected to the West, has commented:

> 'The Soviet Naval Infantry has a very promising future; in the next few years it will receive new types of equipment which will enable it to put large units into action against distant targets. Special combat equipment is being developed for such operations by the marine infantry.'

In the Northern and Baltic Fleets, the naval infantry's primary wartime role is to insert forces behind the NATO lines on the northern flank, in order to support land forces that would be pushing westwards. Their objectives, known as 'choke points', include nuclear installations, ports and submarine bases, the destruction of which would give the Soviet Navy access to the Atlantic. In addition, the securing of the straits commanded by Denmark and Schleswig-Holstein would enable the fleets to break out through the strategic Greenland-Iceland gap.

Naval infantry might even be used to spearhead assault landings on mainland China itself

The Black Sea Fleet would aim to seize control of the Dardanelles Straits and the narrow Bosphorus, while the Suez Canal and its associated oil pipelines represent crucial strategic targets on NATO's southern fringe. The Pacific Fleet, with its steadily growing naval infantry and amphibious element, would need to secure the La Perouse Straits between Japan and the southern Soviet mainland in order to gain access into the vast ocean beyond. If Beijing (Peking) joined with the West in the event of a conflict, the Pacific Fleet's naval infantry might even be used to spearhead assault landings on mainland China itself.

The Baltic Fleet epitomises the Soviet tactical doctrine in terms of amphibious operations. In this theatre, the naval infantry force, with 24 warships, is supported by additional marine elements from Poland and East Germany. Soviet forces, particularly the naval infantry, have been rehearsing their wartime tasks – aimed at overwhelming NATO on the northern maritime axis – for almost 20 years. Their preparations began in 1968, with Operation Sever, the first major amphibious exercise since World War II. Marines were landed on the Rybachiy peninsula, between Murmansk and Norway's northern coastline. NATO holds several installations in Norway,

PT-76 AMPHIBIOUS TANK

The PT-76 light amphibious tank was introduced into service in 1952. The need for an amphibious capability necessitated a hull of all-welded steel construction, with the maximum armour protection (14mm) provided over the front of the hull. Main armament of the PT-76 comprises a 76mm D-56T gun with a maximum rate of fire of eight rounds per minute. Types of ammunition that can be fired include armour-piercing tracer, high-explosive fragmentation, and high-explosive anti-tank rounds. Situated to the right of the 76mm gun is a 7.62mm SGMT machine gun, mounted co-axially with the main armament. More recently, many PT-76s have been fitted with a 12.7mm anti-aircraft gun on the turret roof.

The tank is powered by a V-6 six-cylinder water-cooled engine that can provide a maximum road speed of 27.5mph, and 6mph in water. Before entering the water the trim vane of the PT-76 is erected at the front of the hull and the two electric bilge pumps are switched on. The tank is then propelled by two water jets mounted at the rear of the hull. The PT-76 has formed the basis for a variety of armoured vehicles, including the BTR-50P armoured personnel carrier and the ZSU-23-4 self-propelled anti-aircraft gun system.

Although mainly used as a reconnaissance vehicle ahead of the main units, the PT-76 has also been used for crossing water obstacles in the first wave of an attack, and for artillery support while a beachhead is being established.

During the Vietnam War PT-76s were employed by the North Vietnamese Army and they have also seen combat in South Africa and Angola. When the Indian Army deployed PT-76s for the invasion of East Pakistan in 1971, their amphibious capabilities proved highly effective.

forming the linchpin of the Alliance's northern flank, and Operation Sever illustrated to Western military analysts that this area would be a prime target for the Soviets in the event of war.

Despite being a relatively simple exercise, Operation Sever was poorly co-ordinated. However, in recent years the Warsaw Pact command has enlarged its exercises into impressive displays of amphibious capability, underlining the improved training and tactical deployment of the naval infantry. The scale and complexity of current exercises demonstrate the priority that the Soviets place on the ability to seize and secure strategic 'choke points'.

In the major amphibious exercise conducted by Soviet forces in 1980, Tu-22M Backfire bombers and Mi-24 helicopter gunships supported a landing on Rugen Island, off the coast of East Germany. The exercise incorporated Polish and East German marines, and illustrated the Soviets' ability to co-ordinate large-scale operations. In 1981, 2000 men of the Black Sea Fleet's naval infantry staged amphibious exercises with Syrian forces in the eastern Mediterranean. Naval infantry units have also been deployed with Soviet Navy flotillas off the West African coast, where the navy has a base in Angola, and in the Indian Ocean.

Although the dispersal of naval infantry among the Soviet Navy's four fleets limits the scope of amphibious operations, Soviet naval commanders have consistently made it clear that a large-scale deployment of marines in a role similar to that of the US Marine Corps would be unlikely. The fact that all of the exercises conducted by the Baltic Fleet have been within range of Soviet air bases emphasises the short-range objectives expected of the naval infantry.

Recruits of the Soviet marine force undergo an intensive nine-week basic training course that includes an initiation into commando and guerrilla techniques. Following this, the marines are sent to specialist schools where they are given instruction in the use of heavy weapons, communication equipment, demolition techniques and a variety of other skills. Specialist training may take up to four months, and, upon graduation, some of the recruits are assigned direct to sea duty on one of the navy's amphibious warfare ships.

The extensive reorganisation and modernisation that the Soviet marine force has undergone during the last decade leaves Western analysts in no doubt as to the threat posed by the naval infantry. Noting the introduction of artillery and anti-tank battalions, in addition to new weaponry such as the T-72 tank and the 82mm automatic mortar, sources in the Pentagon readily acknowledge the new-found strength of the Soviet Naval Infantry.

THE AUTHOR Ed Blanche is a journalist of the Associated Press who specialises in military subjects. He has written extensively on many aspects of the Soviet armed forces and on current Soviet military strategy worldwide.

Above: Soviet marines are briefed prior to one of their many training exercises. A very high standard is expected of the SNI, with particular emphasis on their primary role as shock troops (top right).

Right: One of the enormous Aist-class hovercraft skims over the water at a speed approaching 65 knots. Used in conjunction with other elements of the SNI, the emergence of the fast and highly manoeuvrable Aist class has caused the whole concept of amphibious operations to be revised. Far right: Soviet Naval Infantry parade through Red Square in Moscow, displaying the esprit de corps that has resulted in the unit being accorded the elite 'guards' status.

Right: Shock force. Assault rifles at the ready, naval infantry pour out of an Aist-class air cushion vehicle.

708

Operating from floating bases, the Mobile Riverine Force carried out search-and-destroy missions against the Viet Cong in the Mekong Delta

THE MONTH OF June 1967 marked the beginning of intensive operations by the newly formed Mobile Riverine Force (MRF) to subdue the Viet Cong (VC) in the Mekong Delta. On 11 and 12 June the Mobile Riverine Force Base (MRB) left the 9th Infantry Division's HQ area at Dong Tam and sailed some 60 miles to Nha Be, southeast of Saigon. From 13-17 June, strike units of the riverine force operated in the Rung Sat Special Zone (RSSZ), working to clear the region of VC units which were threatening supplies destined for the III and IV Corps Tactical Zones, all of which passed through the Long Mau shipping channel to Saigon. While my battalion commanders controlled the action in the RSSZ, my brigade staff and I planned the next phase, a sweep through the open paddy fields of Can Giuoc District to our south.

Our intelligence co-ordination strongly indicated that Can Giuoc District was being used extensively by the VC regional forces for rest and training. Operations by the 9th Infantry Division had been hampered, prior to the formation of the MRF, by a lack of waterborne mobility, and it had been impossible to enter in force and conduct a thorough search. Now, however, we had the means to move a large complement close into the operational area, and since the VC defences were mostly against airborne attack and had been moved inland, there was a strong likelihood of our landings being unopposed.

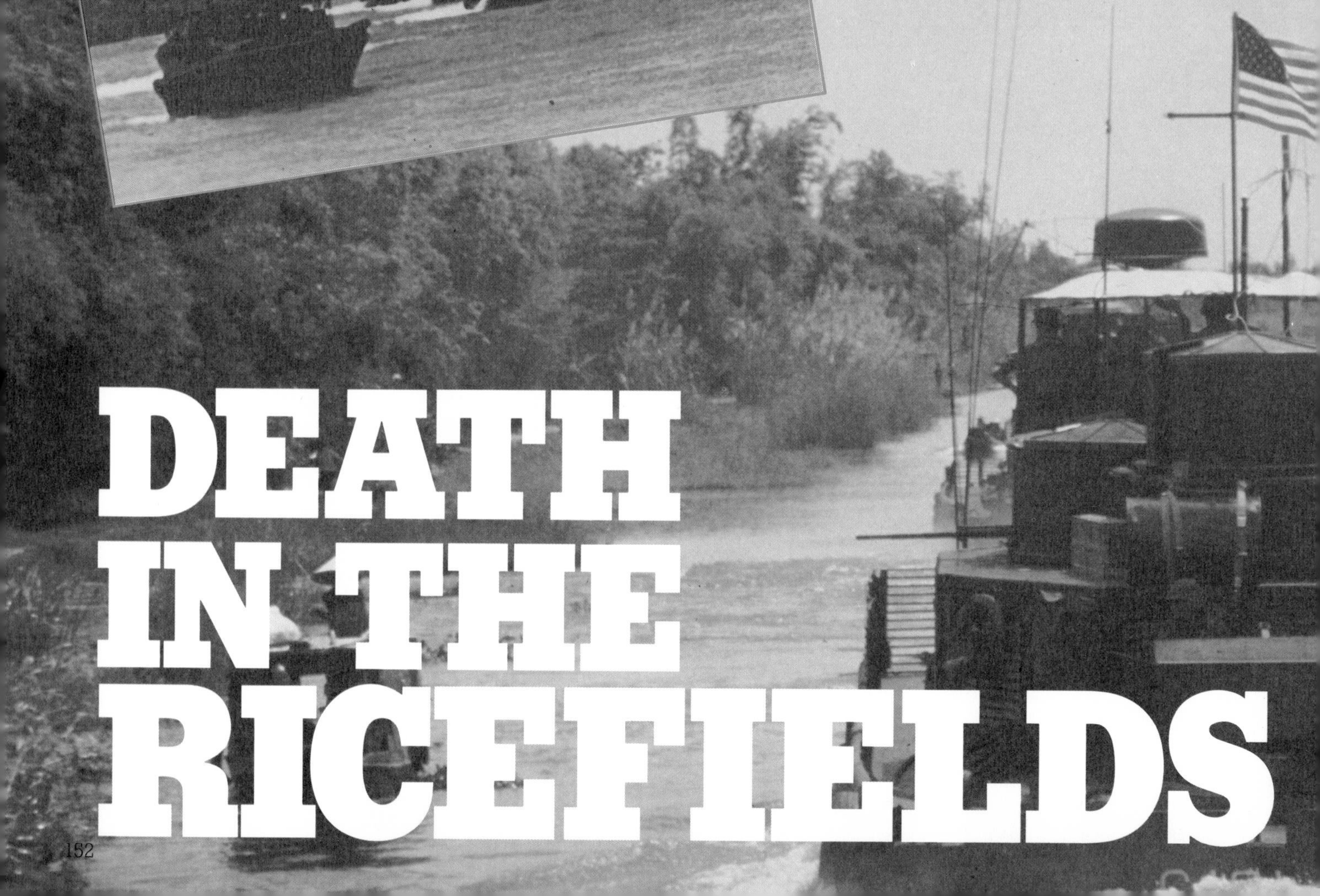

DEATH IN THE RICEFIELDS

On the evening of 18 June the MRB was moved eight miles down river to an anchorage at the junction of the Soi Rap and Van Co rivers, just opposite an old fort, a relic of the previous French regime. On the site of the fort we located a battery of 155mm self-propelled artillery which had been lifted from Vung Tau by Landing Craft Mechanised (LCM). With our base now so close to the target, both the sailing time of our assault craft and the turnaround time of supply and evacuation helicopters and watercraft would be greatly reduced.

Surveying the low, watery country ahead, I was deeply concerned about the changed operating conditions my troops would be facing, for although they had survived well in jungle terrain, this lack of cover demanded a very different approach.

That night, aboard the MRF command ship USS *Benewah*, I communicated my concern to the battalion commanders and Navy River Assault commanders, who had come aboard to present their operational plans to me and Captain Wade Wells, the Navy commander, and to the joint staff. Following this meeting, I decided to do something I had rarely done before, or afterwards for that matter. I decided to go to each of the battalion barracks ships and talk to the company commanders in the presence of their battalion commanders. I took a PAB (Plastic Assault Boat) over to them and covered generally the same points as before, but I dwelt rather more forcefully on the nature of the terrain and how it afforded long range and accurate fields of fire and the potential for excessive and unnecessary casualties unless counter-actions were implemented by ourselves. I cautioned them to use dispersed formations and to move by bounds from covered position to position using their scouts to reconnoitre to the front and flanks, giving the all-clear signal before any movement of the main body, be it a squad, platoon or an entire company.

I could tell from a number of the expressions on the faces in front of me that these young captains were thinking that I should go 'tend to my knitting'. These

The Mobile Riverine Force was formed specifically to oust the Viet Cong from their bunker strongpoints in the Mekong Delta. Men of the 9th US Infantry Division (right) were taken into the combat zone by US Navy brown-water craft (below) and were supported by Hueys operating from barges (left).

MOBILE RIVERINE FORCE

The Mekong Delta, designated the IV Corps Tactical Zone by the US Army, was the last of the four tactical zones in Vietnam to receive a substantial influx of American troops. Situated south of Saigon, it lay away from the critical areas of conflict with the North Vietnamese Army (NVA). By 1966, however, growing activity by the Viet Cong in the area was making a powerful US presence in the Delta imperative if shipping lanes to Saigon were to be protected.

A vast complex of rivers, canals, dykes and seasonally flooded paddy fields, the Delta offered no adequate ground base for a large US defence force. Consequently, a divisional base was constructed with dredged earth near My Tho and named Dong Tam. Meanwhile, in February 1966 the 9th Infantry Division was being activated at Fort Riley in Kansas, specifically for operations in the Delta. Of its three constituent brigades, the 2nd Brigade was selected to become the infantry component of the Mekong Delta Mobile Afloat Force, later renamed the Mobile Riverine Force (MRF).

A joint project of the US Army and US Navy, the MRF possessed flotillas of barracks ships, landing craft, support ships and assault boats. These were used to maintain the 2nd Brigade, including an artillery battalion, as a self-contained, independent amphibious assault force in the Delta, transporting it on strike operations and providing close naval gunfire support. The MRF was active in the Mekong Delta from February 1967 until the gradual handing over of riverine operations to the Vietnamese Navy in 1970.

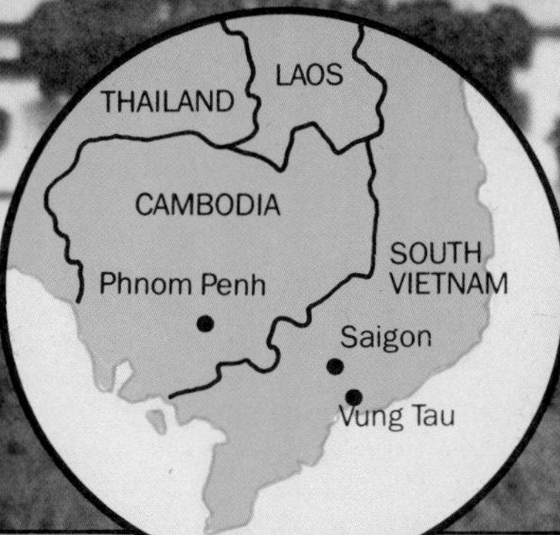
THAILAND
LAOS
CAMBODIA
SOUTH VIETNAM
Phnom Penh
Saigon
Vung Tau

Can Giouc
19 June 1967

In June 1967 the newly-formed joint US Navy-US Army Mobile Riverine Force (MRF) began a series of operations in the Viet Cong-dominated areas of the Mekong Delta and the Rung Sat Special Zone to the south of the South Vietnamese capital, Saigon. On 18 June the MRF moved to a new anchorage on the Soi Rap river ready to go into action against Viet Cong forces in the Can Giouc district.

Mobile Riverine Force

19 June 1000 A battalion-size Viet Cong force is sighted near Objective 20. MRF forces move in by assault boat and helicopter and converge on the VC positions.
1150 As company-size units of the US 47th Infantry Regiment converge on them, the Viet Cong open fire.

PCF-23

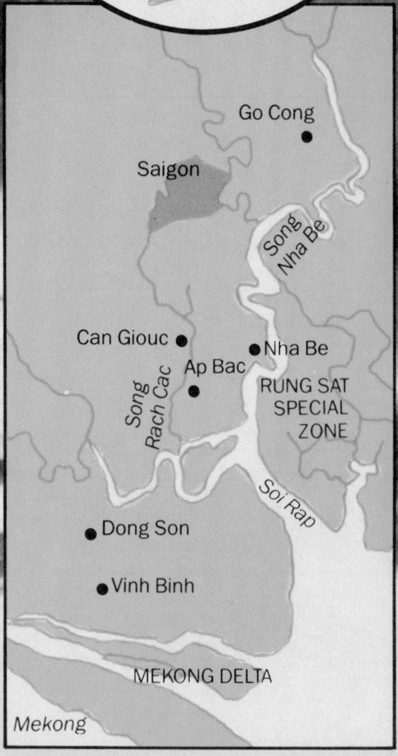
Go Cong
Saigon
Song Nha Be
Can Giouc
Nha Be
Ap Bac
Song Rach Cac
RUNG SAT SPECIAL ZONE
Soi Rap
Dong Son
Vinh Binh
MEKONG DELTA
Mekong

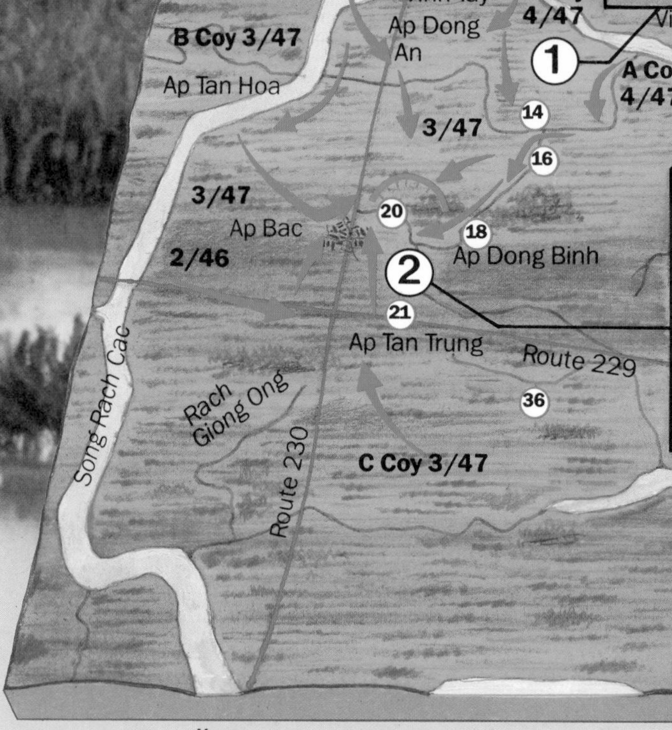
A Coy 3/47
To Can Giouc
Vinn Tay
B Coy 4/47
Ap Dong An
B Coy 3/47
Vinh Thanh
1
A Coy 4/47
Rach Vang
Ap Tan Hoa
14
3/47
16
3/47
20
Ap Bac
18
Ap Dong Binh
2/46
2
21
Ap Tan Trung
Route 229
36
Rach Giong Ong
Song Rach Cac
Route 230
C Coy 3/47
Mobile Riverine Force Base
Song Rach Cat
3/34
Fire Support Base X-Ray

Closing in

With support from artillery, naval gunfire and airstrikes, the MRF infantry close in, but under cover of darkness they move out to the south. MRF forces prepare to renew the fight in the morning.

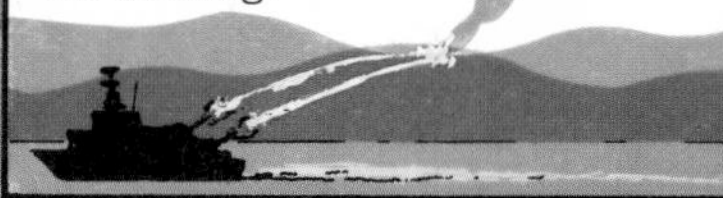

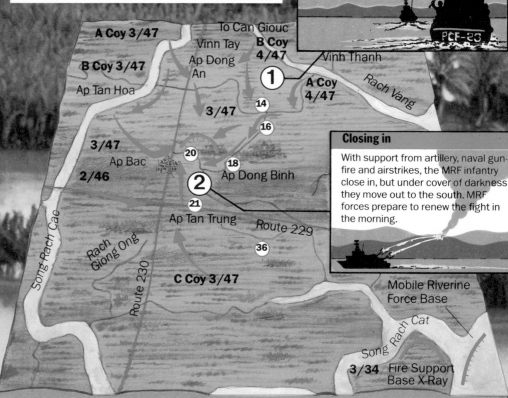

Can Giouc
20-21 June 1967

On 20 June 1967, the MRF troops of the 47th Infantry Regiment swept forward in pursuit of a large Viet Cong force encountered on the previous day. By the following morning, a Viet Cong headquarters had been taken, and the 5th Nha BE Battalion had been effectively eliminated.

Key

- Viet Cong positions
- US forces
- 3/47 US battalions
- 20 US objectives

Renewing the fight

20 June At first light, the MRF infantry move off in pursuit of the enemy, engaging isolated groups as the day progressed.
1700 All MRF companies are in position around the main body of Viet Cong.

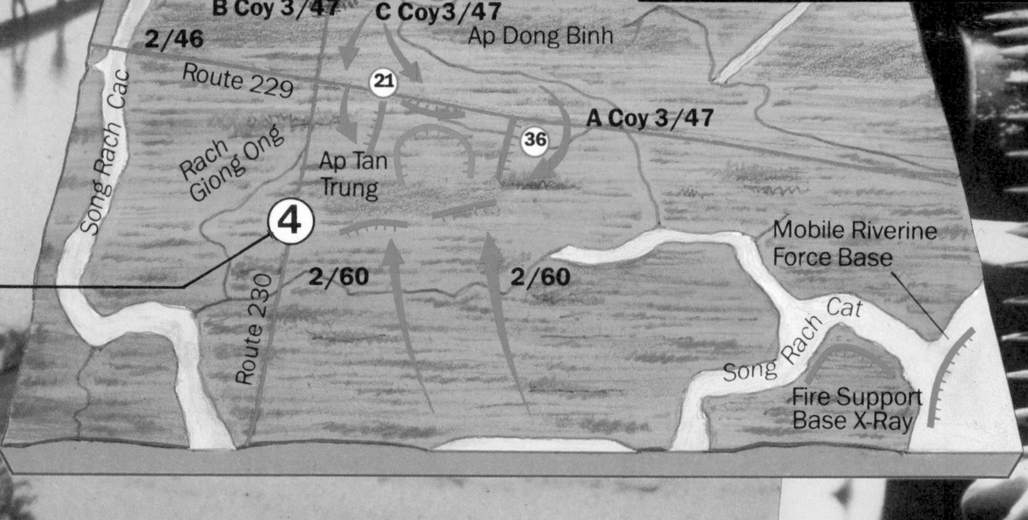
To Can Giouc
14
Ap Tan Hoa
A Coy 3/47
16
3
Ap Bac
20
18
B Coy 3/47
C Coy 3/47
Ap Dong Binh
2/46
Route 229
21
A Coy 3/47
36
Rach Giong Ong
Ap Tan Trung
Song Rach Cac
4
Mobile Riverine Force Base
2/60
2/60
Route 230
Song Rach Cat
Fire Support Base X-Ray

The enemy surrounded

20/21 June Resupply and casualty evacuation is carried out during the night. At first light, B Company, 3/47, sweeps through the enemy position encountering no resistance. MRF forces continue operations against isolated groups of Viet Cong.

Below: The Mekong Delta must rate as one of the worst terrains for modern infantry warfare. VC bunkers, often disguised as huts, commanded uninterrupted lines of fire over the open, flooded paddy fields. Below right: A PBR (River Patrol Boat) crew-member manning an M60 shows the strain of the constant vigilance needed on the waterways.

were men with six months of combat experience behind them and some of them resented my intervention. I then let them know that I respected their experience to date but I reminded them that I'd already fought in two wars before this one and they had better give me their full attention. After repeating my analysis of the tactics I felt would be useful to them the next day, I was sure that they had generally accepted my admonition. Only one company, as it turned out, threw caution to the winds, and it suffered disastrous casualties as a result.

My plan of attack called for a sweep from north to south. For the blocking force in the southern portion I had at my command the 2nd Battalion of the 46th ARVN (Army of the Republic of South Vietnam) Regiment. I agreed with Captain Wells that the assault craft should go up only those rivers and streams that were wide enough to permit them to make 180-degree turns. The boats were to enter the waterways as the tide was rising, permitting greater speed and a longer period at high tide level immediately following entry.

The methods of command that I intended to use had been developed during the past six months of operations with the 9th Infantry Division. By organis-

CAN GIUOC DISTRICT

When the vessels of the Mobile Riverine Force approached can Giuoc District, located in the eastern part of Long An Province, to begin operations in June 1967, they found terrain quite different to that previously experienced by the force in Vietnam. Bordered by large rivers, the low ground contained an extremely good network of navigable channels, permitting small assault craft to penetrate right to the heart of the region. However, it was an area devoted mainly to rice-growing and each tide inundated the paddies in up to two feet of water. Though Can Giuoc District lent itself admirably to riverine operations in respect of transport, it was by no means ideal for the task of flushing out a well established enemy. The force's 2nd Brigade had fought in the jungles of Bien Hoa Province and the Rung Sat Special Zone, and in the fruit orchards and dense undergrowth of Dinh Tuong and northern Kien Hoa Provinces, but here existed wide expanses of exposed paddy land, divided only by isolated patches of vegetation and sparse lines of nipa palms. The open areas gave the Viet Cong extended observation and almost unlimited fields of fire from combat villages sited on artificially built-up ground. The only cover was afforded by the banks of streams and the intermittent dykes separating the paddies. Thus, once they were landed from their assault boats, only the most closely co-ordinated procedures of fire and movement could ensure for the strike units a marginally secure passage across the fields.

Left: Carrying his vital M16 assault rifle and radio equipment well above the water, a GI wades through a stream in the Can Giuoc District. The flow of the tide was a constant factor in Delta operations.

ing the combat area into a large number of intermediate objectives, phase lines and zones, we had the capacity of rapidly changing direction and shifting boundaries. Operational control of the infantry companies could be switched between the battalion commanders, and their actions could be coordinated with all forms of fire support, an essential requirement when closing with a well dug-in enemy. Thus, a simple radio transmission could change the entire direction of a battle, drastically cutting down the volume of supplementary orders normally issued to individual elements of the fighting force.

That same night, the Mobile Riverine Force sent five infantry companies into the area by assault craft. They were drawn from my 2nd Brigade's 3rd and 4th Battalions of the 47th Infantry Regiment (3/47th and 4/47th). The brigade reserve, C Company, 3/47th, under the command of Captain Ron Menner, was to move by water to Fire Support Base Whiskey, which was located at the French fort. This location was also providing a helicopter pick-up zone for a quick reaction when needed. Also under cover of darkness, the 2nd Battalion, 46th ARVN, was picked up on schedule by the Navy assault boats and moved to positions from which to cover their movement objectives and then to establish a blocking position near the deserted town of Ap Bac, oriented to the east. In addition, the MRF's Mobile Intelligence Civil Affairs Team was already operating in Can Giuoc, picking up local intelligence of VC forces in the area and their positions.

The morning of 19 June appeared bright and cloudless and the move of the brigade on the waterways was going smoothly. At about 1000 hours, my command helicopter received intelligence that a battalion-sized VC force was located in the vicinity of Objective 20, which lay to the east of the ARVN battalion's positions along Route 230 near Ap Bac. I immediately decided to commit my brigade reserve, C Company, 3/47th, by bringing them airmobile into a landing zone south of Objective 21. From there they would reconnoitre northeast towards the enemy. Since A Company, 4/47th, had been put ashore near Objective 14, the natural course was to have them proceed south to Objective 18 and establish a block along the bank of a stream just to the north of Objective 20. I gave operational control of C Company to Lieutenant-Colonel Guy Tutwiler, commander of the 4th Battalion, who was already moving the company east in assault boats. Major H. Glen Penny, the acting battalion commander of 3/47th, was instructed to move both of the remaining companies of the 3rd Battalion, A and B, south for possible commitment. Thanks to our methods of operation, it took only a few minutes to get this plan of manoeuvre underway.

At the same time, A Company came upon some Claymore mines suspended in trees

At 1105, Tutwiler's reserve company was in position and pressing northeast. By 1135, C Company, 4/47th, had landed by water on the beachhead to the east of Objective 20. From my helicopter I saw that they were drifting towards the advance elements of the 2/46th ARVN's blocking positions, and I warned the South Vietnamese riflemen not to fire.

It soon became apparent that the enemy position had been mislocated. Elements of C Company, 3/47th, and C Company of the 4th Battalion met after moving through Objective 21 and to the vicinity of Objective 20. At 1150 hours, C Company, 4/47th, was in the process of moving up toward the river bank when the enemy opened fire from across the river with an automatic weapon, causing casualties and the death of Lieutenant Schulman, the weapons platoon leader, who had just disembarked.

At the same time, A Company of the 4th Battalion was moving to put in the block at Objective 18 and came upon some Claymore mines suspended in trees. Despite my previous day's admonition about putting the scouts out sufficiently in advance, the two lead platoons were in line and not more than 100m behind their reconnaissance elements. To com-

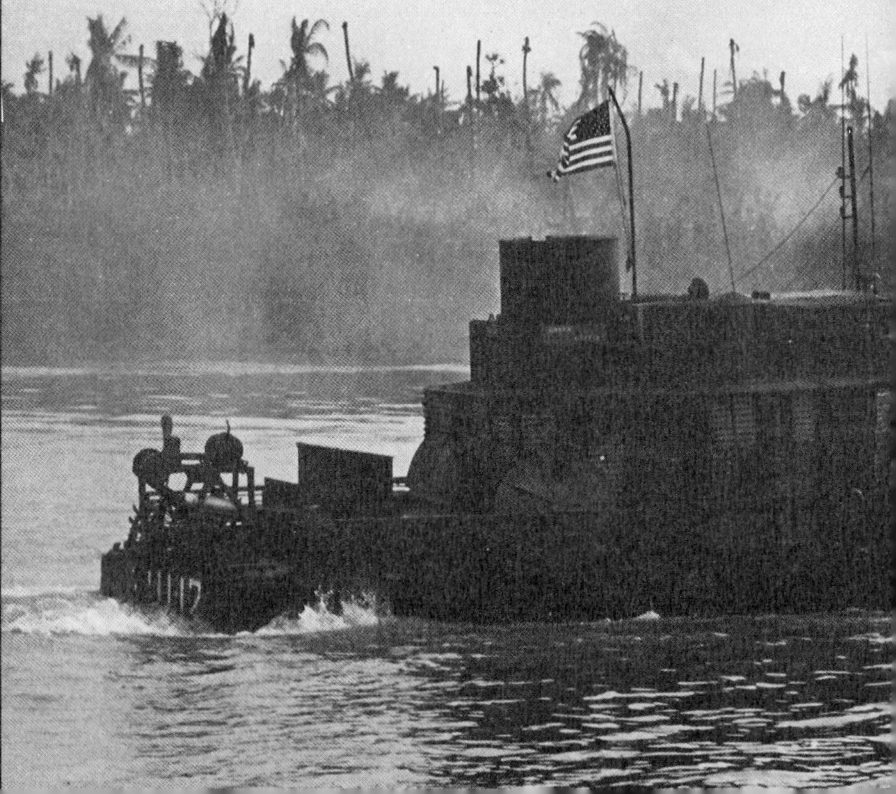

pound the error, all of the company elements were too close to the huts and nipa palms that constituted Objective 18. Just as the recon elements sounded the alarm, the VC opened fire with about six 0.3in machine guns, two 0.5in machine guns and many automatic weapons. The initial fire, coupled with the detonation of the Claymore mines, caused considerable casualties in A Company. Captain Bob Reeves, the A Company commander, attempted to manoeuvre his 1st Platoon to the right in order to outflank the enemy's position. In attempting to do this, the 1st Platoon made what amounted to a frontal attack against a well organised and fortified L-shaped position. The company was receiving fire all along its front and from both its right and left flanks from firing positions that enabled almost perfect cross-fire. Reeves had lost all of his officer platoon leaders and squad leaders almost from the outset of being fired upon, and to complicate his situation, one of the platoon radio operators who was either wounded or dead had his handset permanently keyed, so that Reeves was unable to communicate with any of his platoons on the company command radio net.

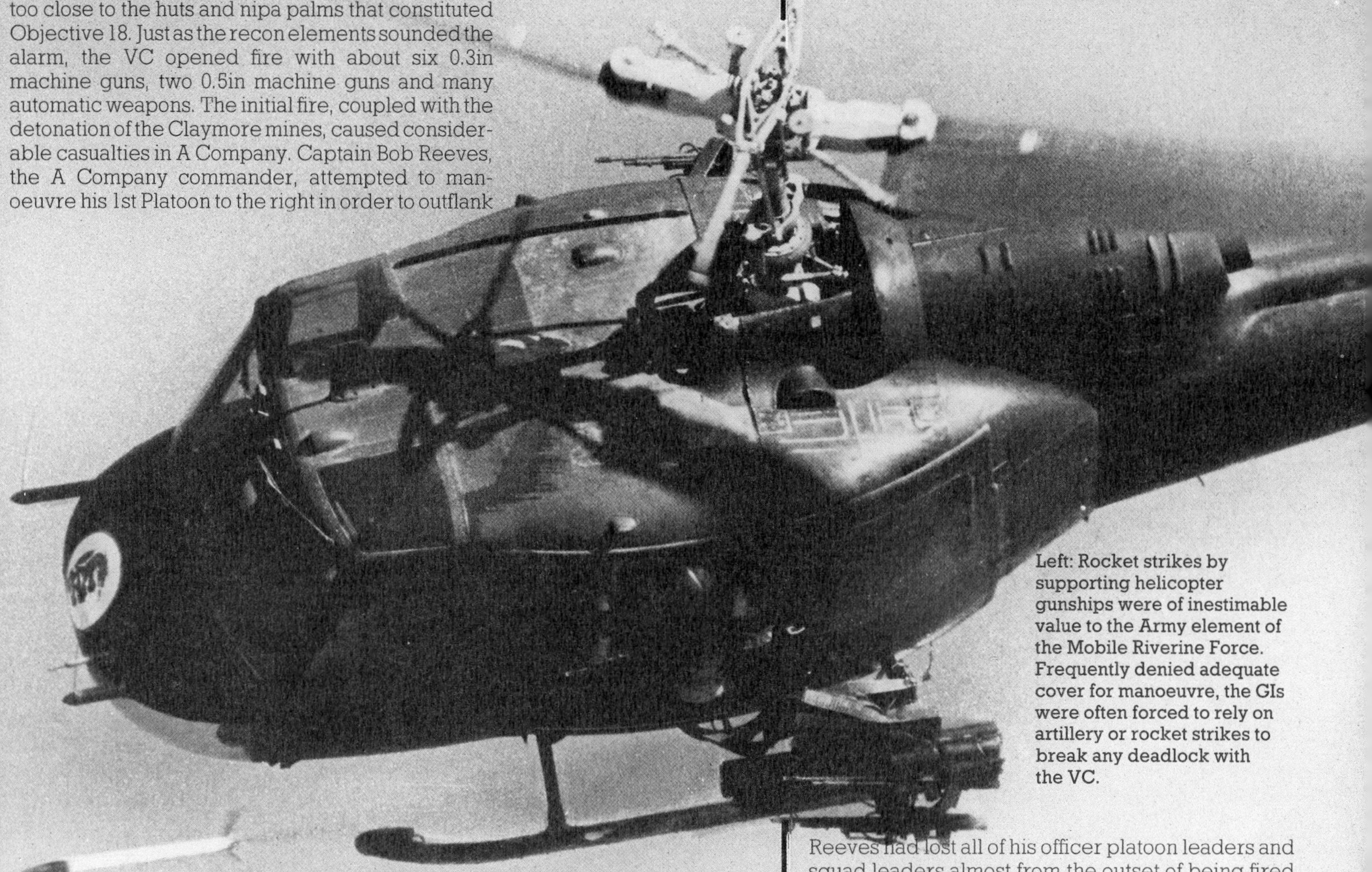

Left: Rocket strikes by supporting helicopter gunships were of inestimable value to the Army element of the Mobile Riverine Force. Frequently denied adequate cover for manoeuvre, the GIs were often forced to rely on artillery or rocket strikes to break any deadlock with the VC.

Below: As dawn comes up, an ATC (Armoured Troop Carrier) ploughs past a mist-shrouded shoreline towards Can Giuoc.

Circling overhead in my command and control ship, I urged Tutwiler to get the artillery cranked up immediately. This took just a little longer than normal, delayed by the difficulty of locating the exact forward positions of the A Company elements. While Reeves was attempting to rally his remaining elements to make an organised fight of it, we finally succeeded in getting significant amounts of artillery on the enemy positions by 1200 hours, which helped to curb the enemy fire against Reeves and his men. We were able to get 105mm artillery fire within 25m and the 155mm fire within 50m of his units without taking undue casualties. With the artillery fire suppressing the VC, three medical evacuation missions by helicopter were made to A Company, 4/47th, but others had to be suspended because of the intense 0.5in fire and the loss of two choppers on the other side of the river in the vicinity of Objective 20. By this time, by the use of radio and recognition panels, we were able to determine accurately A Company's units, and we commenced bringing in air strikes utilising 750lb bombs to within 75m of the forward platoons. All of the fire was co-ordinated by both ground and airborne artillery observers and USAF Forward Air Controllers (FACs). Support was provided by helicopter gunships during the day and night along with naval gunfire from the river.

Colonel Tutwiler immediately shifted B Company of the 4th Battalion, which had been moving on the

battalion right flank, into the area behind A Company to give covering fire and help with the medical evacuation. He ordered C Company, 4/47th, to move up to the river bank along the dyke on the south side of the stream opposite the enemy positions and maintain contact, while he manoeuvred C Company, 3/47th, north across the stream further west, with orders to then fight its way east against the right flank of the enemy positions.

In conjunction with this flanking movement, I directed Major Penny to move his A and B Companies, with haste, to the southeast to link up with C Company, 3/47th, which by now was crossing the river in order to move against Objective 17. Movement was difficult because by this time the tide was starting to come back in, covering most of the area with up to two feet of water. At 1545 hours, I had Penny resume operational control of his C Company and directed that his A Company move into a blocking position just south of Objective 15. B Company, 3/47th, was to join C Company in making its attack.

Navy monitors and ATCs were moving up and down the stream, pouring fire against the bunker lines

Soon B and C Companies, 3/47th, were ready to begin their assault. They were instructed that security took precedence over speed and that reconnaissance by fire was encouraged. Then, preceded by what amounted to a rolling barrage which shifted from position to position ahead of the advancing troops, the companies moved from dyke to dyke, waiting as the artillery hit the dyke line immediately ahead, then moving forward. As position after position was discovered empty of enemy defenders, it became apparent that a line of fortified positions had been turned, forcing the VC southward, possibly to an assembly area.

The co-ordinated attack by B and C Companies, 3/47th, continued until 2000 hours. It was now decided to re-supply and police the battle area. Illumination was brought in over suspected VC positions as helicopters brought in night packs of ammunition, water and combat rations for the following day. The dead and seriously wounded were evacuated by the same helicopters.

Meanwhile, companies of the 4th Battalion, 47th Infantry, had encountered a well defended line of

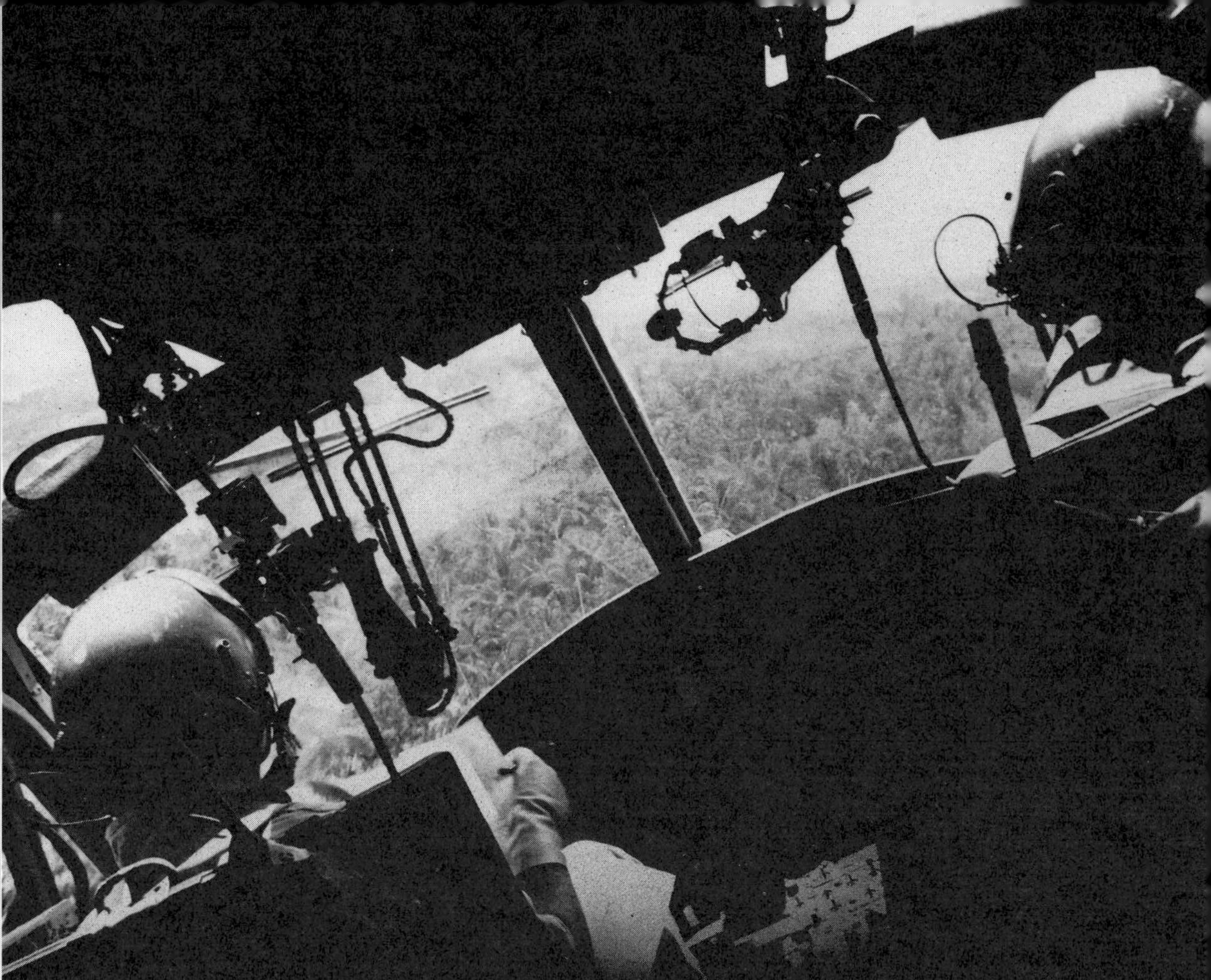

VC bunkers. C Company had begun a systematic destruction of the line, employing a 90mm recoilless rifle and the direct fire support of Navy monitors and ATCs (Armoured Troop Carriers), which were moving up and down the stream pouring both 20mm and 40mm fire against the bunker lines, sometimes at a distance of no more than 25m.

By 2000 hours I felt that we had done the enemy considerable damage with the dual assaults of the rifle companies of both the 3rd and 4th Battalions of the 47th Infantry and with the combined firepower of our artillery, naval gunfire, helicopter gunships and air strikes, all of which were continued after darkness fell. A Company, 4/47th, had taken undue casualties, including almost 40 men killed. We had to take care of this company during the night, especially to provide for the wounded, as we had been unable to evacuate during the day because of the intense enemy fire. Many of those who had been wounded away from the river and the stream on the right of the company zone had to lie in water until night time, and a number bled to death. Some of the more fortunate were evacuated by PAB and by the Navy boats along the river.

My second concern was to try and hold the enemy in his present positions until we could finish him off the next day. This was most difficult because of the numerous rivers and streams and the fact that there was no way to tie my units together to form a continuous perimeter. We used a great deal of illumination, delivered both by the artillery and by the USAF C-47 gunships which remained over our operations area in support.

With the kinds of losses that the brigade had incurred in trying to close with the enemy, I knew that my superior commanders would be looking closely at my operations the next day. I was aware that I would have to land close to this battalion-sized enemy force. I also knew that if the enemy got out by exfiltration he wasn't going to get very far. At around 2300 my units to the north of the enemy position were vigorously probed by small enemy groups, many of

Above: From his command-and-control helicopter, General Fulton was able to maintain close co-ordination between his units. Left: A 9th Division infantryman begins a mission. Above left: Huey gunships comb the waterways for enemy movement, while (inset) two OV-10 Bronco aircraft, armed with Zuni rockets, seek opportunity targets. Far left: Viet Cong guerrillas charge US positions in the Delta.

M-9

whom were killed in the contacts. However, the regimental commander of the 46th ARVN let us know that if the enemy was probing north, the main body would probably go south, in the direction of my Objective 36. Taking a gamble, I directed my staff to make immediate plans to move against this objective in the morning of the 20th. In addition, two fresh companies from the 2/60th Infantry, based to the west in Long An Province, were to be airlifted at dawn to the Fire Support Base, from where they would move by water along the Rach Cat river to beach below Objective 36.

In the meantime, B Company, 3/47th, reported no activity during the hours of darkness. C Company, 3/47th, experienced periodic probes by patrols and smallarms fire until about midnight. They responded with a 90mm recoilless rifle firing Beehive rounds, each of which contained over 8000 lethal flechettes. A Company, 3/47th, who were settled in their blocking position across three small north-south waterways, reported periodic attempts by individual VC to move to the north up those streams. They killed three VC with smallarms fire during the night, and they dropped concussion grenades into the streams at random intervals until dawn.

Just prior to first light, helicopters brought in a hot breakfast for the three rifle companies and lifted out all unnecessary equipment. Just after first light, B and C Companies were directed to sweep the battlefield to their front (east), stopping at least 100m short of the positions held by A Company, 4/47th. No effort was made to open enemy positions collapsed by fire or other means. The number of weapons (especially crew-served and automatic) found, indicated that a local force battalion had been decimated. VC units caught in this position typically disintegrated as individuals or small groups attempted to make their way out of the area. The enemy was, however, highly disciplined to evacuate the wounded, the weapons and the dead, in that order.

One machine gun had been emplaced on an occupied VC spider hole during the night

Since it was considered that most of the escapees had moved through the area to the west of Objective 20, and generally south, the 3rd Battalion, 47th Infantry, was ordered to search in that direction. B Company, 3/47th, was directed to move out of the battle area southwest to Objective 19, and thereafter to the south, parallel to but at least 200m to the east of Route 230. C Company, 3/47th, was assigned an axis through Objectives 20, 33 and 34. A Company, 3/4th, was in reserve, to follow B Company through Objectives 19, 20 and 21 on order.

At about mid-morning, 20 June, B and C Companies moved out on their assigned axes. A Company, 3/47th, consolidating its position and preparing to follow B Company, found that one machine gun had been emplaced on an occupied VC spider hole

Above left: USS *Benewah*, a converted World War II vessel, was one of the mother ships of the Mobile Riverine Force, acting both as a barracks ship and as a command flagship. Moored alongside her floating dock are three monitors (with forward gun turrets) and six ATCs. The 10th craft is an ATC(H), an ATC fitted with a helicopter flightdeck. Above: A monitor brings its formidable armament, including its 40mm forward cannon, against an enemy strongpoint on the waterfront.

during the night. While it waited to move out it turned to searching the area, finding more spider holes, but no more VC.

B and C Companies, 3/47th, moved on their assigned axes, searching carefully and moving slowly; both reported evidence of some kind of movement through the area, and dwellings were empty. The absence of civilians indicated the presence of VC in the area. The populace did not seem to fear either side singly, but didn't want to be caught in the middle. Careful, low-level air reconnaissances were flown in advance of the moving companies, on random directions and intervals.

Air reconnaissance indicated recent activity in an old plantation just north of Objective 36 and a tributary of the Rach Gion Ong. Although there was no sign of life in the area at this time, the dyke lines and trails showed much recent activity. Although most dyke and stream lines in this portion of the Delta had been fortified with bunkers and foxholes at one time or other, there were many recent footprints in the paddy mud and fresh mud had been heaped on the paddy dykes.

Despite the battle of the day before, this was another day and another grid square. The local populace was assumed friendly and reconnaissance by fire was forbidden.

Both B and C Companies, 3/47th, were warned of the suspect location, and to move with greater care as they crossed Route 229 (east-west) and approached the Rach Giong Ong. C Company moved directly towards the position, with the objective of occupying the last covered and concealed position short of the suspect area. They would then be in a position to develop the situation. As they reached the edge of a nipa palm grove and dyke line, Captain Menner, the commander of C Company, reported that he could see emplacements about 100m to his front, but could not tell if they were occupied. At about this time, a rifleman of C Company was forced to fire at a water-buffalo charging him. When he did so, automatic fire broke out from along the front of the suspect area. The rules of engagement promptly changed and artillery and air strikes began immediately. In no time there was a FAC over the area, and there was no shortage of

LIEUTENANT-GENERAL WILLIAM B. FULTON

William B. Fulton was commissioned into the US Army as a second-lieutenant upon his graduation from the University of California ROTC Program at Berkeley in May 1942. During World War II, he commanded a rifle company in the 91st Infantry Division, fighting in Italy from 1944 until the cessation of hostilities in 1945. During the Korean War, he served as a plans officer on the staff of the Advanced Headquarters, Army Forces Far East. When the 9th Infantry Division was formed in early 1966, Fulton activated and trained the 2nd Brigade. In January 1967, the 2nd Brigade entered combat and experienced very heavy fighting in the Mekong Delta region. In June 1967, the brigade and its three infantry battalions teamed up with Navy Task Force 117 to form the MRF. After commanding the 2nd Brigade for 20 months, Fulton was designated the Assistant Division Commander of the 9th Infantry Division, in which capacity he continued to supervise the operations of the MRF, along with those of the 3rd Brigade of the division which was also located in the Mekong Delta area. In 1972, as a major-general, he had the privilege of reactivating, recruiting and training the 9th Infantry Division to operational readiness at Fort Lewis, Washington, where it is still a serving unit in the Active Army. After 35 years of professional soldiering, Fulton ended his military service as the Director of the Army Staff in Washington DC in 1977.

M-91-2
M-91-2

Above: A Mobile Riverine Force convoy, including a monitor and Armoured Troop Carriers, steams down river after a series of search-and-destroy missions near Saigon. The introduction of well-armed flotillas of shallow-draught craft finally gave the US forces the weapon they needed to destroy the communist guerrillas in the maze of Mekong Delta waterways. The tactics evolved, in which infantry sweeps of designated sectors were co-ordinated with naval manoeuvres to block all exits along the rivers, made it extremely difficult for the Viet Cong to escape annihilation.

artillery fire or close air support. At one point there were seven flights of F-100s waiting to make their bombing runs.

B Company, 3/47th, was directed to continue its move southwards to the Rach Gion Ong, and then to move east until it made contact and linked up with C Company. A helicopter airlift was provided to move A Company, 3/47th, to a position northeast of Objective 36, from which it was directed to move west and link up with C Company. Concurrently, I had placed a reinforced company of 2/60th Infantry in position south of the Rach Giong Ong, with the mission of blocking any movement to the south.

B Company, 3/47th, reported periodic sniper fire, and had to clear several concentrations of booby traps as it moved east. A Company, 3/47th, received sniper fire in its landing zone, and as it moved into position south of the river, but reported killing a number of VC attempting to escape south across or along the river.

By about 1700 hours, all companies were in position and had tied in on their flanks. Aircraft, artillery and gunships had fired on the VC position alternately and continuously for nearly two hours. Napalm and rocket fire had removed virtually all vegetation on the perimeter. From this time until dark, efforts were made to advance both A Company to the west and B Company to the east, but each time the artillery fire was shifted and the infantry started to move, the volume of automatic fire from the VC was so intense that a substantial gain without unacceptable casualties was not possible. This situation continued until after darkness. It was then decided to hold in place through the night, firing artillery into the VC area intermittently. Routine re-supply and evacuation of the wounded was conducted during the night.

At first light on 21 June, B Company, 3/47th, swept the area from west to east and found no live VC. Evidence indicated that survivors had floated or swum down river to the southeast. The documents, materiel and weapons found indicated that VC fighting elements and a headquarters had occupied this position.

Very early in the morning, I took my command-and-control group airborne to make an aerial reconnaissance. Coming out of the area at Objective 36, I could see converging footprints in the mud left by the outgoing tide. By a quick estimate, I reckoned that no more than 100 individuals had exfiltrated from the position. I then directed elements of the 4/47th and the 3/47th to conduct sweeps along the streams to find the remnants of the enemy.

During the next few days, units of the 2nd Brigade conducted continuous riverine and airmobile small-unit operations against suspect positions throughout the area. Numerous individuals and small groups from the 5th Nha Be Battalion were captured or killed and several caches of weapons were found. Evidence and prisoner interrogations indicated that the 5th Nha Be Battalion was effectively destroyed on 19-20 June. Its survivors were instructed to hide their weapons and evade capture.

By our count of the enemy dead, we had killed 250 Viet Cong during this short period. Assuming a large number of enemy wounded, we had effectively eliminated the 5th Nha Be Battalion as an effective fighting formation. In addition, numerous personnel from six district companies had been in training under the protection of the local VC force battalion at the time we hit it on the morning of 19 June, and they too had sustained casualties.

Over the period of the next two months, the Mobile Riverine Force returned from time to time to Can Giuoc to hunt the VC. By 1 September, the area was in the process of being pacified and returned to South Vietnamese control, leaving the MRF to drive deeper into the Delta in search of larger quarry, which it continued to find with great success.

THE AUTHOR Lieutenant-General William B. Fulton was commander of the 2nd Brigade, 9th Infantry Division, the US Army component of the Mobile Riverine Force, during its operations in the Mekong Delta in Vietnam.

ON HOSTILE SHORES

Inserted by submarine, the Combined Operations Pilotage Parties (COPP) reconnoitred for many of the great Allied amphibious landings of World War II

OF ALL THE SPECIAL units raised by the Allies during World War II, the 'Coppists' must be numbered among the most valuable. Their vital contribution to the amphibious invasions of North Africa, Sicily, Italy and Normandy was quite disproportionate to their numbers. It is no exaggeration to say that on the work of perhaps no more than half a dozen men hung the fate of thousands of invading troops, who were relying on the beach information COPP supplied and then on being guided in to the landing zones.

The initials COPP stood for 'Combined Operations Pilotage Parties', although 'Combined Operations Police Patrols' was used as a cover name. The teams were the brainchild of Lieutenant-Commander Nigel Clogstoun-Willmott, a specialist navigation officer in the Royal Navy who, in the early years of the war, understood what Combined Operations entailed long before such undertakings became widely implemented. His pioneer reconnoitring of the Rhodes Island beaches – with the founder of the Special Boat Squadron (SBS), Major Roger Courtney – resulted in him training teams to reconnoitre and mark the North African invasion beaches. This in turn

Above: The Royal Navy and Army personnel of Lieutenant Ralph Stanbury's No.5 COPP, photographed at the Combined Operations Pilotage Parties' headquarters at the yacht club on Hayling Island, Chichester harbour. Right: COPP members train in a two-man folbot. These craft were adapted to carry various means of signalling to waiting amphibious forces.

led to a Combined Operations Headquarters (COHQ) meeting on 27 November 1942 which formally approved the formation of COPP.

Willmott had to be very persuasive when putting across his reasons for reconnoitring the Rhodes landing beaches – that the charts varied by as much as a mile was perhaps a conclusive one – and when permission was eventually forthcoming he had to organise equipment and techniques from scratch. Initially, he planned to row ashore in a dinghy launched from a submarine, but after meeting Courtney a collapsible folbot was decided upon. Items such as torches, watches and compasses were waterproofed with periscope grease or naval-issue contraceptives, while the treatment of clothing was even more experimental – heavy sweaters and long-johns were liberally soaked in grease and worn with a waistcoat-type lifebelt. Techniques for swimming ashore unseen and signalling the submarine with infra-red gear had to be worked out, and constant practice was needed to develop ways of moving silently out of the water and around the beach.

Many people in high places were sceptical of his ideas, but Courtney again came to his aid

The reconnaissances were carried out successfully, but the Rhodes landings were cancelled and it looked as if Willmott's ideas about beach pilotage would not be used again. Then, just two months before the invasion of North Africa in November 1942 (Operation Torch), he was summoned to COHQ and asked to raise and train several teams to reconnoitre and then mark the Algerian beaches. Time was desperately short. He was given top priority for equipment and personnel, although Willmott found it difficult to find the right kind of either. Many people in high places were sceptical of his ideas, but Courtney again came to his aid, lending him both men and canoes, while the Chief of Combined Operations (CCO), Lord Louis Mountbatten, after some close questioning, allowed him to take from his staff a number of top navigators and administrators.

A last-minute Admiralty ban on any beach landings prior to the North African invasion made submarine reconnaissance the only method of mapping the landing zones. Two submarines, with Willmott and three of his fellow navigators aboard, spent a fortnight surveying the beaches around Oran and Algiers. Each beach was carefully sketched, and silhouette maps were drawn for the use of every landing craft officer taking part in the landings.

Willmott's 24 men then travelled to their beaches – three around Algiers and one at Oran – in five submarines. These fixed their positions through their periscopes and then dived, surfacing again after dark to release their canoe teams. The COPP navigators took the marker canoes to the correct positions for signalling in the invasion force; from here, at zero hour, they would begin flashing their torches seawards.

In the meantime, the submarines withdrew to a start-line eight miles out to sea and hoisted beacons, around which the invading fleet rallied. The assault craft were then lowered and Willmott and his navigators joined them to take in the assault craft.

Willmott's success in Operation Torch led directly to him being ordered to found COPP. Suddenly enthusiastic after their early scepticism, the authorities requested he train 50 teams for immediate availability. This was quite impossible, but after

Below: Lieutenant-Commander Nigel Clogstoun-Willmott, founder of the Combined Operations Pilotage Parties, demonstrates the watertight, rubberised canvas suit worn by COPP swimmers during beach reconnaissance missions. Below right: Lieutenant Geoffrey Hall, CO of No.7 COPP (left) with (from his left) Sub-Lieutenant Ruari McLean, Sub-Lieutenant W.H. Jennings and Captain Bill Lucas, RE. Below centre: Officers and men of the Malta-based submarine HMS *Uhited* with their 'operational record'. Submarines were used to drop COPP teams close to enemy shores, a somewhat unpopular task with the submariners since it was forbidden to attack enemy targets when the valuable COPP personnel were on board. Below far right: The COPP Depot at Hayling Island. Bottom: HMS *Safari*, the submarine which inserted Lieutenant Neville McHarg's No.3 COPP onto the Sicilian coast in January 1943.

finding a suitable training base – the yacht club c
Hayling Island in Chichester harbour – and suitab
staff, teams, numbered from 1 to 10, were traine
during the next two years. (Teams which we
raised after the first 10 were not given new number
they were used to replace personnel who ha
become casualties, or had returned to general duty
By June 1944, COPP numbered 174 officers and me

The COPP naval personnel wore khaki battl
dress with Royal Navy Commando flashes on the
shoulders. Though trained as thoroughly as othe
commandos, they never wore the green beret. F
administrative reasons, the army personnel in COF
were officially part of the SBS, and wore SBS should
flashes and the green beret.

The intensive training course that Willmott d
veloped took about four months. The messag
scrawled on the blackboard in the lecture roo
startled many newcomers: 'People would rather d
than think. Many of them do.' The pace that Willmc

set was hectic, for he knew that time was short. Without the most thorough grounding in all aspects of COPP work a man had little hope of survival.

This was soon proved when two COPP teams, Nos.3 and 4, had to be despatched, before their training was completed, to the Mediterranean in January 1943 to reconnoitre beaches for the invasion of Sicily. Their leader, Lieutenant-Commander Norman Teacher, had been the navigator off the Oran beaches, but he had never undertaken a beach recce. His two teams were inadequately equipped and the result was disaster. Teacher and two others in No.4 COPP were lost, while No.3 (led by Lieutenant Neville McHarg) lost two canoeists captured.

But these were not the only casualties off Sicily. Two naval teams, formed in the Mediterranean along the lines expounded by Willmott, had also been sent to reconnoitre the Sicilian beaches. When the two groups met it was found that their training and equipment did not even reach the standard of Teacher's two teams. Extra training was quickly instituted and equipment hastily borrowed, but only their leader, Lieutenant Robert Smith, and his paddler survived the reconnaissances. They managed

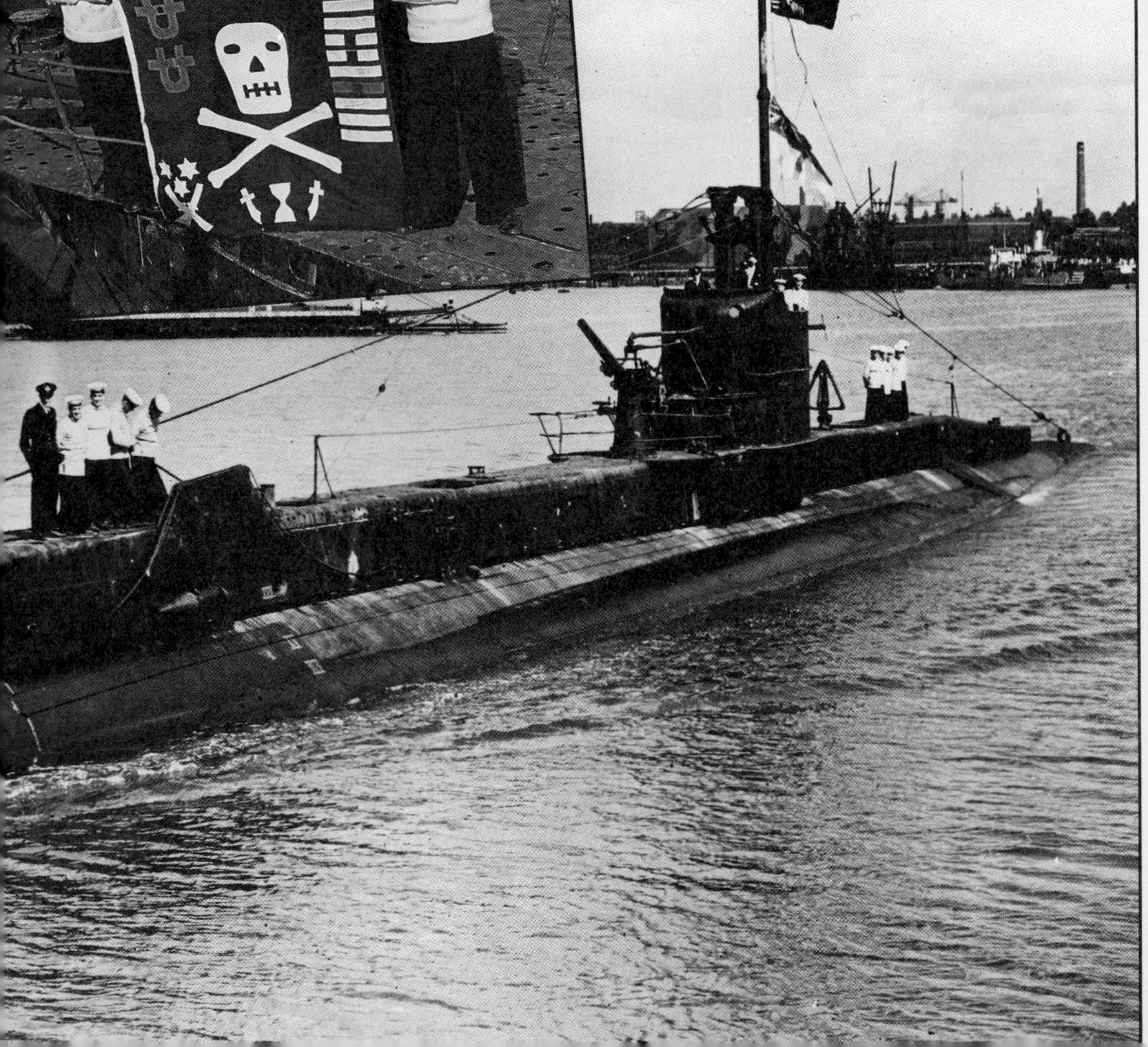

COMBINED OPERATIONS PILOTAGE PARTIES

Each COPP team was an entirely self-contained group of highly-trained specialists, varying in size between 10 and 12 members. The teams were kept small so that they could be airlifted at short notice to any theatre of war. Most jobs were interchangeable, so that if one member was made inoperative the team could still function. The leader, who was known as S/COPP, was a lieutenant-commander or senior lieutenant who specialised in either navigation or hydrography. His assistant, A/COPP, was a lieutenant or sub-lieutenant and was known as the assistant Naval Reconnaissance Officer. The first lieutenant of the team, known as M/COPP, was a lieutenant of the Royal Naval Volunteer Reserve (RNVR). He was usually older than the others and was in charge of maintenance, stores, accommodation, intelligence and welfare, and would go on operations only if the team was fully extended. His A/M/COPP was a sub-lieutenant or midshipman of the RNVR who was also a spare operational Naval Reconnaissance Officer. The Military Reconnaissance Officer, E/COPP, always came from the Royal Engineers and was a captain, though the most senior in a group of teams was a major. Three seaman ratings, petty officers or below in rank, acted as paddlers; an engine-room artificer or mechanic was responsible to M/COPP for gear maintenance; and a Royal Engineers NCO was an operational reserve E/COPP or acted as E/COPP's bodyguard during a land reconnaissance. Later, a draughtsman and a batman and storekeeper were added to the team.

to paddle back to Malta, but two others were lost and four captured.

Despite this early setback, it was becoming evident that the work of the Coppists was vital if any amphibious operation was to succeed. Throughout the early months of 1943 Willmott battled to obtain such basic equipment as adequate suits and a sturdier canoe than the hopelessly inadequate folbot, while at the same time developing techniques for such essential tasks as accurately measuring beach gradients and recovering a team after a beach reconnaissance. He was in constant conflict with the authorities, who still seemed to have little comprehension of what he was doing. When he insisted on having brass anchors for his canoes he was hauled before the Third Sea Lord. Luckily, the Admiral was a navigator and quickly grasped why, with a compass in its bows, a canoe needed an anchor made of non-magnetic material, but not all senior officers were as understanding. Administration was also a constant nightmare. Initially an independent unit, COPP was subsequently made part of the Special Boat Unit and then of the Special Services Group, before finally becoming an independent unit again under the direct control of the Chief of Combined Operations.

Amer's swimsuit was making him too buoyant so he slit it with his commando knife

In the spring of 1943, No. 5 COPP (led by Lieutenant Ralph Stanbury) and No.6 COPP (Lieutenant Don Amer), adequately trained and equipped with proper suits and canoes, were rushed to the Mediterranean to undertake reconnaissances for the revised landings on Sicily. Stanbury surveyed four beaches southeast of Syracuse, where General Sir Miles Dempsey's XIII Corps was to land, while Amer reconnoitred General George Patton's Seventh US Army beaches between Licata and Gela on the southern coast.

During one beach reconnaissance Amer had a very narrow escape. While close to the shore he was spotted by a sentry. He froze, his head and shoulders just above the water. The sentry called another to come and have a look. They probably decided that Amer must be a seal for they started throwing stones at him. Amer's swimsuit was making him too buoyant so he slit it with his commando knife and then managed to slide under the water and escape. Now, however, his suit was weighed down with water and he only just managed to reach the canoe before exhaustion overtook him.

After sketching the landing areas, and going ashore to obtain samples of sand and pebbles, Stanbury's small force guided the landing craft ashore with the aid of motor launches and marker canoes. This accomplished, Stanbury and his team went on to survey several beaches on the Italian mainland, including Salerno, where they again successfully guided in the assault forces. But by now it was acknowledged that the strain on COPP personnel was so great that they could only operate for short periods. McHarg's No. 4 COPP was returned to the UK in July 1943, with Amer and Stanbury following in October.

While Nos. 4, 5 and 6 COPP were in the Mediterranean, the next team to become fully operational, No.7 COPP (led by Lieutenant Hall), was sent to the Far East in June 1943. The team carried out operations in the Arakan and Sumatra until January 1945, when it returned to Britain. No.7 was followed in September 1943 by No.8 COPP (Lieutenant Fred Ponsonby), which operated in the Arakan until March 1945, and by No.10 COPP (Lieutenant Townson). When the invasion of the Andaman Islands, which No.10 COPP was to reconnoitre, was cancelled, it was despatched to the Mediterranean to help mark the beaches for the Anzio landings. In March 1945, No.10 COPP was joined by No.2 COPP (Lieutenant Fyson), which had been taking part in reconnaissances and beach marking for the proposed invasion of Corsica. Both teams did remarkable work in the Aegean and the Adriatic, where, among other tasks, they piloted commandos on raids on the Italian coast.

In May 1943 Willmott's team, No.1 COPP, became the training and development unit at the COPP depot, but towards the end of the year it was made operational again to survey beaches for the Normandy landings. Also involved in this hazardous undertaking were No.6 COPP (Lieutenant Amer) and No.9 COPP (Lieutenant Geoff Lyne).

It was decided – haunted as the top brass always were by the possibility of a landing place being unwittingly betrayed by COPP – to survey the beaches well in advance of the invasion. But then arose the problem of how it was to be done. The heavily mined and shallow waters of the Bay of the Seine excluded normal submarines, and in any case attempting to reach the shore in canoes in midwinter would have been suicidal. Then Lieutenant Nick Hastings, Willmott's right-hand man in No.1 COPP, suggested midget submarines – X-craft. When a civilian from the Directorate of Naval Construction said that it would be impossible to convert any in time, the Admiral conducting the meeting swung round and said: 'Supposing your wife would be made a widow and your house a dung heap if it was not done in a month – what then?' The X-craft were converted at once.

After a preliminary reconnaissance in an LCN (Landing Craft, Navigation), undertaken by Willmott and two swimmers of No.1 COPP, Major L. Scott-Bowden and Sergeant Ogden Smith, the same party returned in an X-craft on 17 January 1944. This time the Coppists were there for several days, though Willmott was not allowed ashore as he knew too much about the D-day plans.

The beaches between St Laurent and Colleville were measured by well-rehearsed techniques that had been methodically worked out at the COPP depot. A stake was driven into the beach at a measured distance from the waterline. From it, running out at right angles to the beach, was a tautline measuring gear attached to a special reel on the swimmer's body: this last had been developed by Willmott from the reel of a salmon rod. Distances from the back of the beach were measured or paced while crawling and direction was kept by taking

Top right: Corporal E.W. Horner of the Royal Marine Boom Patrol Detachment uses an auger to take samples of sand as he assists a COPP survey of a landing beach. Centre right: For the D-day landings the COPP teams made use of converted midget submarines (X-craft) to provide stable points from which to guide in the invasion fleets. As the background photograph shows, the cramped interior of the X-craft had precious little room for the Coppists' equipment. Right: Coppists pose in civilian attire. The COPP organisation was aware that team members would face death if captured, so each man was provided with a 'civvy' photograph which could be incorporated into false identity papers by the French Resistance.

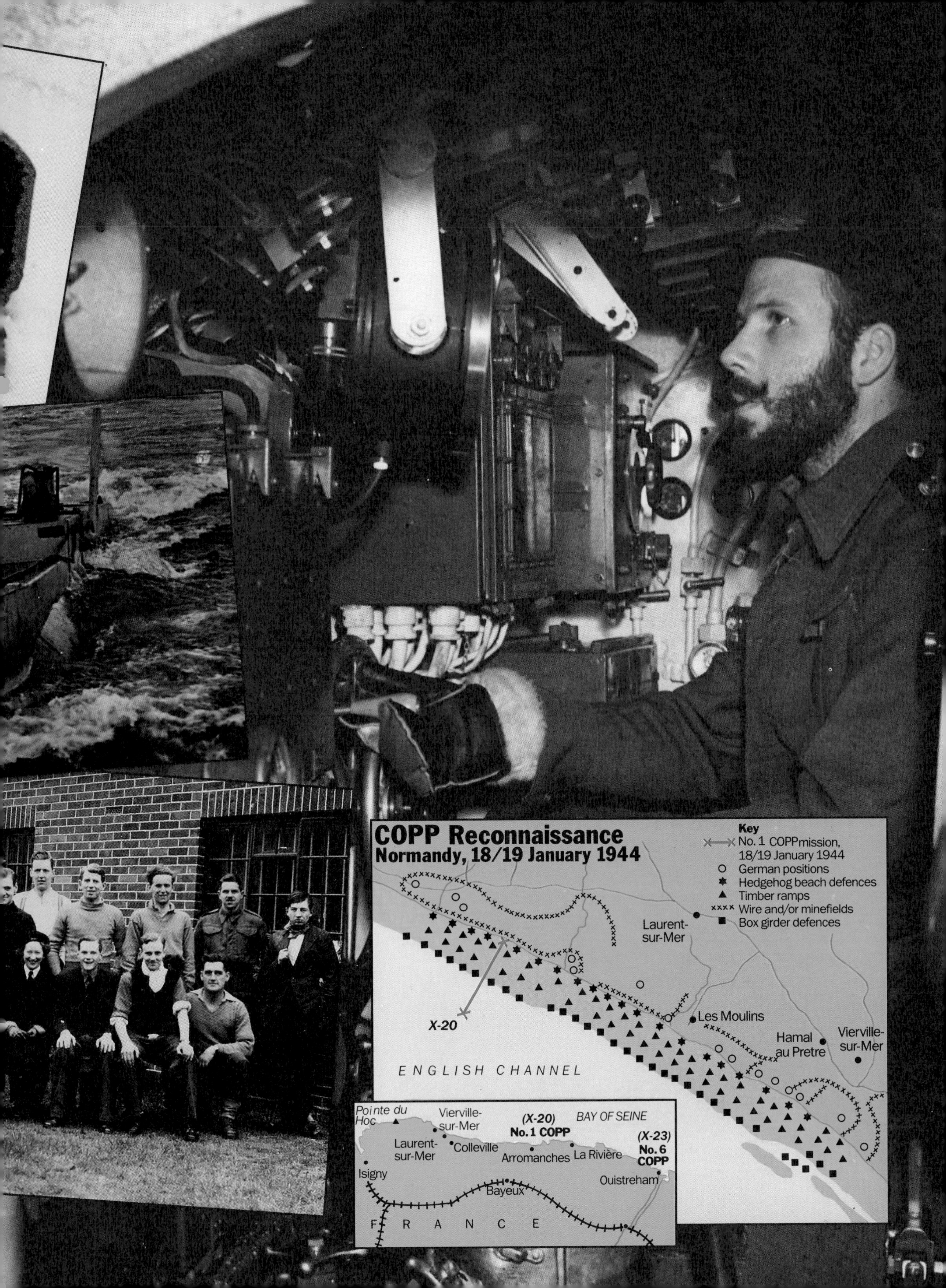

COPP Reconnaissance
Normandy, 18/19 January 1944
Key
No. 1 COPPmission, 18/19 January 1944
German positions
Hedgehog beach defences
Timber ramps
Wire and/or minefields
Box girder defences
Laurent-sur-Mer
Les Moulins
Hamal au Pretre
Vierville-sur-Mer
X-20
ENGLISH CHANNEL
Pointe du Hoc
Vierville-sur-Mer
(X-20)
No.1 COPP
BAY OF SEINE
(X-23)
No. 6 COPP
Laurent-sur-Mer
Colleville
Arromanches
La Rivière
Isigny
Ouistreham
Bayeux
FRANCE

LIEUTENANT-CDR NIGEL CLOGSTOUN-WILLMOTT

Born in 1910 and educated at Marlborough College, Nigel Clogstoun-Willmott entered the Royal Navy at 17 and spent a year as a cadet on HMS *Erebus* before becoming a midshipman. During the 1930s he served in HMS *Revenge* and then in destroyers. He specialised in navigation, a talent which, when war came, led to his involvement in some unusual operations. His participation in the Norwegian campaign of 1940, during which he was Mentioned in Despatches, combined with the reminiscences of an uncle who had taken part in the ill-fated Gallipoli landings in 1915, made him acutely aware of the advantages and drawbacks of Combined Operations. Thus, when he was made the navigator in charge of putting an assault force ashore at Rhodes, he realised the necessity of reconnoitring the beaches first, an operation for which he was awarded the DSO. There followed a period during which he helped in the withdrawal of British troops from Greece and worked with the Long Range Desert Group. Returning to Britain, he was asked to raise beach reconnaissance units for the invasion of North Africa. For his work during this operation he was awarded the DSC, and he gained a bar to it, as well as a second Mention in Despatches, during two COPP reconnaissances of the Normandy beachhead in January 1944. He finished the war as a commander and was promoted to captain in 1951. He now lives in Edinburgh.

bearings of objects or stars with a wrist compass. Soundings were taken by the position of the waterline on the swimmer's body or, if out of his depth, by a special lead and line. An extra-long line of soundings could be taken by joining two reels together, but the current and exhaustion usually made this impracticable. Soundings, the time and the swimmer's position were noted on an underwater writing tablet every 10yds up to 130yds (the limit of the reel), before the whole process was repeated.

All this was accomplished right under the noses of German sentries. One even tripped over Ogden Smith's stake with the wire from the beach gradient reel attached to it. Ogden Smith, gripping the other end of the wire, held his breath, but the sentry just grumbled and moved on. Each morning a periscope reconnaissance was made before the X-craft laid up on the sea-bed. Then, once night had fallen, Scott-Bowden and Smith slipped into the icy water and made for the beach. Besides their beach measuring equipment, each carried a 0·45in automatic with two spare magazines, a fighting knife, wire cutters, a bag for shingle, a bandolier with 12 sample tubes for sand, an earth auger, a torch, emergency rations, and a brandy flask.

Soon after the reconnaissance of the Normandy

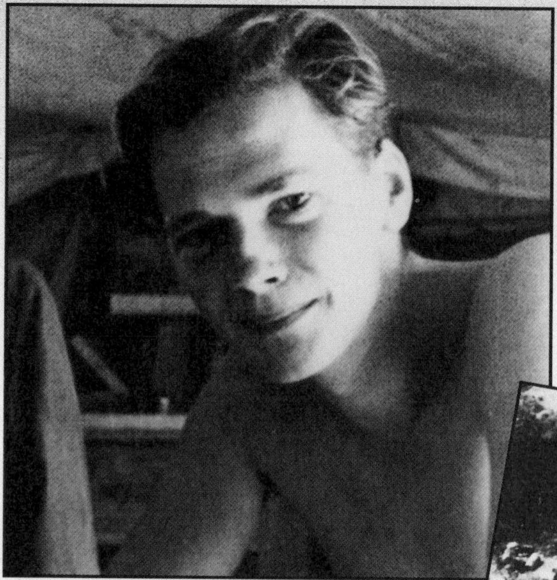

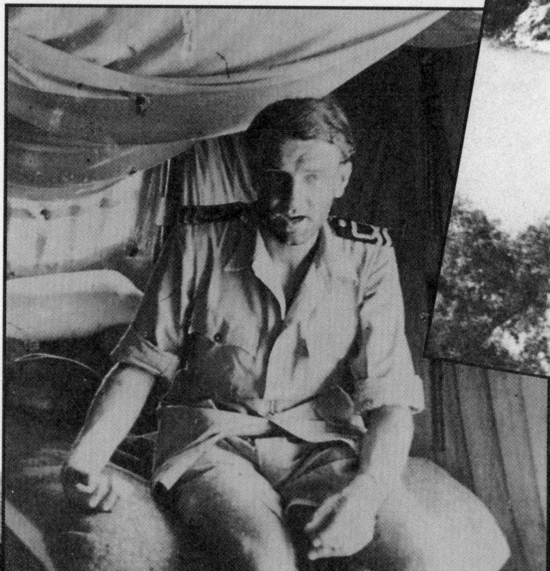

Below: Elements of the Fourteenth Army en route to landing beaches near Ru-Ywa in the Arakan. Operation in the Far East. Right, clockwise from top left: Sub-Lieutenant Robin Hardbud of No.1 COPP; a canoe with an experimental sail; Sergeant Cooke, who acted as Harbud's paddler; and Lieutenant-Commander Peter Wild, CO of No.1 COPP in the Far East. Inset centre: A base on Ramree Island, Burma.

beaches, Willmott, exhausted and suffering from an ulcer, relinquished his leadership of COPP to Lieutenant-Commander Paul Clark. But beach reconnaissance was by now firmly established within Combined Operations as a crucial part in any amphibious landing and when D-day arrived three teams of Coppists guided in most of the armada. Clark (No. 1 COPP) was in X-20, stationed off the beaches between Arromanches and La Rivière; Lyne (No. 9 COPP) was in X-23 off Ouistreham; while members of No.6 COPP, under Amer, and other COPP personnel from the depot, acted as pilots in the motor launches and landing craft that led in the invading fleet.

The two X-craft used for D-day were specially fitted out to act as markers and were equipped with newly-developed gear. Perhaps the most successful item was what was known as the 'bong stick'. Officially called the Rod Sounding Gear, this was nothing more than a simple iron rod which was lowered into the water from the X-craft and hit with a mechanical hammer. The sound could be picked up from as far as 12 miles away by the asdic of the specialist craft leading in the invasion fleet. The bong stick proved a far more reliable homing device than infra-red gear.

In addition to the bong stick, each X-craft used a radar beacon, and a shaded light was displayed from the top of the mast. Nothing was left to chance, and all landed in the right place. This was not true of some of the American beaches, as the Americans had decided against using COPP markers for fear of the landings being compromised. Instead, the US V Corps used Scott-Bowden and Smith as pilots to take them in from the start-line, 12 miles offshore, but as the coastline was obscured by smoke this proved less than satisfactory.

Though now widely accepted and appreciated by the British command, COPP was a highly secret organisation and was thus still regarded in some theatres as being of doubtful value, simply because so little was known about it. Typically, when No.6 COPP and No.9 COPP were deployed to reconnoitre beaches for the invasion of the south of France, they were told that they had arrived too late in the planning stage to be of use. This situation was then rectified by the CCO, who circulated a detailed paper on the uses of COPP to every planning staff, and all COPP matters, other than those dealing with specific operations, were downgraded to 'secret'.

So dangerous was the work, and so secret, that at least one team carried instant death pills. The box was labelled 'to be taken with discretion'

Although Nos. 5 and 7 COPP, both with new personnel, helped the Allied armies cross the Rhine and the Elbe in early 1945, the emphasis on COPP operations switched to the Far East after the Normandy landings. Nos. 1, 3 and 4 COPP, all reconstituted under new leadership, were despatched to Southeast Asia.

The COPP teams in the Far East came under the Special Operations Group known locally as 'Mountbatten's Private Navy'. Mostly they worked in the same way as COPP had in Europe, but often they were involved in other missions as well. Their techniques were similar, too, though there was a much heavier accent on 'skin-swimming ability' using swim-fins. So dangerous was the work – several were killed or executed and a number captured – and so secret, that at least one team carried instant death pills. The box was labelled 'to be taken with discretion', but luckily the pills never had to be used.

The first two COPP teams to reach Southeast Asia, Nos.7 and 8, had had a slow start and had been involved in only four operations over 15 months. But later, during the advance in the Arakan down to Rangoon, teams were used before every landing and two were continually employed in that area. Altogether, 36 operations were carried out by COPP teams in the Far East. In the Arakan alone they carried out 16 separate operations, nearly all involved in scouting up 'chaungs' (swamp channels) to find the next suitable crossing places for the advancing units of the Fourteenth Army.

The importance of COPP in the many vital amphibious landings that virtually won the war in Europe for the Allies cannot be underestimated, and is emphasised by the fact that its personnel were awarded over 90 decorations for their work.

THE AUTHOR Ian Dear served as a regular officer in the Royal Marines, 1953-56. He is now a professional writer on military and maritime subjects and is author of *Ten Commando*, a book on No. 10 (Inter-Allied) Commando to be published by Leo Cooper Ltd later this year.

815

TORPEDO AWAY!

The antiquated Swordfish of the Royal Navy shocked the powerful Italian fleet with a devastating raid on Taranto in November 1940

THE FLEET AIR ARM

The history of the Fleet Air Arm dates back to 1911, when the first four naval pilots were taught to fly at Eastchurch.
Despite official indifference, training continued. In 1911 the first seaplane was built and a biplane was flown off the bows of a stationary battleship. The First Lord of the Admiralty, Winston Churchill, favoured the development of naval aviation and, under his watchful eye, the naval wing of the Royal Flying Corps gained a measure of independence in 1914, becoming the Royal Naval Air Service (RNAS).
The small RNAS played a minor role in World War I, but a few successes pointed the way forward. During the Dardanelles campaign, an aerial torpedo was launched against an enemy surface ship for the first time, and, on 2 August 1917, Squadron Commander E.H. Dunning scored another first when he landed on the deck of a ship at sea.
On 1 April 1918, the RNAS and the RFC were amalgamated to form the Royal Air Force. This loss of independence, however, was brief; in April 1924 the Fleet Air Arm was formed and naval officers began training as pilots. In May 1939, the Admiralty took complete control of the Fleet Air Arm, consisting of seven aircraft carriers and 340 aircraft.
The successful attack on the Italian Fleet at Taranto by Swordfish aircraft of Nos. 815 (whose badge is shown above) and 819 Naval Air Squadrons demonstrated the full value of air power at sea and engendered a revolution in naval tactics.

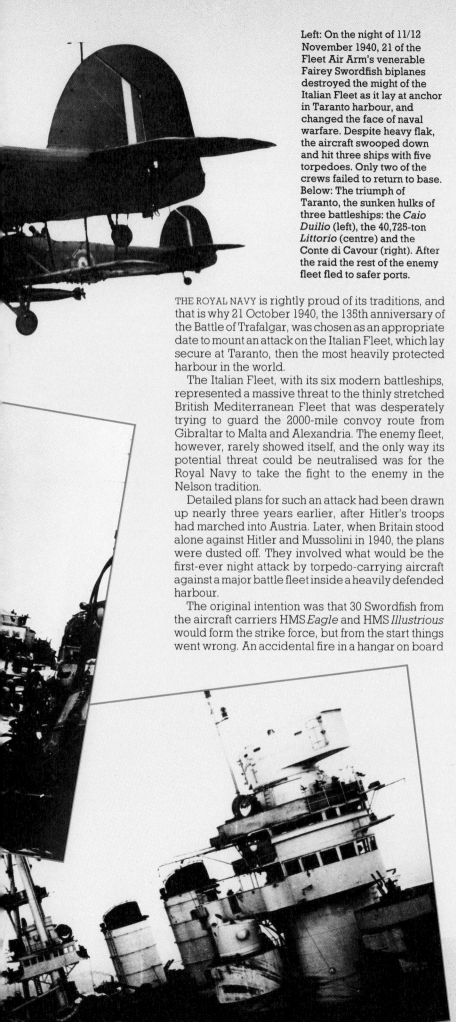

Left: On the night of 11/12 November 1940, 21 of the Fleet Air Arm's venerable Fairey Swordfish biplanes destroyed the might of the Italian Fleet as it lay at anchor in Taranto harbour, and changed the face of naval warfare. Despite heavy flak, the aircraft swooped down and hit three ships with five torpedoes. Only two of the crews failed to return to base. Below: The triumph of Taranto, the sunken hulks of three battleships: the *Caio Duilio* (left), the 40,725-ton *Littorio* (centre) and the Conte di Cavour (right). After the raid the rest of the enemy fleet fled to safer ports.

THE ROYAL NAVY is rightly proud of its traditions, and that is why 21 October 1940, the 135th anniversary of the Battle of Trafalgar, was chosen as an appropriate date to mount an attack on the Italian Fleet, which lay secure at Taranto, then the most heavily protected harbour in the world.

The Italian Fleet, with its six modern battleships, represented a massive threat to the thinly stretched British Mediterranean Fleet that was desperately trying to guard the 2000-mile convoy route from Gibraltar to Malta and Alexandria. The enemy fleet, however, rarely showed itself, and the only way its potential threat could be neutralised was for the Royal Navy to take the fight to the enemy in the Nelson tradition.

Detailed plans for such an attack had been drawn up nearly three years earlier, after Hitler's troops had marched into Austria. Later, when Britain stood alone against Hitler and Mussolini in 1940, the plans were dusted off. They involved what would be the first-ever night attack by torpedo-carrying aircraft against a major battle fleet inside a heavily defended harbour.

The original intention was that 30 Swordfish from the aircraft carriers HMS *Eagle* and HMS *Illustrious* would form the strike force, but from the start things went wrong. An accidental fire in a hangar on board *Illustrious* burnt out three of her Swordfish, and salt-water sprinklers had soaked the remainder so thoroughly that all had to be stripped down, cleaned and then reassembled. This accident meant that the attack, codenamed Operation Judgement, had to be postponed until the next favourable moon, between 11 and 19 November.

Other problems also arose to threaten the operation. Shortly before 11 November, *Eagle* developed serious contamination in her aviation fuel tanks, the result of damage caused by the near misses of bombs dropped by Italian dive-bombers four months earlier. As a result, three of her Swordfish suffered engine failure and crashed into the sea, and *Eagle's* captain decided there was no alternative but to return to Alexandria for urgent repairs, leaving *Illustrious* to go it alone. Five of *Eagle's* aircraft were transferred to *Illustrious*, but the total available force had by then been reduced by a third, leaving only 21 Swordfish serviceable.

Each pilot's chance of survival in the forthcoming raid was rated at less than 50 per cent

Recent aerial reconnaissance had shown an additional hazard that would have to be faced by the Fleet Air Arm aircrews – lines of barrage balloons had been set up across the outer harbour of Mar Grande as an added protection against low-flying aircraft. Each aircrew's chance of survival in the forthcoming raid was rated at less than 50 per cent, but morale amongst the experienced naval aviators remained incredibly high. During the afternoon before the raid, they received the encouraging news that a sixth battleship had joined the other five in Taranto harbour. At 1800 hours on 11 November 1940, *Illustrious*, with Rear Admiral Lyster on board, left its escorting cruisers and destroyers and sailed towards the aircrafts' designated flying-off position, some 170 miles southeast of Taranto.

By 2040, all 12 Swordfish of the first attacking wave had been launched and were forming on their leader at 1000ft, guided by the flashing letter 'K' from a torch held by Lieutenant Norman 'Blood' Scarlett, the observer of aircraft L4A. Piloted by No. 815 Naval Air Squadron's commanding officer, Lieutenant Commander Kenneth 'Hooch' Williamson, this Swordfish, like the others on the raid, carried only a pilot and an observer, the latter crouched in the rear-gunner's seat as his own normal position was taken up by bulky long-range fuel tank. Six of the Swordfish, comprising the main strike force, were armed with one torpedo each. The other six aircraft carried bombs, two of them also being designated to illuminate the scene with flares.

It took some two hours for the lumbering Swordfish to reach Taranto. Long before they arrived, the pilots could see the sky over the harbour filled with an ominous twinkling cone of red, blue and orange flashes. The Italians, aware that a raid was heading their way – their detection equipment had picked up the sound of aircraft engines – were already filling the air with tracer and anti-aircraft shells.

At 2256 the first of the two flare-dropping Swordfish made its run-in at 7500ft. Its mission was to drop a line of brightly burning yellow flares at half-mile intervals to the east of the main harbour to silhouette the line of battleships for the following torpedo-droppers. The flares dropped by Lieutenant Launcelot Kiggell in L4P, with Lieutenant 'Dick' Janvrin as his observer, provided enough

Taranto
Fleet Air Arm, 11/12 November 1940

By early November 1940 – some five months after Italy's declaration of war against the Allies – the Italian navy boasted six battleships, nineteen cruisers and some fifty destroyers, and it was considerably superior in strength to the British Mediterranean Fleet. Decisive action was needed to redress the balance. It came in the form of a historic raid on the main Italian battle fleet at anchor in Taranto harbour, carried out by twenty Swordfish biplanes of the Fleet Air Arm.

Taranto was one of the most heavily defended harbours in the world, protected from air attack by large numbers of barrage balloons and both land-based and shipboard anti-aircraft guns. But by the end of the raid three Italian battleships had been sunk.

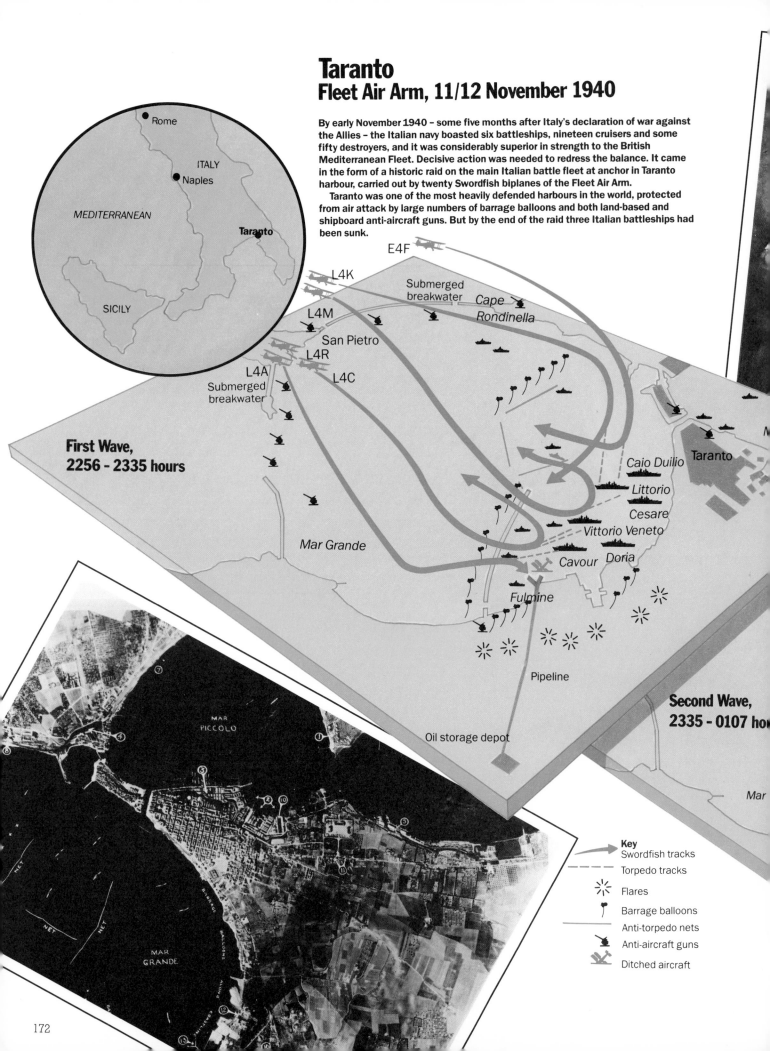

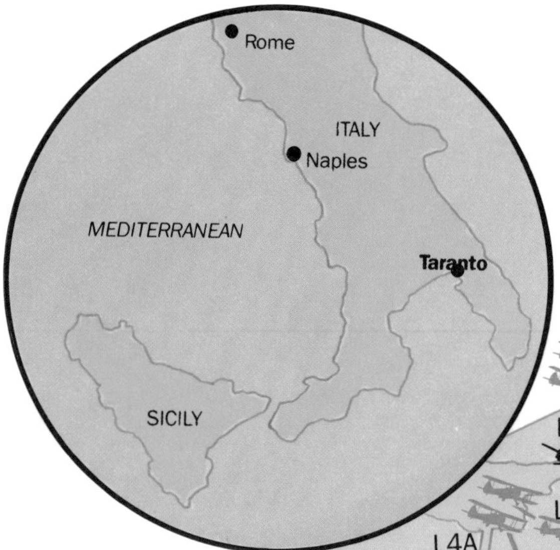
Rome
ITALY
Naples
MEDITERRANEAN
Taranto
SICILY

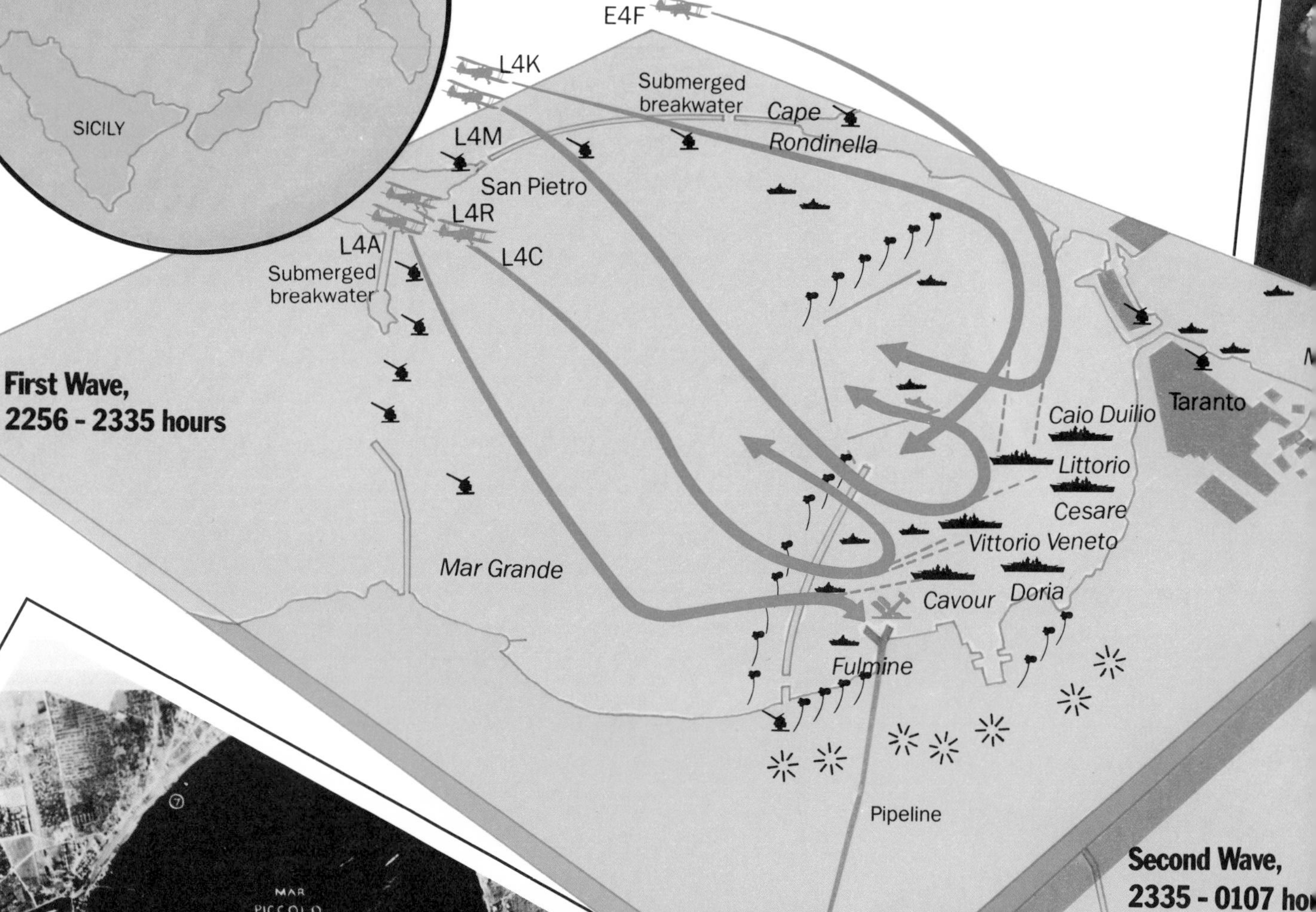
E4F
L4K
Submerged breakwater
Cape Rondinella
L4M
San Pietro
L4R
L4A
L4C
Submerged breakwater
First Wave, 2256 - 2335 hours
Taranto
Caio Duilio
Littorio
Cesare
Vittorio Veneto
Mar Grande
Cavour
Doria
Fulmine
Pipeline
Oil storage depot
Second Wave, 2335 - 0107 ho
Mar
Key
Swordfish tracks
Torpedo tracks
Flares
Barrage balloons
Anti-torpedo nets
Anti-aircraft guns
Ditched aircraft

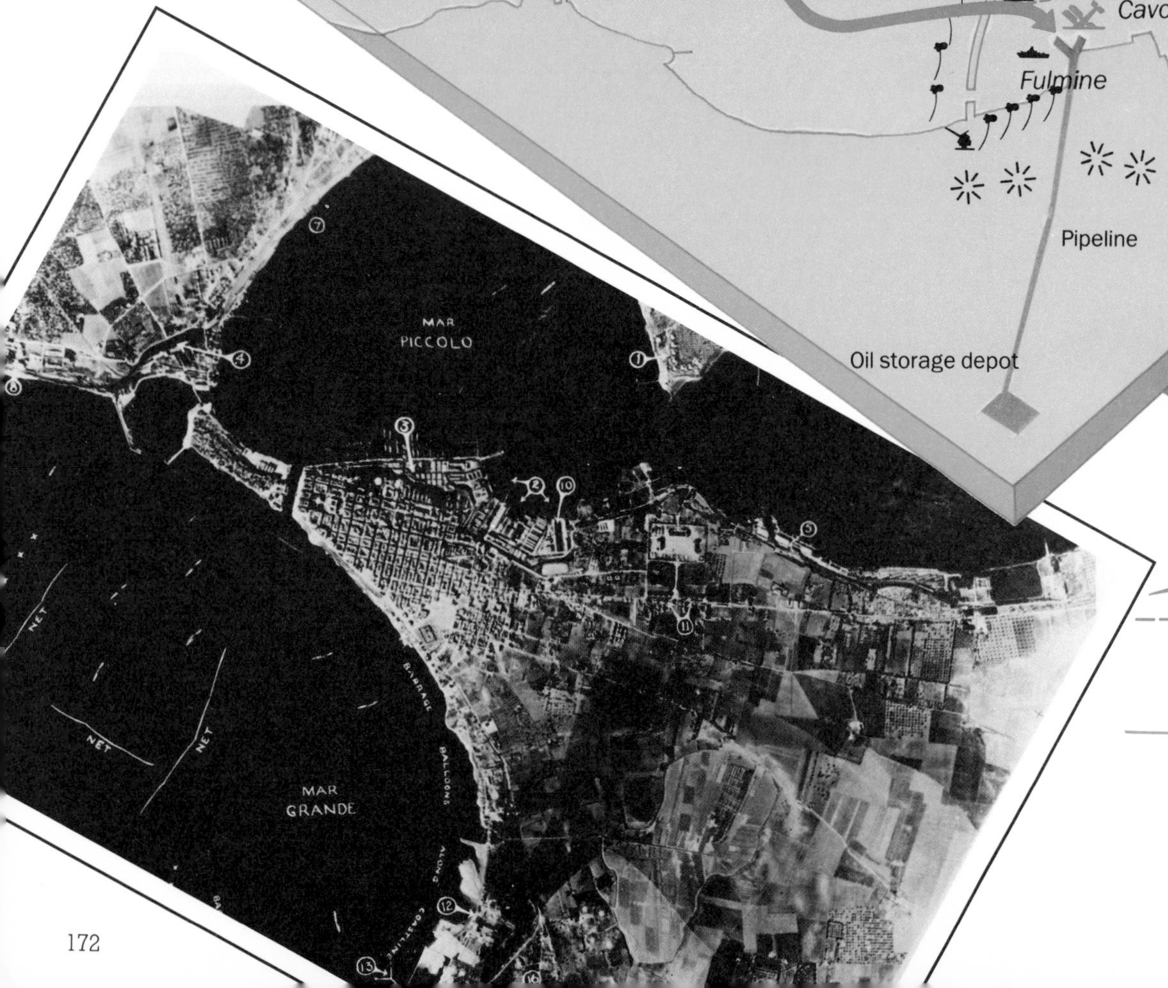
MAR PICCOLO
MAR GRANDE
NET
NET
NET
BARRAGE BALLOONS ALONG

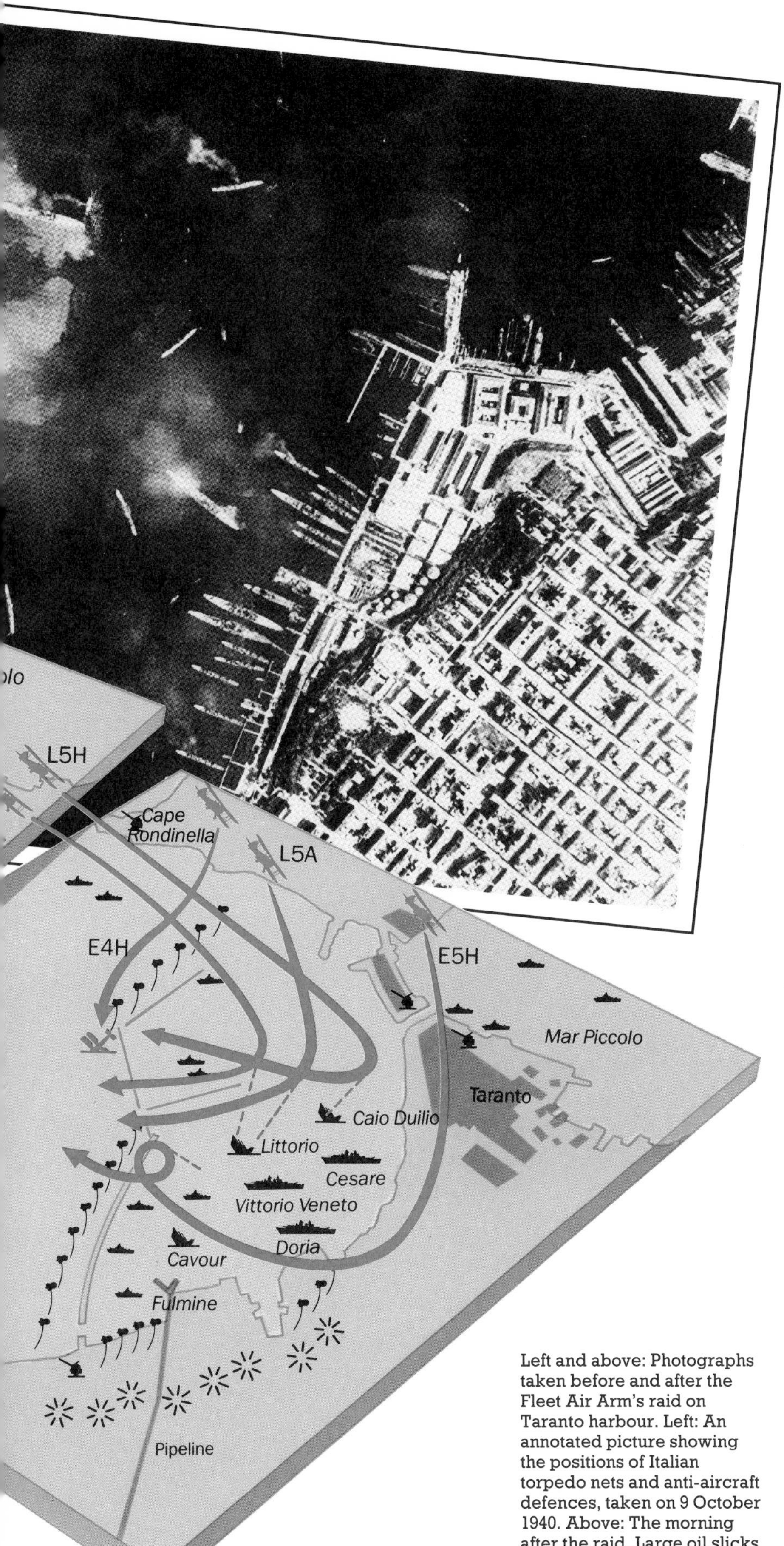
L5H
Cape Rondinella
L5A
E4H
E5H
Mar Piccolo
Taranto
Caio Duilio
Littorio
Cesare
Vittorio Veneto
Doria
Cavour
Fulmine
Pipeline

Left and above: Photographs taken before and after the Fleet Air Arm's raid on Taranto harbour. Left: An annotated picture showing the positions of Italian torpedo nets and anti-aircraft defences, taken on 9 October 1940. Above: The morning after the raid. Large oil slicks surround two of the three battleships hit by torpedoes. Most of the Italian's seaworthy ships left the harbour soon after the attack.

illumination, and the pilot of the second Swordfish, Lieutenant Charles Lamb, with his observer, Lieutenant Grieve, decided to fly straight on to their bombing target, the oil storage depot to the south-east of the harbour.

Williamson and Scarlett were the first to make a torpedo drop. Diving from 4000ft, they flew straight across the three-and-a-half mile length of the outer harbour through intense anti-aircraft fire, jinked their way between the barrage balloons, and then dropped their torpedo just after they had skimmed over the main breakwater.

As they released their torpedo, the Italian destroyer *Fulmine* saw them in the moonlight and opened up with her quick-firing 0.8 and 0.5in guns at 1000yd range. The next thing that the pilot remembered was recovering consciousness still strapped in the cockpit of his Swordfish, which was slowly sinking beneath the waters of the Mar Grande. He released his Sutton harness and shot to the surface, much to the relief of his observer who was wondering if he would ever see his 'boss' again. Despite coming under machine-gun fire as they swam the 150yd to a nearby floating-dock, they managed to scramble safely ashore. An hour or so later they were enjoying a welcome glass of brandy on board the destroyer that had shot them down.

Meanwhile, their torpedo had run true. Exploding magnetically under the 29,032-ton battleship, *Conte di Cavour,* it tore a hole measuring 40 by 27 feet out of her bow. Her fuel tanks were flooded, her bulkheads gave way, and she slowly settled on the bottom.

The other torpedo-droppers followed their leader into the attack. L4C, piloted by Sub-Lieutenant 'Spike' Sparke, DSC, with his observer, Sub-Lieutenant 'Johnny' Neale, and L4R, crewed by Sub-Lieutenants August Macauley and Tony Wray, both chose the same target. Their torpedoes, aimed at the *Cavour,* both missed and ran on towards the *Andrea Doria,* but grounded and exploded before reaching her.

Johnny Neale, who was close enough to the exploding AA shells to smell them, was thankful that he was wearing his best uniform:

'We all realised that this was one of those nights when we had more than the usual chance of being knocked down and I, like most of the others, wore my best uniform. If you were going to be a prisoner of war, you might as well be properly dressed.'

An enormous explosion blew a gaping hole in the 40,724-ton battleship

The fourth torpedo to be dropped was more successful. Lieutenant Neil Kemp and his observer, Sub-Lieutenant Ronald Bailey, in L4K, flew unscathed through the intense fire from the batteries on Cape Rondinella to the north and San Pietro to the south, less than two miles apart. Diving to sea level across the Mar Grande, they could see the shells fired at them by the shore batteries bursting amongst merchant ships lying at anchor in the harbour. Skirting the western line of barrage balloons, they avoided the torpedo nets and made their drop 1000 yards from the *Littorio,* hitting her on the starboard bow. An enormous explosion blew a gaping hole in the bulge abreast of the No. 1 6in gun turret of the 40,724-ton battleship. It was a hole large enough to fly a Swordfish through.

Seconds later, Lieutenant Henry Swayne and Sub-

FAIREY SWORDFISH

Despite its flimsy outward appearance, the Fairey Swordfish torpedo bomber was a massive and very robust structure. Popularly known as the 'Stringbag', it was almost as tall as a double-decker bus on its large, fixed undercarriage. The airframe was all metal; its welded steel-tube fuselage was metal-clad and armour-plated forward of the cockpit area. In comparison with most of its contemporaries, the Swordfish was underpowered; its Fairey-Reed propeller, powered by a 750hp Bristol Pegasus radial engine, was capable of speeds of up to 135 knots, but in strong headwinds this was reduced to between 90 and 100 knots. The Swordfish could carry a potent array of ordnance including a Mark XII torpedo, weighing 1610lb, a 1500lb mine or an equivalent weight of bombs on its under-wing racks. Fully loaded, the aircraft had a range of 540 miles but, with the addition of an auxiliary fuel tank, this could be doubled. Conditions on board the Swordfish were primitive. The three-man crew was seated in an open cockpit and had to endure the buffeting of icy winds which cut through their flying suits. The Swordfish performed a variety of vital roles during World War II and, despite its lack of speed and comfort, was a firm favourite with its crews. Its agility and first-rate dependability engendered a fierce loyalty in aircrews, who knew that, whatever happened, the Stringbag would never fail.

Lieutenant Johnny Buscall took L4M through the same fierce barrage and then approached the *Littorio* from the other side. Their torpedo ripped open plating abreast of the steering compartment, narrowly missing the No. 1 magazine and leaving a hole 23 by five feet.

The sixth and final torpedo dropped by the first wave was aimed at the *Vittorio Veneto.* Released at 1300 yards by E4F, with Lieutenant Michael Maund and Sub-Lieutenant William Bull as pilot and observer, it hit a mud bank and exploded off the starboard quarter of the ship, but caused no damage.

Meanwhile, the bomb-carrying Swordfish had been making their diversionary attacks to confuse the defences. The two flare-droppers, L4P and L5B, had dive-bombed the oil storage depot, each dropping their four 250lb semi-armour-piercing bombs into the complex. As Charles Lamb headed for the open sea, he calmly released his flares across the harbour 'as a rude parting gesture', knowing that the Italian gunners would waste a vast amount of ammunition on them as they drifted down.

The other land target attacked was the seaplane base on the southern shoreline of the inner harbour, Mar Piccolo. As Sub-Lieutenant 'Bill' Sarra pulled back on the stick of L4L at the bottom of his bombing dive, his observer, Midshipman Jack Bowker, wondered whether he should have pulled out of the dive a little earlier: 'I heard the unusual sound of the guns on the ground firing instead of the shells in the sky exploding, and I clearly saw a man near the slipway crane firing a rifle at me.' But the steep dive paid off. There was a violent flash from the seaplane hangar as two aircraft being repaired inside exploded. Sarra's other bombs hit the slipways and stores. L4L's crew felt well satisfied as they departed the scene, since their target was one of the bases from which reconnaissance seaplanes had been shadowing Mediterranean convoys. Next morning, Sarra counted 17 holes in his aircraft.

The other three Swordfish acting as bombers had swept down on the concentration of cruisers, destroyers, torpedo-boats and submarines lying moored in the Mar Piccolo. Captain 'Ollie' Patch, the only Royal Marine pilot on the raid, with Lieutenant David Goodwin as his observer, flew through concentrated machine-gun fire from the banked vessels to bomb two heavy cruisers. Attached to one of the bombs was a pair of well-worn marching boots to let the Italians know that the Marines had paid a visit.

Sub-Lieutenant Tony Forde and his observer, Sub-Lieutenant Anthony Mardel-Ferreira in L4H, not sure that their bombs had released, calmly returned through the barrage to repeat their attack. Lieutenant John Murray in E5Q, with Sub-Lieutenant Stuart Paine in the back seat, obtained a direct hit on the destroyer *Libeccio,* but the semi-armour-piercing nose of the bomb passed straight through the thin skin of its deck and failed to explode.

The first attack was over. Incredibly, for over 30 minutes a handful of frail, slow-flying biplanes had flown at

low level, criss-crossing a heavily defended harbour and the massed guns of the Italian Fleet, yet only one aircraft had been lost. Six torpedoes had been dropped, three had found their target. The *Cavour* had been hit once, the *Littorio* twice.

As the first wave started their return flight to the carrier at 2335 hours, the second wave of Swordfish made their approach over the harbour. Nine had set off, but one had lost its overload tank and was forced to abort the mission. This Swordfish received a 'warm welcome' from the guns of *Illustrious* and the cruiser *Berwick,* who were not expecting anyone back quite so early.

Again, first in were the flare-droppers, L5B with Lieutenant 'Dick' Hamilton and Sub-Lieutenant Weekes, and L4F with Lieutenant Ronald Skelton as pilot and Sub-Lieutenant Edgar Perkins as his observer. Following the pattern of the first wave, they dropped their flares to the east and southeast of the Mar Grande to silhouette the battleships, and then headed southeast to bomb the oil storage depot.

The five torpedo-droppers came in over the northwest of the outer harbour. Leading the attack in L5A was the commanding officer of No.819 Naval Air Squadron, Lieutenant Commander 'Ginger' Hale, who had gained his rugby cap for England before the war, and his observer, Lieutenant 'Georgie' Carline. Flying through heavy anti-aircraft fire from the San Pietro batteries, they turned in over Cape Rondinella and then dived across the Mar Grande to launch their torpedo at the *Littorio.*

At the same time as Hale's attack, L5K, piloted by Lieutenant 'Tiffy' Torrens-Spence, and his observer, Lieutenant 'Alfie' Sutton, who had enjoyed a local broadcast of Italian opera on his radio on the way in, dropped their torpedo at the same target. As they dropped, there was a sudden jarring shock to the aircraft and a column of water shot up in its wake. 'My God, we've been hit,' thought Sutton, but, because they had flown in very low to get under the guns of the battleships, their undercarriage had struck the sea. Lifting to clear the shoal breakwater, they jinked through the barrage balloon cables, and flew straight into heavy point-blank fire from four destroyers. Miraculously, their Swordfish was undamaged as they sped out to the open sea south of the harbour. As Sutton said later, 'None of us really thought we would come out of it alive.'

Which torpedo actually hit the *Littorio* was never established. An unexploded torpedo, which caused Italian divers some anxious moments, was later found embedded in the mud beneath the *Littorio's* keel. The one that hit the battleship blew a hole 40 by 30ft in the ship, just forward of the gaping hole left by L4K in the first raid. Water was already pouring into the stricken vessel, which had settled by the bow, b

Main picture: A lone Swordfish circles the 23,000-ton aircraft carrier HMS *Illustrious.* With a crew of 1392 and a complement of up to 36 Swordfish, the *Illustrious* was one of the most important capital ships in the British Mediterranean Fleet. Bottom right: A deadly warning for the Italians: a rack of 250lb semi-armour-piercing bombs, lined up on the deck of *Illustrious.* One carries the motto, 'Next stop Taranto'. Below: The cockpit of a Fairey Swordfish Mark I. Below left: One of the 'Stringbags' used in the raid, carrying a Mark XII torpedo.

CHARLIE
E
5H
ROYAL NAVY
P3999
TARANTO

then awash. As he made his attack, Torrens-Spence saw a bright orange flash as E4H, believed to have been going for the heavy cruiser *Gorizia,* was hit. The body of the pilot, Lieutenant 'Gerry' Bayley, was subsequently recovered, but his observer, Lieutenant 'Tod' Slaughter, was never seen again.

The fifth success of the raid came from L5H piloted by Lieutenant Charles Lea with Sub-Lieutenant 'Johnna' Jones as his observer. At 20ft above the waves and 800yd out, the target chosen was the 29,391-ton battleship *Caio Duilio.* Their torpedo exploded magnetically nearly 30ft below the surface, blasting a 36 by 23ft hole in her bottom. Sea water poured into her No. 1 and 2 magazines, flooding both. After dropping its torpedo, L5H weaved between the cruisers *Zara* and *Fiume*, narrowly missed the masts of an anti-aircraft vessel, and then headed out unscathed over San Pietro.

Although hit by heavy machine-gun fire, which sent their aircraft temporarily out of control, Lieutenant John Welham, piloting the final torpedo-dropper, E5H, and his observer, Lieutenant Pat Humphreys, who had previously been awarded the George Cross, pressed home their attack, and launched a torpedo at the *Vittorio Veneto.* However, the punishment the aircraft was taking caused the pilot to miss. Although hit again in the port wing by a 40mm shell, Welham coaxed his aircraft back to make a safe landing on *Illustrious.*

The only aircraft acting as a bomber in the second wave arrived over the harbour 24 minutes late. L5F's departure had been delayed due to damage caused by another aircraft crashing into it during take-off. So incensed was the observer, Lieutenant 'Grubby' Going, at the thought of not taking part in the raid, he launched a personal plea to the captain of *Illustrious,* Denis Boyd, and to Admiral Lyster, who said, 'Well, you're flying the bloody aircraft. Off you go.' L5F was quickly repaired.

The warships in Mar Piccolo were to be the target for the pilot Lieutenant Edward Clifford. One of his bombs struck the heavy cruiser *Trento* near the bridge, but again the thin deck-plating of the vessel allowed it to pass straight through without exploding.

Although Clifford's attack ended the raid, the Italian guns continued to fire into the empty sky for 15 minutes after the last Swordfish had cleared the area.

Only two British aircraft had been shot down. The raid was an unqualified success; five torpedoes had hit three of the six enemy battleships and put them out of action. As the last Swordfish touched down on the flight-deck of *Illustrious,* stationed off Cephalonia, there was a deep feeling of relief that the cost had been so light.

The raid had far-reaching consequences. The day after the attack, every major Italian warship capable of steaming left Taranto for the security of Naples and other ports on the west coast of Italy. The threat to British convoys was thus reduced and, for a limited but vital period, the British enjoyed naval superiority in the Mediterranean.

Hale and Williamson, the two strike leaders, and Clifford and Going, who had insisted on taking part in the raid despite a damaged aircraft, were awarded the Distinguished Service Order. Eighteen men received the Distinguished Service Cross, and six others were mentioned in dispatches.

The Battle of Taranto was a milestone in the history of naval warfare. Henceforth, sea-borne aircraft would play a central role in sea battles. The Japanese admiral, Isoruku Yamamoto, carefully studied the results of the Fleet Air Arm attack on the Italian Fleet, and put his knowledge to devastating effect at Pearl Harbor one year later.

THE AUTHOR A.H. Vernon Hillier, FRSA, saw service as a Royal Engineers officer in Egypt, Palestine and Kenya, and later with 56th Armoured Division TA. He is currently Design and Research consultant with the Fleet Air Arm Museum at Yeovilton,

Below: One of only two Swordfish lost during the raid being lifted from Taranto harbour on the morning after the attack.

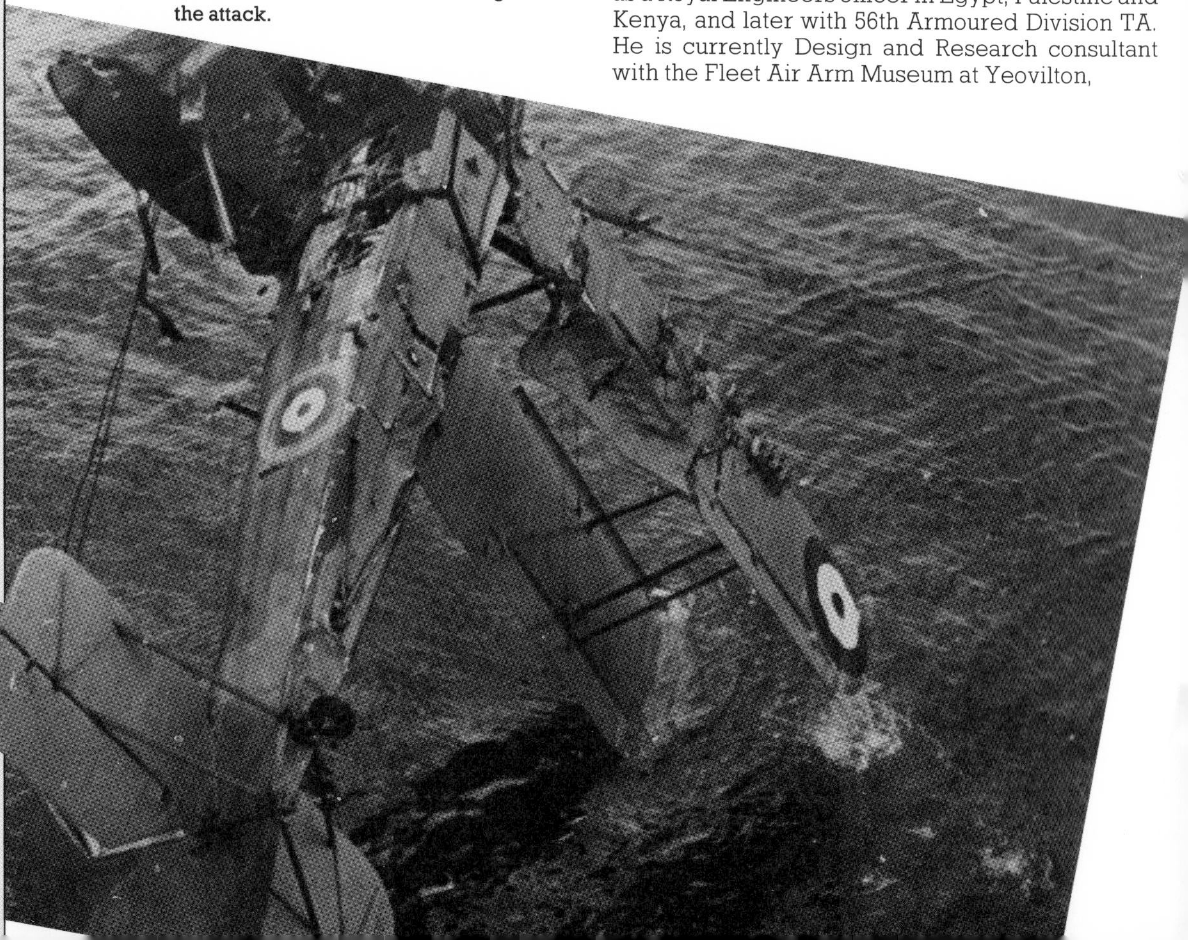

BEATING THE FLAK

One of the most remarkable aspects of the British attack on Taranto was the failure of the Italian garrison to inflict any significant losses on the Fleet Air Arm's torpedo bombers. In an hour-long battle, fought at low-level over one of the most heavily defended harbours of the world in 1940, only two Swordfish were lost to enemy fire.

After the raid, it was estimated that the Italians had fired over 13,000 rounds from the 21 anti-aircraft batteries and 200 machine guns ringing the harbour to inflict this trifling loss. Even this figure was misleading, as it failed to take into account the barrage directed at the Swordfish by the Italian warships at anchor in Taranto's two harbours.

The failure of the defences was the result of several factors; most notably, Italian inexperience in dealing with torpedo attacks, and the skill of the British pilots. Although Italian sound-detection equipment had identified the first wave of Swordfish, much of the subsequent defensive fire was poorly co-ordinated and inaccurate, with battleships hitting cruisers and cruisers firing at several of the merchant ships at anchor in the harbour. Many shore-based batteries had to fire high to avoid the ships and consequently missed the low-flying aircraft making their bombing runs. More sophisticated early-warning systems, searchlights and interlocking fire zones might have increased the number of kills.

Despite the inefficiency of the Italians' defensive measures, much of the credit for the raid must rest with the British pilots and their aircraft. Pilots performed prodigious feats to avoid both barrage balloons and anti-aircraft fire before dropping their torpedoes, and the dependable Swordfish kept flying despite receiving many hits.

The Fleet Air Arm's raid also had the advantage of originality; never before had a large formation of torpedo bombers been used to strike at an enemy fleet stationed at a home port.